Venini. Catalogue Raisonné 1921–1986

Anna Venini Diaz de Santillana

Venini
Catalogue Raisonné 1921–1986

SKIRA

Editor
Valerio Terraroli

Art Director
Marcello Francone

Editorial Coordination
Franco Ambrosio

Editing
Emma Cavazzini

Layout
Sara Salvi

Translations
Andrew Ellis
(from Italian language)
Jane Marret Glees
(from German language)
Susan Wise
(from Italian language)

Iconographical Research
Massimo Zanella

Cover
Paolo Venini
'Murrina' vase, c. 1950
New York, Barry Friedman
Collection

Back cover
Fulvio Bianconi
'Pezzato' vase, 1948–49
New York, Barry Friedman
Collection

First published in Italy in 2000
by Skira Editore S.p.A.
Palazzo Casati Stampa
via Torino 61, 20123 Milano,
Italy

© 2000 by Skira editore

Printed and bound in Italy.
First edition

ISBN 88-8118-651-9

Distributed in North America
and Latin America by Abbeville
Publishing Group,
22 Cortlandt Street,
New York, NY 10007, USA.
Distributed elsewhere in the
world by Thames and Hudson
Ltd., 181a High Holborn,
London WC1V7QX,
United Kingdom.

*My heartfelt thanks go to Massimo Vitta Zelman,
for his constant encouragement in putting together
this book on Venini glass; and to Stefano Piantini,
who helped me plan and devise the book, always
with the useful advice of a good friend.
Fondest thanks also to Valerio Terraroli, for his insights
and extensive knowledge on the period discussed –
working alongside him has been immensely rewarding.
Thanks also to Maria Novella Benzoni, for her
concerted effort in researching and compiling the
catalogue entries and contacting collectors for details
– to her my fond regards and best wishes for a brilliant
career as an art historian and expert in the art
of glassmaking.
For publishing matters it was an honour to draw on
the expertise of Franco Ambrosio and all the editorial
staff of Il Faggio.
Special thanks go to Simona Cocchi, always a patient
and knowledgeable friend who provided photographs,
news items, and assistance of every kind.
I am also indebted to the museums, collectors, and
gallery owners who generously supplied information
and illustrations for this book, notably:
Marco Arosio, Milan
Victor Edelstein, Venice
Barry Friedman, New York
Odetto Lastra, Union City, New York
Angelo Gino Levis, Padua
Nancy Olnick and Giorgio Spanu, New York*

*In loving memory of Paolo and Ginette Venini,
and Ludovico Diaz de Santillana*

Anna Venini Diaz de Santillana

Table of Contents

9   The Venetian Legacy and the Foundations
of a New Glassmaking Tradition: Venini 1921–1942
Helmut Ricke

17   Paolo Venini and the Metamorphosis
of Modern Style during the 1920s
Valerio Terraroli

27   The Venini Glassworks: a Brief History
Rosa Barovier Mentasti

33   Venini and 'Studio Glass': American Fascination
for Murano Glass
Victoria Milne

39   The Critical Acclaim for Venini Glass
Maria Novella Benzoni

45   The Venini Glassworks 1921–1986:
a Passion for Glass
Anna Venini Diaz de Santillana

Catalogue Raisonné 1921–1986
58   Colour Plates
192   Entries

Historical Catalogues
235   Catalogo blu
268   Catalogo rosso
287   Catalogo verde

Appendix
305   Chronology
307   Designers for Venini
309   Glossary
311   Exhibitions
313   Bibliography
317   Index of Names
319   Index of Places

The Venetian Legacy and the Foundations of a New Glassmaking Tradition: Venini 1921–1942

From the fifteenth through well into the seventeenth century it was commonly held that Murano glass was the finest and most artistic in the world. Its quality was matchless and, indeed, considered insuperable. To be of Venetian origin was considered a prerequisite for wares and artefacts fashioned from glass destined for Europe's nobility and courts – and if not from Venice itself, then at least blown *à la façon de Venise*. The international standards for the glassmaker's art were moreover virtually decreed by Venice. Without doubt the beauty and appeal of Venetian production was entirely due to the natural ability and expertise of the Murano glassblowers, whose consummate skills were made manifest at the mouth of the furnace itself. The use of moulds or successive workmanship of cutting or engraving were of secondary importance. The only 'cold' technique consented was diamond engraving, which remained nonetheless an auxiliary phase for accentuating and highlighting the basic form with which each article had already been endowed in the course of blowing. Enamelling was the only cold-working technique that developed with any freedom, though well within the confines of its specific field of application.

The distinctive lightness, elegance and dynamic tension given to the vases and objects during their fluid progression through the various phases of workmanship in the glass factory have always been the distinguishing features of glassware from Murano. The essence of Venetian glass art lies in a self-assured ability in modelling the incandescent material, an ability that established a qualitative standard for glass workmanship that has lasted up to our times, and reaches far beyond the compass of Venetian production, so perfect that one is tempted to affirm that the art of freehand blowing of molten gather freshly drawn from the furnace – without the use of casting and moulding – is the connatural principle of Venetian glassmaking.

In the eighteenth century, however, following the immense success of Bohemian crystal with its thick walls

of clear matter, it became questionable if this principle would be able to withstand the brutal collision with the sweeping changes in glassmaking techniques, and the consequent, profound rewriting of aesthetic values. The question remains: fraught as it was with financial difficulties, would glass manufacturing in Murano have managed its transition into the modern world if it had remained true to that principle, i.e., of freehand blowing.

In the 1860s a return to the glorious past was considered the right direction. Antonio Salviati's attempts to retrieve bygone greatness was a response to the needs of the times, and was crowned with undisputed success, though his enthusiastic use of decoration turned out to be a blind alley. The glass mosaic technique, which had been resuscitated by numerous artists including Vincenzo Moretti and Giuseppe Barovier, was the only development that would outlast the period.[1] Art Nouveau in France and Jugendstil in Bohemia and Germany followed completely different, often even contrary, paths to the Venetian principle of freehand blowing. Glass became a medium of artistic expression, transcending pure formal beauty and matter. Despite their future importance to Murano, as yet there was no trace of these developments: the island's sole contribution to art at the turn of the century consisted again in its glass mosaic vessels, such as the *murrina* works by Teodoro Wolf Ferrari and the Artisti Barovier craftsmen, techniques which did not came into their own until the late 1930s.

During these years of radical change, the Murano craftsmen became painfully aware that despite the perfection of their skills, these could no longer guarantee their products' success if not adapted to the spirit of the time. Somewhat behind their counterparts north of the Alps, a growing number of Venetian firms started to look for the help of artists, and painters, sculptors and architects who had come into contact with the ideas of the Austrian and German Werkbund finally began to take the

9

production of utility and ornamental glass objects seriously.

In the immediate post-war period the crisis affecting Murano's beleaguered glasshouses had reached a new head. There was nothing to suggest that someone like Paolo Venini – a lawyer and business man from Milan – could possibly become the central figure for a solution. Interested in art but without any experience in glassmaking, Venini developed a quite simple artistic program for his new company Vetri Soffiati Muranesi Cappellin Venini & C., working in partnership with the antiques dealer Giacomo Cappellin and the painter Vittorio Zecchin. It was hardly a revolution, but it ushered in a return to that old, solid foundation, the Venetian principle of freehand glassblowing.

This evocation of the golden age of Venetian glassmaking – the Renaissance – was typified by such items as Venini's *Veronese* vase, chosen as the firm's emblem (cat. no. 1). Lacking any other truly innovative solutions, this return to the past symbolised an attempt to redeem the situation. On its own, the *Veronese* vase does not provide a proper idea of the early sets of glassware. The production program the two partners Cappellin and Venini set up in the 1920s consisted of three lines of practically equal importance. In addition to evoking Venetian glassware of the sixteenth and seventeenth centuries, ancient Roman glass was also used as models for new formal solutions. The importance of this second plunge back into the past is evident in the *Catalogo blu*, which documents the first year's production.[2]

The third line of the firm's production focused on the present, drawing on a repertoire of forms, with their conical or slightly bell-shaped bowls on raised feet. They had already been developed before the war at the Viennese School of Arts and Crafts and the glassmaking schools of north Bohemia by key figures such as Josef Hoffmann, Michael Powolny and Otto Prutscher.

Notwithstanding the firm's production for the period 1921–28 conformed in full with the Venetian principle and presented few innovative ideas,[3] this was not so apparent to their contemporaries: the glasshouse's early success stems from the fact that the 'historical' forms they borrowed were actually considered modern in taste, and consonant with the period's evolving ideals of form. With their lean silhouettes and economy of line, they addressed the preference for spare, essential forms, a period in which functionalism was steadily gaining acceptance. This new elegance was notably manifest in the forms borrowed from Renaissance sources.

The trend did not last long however, and attempts to rekindle past glory had the same outcome as Salviati's efforts, failing to ensure further developments of the art of Venetian glassmaking.

Venini and Cappellin's Venetian revival was out of step with developments across Europe. The Venetian *façon*, though followed keenly by Sweden, England, Germany and Austria, was an integral part of a broad movement of developments in glassmaking, in which such Venetian companies as Fratelli Toso fulfilled the purely executive role of manufacturing articles to designs by northern artist.[4]

The revival of Roman forms took quite a different course. In this case, the backward look at early glass was in tune with the growing fixation for Antiquity, whose appeal was also reflected in political movements that wished to emulate the Roman Empire.

Throughout the 1930s this trend affected artistic currents all across Europe, and not only in countries dominated by Fascist regimes. In this way, the pioneering path followed by Italian glassmaking in the 1920s is an early precursor of the evolution under way.

In the 1920s the third source of Venini and Cappellin's inspiration – the movements flourishing in Viennese cultural circles, conforms to the new idea of form prevalent in German-speaking countries at the time. This interest in developments north of the Alps is hardly surprising, given northern Italy's long-standing ties with the Habsburg monarchy. The perception of form and solid grasp of materials evinced by Viennese designers were more akin to Murano's own traditions – irrespective of the historical ties – than to contemporary developments in other countries.

There was an undeniable affinity between the formal solutions of the Viennese School with its love of clean, unfussy lines, and the resurrection of the pure, classical forms of the Renaissance. The permeable borderline between these two approaches to pure form originated a reciprocal overlapping that produced fascinating results.

At the time Murano was not yet prepared to challenge the sanctioned Venetian methods of hot-working thinly walled vessels, nor to succumb to the lure of the new European movements. And while the production of Venini glassworks bears no trace of the young Swedish, Dutch or the otherwise still strong French glassmaking, all emphasising an equilibrium of form and decor with an accentuation of volume, mass and weight, the pieces produced between 1921 and 1928 can be traced back more or less to any one of the three sources of reference above.

As long as the neo-Venetian line pursued in the 1920s remained commercially successful, the necessity to reconsider traditions did not arise. Towards the end of the decade, continuing public appreciation of Venini's production north of the Alps induced the competing Bohemian firm Joh. Lötz Witwe to subscribe to the Murano glasshouse's standards with its own versions of the 'Veronese' and the 'Libellula' (Dragon-fly) vase series.[5] The firm's formal canon for these years was given its fundamental imprint by the strong-minded designer Vittorio Zecchin and by Giacomo Cappellin, a man familiar with art history; for the time being Paolo Venini's input to the decision-making on artistic and formal matters was minimal. For him it was still a period of intense learning, a period during which he steadily acquired the resources that would earn him with that infallible sense of form and expertise with the material which informed his activity in the years that followed.

The break-up with Cappellin took place in 1925, and marked Paolo Venini's first step towards greater independence. The real start of the firm's extraordinary success only began about 1928 when Paolo Venini empowered his artistic director, the sculptor Napoleone Martinuzzi to make radical changes to the manufacturing program. It was at this moment that Venini – ostensibly an outsider, an 'immigrant' lawyer from Milan – felt sufficiently confident about his understanding of Murano's complex structures and traditions to refine and consolidate areas of proven excellence, eliminating the weaker elements, and finally embark on completely new lines of production.

His Milanese background and the indelible ties he maintained with this city, the country's most vibrant and creative cultural centre, afforded Venini greater breadth of vision than that of the local glassmasters of his adopted Murano, enabling him to shore his own ideas against the entrenched traditionalism of the island's craftsmen. To some extent, the history of Murano glassmaking was repeating itself: as before, the problem was that, in order to become really creative, traditional Venetian glassmaking skills needed new input from developments taking place abroad.

Whilst Cappellin remained loyal to the Venetian principle – initially with Zecchin, who was to work for him until the end of the 1926 and then with the young Carlo Scarpa, and eventually encounters commercial failure in 1932 – in Venini's new firm Martinuzzi did not simply jettison traditional values, but challenged them, finding ways to bring production in line with the spirit of the times. Furthermore, by choosing a sculptor as artistic director, in 1925 Paolo Venini now had a designer capable of translating volume, mass and body into form – an aspect that gained strategic importance in the 1930s. The designs turned out from 1928 on broke with the traditional emphasis on line and profile, and opened the way to a multitude of new and varied possibilities that Martinuzzi exploited with courage and determination.

Jointly, Martinuzzi and Venini instituted a genre of sculptural glass that was novel to Murano, a completely new tradition that has endured to the present day. The new designs were particularly popular in the 1930s thanks to numerous creative minds such as Flavio Poli, Ercole Barovier, Archimede Seguso and Alfredo Barbini. Where sculptural inventions in Venetian glass production had once been limited to flame work in small format, or to decorative elements for extravagant detailing – such as dragon stems for drinking vessels or elaborate decoration for vases – the new objects were emancipated from pure functionality by the efforts of Martinuzzi. Although they maintained their decorative nature, they could now stand alone, as self-sufficient sculptural objects, affiliating themselves to the forms of the incoming Art Déco movement so popular in Paris.

With his 'Piante grasse' (Cacti) series (cat. no. 54) Martinuzzi applied the concept of Art Déco 'cactus style' to the letter. For this he modelled pieces of solid or opaque glass straight from the furnace with pincers or

shears, creating sets of ornamental objects and animals – a radical departure from the transparency and airiness of Zecchin's vases of the 1920s. Perhaps even more revolutionary in approach was Martinuzzi's interference with the very composition of the molten glass: no one in Murano had ever dared subvert the crystal purity of the glassmaker's basic material, and suddenly this was no longer sacred. An entirely new type of glass with a textured, bubbled-filled mass, was created. The new material, known as *pulegoso*, had properties similar to ceramics. Aspiring to Roman forerunners, vases wrought with the new method were welcomed as strikingly modern and hence very fashionable.

With the new lines created in 1928 Martinuzzi and Venini had caught up with the international design vanguard, making their own inimitable contribution. Suddenly Vienna was no longer the sole point of reference for Murano, as craftsmen began seeking inspiration from developments further afield in glassmaking centres in France, Sweden and Holland.

Napoleone Martinuzzi's work was only a beginning, however, and not a complete breakthrough. His transgressions were bold revisions, but all in all this spurt of invention was too brief and his style too flamboyant and individualistic to have a lasting effect. This way, like Tomaso Buzzi, who worked for Venini for a brief period in Milan, Martinuzzi was above all harbinger to Carlo Scarpa, who became the firm's most important designer of the 1930s and the early '40s. He had been

at Venini's side since 1933–34, and eventually gave the firm its distinctive identity, making Venini a hallmark of new European glass design.[6]

The young architect Scarpa's work brought clarity and coherence to Venini's range of designs. The firm's lines subscribed to simplified, often three-dimensional forms. (Occasionally they admitted east Asiatic models).

From the outset Scarpa showed a preference for vessel design over sculpture. Their forms Paolo Venini entrusted to the Swedish ceramist Tyra Lundgren. Meanwhile, with astonishing self-confidence, Scarpa transposed new achievements in European glass of the 1920s and early '30s to the Venetian milieu, disregarding the phase of development marked by the work of Maurice Marinot in Troyes in the mid-1920s.[7] On occasion, Scarpa reverted to a somewhat heavy, almost archaic approach in his creations, advocating, like Marinot, thick, colourless vessel walls, but left aside any exploration of their interior space – a direction he left to the firm's competitor, Ercole Barovier, to develop.[8]

In his early phase with Venini, Scarpa focused on the study and analysis of current trends, mainly the possibility of exploring uses of solid glass. This is clearly demonstrated by his first designs in the *bollicine* glass, developed from Martinuzzi's *pulegoso*. This new direction was further explored through the series of objects using the *sommerso* (submerged) technique, which saw a very individual application of layers of bubble-glass flecked with gold leaf – a return to classic Venetian methods, but highly innovative (cat. nos 116–17).[9] With the 'Sommersi' series of 1933–34 Scarpa proved to be one of the most progressive glass designers in Europe. Previously, works of this kind were only to be found in the Dutch glass factory Leerdam, designed by Andries Dirk Copiers.[10]

Be that as it may, the decisive step towards a total freedom of form was still to be taken: by forgoing the traditional reverence for glass's smooth, fire-polished surface, Venini and Scarpa were transcending a secular Venetian law. Despite half-hearted attempts at revival in the eighteenth century, nothing could stanch the flood of engraved glass produced north of the Alps, which plunged Murano into a decline from which it never fully recovered. Nor had any serious efforts been made to provide skills in the various forms of cold-finishing glass. Throughout the twentieth century only one manufacturer, s.a.l.i.r., explored these new possibilities of glass decoration. The gaffers and their teams of practised glassblowers were highly sceptical, and viewed such techniques as utterly alien to the Venetian tradition.

To initiate a process of reassessment, a determined entrepreneur was needed, someone free of preconceptions and with the courage to foster new ideas, and a designer who was slave neither to current fashions nor to 'inviolable' traditions but had a deep acquaintance with the rules of form and decoration developed over centuries in all cultures.

Paolo Venini and Carlo Scarpa were the personification of these two figures, and together they managed to transcend traditional prejudice, undermining Murano's diffidence towards cold-finishing techniques.

The introduction of surface finishing gave Venini's production an altogether new cast. The new *corroso* (corroded) glassware ushered in a new form of coloured opaque glassware with a characteristically weathered finish, rough to the touch, produced by a treatment involving sawdust soaked in hydrofluoric acid.[11] Iridised finishes were also frequent, together with the addition of sculpted relief elements that lent rhythm and articulation to the surface of the vase (cat. nos 120–23).

This new approach to surface treatment came into its own with the introduction of *battuto* (beaten) and *inciso* (incised) wares (cat. nos 135–37).[12] Techniques of working glass when cold were gradually conceded in Venice and Murano as a valid, practical means of styling – a change of course that was very significant for Murano's future development. The island had broken free of the Venetian principles without exactly relinquishing them, thereby creating new opportunities and markets of international recognition. The techniques of cutting and engraving – long since accepted by glassmakers abroad – guaranteed Scarpa's skilfully wrought and sculpted vases a place alongside the leading names in European glassware.

Thanks to the pioneering efforts of Venini and Scarpa, glassmakers all across the lagoon adopted the technique of cold surface decoration. The result was not a mere reworking of northern influences previously alien to Murano – this could only be said for some designs produced by the S.A.L.I.R. – but something specifically Venetian.

With this novel starting point, the entire tradition of Venetian ornamental techniques could be given a facelift. While the technique of *mezza filigrana* (cat. no. 118) kept its traditional use of filaments of opaline glass trailed through the transparent medium, the *tessuti* (weave) lines lead to a complete revision of the ancient techniques of filigree decoration (cat. nos 129–30). Scarpa's novel use of parallel trails evinced a consistent use of chromatic effects and a conscious rebuttal of the virtuosity of traditional manufacturing with its complex lattice and imprisoned air bubble effects.

The same thing is true for the reintroduction of 'mosaic' glass, which, despite promising development during the late nineteenth and early twentieth centuries, had been abandoned, for reasons as yet unclear. Paolo Venini launched its revival with great success, commencing with his imitations of Roman murrhine glass in the *murrina* wares of 1936 (cat. no. 68) and concluding with the subtle vases, plates and glasses of 1940 (cat. nos 142–43)[13] that were not always easily recognisable as mosaic glass: the pattern of the individual inserts is kept utterly simple, and the final striking effect is due to the sheer number of the welded glass pieces and particularly to the final grinding of the surface to produce a semi-opaque finish. The same is true for the designs involving the *tessuto* technique.

Observing today the striped models of the 1940s (cat. no. 144), including the expressive *pennellate* glasses (so called because of their expressive brush-stroke effects; cat. no. 145) and above all the *macchie* (flecked) glasses decorated with irregular flecks (cat. no. 146), one grasps the impact of Carlo Scarpa's approach on Venini's development: all the formal elements intrinsic to the works of Scarpa's young and lively successor Fulvio Bianconi had already been developed and anticipated by Scarpa himself.

Paolo Venini's insightful choice of his collaborators can be seen in the fact that, in those decisive post-war years he did not look for a 'replacement' Scarpa figure, but instead decided on the slightly eccentric young painter and graphic designer. With imaginative flair and inexhaustible creativity, Bianconi drew directly from the existing well of technical and formal possibilities, bypassing the long and tiresome learning processes and technical experimentation. After the methodical architect Scarpa, who had known how to combine a sensitive and poetic creative process with material experiments that controverted local traditions, Venini could now allow himself to give the task of designing to an artist who had spiritual sensitivity and a feeling for the new era. This is how the door that lead to the creative explosion of the 1950s opened.

Without Carlo Scarpa's preliminary work, Venini's immense success in the post-war years would have been unthinkable. And Carlo Scarpa could not have wrought such change without the continuous dialogue and encouragement that Paolo Venini unswerving accorded him. As a result, one might say that Scarpa's works are to a large degree also Venini's. Works of such artistic élan could only have be achieved by someone who – despite his passion and esteem for the Murano glassmaking tradition – was neither encumbered by convention nor hindered by the virtuoso glassblowing tradition. While not belonging to Murano, Paolo Venini's earnest conviction of being able to turn the island's legacy to account enabled him to find new in the old, and to reach this goal he intuitively brought in and nurtured new collaborators whose horizons broke the island's creative deadlock.

Showing great determination, Paolo Venini made the unprecedented step of inviting guest designers from abroad, at a time when the island's craft was allegedly still a 'secret', to be protected from the outside world.

In this way the Venini label became synonymous with a bold divorce from the hitherto unassailable Venetian principle of glass production, a dissociation that ushered in an era of rebirth for Murano. By indomitably embracing outside influences, Paolo Venini was the harbinger of Murano's present modern practices, which are in constant and rapid evolution to this day. The achievement of that transformation remains Venini's inextinguishable legacy: he guided Murano out of its self-imposed isolation, striving to make the voice of new Venetian glassmaking stand out amid the trends across Europe, and lead the island, with all its age-old tradition, to new and unforeseen greatness.

[1] Salviati: cf. G. Sarpellon, *Salviati il suo vetro e i suoi uomini*, Venice 1989; *murrina*, cf. G. Sarpellon, *Miniature di vetro: Murrine 1838-1924*, Venice 1990.

[2] Cf. F. Deboni, *Venini Glassware*, Milan 1996, appendix S, pp. 1ff.

[3] This is more true for Venini than for Cappellin; after Venini's break with the firm in 1925, Cappellin continued along the established path of success, but called in the young Carlo Scarpa; despite a basic loyalty to the Venetian principle, the firm introduced many new ideas and solutions. Cf. M. Barovier, *Carlo Scarpa. I vetri di un architetto*, exhibition catalogue (Palazzo Martinengo, Brescia), Milan 1997, pp. 54–99.

[4] Cf. H. Ricke, "'Stile Novecento" and "Forme Nuove". Italy's Contribution to European Glass Culture in the Twentieth Century', in *Italian Glass. Murano-Milan 1930-1970*, The Collection of the Steinberg Foundation, edited by H. Ricke, E. Schmitt, Munich/New York 1997, pp. 11–34.

[5] Cf. Lötz, *Böhmisches Glas 1880-1940*, Vol. 2, *Katalog der Musterschnitte*, Munich/New York. 1989, pp. 256–57, nos 3869, 3923.

[6] For more on Scarpa, see. M. Barovier, *op. cit.*

[7] For Marinot's works, see e.g. M. Hoog, C. Giraudon, *Maurice Marinot peintre et verrier*, exhibition catalogue, Paris 1990.

[8] Cf. among others A. Dorigato et al., *Art of the Barovier Glassmakers in Murano 1866-1972*, Venice 1993, pp. 128–31.

[9] Cf. M. Barovier, *op. cit.*, pp. 104–11.

[10] For Copier's works see among others, R. Liefkes, *Copier*, Den Haag 1989 and *Leerdam Unica*, exhibition catalogue (Kunstmuseum, Düsseldorf), Düsseldorf 1977.

[11] The use of acids for surface effects was without doubt greatly boosted by the work of the Swedish ceramist Tyra Lundgren; her early fish pieces already had surfaces treated this way.

[12] Cf. M. Barovier, *op. cit.*, pp. 120–27 and 150–61.

[13] Cf. ibid., pp. 145, 164–70, 171.

Valerio Terraroli

Paolo Venini and the Metamorphosis of Modern Style during the 1920s

The facile, all-inclusive term 'modern style', referring either to Modern as a concept, to the Italian Novecento style, or simply to Rationalism, seems at first to conveniently encapsulate the multifaceted panorama of creativity in the first half of the twentieth century. Upon closer scrutiny, however, it proves to be an almost recklessly ambiguous term, inadequate to encompass the inventive dynamics it claims to define, those abrupt shifts of taste. Above all, it fails to provide a rational system of styles. This fact becomes even more cogent when one envisages the sheer diversity of production in the field of the decorative arts, and similarly in design for industry where, necessarily, executive and draughting skills consonant with a tradition of high-level craftsmanship meet and merge in serial production, with formal devices informed with high-key identities, engendering products that faithfully reflect the lurching, transient canons of taste.

Precisely taste – or, better, the *variability* of taste – at once conditions and influences the choice of both material and form for articles related to everyday life and furnishings, more so than in the case of painting or monumental sculpture.

To apply the expression 'Modernism' to international Modernity in its broadest sense (including such phenomena as the Italian style known as 'Liberty', for instance), implicates the real validity of the term itself – a term used widely in journals, advertisements and critiques in reference to the artistic production of the early 1920s. While in some cases that production became a hackneyed, repetitive pursuit of the Liberty *esprit*, it was accompanied by a strong, meaningful resurgence of traditional academic knowledge, triggering notable episodes of revival eclecticism. By contrast, elsewhere in central Europe, Holland, and the United States, areas of production more drawn to the new dictates of Abstract and function-oriented art and architecture were steadily gaining ground.

Despite such a fluctuating, highly diversified situation, abounding in cultural cross-references and well-estab-

lished models, a coherent line of taste nonetheless came into being. Though short-lived and affiliated with Liberty, it entailed an amalgam of the more radical, geometric Wiener Werkstätte mode and the Novecento aesthetic. The 'style' had assumed identifiable characteristics by 1920–21, reached its climax in 1925 (on the occasion of the Paris Exposition des Arts Décoratifs et Industriels), before quickly petering out with the 1929 world crisis and the beginning of the 1930s.

Art Déco, also known as '1925 style', is indeed a style in its own right having an international matrix, but with regional variations. Hence, properly speaking it was not a *style*, as it was not rooted in ideological foundations as such. Nor was it motivated by 'educational' premises, or aimed at socio-cultural transformation. Nevertheless, it was a highly refined mode of expression, involving a sapient cross-pollination of classical aesthetics with the bold, playful graphism of the Futurist tradition. Liberty stressed the intrinsic luxury of manufactured articles through the preciousness of the materials used, through a complacent aloofness in the forms proposed, through the absolute modernity (subscribing therefore to so-called Modernism) of its forms and decorative inventions. Last of all, it unabashedly emphasised the utter *futility*, however appealing, of its products.[1] Today, Déco taste provides a portrait of a hedonist society that wished to cancel the tragic memory of World War I, heedless of the clouds of international conflict gathering once more on the horizon, blithely convinced of the coming fortune and magnificence afforded by industry and technology. While it culled whatever possible from classical spheres for reuse in the modern lifestyle, the new aesthetic underwent a distillation and revision prescribed by the emerging, innovative visions of the avant-gardes. It was in this atmosphere of exceptional creative fervour – a phenomenon which largely connotes production on both sides of the Atlantic at the time – that Paolo Venini's glassworks, founded with Giacomo Cappellin and

Vittorio Zecchin in 1921, first saw the light. The story of the firm's creation, admirably rehearsed elsewhere,[2] takes us from Murano to Milan and back again: inasmuch as Murano and Venice together are ritually archetypes of tradition and romanticism – and as such the bane of the Futurists – they are also synonymous with the production of art glass, while Milan itself was midwife to the Italian version of Déco, Liberty, and nurtured it over a couple of years.[3]

The firm Vetri Soffiati Muranesi Cappellin Venini & C. personified the new productive energies prevailing in the early post-war years. The newly founded company was a winning fusion of specific skills, but the beginnings were clouded, however, by the sudden death of the master glassmaker Andrea Rioda, a compelling interpreter of the Modernist style, whose designs were continued in replica. These events determined the setup of the new glassworks: Cappellin embodying the continuity of tradition of art glass; Zecchin as designer hailing from the Ca' Pesaro Secession glass and Venetian Liberty; and the young Venini as administrator, Milan-born and freshly graduated in Jurisprudence.

From the outset Paolo Venini's role was to deal with the marketing and promotion of the glasshouse's production. He was to extend the firm's frontiers at both artistic and sales levels, principally by growing new markets. Showing great intuition, he successfully overhauled the product range, creating an essential, clean-cut line or glasswares without compromising the Murano legacy, while refocusing the traditional skills and multiplying the technical processes of production. Meanwhile he fostered a healthy interchange with Italy's new generation of architects, in whose designs glass was no longer just a separate article of interior furnishing but included items of everyday use, an element that enhances and integrates with the interiors by means of coherent overall decorative formulas.

Members of the highbrow milieu of creative minds in Milan felt the need to bridge the enduring schism between high-level craftsmanship and industrial production.[4] They therefore essayed to circumscribe a class of product designs having a functional role in everyday life, products with a wide diffusion therefore, but which nonetheless expressed elegance through their select forms and materials; such articles were to entail links with traditional Italian designs, while being patently modern. With these premises as their guide, Venini and Cappellin made all their decisions, tailoring them to the environment of Venice, the 'womb' of the centuries-old tradition of Murano glassmaking, which they wished to entirely renovate in its products while preserving its tech-

nical skills, and nurture links with contemporary historical trends and art movements.

The distinction the so-called applied arts had achieved since the end of the nineteenth century, carried forward now by the tide of international Modernism, was formulated in the new theories put forward by the Vienna School, and in particular the writings of Alois Riegl.[5] The tide of renovation saw the creation of art schools and important production centres (the above-mentioned Wiener Werkstätte), and the establishment of museums devoted to the history of the applied and decorative arts, proposed as focuses of training for the new generations of workers in the sector.

On Murano the Museo Vetrario played a major role in fostering new talents. Among its directors was the sculptor Napoleone Martinuzzi, who for an important spell was in charge of design at the Venini works. But these years also saw a widespread rediscovery of Venetian painting, particularly of Renaissance Venice, with Giuseppe Fiocco publishing *catalogues raisonnés* of various artists, including the complete works of Paolo Veronese (in 1928). Another influential event was the reappraisal of simplicity and formal exquisiteness of objects featured in those same Renaissance paintings. The painter Mariano Fortuny y Madrazo sought to replicate the exquisite sixteenth-century silks and velvets that appeared in the works of Titian, Veronese, and Tintoretto, using less expensive modern production methods. Meanwhile, the wave of sixteenth-century revival prompted cabinetmakers and carpenters to include replicas of antiques in their production.

Working from drawings by Zecchin, Giacomo Cappellin began producing sets of clear, transparent wares in a very thin lightweight glass inspired by famous paintings. This heralded the 'Veronese', 'Holbein', and 'Tintoretto' series of vases, which opportunely became signature articles of the company. These, more importantly, were immediately followed by a new range of pieces conceived by Vittorio Zecchin for production in series (still in limited quantities, to guarantee quality): the novelty was that the new items were skilfully adapted for modern everyday use. This brought new ensembles of tableware composed of compotes, glasses, bowls, vases, and not least chandeliers modelled after eighteenth-century specimens that had never been omitted from traditional Muranese production. These were resurrected with a rigorous simplification of form, and elimination of decoration. Nonetheless, while the forms adopted from 1921 to 1925 are rooted in imitation, quoting, as it were, from the paintings of the Venetian masters – therefore in line with the eclectic bent of 1920s – the resulting articles exuded a spirit of modernity, a wholly contemporary answer

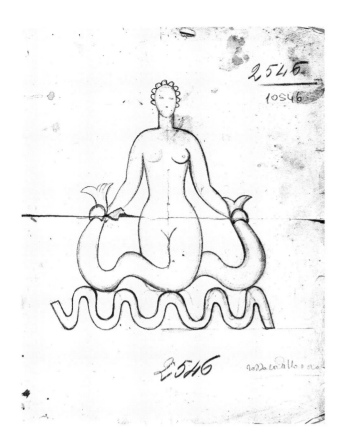

to Art Déco. Among these new designs, the *Libellula* (Dragon-fly) bowl, later repeated even by Martinuzzi, epitomises the metamorphosis of a form copied from sixteenth-century tradition, to which the highly elegant though perhaps redundant swirls and large round base bestowed a look at once of lightness and gracious monumentality. The same can be said of the oval vases and the tiny flasks fitted with lids and stoppers and phytomorphic handles: little apples, tiny mottled pears, lemons, fruit that recurs in larger sizes as fillers in a kind of modern, vitrified still life, for large bowls with cone-shaped bases; added to these came fruit stands or large, extremely light, almost impalpable sky-blue platters.

It is worth noting Zecchin's adherence to the winning formula of Liberty tradition, and to a sense of lightness that yields to the more explicitly Déco opulence expressed in the utter essentialness and total absence of painted or added decorative features, as in the choice of bold colours such as violet and deep blue.

The acclaim accorded the Cappellin Venini & C. glass exhibits at the first Monza Biennale in 1923 was formulated by Roberto Papini, who re-evokes the Muranese tradition: 'It was and is the paroxysm of manual skill [...]. Zecchin, one of the most accomplished artists in Italy today, should be recognised as the first to have grasped the two essential qualities of Murano glass: lightness and transparency, all the more evident and splendid for being em-

bodied in forms of elegance and harmony.'[6] Venini's success was repeated in 1925 in Paris at the huge fair devoted to the decorative and industrial arts: among the firms representing Italy were the Richard-Ginori ceramics group, whose production designer was Gio Ponti (awarded first prize); and Venini & C., which presented designs by Zecchin of arboreal compositions with stylised curlicues and symmetrical flourishes, plus a monumental chandelier where both the campanula-shaped bowls and the elements inspired by acanthus swirls, were blended in rigorous, sober geometric forms, in the purest Déco style.[7] That same year proved to be a critical one: the company broke up in May, Giacomo Cappellin left to set up a new glassworks bearing the title Maestri Vetrai Muranesi Cappellin & C., taking with him Venini's chief designer, Vittorio Zecchin.

In the meantime, Paolo Venini had accumulated some solid business experience, not just in marketing but also in matters of production practices. This new asset gave him the managerial independence he had probably sought from the beginning. He retained the ownership of the glassworks and two of the main sales outlets: one in Venice close by St Mark's; and one in via Montenapoleone, Milan. At the same time he took on a group of master glassblowers preparing to open a new workshop headed by the Muranese sculptor Napoleone Martinuzzi, then also director of the Museo Vetrario. Mar-

tinuzzi had close ties with Gabriele D'Annunzio and other members of Venetian cultural circles, including the De Maria and Cadorin families.[8] Well-versed in the established technical traditions he had been able to observe among the museum's collections, including open-mould reliefs and half-moulds, and the method of sculpting the material and producing large-scale pieces, Martinuzzi effected a gradual transformation of the product range his forerunner Vittorio Zecchin had assembled, introducing a change of taste aligned to the more accepted Déco typologies, which in the early 1930s was expressed in a Novecento idiom.

Meticulously supervised by Paolo Venini, the firm's production went from strength to strength. Success abroad compounded the healthy returns from the Venice and Monza Biennales (the latter becoming the Milan Triennale in 1930) and Rome Quadriennale exhibitions, events for which Venini proposed certain new compositions in large-scale format such as fountains and flowering trees. But the firm's chief accomplishments lay in the conscientious replication of models created by Murano's past-masters. Indeed, glassworks all over the island took Venini's cue, and began producing the kind of art glass that was garnering a large market, emulating both the materials used, but above all Venini's choice of forms. The Venini trademark became synonymous with Modernism. The firm's role as bellwether was as acknowledged

at home as it was abroad. At the 1927 Monza Biennale, Gio Ponti invited the Venini glassworks to join company with the 'Labirinto' (Labyrinth), an association of architects comprising Tomaso Buzzi, Emilio Lancia, Michele Marelli, the glassmaker Pietro Chiesa and Carla Visconti di Modrone. It was no coincidence that the group's address was the Venini store in via Montenapoleone, Milan.

The new firm's explicit objectives – which deserve a more in-depth discussion than is possible here, given the impressive show of creative input manifested in such a brief lapse of time – was to create a line of items with a unifying, coherent style tailored specifically for designer interiors and modern architecture. This was the 'Italian-style home' tirelessly advocated by the Milanese architect Gio Ponti, an idea made concrete in 1928 with the founding of the magazine *Domus*.[9] Venini glass (house furnishings, tableware, and light fittings) addressed Ponti's appeal by designing tableware in synergy with the elegant Richard-Ginori porcelain products, designed by Ponti and modelled by Gariboldi, Griselli, Cibau, Andreotti, and Saponaro. Other evidence of a cohesive aesthetic included: monumental majolicas; neo-rococo furnishings by the Lancia auto manufacturer; the ingenious, Futurist-style items by Portaluppi; Pietro Chiesa's stained-glass windows (much praised by Gabriele D'Annunzio); the elegant and unjustly overlooked cre-

ations of Tomaso Buzzi, who worked briefly directly for Venini from 1932 to 1934.

Towards the end of the 1920s, first the Milanese and then the Romans began to take notice of Paolo's intuitive outlook. Important public buildings – post offices, railway stations, and government offices – were accoutred with Venini light fittings and decorative glass installations. Other major contributions include: glass fittings for patrician residences (Villa Barbaro Volpi at Maser) and hotels, notably the four fabulous, monumental chandeliers in the salon of the Hotel Vittoria, Brescia, designed by Egidio Dabbeni as part of the larger project by Marcello Piacentini for piazza della Vittoria, completed in 1931; here Napoleone Martinuzzi devised a singular reworking of Zecchin's model for the 1925 Paris exhibition, in which the airy lightness of forms is replaced by grandeur and an impressive array of materials, generating a manifest link between Art Déco and the Novecento manner.

Napoleone Martinuzzi's spell at the Venini firm from 1926 to 1932 saw a complete makeover, during which the product range was definitively brought up to date. Paolo was keenly aware of the course they had taken, and extended *ad libitum* the possible applications of glass, passing from picture frames, mirrors, and clocks, to monumental sculpture (such as the ingenious *Josephine Baker* figure styled by Martinuzzi in two versions in 1928 and 1929); this led to a rediscovery of the natural world, with amazing cacti, exotic animals and aquariums, supports for lamps and light fittings, a musical fountain, furnishings, and not least a stained-glass window resembling an antique tapestry.

The fundamental record for these inventions is still the so-called *Catalogo blu*, a series of sheets of blue paper (the same colour as that used by the Tiepolos), illustrated with the outlines of the pieces, each with its serial number, pieced together in the early 1930s (in all probability 1933–35), after Napoleone Martinuzzi's departure from the firm. That *taccuino* is reproduced in full here, testifying not only to the creative diversity characteris-

ing articles produced by Venini in the 1920s, but also of the continuity, for some of them, of the Cappellin-Zecchin inventions (a firm that wound down in 1929 owing to the world economic crisis). An essential nucleus of pieces Martinuzzi produced either for Venini or for Francesco Zecchin is conserved at the Vittoriale on Lake Garda, the mausoleum-home built by Gabriele D'Annunzio over the period 1921–38. A great deal has been written about the poet D'Annunzio's links with Venetian cultural circles in the 1910s and '20s, and about the authentic variant of Déco forged specifically for the villa's furnishings, though somewhat lost amid the poet-collector's somewhat grandiose, inimitable eclecticism.[10] What is significant is the importance D'Annunzio ascribed to glass as a material. The forms and models he solicited were in precise keeping with the tastes of the day. He personally kept in touch with Napoleone Martinuzzi and Vittorio Zecchin, whom he had met during his stay in Venice. Oddly, in the D'Annunzio archives there is no trace of correspondence with the Venini firm,

nor with Paolo himself, who must have been delighted that Venini articles were admitted to the poet's home (what better means of publicity?), despite the latter's exigent preferences – typical also of the 'Labirinto' group. D'Annunzio was an esteemed taste-maker, an authority on style and fashion and, with all these Venini-produced furnishings arranged through the poet's lakeside villa, Paolo found a formidable ally in the engineer Ruggero Maroni (brother of the architect Gian Carlo Maroni who had conceived the entire Vittoriale ensemble), a close friend of several eminent figures from the Venetian art world, including Martinuzzi, the Cadorin family, and Del Giudice.

An unpublished letter from Ruggero Maroni to D'Annunzio, whom he addresses as *Comandante* (Captain), dated 28 May 1925,[11] implies that Martinuzzi himself was *magna pars* in founding the new concern. He asked Gabriele D'Annunzio for an endorsement, for national and international recognition of the firm's drive to revitalise the arts and craftsmanship in a new, progressive spirit: 'CAPTAIN, as per agreement, I take the liberty to inform you that I am leaving tomorrow for Turin for a few days. If you have some errand to entrust me, I am at your disposal.

'Later, around June 10th I shall go to Venice to attend the inauguration of the new company "Vetri Soffiati Muranesi" which has been formed by absorbing the commercial assets of the old V.S.M., which, under the artistic guidance of Napoleone Martinuzzi, and in league with a staff of skilled master glassworkers, intends to raise the art of glass to its former glory.

'Spurred by your encouragement, Martinuzzi has managed to assemble this creation, always keeping in mind your verbal agreement whereby you will be willing to give new instructions as *Grande Maestro del Fuoco* [Grand Master of Fire]. This glasshouse should represent a branch of the arts of the Vittoriale, which should soon be able to transfer here the premises of your planned Village of the Arts.

'Regrettably, the art of glass is under a grave threat. National speculators are trying to take abroad the few skilful workers we still have, causing serious artistic and financial harm. Artistic: owing to the foreign atmosphere and the absence both of the traditional local spirit and of the worthy examples of the Muranese past-masters' handiwork. Financial: owing to the reduction of personnel, exports, and income. Let us hope that common sense and a yearning for their smoky island will avert this calamity. Surely, at our ceremony your presence, even if only in spirit, will not fail to fuel the spirit and fervour of the masters of the sacred fire. Ever at your command, your most devoted servant, Engineer Ruggero Maroni. 28.V.1925.'

The 'Village of the Arts' cited in the letter, one of D'Annunzio's grandiose dreams, never came about. Nor did the poet's auspicated endorsement of the new firm directed by Paolo Venini. Nevertheless, there was a constant exchange, passing through the art director, Martinuzzi: 'To the Muranese master, who fashions glass and marble with the same artistic spirit, who treats glass and bronze alike with the same fire, I offer the emblem of the rooster, endorsed with the motto '*Excalant iunctam con viribus artem*' – 27.1926, Gabriele D'Annunzio, sculptor and glassmaker.'[12]

With this redoubtable dictum the poet sanctioned his alliance with the creator of the beautiful glass articles that adorn the Vittoriale: chandeliers in violet, emerald green, and yellow-green blown glass restyled on designs by Zecchin (flare-rimmed bowls, ornamental swirls, oval pendants) with echoes of antique artefacts such as Roman lamps (lamps in the Office Cheli and Bagno delle Ospiti), as well as prestigious sets of glassware and table-ware either in yellow-green, green, transparent, or in pink, coral, black paste and *pulegoso* glass, unusual pumpkin-lamps for the Stanza della Musica or di Gasparo, fashioned by Martinuzzi along with the glass baskets of fruit between 1926 and 1927; and the glass 'bestiary' (blue and red elephants with gold leaf, red bears, a transparent glass gazelle, all pieces Francesco Zecchin produced at the Venini furnace), and the two fabulous cornucopia chandeliers (Stanza del Mascheraio and Stanza Verde), especially made for D'Annunzio around 1928–30 such as the renowned *Vaso pulegoso ad anse dorate* eloquent harbingers of the coming Novecento style, and also produced at the Venini works.

The collection of drawings in the *Catalogo blu* (Venice, Anna Venini Collection) reveal the sculptor-glassmaker's creative vitality. His elegant designs are never hackneyed. Presaging trends about to take off in the 1930s were his various cacti pieces, and the monumental flowering cacti for the Bergamo post-office building (two elegant, scaled-down versions can be seen in the Stanza della Leda in the Vittoriale), ideas that reflected international trends, including developments in North America in 1928–30. In a provoking display of essentialness, new production included bird-figures perched on columns, exotic animals, lamp bases resembling small household aquariums filled with water, in which sea fauna are reflected and deformed; but also cacti and abstract spirals. Martinuzzi had completely overhauled the Venini product range. The change also affected the choice of materials and production techniques, with a wide use of the heavy-looking *pulegoso* glass, full of air bubbles like dew immersed in a deep greenish glass; new designs based on nature ensued, more the handiwork of a sculptor, crafted in heavy, strong body of glass, less of the ethereal, weightless articles favoured by Cappellin and Zecchin; and last of all, the very concept of the material altered, with the introduction of variegated glass, the inclusion of gold leaf, the folding of layers in imitation of chalcedony, jade, and antique cameo glass. These ideas were subsequently explored further by Tomaso Buzzi, who created an imaginary, pseudo-natural world – works that evidently delighted the poet D'Annunzio: 'My dear Napè, Your fruits were delicious – but have not sated me. I devoured them all that very evening. So now I need a new basketful. But you risk straining – or breaking – our friendship with your stubbornness in refusing to consider me a true *customer* of your glassware. A 'recipient' soon tires of being repeatedly overwhelmed by lavish gifts – *do you hear?* I hereby engage you to make six illuminated fruit baskets – but as a *customer*, mind you. The round base should not exceed *15–20* centimetres (in diameter). That is my sole requisite. I leave it to you to decide the form itself of the baskets, which should be in *opaque* glass, in the yellow or reddish hue of cane or wicker, so that the pile of fruit *alone* is resplendent. The light bulb will be inserted through the base and set in a wooden disk. I venture to enclose a somewhat clumsy sketch, which you will turn into a miracle of brilliant grace. As for the fruit, let colour abound, *à la Venise…*'[13]

The crisis that overtook the world in 1929, and particularly the repercussions on the market in fine glass over the ensuing three years, led to countless firms folding, including the Cappellin & C. glasshouse. Venini's resisted, but Napoleone Martinuzzi and Francesco Zecchin, relieved of their duties to the company, went off to open their own factory.

For his part, Paolo Venini stoically inaugurated a new phase of production characterised by Tomaso Buzzi's earnest, refined two-year presidium of the design department: it was the swan-song of the graceful, stylish Déco taste, henceforth replaced by the grandiloquent, sculptural Italian Novecento style. And a refined swansong it was, with its ironically ornamental forms and figures (like the renowned *Mani* bowl with clasped hands and the twin-spouted vase, now in a private collection, Padua), for which Buzzi made good use of opaque *lattimo* glass and *alga*, with forceful hues of aquamarine, amethyst, brown and grey highlighted with minute gold flecks. The well-to-do, erudite – but ultimately limited – market of middle-class patronage was supplanted by the need to open out the market to a wider public, which required a constant reinvention of forms and models to keep up with the radical changes in fashion and style, orienting the factory's forces to production in series, in keeping with the emerging trends in architecture, be it Rationalist or Classicising. It was at this juncture that a new figure entered the scene: the architect Carlo Scarpa (in 1934). He found an equitable partner in Paolo Venini who, himself having begun to design and put those ideas into practice, worked in admirable harmony with Scarpa to create the new 'Venini' line, once again in an entirely new, path-breaking 'modern style' that had always been the firm's unmistakable hallmark.

[1] Bibliography on *Art Déco* is by now very plentiful, but for a systematic general survey see: *L'Art Déco*, Geneva 1974; D. Klein, N. McClelland, M. Haslam, *L'esprit Art Déco*, Paris 1991, and B. Hillier and S. Escritt, *Art Déco*, Milan 1997. For Italy, another point of reference is R. Bossaglia, *Il "Déco" italiano. Fisionomia dello stile 1925 in Italia*, Milan 1975.

[2] For the precise reconstruction of Muranese events from the early twentieth century onwards, see R. Barovier Mentasti, *Il vetro veneziano. Dal Medioevo al '900*, Milan 1982, 2nd edn Milan 1988, pp. 231–68; for Venini in particular, see A. Venini, 'La famiglia Venini', in *Gli artisti di Venini. Per una storia del vetro d'arte veneziano*, exhibition catalogue edited by the Fondazione Giorgio Cini, Milan 1996, pp. 47–55, and R. Barovier Mentasti, *Venini a Murano e nel mondo*, ibidem, pp. 13–27.

[3] As regards the traits and modalities of the development of Art Déco taste in Italy and in Milan in particular, see recent publications: *Milano déco. Guida alla mostra diffusa*, edited by R. Bossaglia, V. Terraroli, Milan 1999, and V. Terraroli, 'Milan déco: le arti decorative e industriali tra il 1920 e il 1930', in *Milano déco. La fisionomia della città negli anni Venti*, edited by R. Bossaglia, V. Terraroli, Milan 1999, pp. 29–155. On the connections with the magazine *Domus*, see V. Terraroli, *Le arti decorative in Lombardia nell'età moderna 1780-1940*, edited by V. Terraroli, Milan 1998, pp. 345–69.

[4] In particular V. Terraroli, 'Le arti decorative in Lombardia tra Ottocento e Novecento nel dibattito tra artigianato e industria. I ferri battuti e le vetrate artistiche', in *Le arti decorative in Lombardia…*, cit., pp. 8–47.

[5] On the discussion undertaken by the Vienna School on the importance and the role of 'industrial' art in the development of human culture see G.C. Sciolla, *La critica d'arte del Novecento*, Turin 1995, pp. 3–49. By Alois Riegl note in particular *Stillfragen*, published in 1893 (*Problemi di stile*, It. transl. Milan 1963) and *Volkskunst, Hausfleiss, Hausindustrie*, published in Berlin in 1901.

[6] R. Papini, *Le Arti a Monza nel MCMXXIII*, Bergamo 1923 quoted in R. Barovier Mentasti, *Venini a Murano…*, cit., p. 15.

[7] The lighting equipment, offered by Paolo Venini, was recently recovered in the storage space at the Musée Nissim de Camondo in Paris. The fittings are published in the official catalogue of the Italian Pavilion at the 1925 Paris exhibition, edited by U. Ojetti and M. Sarfatti, plates VII, VI-II, XIV, XVI.

[8] Napoleone Martinuzzi's connections with D'Annunzio are dealt with in the book by R. Barovier Mentasti, *Napoleone Martinuzzi vetraio del Novecento*, Venice 1992 and especially the essay by A. Rossi Colavini, 'Martinuzzi alla "corte" di D'Annunzio', pp. 2–23; the booklet by P. Martinuzzi, *Napoleone Martinuzzi*, Venice 1990; and in 1989 the index of Martinuzzi's works conserved in the Vittoriale in *Gabriele D'Annunzio e la Promozione delle Arti*, exhibition catalogue (Villa Alba, Gardone Riviera), edited by R. Bossaglia, M. Quesada, Milan-Rome 1988.

[9] See V. Terraroli, 'Le arti decorative in "Domus" 1928', in *Le arti decorative in Lombardia…*, cit., pp. 345–69.

[10] On the relationship between Venetian culture and D'Annunzio, see R. Bossaglia, 'D'Annunzio e gli artisti delle Venezie', in *D'Annunzio e Venezia*, proceedings of the seminar curated by E. Mariano, Rome 1991, pp. 303–13, and in particular concerning the letter dated 4 June 1922 and signed not only by Martinuzzi himself, but by Astolfo De Maria, Bartolomeo Sacchi, Guido Cadorin, Brenno Del Giudice and Mario Marenesi, transcribed and published by V. Terraroli, 'Cadorin, D'Annunzio e la stanza dei "sonni puri"', in *Guido Cadorin. 1892-1976*, exhibition catalogue, Milan 1987, p. 106. The catalogue of the D'Annunzio collection (in press, edited by V. Terraroli) has revealed numerous hitherto unknown examples of Martinuzzi's work (including some monster-animals in *pulegoso*).

[11] Gardone Riviera, Il Vittoriale degli Italiani, Archive of correspondents, Maroni Ruggero file. The brother of Gian Carlo Maroni, who distinguished himself during the world war, took an active part in the early stages of the construction of the Vittoriale; in 1925 he became a partner in Vetri Soffiati Muranesi Venini & C., and died after a brief illness in 1928. A letter of sympathy to his architect brother, dated 16 January 1928, on the Muranese firm headed notepaper, indicates the relevance of the role Maroni had played. The letter, signed by Alberto Franzini, quotes Napoleone Martinuzzi and the entire body of the master glassmakers.

[12] Gardone Riviera, Il Vittoriale degli Italiani, Archivio dei corrispondenti, Martinuzzi Napoleone file, 1926.

[13] Gardone Riviera, Il Vittoriale degli Italiani, Archivio dei corrispondenti, Martinuzzi Napoleone file, 1926.

10802

Rosa Barovier Mentasti

The Venini Glassworks: a Brief History

Although the name Venini and all it represents is deeply rooted in the great Murano tradition of glass craftsmanship, it stands apart, a tradition in its own right. The extent of innovation represented by Venini glass production within the historical context of Murano must take account of the extraordinary legacy of workmanship that the technicians and the glassworkers of the island offered the two businessmen who came to the island to set up the Venini firm. That legacy included countless superb specimens of the island's past-masters of glassmaking. Venetian glassmaking goes back as far as the tenth century A.D., as testified by an early record, dated 982, containing the first known mention of the name of a glassmaker. While Venetian glassmaking may have originated with the Romans, its ties with medieval Islamic and Byzantine glass production were essential to its becoming, in the twelfth century, a highly refined art. Ever since those times, a portion of Murano's production has been intended specifically for export, and is to this day associated with an exceptionally high quality of clear or gloriously coloured glassware, and with peerless technical skill in fashioning molten glass.

Such technical skills are synonymous with an innate feeling for glass almost unique to Venetian craftsmen, who saw how, when molten, glass lent itself to being blown and shaped in endless variations. In their choice of techniques, the master glassmakers of Murano have always remained loyal to the material's matchless ductility, taking a different approach to that of the Bohemians, who, from the seventeenth century on saw glass as a substitute for semi-precious stone, to be worked in rough while still incandescent, and then cut and engraved once cool. Here in the glasshouses on the Venetian lagoon, master glassblowers attained levels of extraordinary dexterity in fashioning glass while molten, inventing new techniques which they took with them to other countries: *mezza filigrana*, *retortoli* and *reticello* technique, *vetro ghiaccio* (ice glass), *incalmo* (welded), and *millefiori*. Furthermore, types of glassmaking practised in ancient times were rehabili-

tated, such as *murrina*, enamel and gold leaf graffito decoration, the so-called *fenicio* technique (threads trailed onto the surface and combed into festoons).

At the time of the founding of the Vetri Soffiati Muranesi Cappellin Venini & C., the island's glasshouses had assimilated the nineteenth-century advances in colour technique, achieving an extremely rich range of hues, while the masters themselves were the same virtuosi glassblowers of the nineteenth century, or their sons or pupils. Prompted by the avant-garde work of the 'non-conformist' Ca' Pesaro artists, in the years just before World War I; forays into new, modern realms of glass had been attempted, resulting in marvellous inventions, especially in *murrina* glass. These innovations had not been followed up, however, as war had put an end to the Nouveau and Secession decorative styles. When Giacomo Cappellin and Paolo Venini arrived on Murano in 1921, they did not find so much a *métier* in decline as a craftsmanship exhausted by its own technical over-refinement, and unable to assert its rightful place in a decade rife with innovation, ferment and contrast. The revolution of the decorative arts and furnishings sector with the introduction of industrial production – i.e., the Functionalism, as epitomised by the Bauhaus – and with the arrival of the essential, exclusive élan of Modern style, involved an aesthetic reworking of articles made of rare materials with skilled craftsmanship.

Of course, the solution was not to discard the Murano traditions. That would not only have meant wasting something of great value, but would have been a mistake: purely industrial practices were doomed to be short-lived on an island whose wealth depended entirely on the traditional skills of its population. The solution was therefore to enhance the very profession and tradition those men embodied, encouraging them to cater to this new and demanding clientele – the Milanese bourgeoisie – whose tastes were attuned to the neoclassical architects at work in the Lombard capital, architects who were bent on effecting a stylistic

Napoleone Martinuzzi, *Vase with trapped bubbles*, 1930
Location unknown

transformation of the decorative arts as a whole.

As witnessed at the first Mostra Internazionale delle Arti Decorative, held in Monza in 1923, attempts to revive regional crafts traditions risked lapsing into parochial 'folk-lore' mannerisms – precisely what Cappellin and Venini wished to avoid. The new glass company had four partners, only two of whom were personally involved in the business side of the new concern, Cappellin and Venini, the latter with no previous experience in production or commerce. Giacomo Cappellin, who since the war had run a gallery of antiques and art works in via Montenapoleone, Milan, had already run into the problem of supplying the Milanese public with quality Venetian blown glass. So he decided to commission the Murano craftsmen to make replicas of glassware featured in paintings by the great artists of the Renaissance. The success of this imaginative venture determined the stylistic and technical development of the new company: peerless workmanship was paired with fine-art glassware in classical style (hence far removed from the feared mannerisms), which, while in keeping with the 'sophisticated simplicity' dictated by Modern style, was identified with the period of Venetian glass's greatest success, the sixteenth century. Newly appointed to prepare the Cappellin-Venini production catalogue, the Murano-born painter and designer Vittorio Zecchin suggested a selection of specimens drawn from period paintings, an idea that led to the creation of the famous 'Veronese' reproductions. In addition, Zecchin designed new items that emulated their antique counterparts in the use of transparent, clear glass and an essential grace of form. Other innovative elements – the unusual, stylised handles or wide flat bases, elegant colours invented by the master glassblower Giovanni Seguso (called Nane Patare), and large works designed to stand out amidst interior furnishings – were characteristic of the collections Vittorio Zecchin created. He likewise overhauled traditional Venetian tableware and lamp designs.

Admittedly, the person chiefly responsible for this change in the firm's stylistic bearings was Giacomo Cappellin. Though a man of exquisite taste, he proved to be a poor administrator, however, while Paolo Venini, showed himself a more flexible and adventurous pupil. Zecchin's talent as a designer is beyond criticism, but the absence of ornament that even today makes the jointly designed Cappellin-Venini pieces so up-to-date, must surely have been dictated by his partner Venini, given that at all the major shows during those same years Zecchin presented blown-glass pieces with elaborate flourishes in enamel and gold in late Secession style, as well as precious motifs of gold detailing for rustic furniture.

The impact of the two men's ideas on Murano was im-

mediate: their visionary approach broke the impasse that had begun to stigmatise the island's production.

The new firm was made official in November 1921, work began right away, and Cappellin's shop in via Montenapoleone was soon decked out with the new production. The success was such that on Christmas Eve the store was allegedly 'left nearly bare'. At the 1923 Monza Triennale, divided up by region, the firm's pieces stood out for their distinct classicism. The critic Roberto Papini was enthusiastic, and in *Emporium* (July 1923) he remarked: 'A resurrection in the art of glass is taking place […] Cappellin & Venini's glass has many followers.' In response, other glassworks began producing large clear blown-glass pieces in plainer forms, and the philosophy of basing a firm's entire production on the creations of a single designer – without being a slave to the trademark's traditional output – began to gain general acceptance. The strong bond between Murano and Milan was to remain a constant of the Cappellin-Venini glassworks, even when the name changed to Vetri Soffiati Muranesi Venini & C. on Giacomo Cappellin's departure in 1925. This occasioned a merger of the refined Venetian glass techniques with the stylistic trends of Milan's new generation of architects.

When Vittorio Zecchin also left the firm, Paolo Venini formed a partnership with the Murano sculptor Napoleone Martinuzzi, who was appointed art director. At first Martinuzzi followed his predecessor's ways, and then introduced pieces in the Novecento style. Far from conceiving interior furnishing as a functional whole, this production entailed individual, elementary volumes, an approach epitomised by Martinuzzi's insistence on separate stereometric forms: solid classicising vases, outsize stylised cacti, animal figures, and fruit. These he created either in opaque glass or in an unusual bubbled glass, termed *pulegoso*, which, though quite fragile, had a rough, robust appearance. It was a brilliant solution to conveying a sense of volume and solidity that thin transparent glass could not provide, and was akin to experimental techniques applied in the late nineteenth century. For a while the courage of other craftsmen on Murano wavered. At first attracted to the new ideas, then discouraged, they eventually copied the Venini models and adopted *pulegoso* glass. Even the Seguso Vetri d'Arte glassworks, at the time Venini's most worthy competitor, subscribed to the *pulegoso* technique.

Links with Milan loomed large once again when Martinuzzi's collaboration with the firm came to an end, and the architect Tomaso Buzzi, who worked in Milan, was called in as art director in 1932. He had meanwhile joined the 'Labirinto', a group of architect-designers composed of Venini, Pietro Chiesa, Emilio Lancia, Michele

Paolo Venini

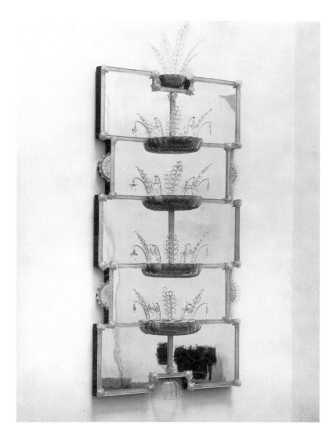

Marelli, Gio Ponti, formed around Carla Visconti di Modrone to further 'the spreading of modern decorative arts into the home'. The items proposed by Buzzi, in *mezza filigrana, reticello*, relief glass, *incamiciato* (multi-layered glass), were soberer than Martinuzzi's and addressed the new middle-classes' fondness for formal élan. In 1934 Buzzi's place was taken by the Venetian architect Carlo Scarpa, who had accumulated experience in glassmaking earlier in the factory that Cappellin had founded after parting company with Venini. Scarpa worked in perfect accord with a now mature Paolo Venini in fine-tuning the company's aesthetic orientation. His first works were in *mezza filigrana* and *lattimo* (milk glass), the latter styled on Chinese porcelain. His aptitude as a designer has perhaps been overstated, as his forms were very often plucked from the decorative arts of the Orient. However, in bringing oriental forms to Murano, he applied them mainly for opaque monochrome glassware, or glass rendered opaque by inserting an inner layer of *lattimo*. On the one hand he created highly refined models suited to the decorative skill of the Muranese, on the other he found the way to produce monochrome vases of outstanding refinement at feasible prices, a solution still being used today and long ago taken up by other glasshouses.

The *lattimo* and the *mezza filigrana* pieces of 1934 ex-

emplify a method of glassmaking that became standard practice in the Venini factory: in a subtle interplay between harmony and contrast in smooth forms that were in no way indebted to the formal Venetian tradition, the emphasis was on the material, which had to be traditional and refined, in this case *filigrana* and *lattimo* of the utmost purity. The practice became a constant in the 1950s. Earlier in the Novecento period it was not always observed, however, because from 1934 to the war years Murano was under the sway of a style far removed from tradition. Opaque *pulegoso* glass was set aside, as it could be confused with other materials. Murano wanted to revive transparent glass and, to obtain plasticity, they turned to a thicker type of transparent glassware, in dull, aqueous or autumnal colours, introducing *sommerso* (submerged glass) techniques, speckling with gold leaf, tiny bubbles, and corroded surfaces. Never had Murano glassmaking so betrayed its tradition as in this period, and yet glass continued to be fashioned while molten, and was always accompanied by the technical legacy of the island's past-masters.

At the end of the 1930s Carlo Scarpa turned from using thick glass in muffled tones and shaped in plastic forms, and unexpectedly began making thin-walled vases in bright, contrasting colours, re-applying techniques that had been in disuse for a decade, including *murri-*

na glass. His idea, however, was foreshadowed by Paolo Venini himself, with his 'Murrine romane' series of 1936. In these new collections elaborate techniques are mapped closely onto elementary forms. Nevertheless, the *murrina* technique was not used in view of obtaining decorative perfection, as was the general custom on Murano. Instead, it sought to achieve the 'primitive' flavour of African woven fabrics. Other collections followed, playing on colour contrasts and techniques unusual at the time. Entirely original were the *battuto* (beaten) and *inciso* (engraving) techniques, derived from finishing applied to the *murrina* wares, techniques that were intended to be discreet but which Scarpa used as decoration in their own right, to confer new tactile qualities to the artefact. Harbinger of the coming fashions of the 1950s, at first Venini production was not copied by other glassworks, perhaps because it was not quite understood. A recent revival of interest in Scarpa's work has, however, had a marked influence on contemporary glass, and *battuto* glass in particular has been so widely copied it has all but lost its original appeal.

After the war Murano reaffirmed its links with Milan, but look to Europe and the United States, whence came designers to collaborate with Venini. The factory's chief designer was nevertheless Milanese by choice, Fulvio Bianconi. Even in his most openly provocative work, the modernity of the forms always dovetails with the characteristically exacting Venetian artistry. Among the fruits of this propitious merger were the *Fazzoletto* (Handkerchief), a vase fashioned in delicate *zanfirico*; the 'Pezzati' vase series, intentionally irregular in shape, in polychrome glass patterned with patchwork; the vases invested with a female form in *merletto*; and the 'Occhi' (Eyes) series by Tobia Scarpa, like children's building puzzles, in *murrina* glass. Seemingly of random invention, these articles exuded a welcome freshness of approach that in truth resulted from careful research and specialist skills. That inventive *esprit du temps* can be found in many articles designed in the 1950s, but is particularly noticeable in Venini glass.

Subscribing to a common practice in Murano businesses, Paolo Venini took a good look at the catalogues of other glasshouses. Venini's signature piece, the *Zanfirico mosaico* of 1954, with its patchwork of *zanfirico* canes, was undoubtedly a more sober and refined interpretation of the polychrome 'Zanfirici' series which Dino Martens had designed several years earlier; whereas Venini's *Zanfirico reticello* drew its inspiration from the 'Merletti' types by Archimede Seguso, albeit with a different technique. Nonetheless, Venini's trademark products served as models for other companies, although the sheer complexity and costs of production were prohibitive. Witness to the firm's innovative outlook in the line of lighting installations is the 'Poliedri' series of 1958, which involved modules of moulded blown glass that admitted virtually unlimited combinations of form and dimension. Since then, factories all over Murano have designed similar modular elements.

After Paolo Venini's death in 1959, Ludovico Diaz de Santillana endorsed the firm's hallmark style, while introducing novel ideas related to his training as an architect. Those were the irreverent 1960s, during which the temptation was to experiment at all costs, even if that meant disregarding the rules of business. Several one-off collections, such as the 'Facciate di Venezia' (Venice Façades), created by the American designer Thomas Stearns and presented at the 1962 Venice Biennale, were not copied by other glassworks, and even Venini waived production owing to the difficulties of their acceptance. By contrast, due to the 'anti-decorative' mood that clouded these years of Minimalism, up until the 1970s there was extensive use of '*a fermo*' (fixed) moulds, first tried out by Toni Zuccheri in his 'Ninfee' (Nymphs) series of 1964 and 'Tronchi' (Trunks) of 1966; and likewise by Bianconi in his 'Informale' sets of 1968. The work of Tapio Wirkkala, whom Ludovico Diaz de Santillana invited to Murano in 1965, exerted a formidable influence on Murano glass production. Hailing from a glass industry that was very removed from developments in Venice, Wirkkala became deeply appreciative of the Venetian approach to art and glass. It was Wirkkala who revived the use of *incalmo*, a system invented in the sixteenth century but never used to full advantage; this he often combined with the *mezza filigrana* technique or *murrina* in platters and vases with forms of characteristic Nordic simplicity. In its day, the 'Wirkkala effect' was decisive, and is perceivable even in today's production. Alessandro and Laura Diaz de Santillana have both followed his working procedures, the latter designing superb creations in *murrina* in the 1970s, forged by combining the intricate techniques of yesteryear with the spare aesthetics of modern design. That spirit is typified by her utterly original 'Numeri' piece in *murrina* glass, with its delightful touch of *naiveté*.

When the Venini family withdrew from the company, the new ownership vouched to honour the Venini hallmark style, established back in 1921 by the founders Cappellin and Venini, and uphold the long-standing dialectic between modern design and the refined glassmaking techniques of Murano's forebears. Since the firm was handed over, important new collections have issued from the furnaces, though it is too early to assess the distinguishing features of current production.

Victoria Milne

Venini and 'Studio Glass': American Fascination for Murano Glass

In describing the influence of Venini s.p.a. in the United States, this essay should also convey the breath of truth passing by, a shiver in the drama of human striving that is in this story and every other one worth recording.

The breath of truth lies, here, in beauty itself. It lies in the fact that the Venini company made beautiful things, that this is rare, and that the world saw and appreciated that. This expression of beauty has done what that form of truth almost always does: affect others, and move our human project forward, in a poetic, lovely way.

That is the short version of why it is worthwhile to write or think, or read about anyone who makes... vases, for instance. Doing that well is the glassmaking and design manifestation of the human spirit, just as writing an essay well is the writer's manifestation of the human spirit, and appreciating the glass, through seeing or owning or emulating, is another form.

So, now that we are correctly aligned to approach our subject, how has Venini influenced the United States? 'Insufficiently', would be the best one-word answer.

But this is the response of a Venini partisan, for whom the more glass resembles something by Carlo Scarpa, the better it is. And despite this country's charms, that resemblance is not strong enough in the United States yet. The good news, however, is that the Venini spirit is not absent here; it is reinterpreted, carried on, changed and revered, as it should be.

There are two threads that connect America directly to the Muranese Venini hotshop: one is knowledge and the other is appreciation. Knowledge is what passed, as a direct effect of the generous personalities of Paolo Venini and Ludovico Diaz de Santillana, to others. This knowledge is like a floodgate; small movements at the source had broad and deep consequences. Appreciation, which is the activity of the many American collectors and admirers of Italian glass, has a different kind of link to the firm.

While there are now innumerable collectors of Venini in the United States, and enthusiasts who will follow it at auction, and write about every historical interpretation, there is something almost obvious about mentioning them: who, after all, would not naturally admire such beauty? But Americans have not always appreciated this glass. In certain phases, the firm's American distributors focused on lamps, for instance, and were commercially oriented; the vases and tumblers were left at home. And, the embarrassing truth is that Americans have not always been sensitive enough to elegant design to appreciate what they saw. However, they do now, in droves, and not a moment too soon. While the American admiration of Venini may be surprising for having ever been absent, the flow of knowledge from the firm is more surprising because it happened at all.

To get a sense of the impact of the knowledge in the United States, one must first have a general sense of the recent history of high-end glass here. The material became a medium for artists when what is now called the 'Studio Glass' movement began in the early 1960s. The movement started in a climate of artistic experimentation, with a lot of exuberance and an appreciative audience for anything that could be accomplished in the mysterious medium.

These experimenters, led by Harvey Littleton and Dominick Labino, set a tone in their glassmaking that is very American, and which still colors glass work in this country. First of all, they declared themselves artists. With the wind of the American Craft movement in their sails, and a complete indifference to European class distinctions, they made Art from glass. The model that began with Littleton was to have one's own shop, and to make one's own work.

This seductive independent formula caught on; the artists attracted students, and the students wanted to know more. This next generation, loosely defined, included Dale Chihuly, James Carpenter, and Dick Mar-

Richard Marquis, *'Murrina'*
tea- and coffee-pot, 1984
Private collection

Richard Marquis, *American LSD Acid Capsule*, 1969–70
Seattle, Pam Biallas Collection

Richard Marquis, *Marquiscarpa #98-5 (homage to Scarpa)*, 1998
Seattle, Richard Marquis Collection

quis, among others. Being both curious and devoted, they learned that glass was taken very seriously in Venice, and each of them set out to Italy to learn. These three were among the few Americans who were invited, separately, to work at Venini as visiting artists or designers. While they went out of personal interest, and intended, in a sense, to be drinking at the fountain of knowledge, they cannot have known then exactly how powerful a role they would play in the history of contemporary glass in the United States. They became leaders in their generation, and were followed by Benjamin Moore, Michael Scheiner and, later, Dante Marioni. Now, the tomato plant, I am told, came from the United States to Italy… but we all know how important tomatoes are in Italian food today. It is exactly the reverse with Venini in the American Studio Glass movement. It is as though these visitors in Murano returned with the seeds of a plant that overtook the United States. The 'fertile soil' was in select spots: the Rhode Island School of Design glass department, and then the Pilchuck Glass School in Washington State. But where that soil was, it was fertile indeed.

At the time of these visits, in the late 1960s and early 1970s, the skill level in glassmaking in the United States was very low. Almost all of it was being done in molds and in factories. When James Carpenter was invited into the hotshop at Venini by Ludovico Diaz de Santillana he had never seen glass handled loosely before. The new tools included a marver, hand shaping, gravity, centrifugal force and others, but what they meant was that the material was allowed to show its character. This glass, suddenly out of the mold, became free and lively.

Today, three decades later, there are thousands of glass artists in America, and thousands blowing glass in factories. All of the glass artists and many of the factory workers use these Italian techniques. They did not learn it from their fathers, and they were not allowed to work in Venetian factories, at least, very very few. They learned it, directly or indirectly, from James Carpenter. And from Dale Chihuly and from Dick Marquis, and from Ben Moore; from the Italian teachers who they in turn invited to come to Pilchuck, and then from the generations of students who learned from those who preceded them.

Dante Marioni is one of the States' best glassblowers, and his work is very Italian. But he did not work at the factory. 'Venini is the story I grew up on', he says. 'I began blowing glass in Seattle at fifteen or sixteen, and when I was twenty I went to Murano. It was like going to the Holy Land for me. I was allowed into the Venini factory to watch, where I saw Checco Ongaro [the maestro] making a piece designed by Jamie Carpenter. Jamie Carpenter had been Benny's teacher [Benjamin Moore] and Benny was my teacher. It all just fell into place in that moment.'

And Marioni is by no means the trickling end of what

James Carpenter, *Crystal bowl*
Corning, The Corning Museum of Glass

Benjamin Moore, *Vase and platter*, 1997
Seattle, Benjamin Moore Collection

Dante Marioni, *Mango coloured
goosebeak pitcher and chalice
with red wraps*
Seattle, Dante Marioni Collection

came from that floodgate opened by Carpenter and de Santillana; he has himself been teaching for fifteen years, so another generation already follows his first visit.

But it is the floodgate we are speaking of here; Venini itself. The firm had this effect because it made, one may argue, the most beautiful glass in Italy. But even if that were absolutely true, that is not all of it – or rather, that is itself another symptom of the real reason. The real reason is a generous spirit, which found its manifestation in supporting the best glassblowers, then inviting designers into the factory to develop designs with them. By all accounts, this spirit belonged to Paolo Venini and was carried on by Ludovico Diaz de Santillana.

It was Paolo Venini's fundamental willingness to work with designers that led to great design, and that led to the Americans learning what they have. Now, to anyone familiar with the star system in design, it is difficult to imagine how unimportant designers were at that time. Venini can only have brought them in because he thought that they made the glass better, and he was right. Massimo Vignelli was a young designer at the factory then, who became close with Venini. 'One time a friend of mine in London sent me a letter saying that he had put some of my lamps on a television show. I showed this to Paolo thinking he would be proud, but he said "There is no such thing as a Massimo Vignelli lamp! There are only Venini lamps!" and he fired me right there. (But when I came in to work the next day, he took me back.)' At the time a designer's name was never attached to the product.

Vignelli is an Italian designer who has spent most of his career working in New York, where he has built an extremely influential practice. Though he focuses on graphic design and product design in his office, he is another example of the Venini influence in the United States. 'I learned a lot from glass', he says. 'I came to understand a kind of freedom within restraint that you can have with the material. I was always working to keep the fluid nature of the glass present even when the design would ultimately be molded for consistency.'

This tension between freedom and discipline is common to all the arts, but it is especially vivid in glass. On the literal level, a gooey material must be made to conform. On the personal level, those who work glass have a very high standard to meet in the balance of skill and expression, the skill that cannot come without discipline, and the expression that is freedom itself. These themes also mix on this largest scale in this story, through the relationship of American culture and Italian culture.

To use another simile, it is true that in Latin America, the Word, as Catholic missionaries brought it from Europe, mixed with indigenous religions. As a result, in the current religion there, icons of a woman are floated out to sea in a ritual that mixes a sea goddess with the Virgin Mary. This is also something like what has come of the Italian glass tradition in the United States. In our American excitement, we have created a glass working culture that in some respects, may be considered at least pointless and at worst sacrilegious to

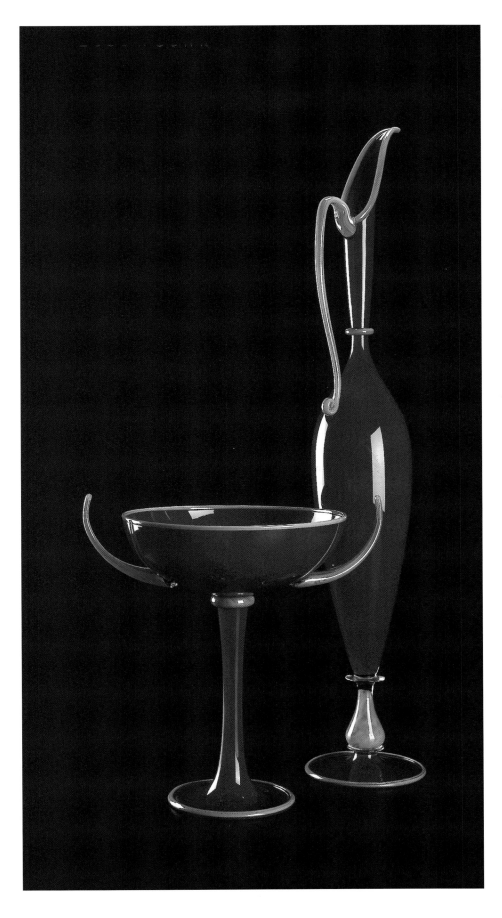

the old world of Murano. The culture this glass artist – who is not always a man – is inculcated in is not factory work but a chosen art career. Students at the Pilchuck Glass School are known for orchestrating 'performances', in which the chief entertainments seem to be beer and throwing molten glass around in the dark. (As with Haitians biting the heads off of live chickens, this is best understood by initiates.)

However, in the hands, and in the hearts, of these heathens, the Word endures. The Word of the Italian glass masters, that is. Moore, Marquis, and especially now Dante Marioni are glassblowers whose very seriousness shows their debt to what was able to be learned at Venini.

Carpenter, and the earliest American glass students, came from a place with no living glass tradition. They went to Venice where glass was a tamable wild animal. What they learned, that changed everything here, was that a great deal of beauty can come from the meeting of wildness and a master of that wildness. That was the lesson from Italy, and the lesson from Venini.

America, though, is itself famously wild. Yet young men and young women, went to Italy to learn about tradition and technique. Just as, in the hands of Venini's famous maestro, Mario Grasso, the glass seemed to want to become lovely, some part of America wanted to be tamed by knowledge, and devotion, and skill. The result, in both cases, has been beauty.

The Critical Acclaim for Venini Glass

When, in 1921, in partnership with Giacomo Cappellin, Paolo Venini started the firm that was to become his lifework, he probably nurtured the hope that some day the Vetri Soffiati Muranesi Cappellin Venini & C. would become a glasshouse of world renown. That dream indeed did come about, as testified by the fact that it is through his very work that we are now able to retrace the shifting tastes and fashions of the day. This invests the man's achievement with a meaning far beyond his original expectations, as it assumes the status of a creative phenomenon in its own right.

'Quite unexpectedly', wrote Robert Linzeler in 1923 in his description of the two partners and their separate approaches to glass, 'two men came together to revive its bygone beauty [...]. One of this team, Cappellin, is the source of inspiration, the creator, the technician; the other, Venini, sharp-witted, well-educated, knowledgeable of men and of the affairs of his times, is the administrator, the true "man of action".'[1]

On the occasion of the first Mostra Internazionale delle Arti Decorative, held in Monza in 1923, Roberto Papini explained the trend the new artistic director Vittorio Zecchin had established in 1921: 'In the entire exhibition I cannot find a more clear-cut process of clarification than the one Vittorio Zecchin's inspiration brought about in the glass articles produced by the furnaces of Messrs. Cappellin and Venini. [...] Only yesterday, speaking of Murano glass, meant weirdly complicated forms, curlicues, filaments and spirals. [...] Vittorio Zecchin, one of the most refined artists in Italy today, must be acknowledged as the first to grasp once again that Murano glass has two essential qualities: lightness and transparency, all the more evident and joyful when embodied in such elegant and harmonious forms.'[2]

When the Venini company won the 'Gran Prix' at the Exposition Universelle in Paris in 1925, the same critic endorsed his previous appraisal of the glasshouse: 'What I wrote two years ago spares me the necessity of speaking at length of how Venini and his partners brought about the renaissance of the art of Murano by simplifying forms and using glass in a logical and rational way.'[3]

Years later, on the occasion of the one-man show of Vittorio Zecchin's work, Guido Perocco qualified it as 'typically Muranese owing to the purity of imagination consistently present in his poetics, committed to the magic of glass and the illusory translucence of crystal, [Zecchin] fully realised that the mastery over a material rendered malleable by heat, often tempted the craftsman into self-indulgent virtuoso displays of his skills.'[4]

The year 1925 saw the separation of Paolo Venini and Giacomo Cappellin, who left with Vittorio Zecchin and opened another glassworks, entitled Maestri Vetrai Muranesi Cappellin & C.

Taking his place at Venini's factory was Napoleone Martinuzzi, a Muranese sculptor, who associated the task of fashioning glass with that of sculpture. 'Among the characteristic and grotesque animals the Venini furnaces presented at the latest Venice Biennale', noted Gio Ponti, 'one has to acknowledge Napoleone Martinuzzi's temperament, unsure as to whether one should admire him more as a sculptor or as a creator of glass.'[5]

Despite the reshuffle, Carlo Alberto Felice observed: 'The V.S.M. of Paolo Venini and C. is the one glasshouse that is decidedly faithful to its lofty programme – from which it draws growing authority and nobility – and that is capable of maintaining its articles, despite their greatly varying commercial value, in an absolute unity of style.' Napoleone Martinuzzi's glasswares expressed another artistic ideal that was well suited to the prevailing Novecento style: 'Having a solid classical form, shrewdly highlighted by interesting material, handled with the utmost expertise, they are and will remain among the most noteworthy testimonies of our return to good taste.'[6]

What Carlo Alberto Felice indicated as 'interesting material' was the *pulegoso* glass. While it addressed the evolving tastes of the period and was inseparable from the prevalent Novecento style, it went against the Mu-

Paolo Venini, *'Fazzoletto' vase, c.* 1955
Toledo, The Toledo Museum of Art

Vittorio Zecchin, *Group of blown-glass objects* Monza, Prima Mostra Internazionale delle Arti Decorative, sezione triveneta, 1923

ranese ideal of 'purity' in glass and glassware. 'Murano is not lacking in those who still long for the old forms and the old glass techniques', noted Ugo Nebbia, 'people who cast a somewhat suspicious, sceptical eye upon articles that issue from the nonetheless famous and respected furnaces of ours; […] but we should not object if the characteristic transparency, fragility, and specimens of virtuoso glassblowing momentarily yield to the demands of fashion – of the market, that is – admitting new technical and formal variants, new mixtures and palettes, and, even allowing crossovers of taste as regards the pure art of glass. […] Lining the grand stairway of the Villa Reale, aside from the dubious taste they betray, those famous 'light fittings' of the V.S.M. Venini of Murano clearly declare that they were not designed by a glassmaker.'[7]

A great admirer of Napoleone Martinuzzi, the poet-playwright Gabriele D'Annunzio commissioned him to make a set of illuminated pumpkins and baskets of fruit for the Stanza della Musica at the Vittoriale, his monument-villa on Lake Garda. The villa was an embodi-

ment of the state of the decorative arts at the time, and next to Martinuzzi's were works of other artists such as Guido Marussig, Guido Cadorin, Mariano Fortuny, and Renato Brozzi.

On the occasion of the 1932 Venice Biennale, where Venini glass by Tomaso Buzzi was presented, Ugo Nebbia praised the rediscovery of the 'linear simplicity of that delicate blown glass, turquoise with black, green and gold decoration, and, especially, the utterly transparent and aristocratic Venini white and silver.' And although he does not name the designer, later, regarding the piece entitled *La mano di Atlante* (The Hand of Atlas), he notes how, 'with far different improvisational skill and refined sensibility and deliberation, Tomaso Buzzi has once again created for Venini a piece that arouses keen interest.'[8]

The importance of the 1932 Venice Biennale cannot be stressed enough. It was the inaugural year of this biennial exhibition, a long-awaited event appointed exclusively to the decorative arts.

In 1933 Papini wrote a long article on the Milan Trien-

Michele Marelli,
Floor lamp, 1930–35
Location unknown

Napoleone Martinuzzi,
Lamp in 'pulegoso' glass, 1930
Monza, Triennale, 1930
(Milan, Triennale, Archivio Fotografico)

nale, and of course did not omit Paolo Venini: 'In the art of glass Venini offers the finest experiments [...]. Today he triumphs because he has understood that the outer appearance is not enough if you fail to achieve ever-new effects that highlight the material itself.'[9] It is amazing that not even Papini mentioned the author of the new Venini collections; the architect Tomaso Buzzi seemed to stay in the background, the warranty being Paolo Venini's name.

Venini's inspired receptiveness towards other fields of art and the urge towards constant renewal he methodically put into practice is testified by the steady stream of artists from abroad, among whom the Swedish ceramist Tyra Lundgren.

Tyra met Paolo for the first time when she took part in the 1936 Milan Triennale. Like the Milan Triennales and other major exhibitions across Europe, the Venice appointment offered artists who were able to travel excellent opportunities and new contacts. Paolo Venini invited the Swedish ceramist to Murano and put at her disposal his leading master craftsmen. Tyra, who had worked for Swedish magazines ever since the 1933 Triennale, had noticed Venini glass and described as 'the most beautiful to be seen today.'

During those years the decorative arts became more and more prominent, and among the artists and organisers of these events there was often a communion of mind, a sharing of ideals. It is worth remembering that the 1930 Triennale heralded a radical change in management and programme aims. An executive board formed by the architects Alpago-Novello and Gio Ponti, by the painter Mario Sironi, with Carlo Alberto Felice in the role of secretary, had been appointed for that year's exhibition. Setting aside the former subdivision by regions, the new board endeavoured to emphasise the importance of the applied arts as a reflection of modern times.[10] Paolo Venini, as well as Gio Ponti, had joined the 'Labirinto' (Labyrinth) group; the Milanese architect was to design several articles for Venini and as director of *Domus* he never neglected to praise the glassware the Venini furnace constantly produced.

Around 1934 Carlo Scarpa was brought in alongside Paolo Venini as art advisor to the glassworks. His debut at the 1934 Venice Biennale was recorded by Roberto Papini: 'Utterly select and novel the new Venini production with its polished, filigree and plastic glass, where there is imagination, taste and an admirable exquisiteness of technique, both classical and original, such a production is in the forefront of modernity.'[11] It is worth noting that Papini devoted an entire page to Paolo Venini, following his article on the decorative arts of the 1934 Biennale, where he explained the great success of the glassware: 'Paolo Venini's personality, his taste, his imagination, his sense of balance, indeed that glassworks has always remained the first, the constant creative force, with untiring youthfulness. *El pregio xe nel manego* [in local dialect: its value lies in its dexterity], we can say in speaking to the Venetians, certain of being understood.'[12]

At the 1938 Biennale and above at those held in 1940 and 1942, Carlo Scarpa took an unabashedly avant-garde stance and presented a new collection that derived from his utterly personal technical research, and had nothing to do with the trend current on Murano, departing instead from the Novecento style. His offering included works using numerous techniques: *tessuti a canne*, wheel-ground opaque *murrina*, *iridati*, *granulari*, *pennellate*, polychrome, bicoloured, *a battuto*, engraved, *soffiati a fili*. 'No longer soft nuances, but strident contrasting colours; no longer thick *sommersi* with beguiling effects but the return to traditional techniques in thin layers.'[13]

'Carlo Scarpa stood apart from the others, [...] on the whole his collection was not well received by the press, nor even by the Muranese. He actually presaged the Murano glass of the 1950s.'[14] As Astone Gasparetto observed, 'Carlo Scarpa's fabulous new *murrina* wares represent perhaps the highest refinement ever achieved with this technique, a process of embedding gesture and colour in the material.'[15]

In 1940 Enrico Motta enthused about Carlo Scarpa's new creations, which had achieved such refinement they defied imitation: 'A collection of superb pieces in such techniques as *granulare*, *a bugne*, *a bollicine*, *a tessuto*, *sommersi* with inimitable iridescence, ground and engraved glass, *murrina* bowls, black and red with an exotic flavour and a vitreous *pasta* that looks like enamel, splendidly coloured monochrome glass, bright yellow and scarlet, lead glass imitating the texture of metal. A chandelier in white glass seems to pour out of the rim of a vase countless stems overflowing in red and green-striped corollas, an exceptional piece for its lightness and fantastic design.'[16]

At the 1948 Venice Biennale, Venini exhibited a set of figurines based on Commedia dell'Arte characters designed by Fulvio Bianconi. Thus began a long collaboration with Paolo Venini that was to spawn astonishing new designs. 'The return to the theme of the masque and the theatre was glaringly appropriate for Venice. But we must not forget that it was an iconographic, expressive trend typical of the early 1950s, one that blossomed above all in the circles that had practised fashion illustration and graphics with nonchalant skill.'[17]

'The Venini glasshouse began in 1948 with stylised fig-

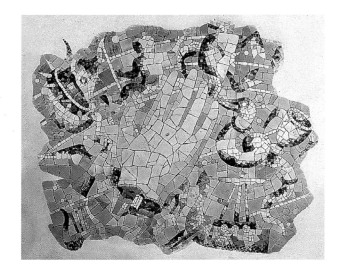

urines that had a touch of harmless kitsch, and with highly coloured vases (the 'Pezzati', 'Fasce', 'Scozzesi', 'Forati', 'Merletti', and 'Rete' series) where the designer Fulvio Bianconi perfectly demonstrated his talent as a supreme colourist, graphic artist and cartoonist.'[18]

The assuredness in the firm's aesthetic choices was not only due to Paolo Venini, but also to his wife Ginette Gignous, who declared in an interview in 1963: 'In 1949, when Paolo was seriously ill I offered to replace him for the first time, because it was tradition in our company for every single article to pass through the hands of a member of the family before leaving the works. Paolo was pleased, and ever since then I have worked alongside him.' When in 1959 Paolo died, she added that 'taking his place was natural – my duty, even, after he passed away.'[19] She had been his loyal collaborator, she was the first to whom her husband revealed a new design, the first to see and judge the sketches and choose the colours, and would continue to do so with her son-in-law Ludovico Diaz de Santillana.

'Venini's novelty is the series of large new stained-glass windows composed of elements of mosaic glass, and some with elements of monochrome or *pennellate* glass: Venini got the idea of the stained-glass windows during a trip abroad, while observing the structure of some old walls on the island of Delos.'[20] Those windows, designed in collaboration with the architect Oscar Stonorov, were among Paolo's last works, but we should also recall the handsome velarium covering the inner courtyard of Palazzo Grassi, crafted in 1954 out of *ballotton* glass of various sizes mounted *a collana* (linked), unfortunately now replaced, and the polyhedral chandelier for the 1958 Brussels Fair: 'A jewel of decorative lighting at the Brussels Expo must be mentioned: the enormous chandelier in the grand hall of the Italian pavilion.'[21]

'Sixty years on, the firm of Venini still continues the same philosophy in family hands, headed by Paolo Venini's daughter Anna, and her husband Ludovico Diaz de Santillana (originally an architect, but now a Venetian glassmaker by adoption).'[22]

The glass collections that were created under de Santillana's supervision were at the same time traditional and innovative, arising from the collaboration of famous international artists, architects and designers, each of whom created original, sophisticated forms and tried out new colours and technologies. Returning to its old traditions, the firm developed more and more collections of limited editions, especially in the lighting sector, which made it famous all over the world.

'Ludovico de Santillana has inherited a company at the height of success and endowed with a strong market identity, […] we see a different Venini about to emerge, with a receptive attitude to outside glassmaking practices.'[23] The collaboration between Tapio Wirkkala and Venini began in the mid-1960s, when he was already world-famous as a designer, and after his first experience with glass with Iattala in Finland.

Although Wirkkala and Venini met in the early 1950s, perhaps at the 1951 Triennale, where Paolo must have noticed his glass sculptures on display in the Finnish section, Wirkkala's collaboration with the Venini company did not start until the 1960s.

'In Murano, Wirkkala found himself faced with a very different glass heritage. […] The traditional techniques of Venetian glass gave Wirkkala new opportunities for experimentation. […] The material alone makes Murano glass something special. The quartz sand, soda and lime and the other constituents are stored underneath the works.'[24]

In the early 1960s meanwhile Americans began to flow into the Venini factory, Thomas Stearns being the first, followed by Dale Chihuly, Richard Marquis, Ben Moore, and James Carpenter. 'We used to have large gatherings in our home with that group of young people', recalls Anna Venini, 'discussing all sorts of things – art, politics, and the countless problems of change taking place in the 1960s and reflected all over the world.'

But the great impetus given by Ludovico Diaz de Santillana was above all in lighting installations: cascades of glass in polyhedrons, drops, listels, canes, made in Italy, in Europe, all around the world.

De Santillana was foremost an architect endowed with flexible tastes, receptive to outside cultures and influences: for Paolo Venini first, and then for Ludovico, the conception of art glass 'did not have outlets on the usual markets, since its cost, no matter how contained, was far higher than any other glass, the only possible market being that of Art. The Venini–de Santillana combination was the forerunner of New Glass, of Haute-Couture Glass.'[25]

At the end of the 1970s, freshly graduated from the School of Visual Arts of New York, Laura Diaz de Santillana joined the workforce at the family firm; her brother Alessandro followed in the early 1980s; both continue their work in the field of glass as masters of their craft, natural heirs to the Venini family tradition.

[1] R. Linzeler, 'Les Verreries de Cappellin et Venini', in *Art et Décoration*, March 1923, pp. 79–84.
[2] R. Papini, 'La Mostra delle Arti Decorative a Monza', in *Emporium*, LVIII, July 1923, pp. 3–21.
[3] R. Papini, 'Le Arti a Monza nel 1925. II Dalle ceramiche ai cartelloni', in *Emporium*, October 1925, pp. 223–43.
[4] *Vittorio Zecchin*, exhibition catalogue edited by G. Perocco (Museo d'Arte Moderna Ca' Pesaro, Venice), Milan 1981.
[5] Dir., 'Vetri di Murano', in *Domus*, February 1929, pp. 31–33.
[6] C.A. Felice, 'Le arti decorative. Vetri di Orrefors e di Murano, argenti di Feragotti, la scuola d'arte di Padova', in *Domus*, July 1928, pp. 29–33.
[7] U. Nebbia, 'I Veneti alle Arti Decorative di Monza', in *Le Tre Venezie*, June 1930, pp. 10–16.
[8] U. Nebbia, 'L'Arte decorativa alla Biennale', in *Le Tre Venezie*, May 1932, pp. 305–9.
[9] R. Papini, 'La Triennale milanese delle arti', in *L'illustrazione italiana*, Milan 4 June 1933, pp. 850–76.
[10] On the history of the Biennales and Triennales of Monza and Milan see G. Mori's essay, 'Le Biennali e le Triennali di Monza e Milano (1923-1936) viste dalla stampa', in *Il Vetro Italiano a Milano 1906–1968. Tra creatività e progettazione*, exhibition catalogue, edited by R. Barovier Mentasti, M. Chirico, G. Mori, A. Pansera, C. Salsi (Castello Sforzesco, Milan), Milan 1998, pp. 25–29.
[11] R. Papini, 'L'arte decorativa', in *Le Tre Venezie*, May 1934, pp. 275–78.
[12] R. Papini, 'Vetri di Paolo Venini', in *Le Tre Venezie*, May 1934, p. 279.
[13] R. Barovier Mentasti, 'Il Novecento muranese', in *L'arte del vetro. Silice e fuoco: vetri del XIX e XX secolo*, exhibition catalogue edited by M. Quesada (Palazzo delle Esposizioni, Rome), Venice 1992, p. 200.
[14] R. Barovier Mentasti, *Venini a Murano e nel mondo*, in *Gli artisti di Venini. Per una storia del vetro d'arte veneziano*, exhibition catalogue edited by Fondazione Giorgio Cini, Milan 1996, p. 21.
[15] A. Gasparetto, 'Dalla realtà archeologica alla contemporanea. Il Novecento', in *Mille anni di Arte del Vetro a Venezia*, exhibition catalogue edited by R. Barovier Mentasti, A. Dorigato, A. Gasparetto, T. Toninato (Palazzo Ducale, Venice), Venice 1982, p. 38.
[16] E. Motta, 'Vetri e merletti', in *Le Tre Venezie*, XVI, May 1940, pp. 240–44.
[17] R. Bossaglia, *I vetri di Fulvio Bianconi*, Turin 1993, p. 13.
[18] R. Barovier Mentasti, 'Il Novecento muranese', in *L'arte del vetro…*, cit., p. 202.
[19] 'Dalla "haute couture" ai vetri soffiati', in *La Nazione*, 11 October 1963, p. 18.
[20] 'Venini vetrate', in *Domus*, August 1957, pp. 47–50.
[21] 'A Venini Chandelier', in *International Lighting Review*, n. 6, June 1958, p. 194.
[22] D. MacNeil, 'The Noble Tradition of Murano revived by a Milanese Lawyer', in *House and garden*, November 1981, pp. 178–79.
[23] A. Venini, 'La famiglia Venini', in *Gli artisti di Venini…*, cit., p. 54.
[24] T. Keinänen, 'Wirkkala and Venini', in *Tapio Wirkkala. Venini*, exhibition catalogue (Finnish Glass Museum, Riihimäki), Riihimäki 1987, pp. 24–27.
[25] S. Tagliapietra, 'Ludovico Diaz de Santillana', in *Giornale Economico*, 1989, pp. 29–32.

Anna Venini Diaz
de Santillana

**The Venini Glassworks 1921–1986:
a Passion for Glass**

Paolo Venini in front of a window
display of blown-glass objects

Paolo Venini, 'Murrina' vases,
c. 1955
Location unknown

In 1921 Paolo Venini created the glassworks originally entitled V.S.M. - Vetri Soffiati Muranesi Cappellin Venini & C.

Co-founder with Venini in this enterprise was Vittorio Zecchin, designated as art director. The third partner cited in the firm's title, Cappellin, was a Venetian antiques dealer.

For years Paolo had had the utmost esteem for the craftsmanship of Murano glassblowers, and this admiration must have kindled the desire to restore glass to its essence, to shed the accumulated trammels of decoration which, Astone Gasparetto notes, 'marred its elegance'. Zecchin heeded his partner's inclination and together they decided to orient the firm's output to the style of glass production prevalent in the Italian Cinquecento, when Murano glass was at the acme of its renown.

Their decision gave rise to the delicate *filigrana* blown-glass pieces, borrowed directly from sixteenth-century master paintings, including canvases by Paolo Veronese, whose *Annunciation* features a striking piece of glassware, and the series of two-handled 'Holbein' vases featured in the painter's *Portrait of Georg Gistze*, now in the Staatliche Museen in Berlin. Other artefacts that emerged from this process were the exquisite, almost weightless lanterns, the vases and goblets – eloquent tokens of the men's rediscovery of a past world.

But Paolo also kept a keen eye on the shifting fashions and trends around the world, and realised that glass was taking new directions. His first influence came from France: at the second session of the Salon des Artistes Décorateurs held in 1925, he witnessed the works of the great French master of glass, Maurice Marinot, who would later exhibit at the Venice Biennales of 1932 and 1934.

It was Marinot's art that enthralled Paolo Venini most. A peerless craftsman, Marinot performed the creation of his pieces himself, foreshadowing the American style known as New Glass, of some years later. Marinot demonstrated unprecedented liberty in designs of remarkable softness. Besides Marinot, Paolo met with other glassblowers and painters, and saw the furniture of Paul Durand-Ruel, and realised the approach the Venini glassworks ought to adopt, namely, to create a distinctive modern style of discerning elegance.

It was, however, during this Salon in France that Venini broke with Cappellin. The exact reasons for the rift are not known, though my mother told me it was irreparable.

Cappellin took the team of master glassblowers with him, including Vittorio Zecchin, an accomplished craftsman but so intensely attached to the Murano tradition he was unable to conceive of how established techniques could be combined with new expressive means that took their cue from the emerging canons of modern art.

A man of great determination, Paolo also had luck on his side: he founded a new factory where he joined in partnership with another Zecchin (a relative of Vittorio), and a group of master glassblowers of outstanding talent.

Leading this new cadre of glassworkers was the young Boboli (Arturo Biasutto), already a precocious master of his craft by the time he was thirty: Boboli remained a close ally for many years, bringing his boundless enthusiasm to each new innovation Paolo proposed.

Mastery of glassblowing only comes with experience, and one of the greatest challenges was the application of colour: like an alchemist's apprentice, Paolo had yet to fathom the many arcane methods and techniques of the craft.

Incidentally, within the organisation of glassworks in Murano, the chemist was on an equal footing with the master glassblower. The proprietary formulas for certain techniques and types of glass varied from factory to factory, enabling each one sporadic advantages over its competitors. Secrecy was therefore paramount, and consequently the Venini glassworks kept its exclusive colour formulas locked away in a little black notebook that was handed down from father to son.

The new art director appointed to the refounded Veni-

Napoleone Martinuzzi,
Foal and cacti, 1932–33
Location unknown

Napoleone Martinuzzi, *Chandelier*
Venice, Biennale, Italian Pavilion, 1926

ni works (now just V.S.M.) was Napoleone Martinuzzi, a man of eclectic nature and a native of Murano who held the directorship of the Museo Vetrario on Murano.

Martinuzzi was a close associate of the poet and novelist Gabriele D'Annunzio, and his first creations were an ensemble of superb glass furnishings and lamps in glass for the writer's villa on Lake Garda, the Vittoriale.

In this period he also created a new kind of glass, known as *pulegoso*, obtained by pouring petrol into the liquid glass paste. With the utterly new type of material thus obtained, Martinuzzi proceeded to devise vessels in the style of early Roman glass (inspired most likely by the large ollas for transporting oil), together with lamps and chandeliers of unusual and ingenious design.

Under Martinuzzi, the Venini glassworks provided lighting installations for various post-office buildings in cities all over the country, most notably for the one in Bergamo, built to designs by the talented young Mazzoni, who was much reviled by Marcello Piacentini, an architect particularly active during the Fascist period.

For the Bergamo post-office building Venini and Martinuzzi devised the ingeniously essential light fittings in metal and glass, which would subsequently become a standard in post-office buildings throughout the country.

With keen imagination, Martinuzzi also designed a superb glass cactus-shaped installation with flowers and leaves formed from the new *pulegoso* glass.

In this same period Paolo Venini and the architect Piccinato jointly created the lighting installations for Palazzo Accursio, formerly the Stock Exchange building in Milan.

Of primary importance at this time was Venini's participation in the group of architects known as the 'Labirinto' (Labyrinth), whose number included Gio Ponti (later one of his closest friends), Pietro Chiesa (founder of Fontana Arte), Michele Marelli, and Tomaso Buzzi. The Venini glassworks thrived in these years and made a vital contribution to the architecture of the day, keeping a keen eye on the new trends emerging in the field of art and design.

Martinuzzi's role was crucial, but not entirely determining: his works for D'Annunzio, his ingenious cactus installations, were wanting innovative drive. This notwithstanding, he completely redesigned the blownglass collection, accentuating their form and colour, producing an entirely novel item for the Venini catalogue, namely, his animal series: elephants, fish in white and green *pulegoso*, ducklings, a dove in white *pulegoso* tricked out with a narrow blue collar, and the comical red dachshund.

While the 'spirit' that characterised the output of the Venini glassworks eludes a precise definition, the artists who joined the team immediately perceived something in the air: the atmosphere was quite unlike that of other factories. There was an air of responsiveness and innovation, a requisite dovetailing of decorative arts, painting, and architecture to form a harmonious unified style in its own right, a style that was unmistakably Venini, and which was made possible by discerning managerial guidance and coordination – first under Paolo Venini, and then under my husband Ludovico Diaz de Santillana who, like his father-in-law, opted not to sign the innumerable creations that issued from his hand.

With considerable headway on practices current at the time, Venini created the very first designer trademark in which it was unimportant who the creator or designer was, because the article thus created was irrefutably and immediately identifiable as a product from the Venini glassworks.

In 1932 Tomaso Buzzi was appointed art director. Buzzi ushered in new forms of the purest design, whose natural elegance was expressed principally in a brilliant palette of his own invention, layered into the glass and often overlaid with leaves in gold or silver.

As a consequence, the entire range of Venini's production took an intriguing change of tack: when he took over from Martinuzzi to my mind Buzzi gave new bearings to the firm, reorienting it to the aesthetics of the furniture and ceramics of Gio Ponti. Moreover, I might add that Buzzi's ideas foreshadowed the work of Carlo Scarpa.

A superb coloured *sommerso* glass ball designed by Buzzi was reproduced in *filigrana*.

The signature Venini cup bearing a pair of hands was ingeniously reworked by Buzzi, who enclosed the entire piece in similarly joined bronze hands embracing the two columns, also in bronze, supporting the bowl itself, presented at the glass salon in Villa Barbaro in Maser, near Treviso.

Although he was called back to Milan to resume his work as an architect, during Buzzi's tenure, Scarpa made regular visits to the Venini glassworks.

A close study of Carlo Scarpa's work reveals a telling emphasis on materials, as against the forms themselves, just as he applied in his architecture, more often than not contriving variants of the classic Venini inventions. It is revealing to look through the Venini *Catalogo blu*, the first to which Scarpa contributed. Most striking is the purity of the successive shapes Scarpa introduced, each one explored and re-interpreted.

His arrival at the glassworks marked the onset of a close communion of minds with Paolo Venini, who was ever fascinated by the work of his new colleague. In addition to providing new designs, Carlo followed his own creations through the factory alongside the craftsmen, nurturing a hands-on collaboration that entailed the introduction of new colours and a wide array of forms. The new techniques being brought into play charmed all those involved. One such invention, *bulicante*, or bubble-glass, and glass with submerged pockets of air, endowed each piece with a novel, unusual luminescence. Another procedure of recent acquisition involved the technique of corrosion, an invention of the Middle East

(perhaps Lebanon) that had made its way up the Italian peninsula to Murano. Glass of Roman manufacture exemplifying this technique is documented in the mid-first century A.D.; excavations in Pompeii unearthed a white, hand-blown goblet in opalescent glass, its surface detail achieved on the lathe with extraordinary delicacy.

Not surprisingly, such techniques spread steadily up the peninsula.

It was this critical appreciation of past methods of glassworking that brought Carlo Scarpa and Paolo Venini even closer in spirit.

The years before the outbreak of World War II witnessed intense, fertile activity at the glassworks at both creative and intellectual levels.

The Venice Biennale exhibitions were a hive of new energy. One of my childhood memories is of the bookstore 'Libreria del Campanile' in St Mark's Square, run by the Israeli Ugo Ravenna and a focal point for Venice's intelligentsia.

Our visits to the shop were frequent, and when it suddenly closed down, I received only vague answers to my questions. It was suspected that Ravenna had been deported.

But life continued, and activities at the Venini glassworks progressed, unremitting.

Indeed, this was perhaps Carlo Scarpa's most fecund period, and his creative output seemed boundless.

After the 'Corrosi' sets came the opaque 'Murrina' pieces with coloured patterns borrowed from oriental pottery, accompanied by lanterns and glass platters designed for the Milan Triennale.

To this was added series of 'Tessuti', or textured wares in a range of dynamic tones, including a highly expensive piece in which the glass was textured both inside and out.

It is perplexing to note how the menace of war looming on the horizon in the mid-1930s barely dented the constant flurry of creativity in artistic circles then under way in Italy.

At this time Venice received a visit from the wife of the Finnish architect and designer Alvar Aalto, who was immediately enthralled by Venini glass. Her visit marked the firm's first links with Northern Europe, and heralded an enduring connection felt in both human and artistic terms.

Under the direction of Pietro Chiesa, in 1942 the Milan Triennale organised an exhibition at the Nationalmuseum in Stockholm. The exhibits were transported on an eventful odyssey by train through war-torn Europe, and met with resounding success in Sweden.

For Carlo Scarpa, these were perhaps the most charmed years of his career: his gift for invention brought forth the vase series in drawn threads, plus the

The Venini stand at the 1930 Monza Triennale (Milan, Triennale, Archivio Fotografico)

Paolo Venini in Sweden; note the polyhedral lamp in the background

rare cut glasses (on which the Bohemian engraver Franz Pelzel worked), all put on a spacious display at the Venice Biennale.

Alongside the 'Diamanti' and 'Murrine romane' glasses by Paolo Venini – whose inimitable modern slant lay in their regular, composed simplicity – Carlo Scarpa presented a throng of exquisitely refined pieces, ranging from the 'Corrosi', to the 'Sommersi', to the 'Granulari', whose delicate fragility stemmed from the tiny pearl inserts.

He meanwhile created a series of orientalizing wares – known as 'Cinesi' – where one can perceive working in tandem the minds of Scarpa and Venini, who had studied many exemplars of this variety in museums.

One of Scarpa's later works with Venini, or should I say his very last, is the superb centrepiece commissioned by University of Padua from three different Murano firms, and awarded to the Venini glassworks by means of a competition thanks to the sapient mediation of the sculptor Arturo Martini.

Venini proposed a series of mythological animals that stood for the various fields of study (the leading one being the *Bò*, or University of Padua), executed in glass iridised with gold.

When the bombing of the Ponte della Libertà left Venice cut off from the mainland, transport had to be improvised with the assistance of the university caretakers, who undertook the centrepiece's safe conduct to Padua.

Owing to the war, that centrepiece fell into neglect, and it was not until several years later that it was brought back to light by the rector of the University, Mario Bonsembiante.

Production at the glassworks was brought to a halt for two years. In 1945 activities were slowly revived in the manufacture of light-bulbs. Though haltingly at first, Venini signature glass also came back into production. Once the war was over, the glassworks experienced a singular upsurge in productivity: the new-found thrill of the creation was manifested not just at the Venini glassworks, but in the decorative arts throughout the country.

The first Triennale exhibition held in a bomb-scarred Milan intent on piecing itself back together showcased the state of the decorative arts. Chief organiser was Gio Ponti, who made his selection of entrants on the basis of admiration. Admiration, he averred, led straight to promotion: promotion itself is part and parcel of design (*progetto*, from the Italian word *progettare*, also denotes 'planning'), and derives from an attention to the present (i.e., 'So you appreciate this artist's work? – then buy his paintings. You admire this architect? – then enable him to realise his designs', L. Licitra Ponti, 'Ritratto', in *Gio Ponti. L'opera*, Milan 1990, p. 17). Such was Gio Ponti's *modus operandi*, and the magazines he founded, *Domus* and *Stile*, were a vibrant record of emerging talent – and an appeal for an audience – guaranteed by his vision and experience alone. He was spurred by his faith in the new, in the possible. He saw this confidence itself as an element of genius. Given such character traits, Gio Ponti was one of the finest directors of the Triennale's long history, and his enthusiasm acted like a magnet, attracting talent from far and wide. The Venini firm likewise drew artists from all over the world, encouraged by Paolo's heart-felt embrace of the creative spirit: at this point he seemed to feel entirely responsible for the creative drive of the firm. In this he cor-

responded with the past masters of Murano, but with an even greater breadth of vision of the world's offering. These were the Venini glassworks' finest years. It had finally gained a foothold in the world of Murano glass-making, despite its founder's origins, a provenance that had long kept him at arm's length as an outsider, as one not of the island.

I remember this period very well. For me it signalled my arrival at the factory, where I followed Paolo around, trying to familiarise myself with the craft, little suspecting that this would shortly become my entire life. At this point Fulvio Bianconi made his appearance, a man brimming with ideas, colours and forms. He dusted off the traditional Murano figurines of players from the Commedia dell'Arte, and fine-tuned them in a modern key.

With his 'Pezzati' Bianconi showed how even the *murrina* pieces could be rescaled and coloured differently from the traditional way.

On Bianconi's heels came Eugène Berman and Gio Ponti, who faithfully kept up his working relationship with the glassworks. But it was largely Paolo the creative mind behind production, rehearsing old techniques and classical forms with unerring intuition and elegance. Dazzling new creations on the product line were the vases in *zanfirico scozzese, tessuto incrociato, murrina,* and not least his celebrated *Fazzoletto* (Handkerchief), which would find its place in the Museum of Modern Art, New York. These and other pieces express better than words the astounding innovation that characterised the Venini label. With the '4000' series of lamps designed by Massimo

Vignelli, in 1954 the Venini garnered its first 'Compasso d'Oro', the coveted design award assigned by the Milan Triennale.

There come to mind many of his designs, particularly the delightful brightly coloured piece he devised in Detroit in 1957 with Oscar Stonorov, and the slightly more essential one for the Salon d'Honneur in the Brussels Expo of 1958. This exhibition saw the arrival of the first polyhedral lamp, a work of extraordinary modernity. Paolo Venini was the first to grasp how to best apply conventional Murano glassmaking techniques to fashion multi-coloured pieces without employing lead joins. Prematurely taken from us in July 1959, Paolo left many things as yet undone. Remaining at the glassworks were his wife Ginette, daughter of the painter Eugenio Gignous, whom with considerable zest would oversee the quality of the colours and production until her death in 1981. Soon to take his place alongside this woman was Paolo Venini's son-in-law, the architect Ludovico Diaz de Santillana, who had to shoulder the role of his predecessor, a man by all accounts deemed irreplaceable.

In his dedicatory encomium of Paolo Venini, the architect Gio Ponti highlighted 'his teaching and sheer drive, his creative and productive verve' which, combined, secured international recognition and status for both the man and his trademark glass, 'enhancing the very perception and identity of Murano and Venice worldwide.' Such was the impact of his efforts that the name Venini remains engraved in the annals of glass: the 'Veniniana' exhibition set up at the Triennale in 1960 was not 'a mere

9
Napoleone Martinuzzi,
Ansate vase, 1925–28
h 46 cm, Ø 44 cm
Gardone Riviera, Il Vittoriale
degli Italiani, Prioria,
Stanza del Lebbroso
(cat. no. 17)

10
Napoleone Martinuzzi,
Tall blue amphora, 1925–31
h 74 cm
Padua, private collection
(cat. no. 19)

11
Napoleone Martinuzzi,
Pheasant, 1926–30
h 17.5 cm
Treviso, private collection
(*cf.* cat. no. 22)

12
Napoleone Martinuzzi,
Glass-drop chandelier, 1926–30
h 103 cm, ⌀ 78 cm
Gardone Riviera, Il Vittoriale
degli Italiani, Prioria, Bagno Blu
(cat. no. 23)

13
Napoleone Martinuzzi,
Glass-drop chandelier, 1926–30
h 76 cm, ⌀ 70 cm
Gardone Riviera, Il Vittoriale
degli Italiani, Prioria, Stanza Cicerin
(cat. no. 24)

14
Napoleone Martinuzzi,
Striated chalice-vase, 1927
h 32 cm
Venice, private collection
(*cf.* cat. no. 26)

15
Napoleone Martinuzzi,
Striated chalice-vase, 1927
h 24 cm, ∅ 21 cm
Padua, private collection
(cat. no. 26)

16
Napoleone Martinuzzi,
Duckling, 1928
h 30 cm
Murano, Museo Vetrario
(cat. no. 27)

18
Napoleone Martinuzzi,
Fruit-stand with fruit, 1928–30
h 37 cm, ∅ 37 cm
Gardone Riviera, Il Vittoriale
degli Italiani, Prioria,
Stanza della Musica
(cat. no. 31)

19
Napoleone Martinuzzi,
Fruit-stand, 1928–30
h 16 cm, ∅ 21 cm
Gardone Riviera, Il Vittoriale
degli Italiani, Prioria, Stanza Cicerin
(cat. no. 33)

20
Napoleone Martinuzzi,
Pumpkin, 1928–30
h 87 cm, ∅ 40 cm
Gardone Riviera, Il Vittoriale
degli Italiani, Prioria,
Stanza della Musica
(*cf.* cat. no. 29)

21
Napoleone Martinuzzi,
Large chandelier, 1928–30
h 122 cm, ⌀ 90 cm
Gardone Riviera, Il Vittoriale
degli Italiani, Prioria,
Stanza del Mappamondo
(cat. no. 34)

22
Napoleone Martinuzzi,
Chandelier, 1928–30
h 62 cm, ⌀ 34 cm
Gardone Riviera, Il Vittoriale
degli Italiani, Prioria,
Bagno delle Ospiti
(cat. no. 36)

24
Napoleone Martinuzzi,
Large 'leaf' chandelier, 1928–30
h 160 cm, ⌀ 110 cm
Milan, private collection
(cat. no. 35)

25
Napoleone Martinuzzi,
Volute chandelier, 1928–30
h 140 cm, ⌀ 45 cm
Gardone Riviera, Il Vittoriale
degli Italiani, Casseretto,
Gian Carlo Maroni's study
(cat. no. 37)

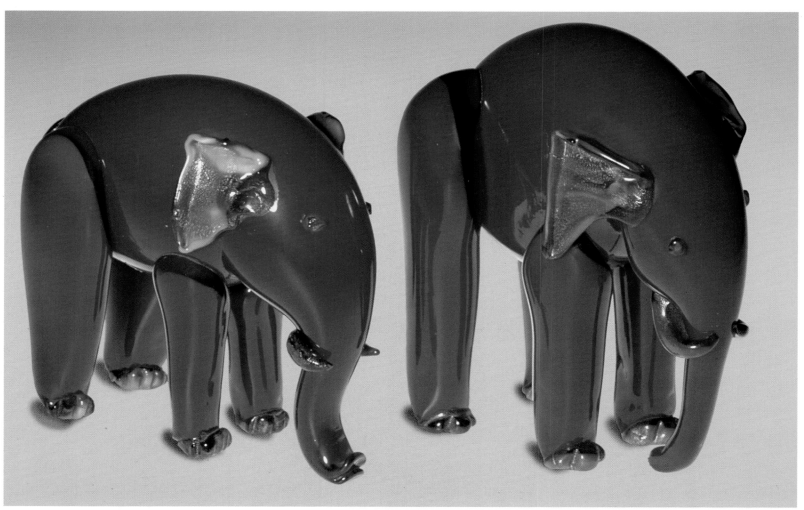

26
Napoleone Martinuzzi,
Foal, 1929–30
h 27 cm
Asti, private collection
(cat. no. 40)

27
Napoleone Martinuzzi,
Unicorn, 1930
h 21 cm
Murano, Museo Vetrario
(*cf.* cat. no. 40)

28
Napoleone Martinuzzi,
Two elephants, 1929–30
h 18.5 cm; h 22 cm
Paris, private collection
(*cf.* cat. no. 41)

29
Napoleone Martinuzzi,
Elephant, 1929–30
h 19.5 cm
Padua, private collection
(cat. no. 41)

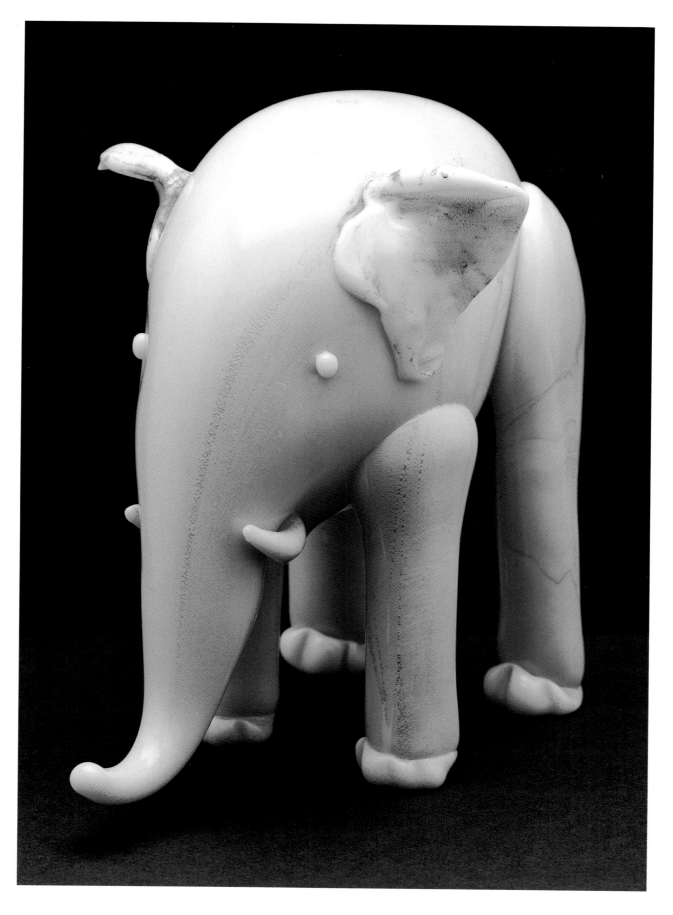

32
Napoleone Martinuzzi,
Amphora with five handles
of grooved ribbon, 1930
h 34 cm
Gardone Riviera, Il Vittoriale
degli Italiani, Prioria,
Stanza della Zambracca
(cat. no. 44)

33
Napoleone Martinuzzi,
Bowl in 'pulegoso' glass , 1930
h 7 cm, ∅ 20 cm
Turin, private collection
(*cf.* cat. no. 44)

34
Napoleone Martinuzzi,
Vase in 'pulegoso' glass , 1930
h 40 cm, ∅ 25 cm
Turin, Galleria Ecodiforme
(*cf.* cat. no. 44)

35

Napoleone Martinuzzi,
Dachshund, 1930
l 40 cm
Paris, private collection
(cat. no. 45)

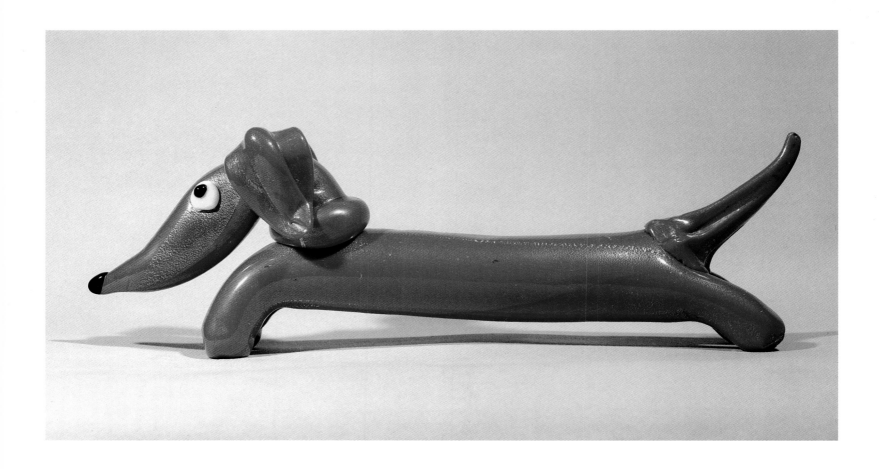

36
Napoleone Martinuzzi,
Mermaid, 1931
h 24.5 cm, l 29 cm
Piacenza, private collection
(cat. no. 52)

87
Napoleone Martinuzzi,
Dolphin, 1930
h 35 cm
Gardone Riviera, Il Vittoriale
degli Italiani, Prioria,
Stanza della Zambracca
(*cf.* cat. no. 46)

39
Napoleone Martinuzzi,
Banded vase, 1930
h 32 cm
Venice, Anna Venini Collectio
(cat. no. 50)

40
Napoleone Martinuzzi,
Flowering plant, 1930
Milan, Biblioteca Ambrosiana
(*cf.* cat. no. 54)

41
Napoleone Martinuzzi,
Cactus, 1930
h 20 cm
Gardone Riviera, Il Vittoriale
degli Italiani, Prioria,
Stanza della Leda
(*cf.* cat. no. 54)

42
Napoleone Martinuzzi,
Large cactus, 1931–32
h 225 cm
Bergamo, Post-office building
(cat. no. 54)

43
Gio Ponti, *Chandelier*, 1946–50
h 70 cm, ∅ 50 cm
Milan, Marco Arosio Collection
(cat. no. 56)

44
Gio Ponti, *Lamp in 'corroso'
glass, c.* 1950
h 38 cm
Turin, Galleria Ecodiforme
(cat. no. 60)

45
Gio Ponti, *'Crinolina' vase*, 1950
h 13 cm, Ø 12 cm
Turin, Galleria Ecodiforme
(cat. no. 59)

46
Gio Ponti, *Cane glasses*, 1955
h 12 cm each
Turin, Galleria Ecodiforme
(cat. no. 61)

Following pages:

47
Paolo Venini,
Engraved bottles, 1950
h 21.5 cm; h 19 cm; h 27 cm;
h 40.5 cm; h 31.5 cm;
h 21.5 cm; h 29 cm
Venice, private collection
(cat. no. 75)

48
Paolo Venini,
Trailed-spiral bottle, 1952
h 23.5 cm
Turin, Galleria Ecodiforme
(*cf.* cat. no. 78)

49
Paolo Venini,
'Tartan' vase, 1952–53
h 18.5 cm
Milan, Galleria In. Arte
(*cf.* cat. no. 84)

50
Paolo Venini,
Waisted vase, 1952
h 28 cm
United States, Millennium
Pictures Collection
(*cf.* cat. no. 77)

51
Paolo Venini, *Bottle*
in 'zanfirico' mesh, 1954
h 39 cm
Zurich, Museum Bellerive
(cat. no. 82)

52
Paolo Venini,
Cane bottle, 1952–56
h 27.5 cm
Union City, Odetto
Lastra Collection
(cat. no. 80)

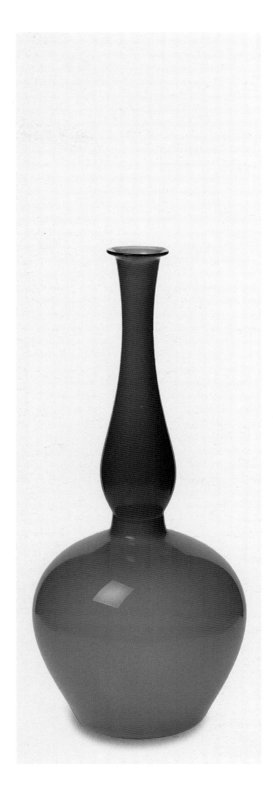

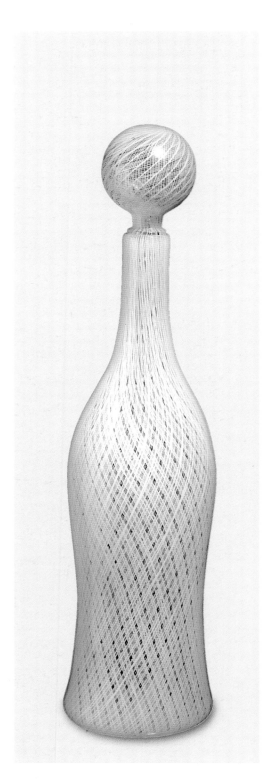

53
Paolo Venini,
'Murrina' vase, 1954
h 31.7 cm
New York, Barry
Friedman Collection
(cat. no. 83)

54
Paolo Venini,
Mosaic 'zanfirico' vase, 1954
h 24.8 cm
New York, Barry
Friedman Collection
(cat. no. 84)

55
Paolo Venini,
'Zanfirico' vase, 1950–55
h 24.8 cm
New York, Barry
Friedman Collection
(*cf.* cat. no. 84)

56
Paolo Venini, *Group
of 'zanfirico' vases*, 1950–55
Location unknown
(*cf.* cat. no. 84)

57
Paolo Venini, *Tableware
for Ginette*, 1950
h 17 cm (jug); h 14 cm (small jug);
h 15 cm (vase); h 9 cm (wine);
h 10 cm (water); h 25 cm (bottle)
Venice, Anna Venini Collection;
Boston, Laura Venini Hillyer Collection
(cat. no. 74)

59
Paolo Venini,
'Murrina' bowl, 1954
h 12.7 cm
New York, Barry
Friedman Collection
(cat. no. 87)

62
Tomaso Buzzi, *Cased
'laguna' vase*, 1932–33
h 28 cm
Milan, private collection
(cat. no. 98)

63
Tomaso Buzzi, *Cased bowl
with light silver-leaf flecks*, 1932–33
h 18 cm
Lugano, private collection
(*cf.* cat. no. 98)

64
Tomaso Buzzi, *Twin-spouted
vase*, 1933
h 16 cm, ⌀ 20 cm
Padua, private collection
(cat. no. 99)

67
Tomaso Buzzi, *Pink cup*, 1932
h 10 cm, ⌀ 20 cm
Milan, Galleria In. Arte
(*cf.* cat. no. 102)

68
Tomaso Buzzi, *'Laguna' cup*, 1932
h 11 cm, ⌀ 31.3 cm
Zurich, Museum Bellerive
(*cf.* cat. no. 102)

69
Tomaso Buzzi, *'Laguna'*
cup, 1932
h 14 cm, ⌀ 25 cm
Padua, private collection
(*cf.* cat. no. 102)

70
Tomaso Buzzi, *'Laguna'*
vase, 1932
h 50 cm
Turin, private collection
(*cf.* cat. no. 102)

71
Tomaso Buzzi, *Table lamp*
in silver-flecked 'laguna'
glass, 1932
h 29 cm, Ø 23 cm
Milan, private collection
(*cf.* cat. no. 102)

72
Tomaso Buzzi, *'Chiocciole'*
amphora, 1933
h 13 cm
Asti, private collection
(cat. no. 103)

73
Tomaso Buzzi,
'Alga' vase, 1933
h 20 cm
Turin, Galleria Ecodiforme
(cat. no. 104)

74
Tomaso Buzzi,
'Bugnato' vase, 1933
h 18 cm
Piacenza, private collection
(cat. no. 105)

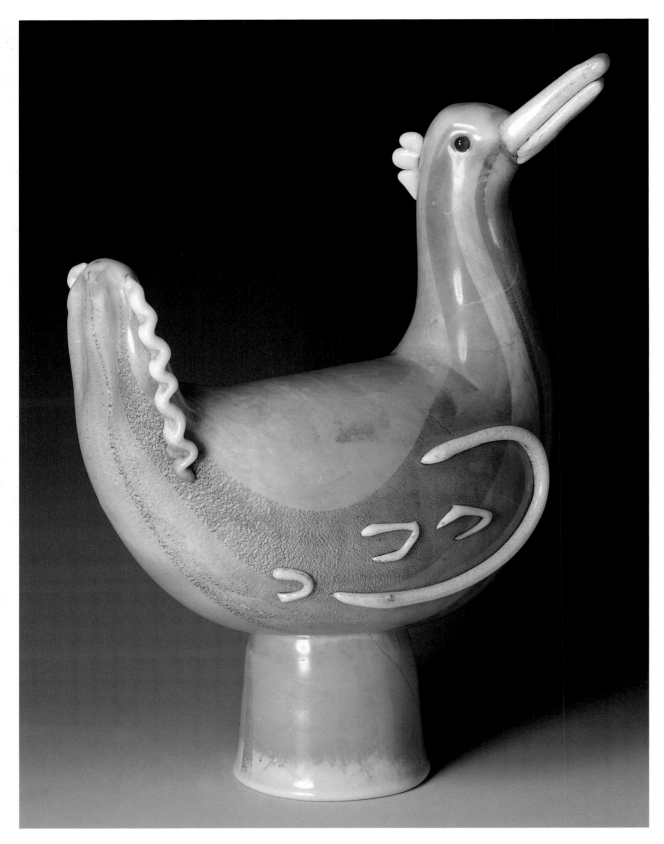

75
Tomaso Buzzi, *Duck*, 1933
h 20 cm
Milan, Galleria In. Arte
(*cf.* cat. no. 106)

76
Tomaso Buzzi, *Cockerel
and hen*, 1933
h 21 cm; h 18 cm
Union City, Odetto Lastra Collection
(cat. no. 107)

77
Tomaso Buzzi, *Turquoise
and black vase*, 1933
h 36 cm
Tarzana, Artur Liu Collection
(cat. no. 110)

78
Tomaso Buzzi, *Turquoise
and black vase*, 1933
h 40 cm
Milan, Galleria In. Arte
(*cf.* cat. no. 110)

79
Tomaso Buzzi, *Pear*, 1933
h 8 cm
Zurich, Museum Bellerive
(cat. no. 108)

80
Tomaso Buzzi, *Table lamp*, 1933
h 25 cm, Ø 30 cm
Treviso, private collection
(cat. no. 111)

81
Tomaso Buzzi,
'Egg-shell' vase, 1933
h 35 cm
Piacenza, private collection
(cat. no. 113)

82
Tomaso Buzzi,
'Alba' vase, 1933
h 40 cm
Turin, private collection
(*cf.* cat.n. 112)

83
Carlo Scarpa, *'Sommerso'*
bubble vase, 1934
h 28 cm
Union City, Odetto
Lastra Collection
(*cf.* cat. no. 116)

84
Carlo Scarpa, *'Sommerso'*
bubble vase, 1934
h 21 cm
Turin, private collection
(cat. no. 116)

85
Carlo Scarpa, *Vase with*
'egg-shell' milling, 1938
h 40 cm
Milan, private collection
(*cf.* cat. no. 135)

Following pages:

86
Carlo Scarpa, *'Sommerso'*
bubble vase, 1934
h 18 cm
Turin, Galleria Ecodiforme
(*cf.* cat. no. 116)

87
Carlo Scarpa, *'Mezza filigrana'*
vase, 1934
h 22 cm
Turin, Galleria Ecodiforme
(*cf.* cat. no. 118)

88
Carlo Scarpa, *'Corroso' goblet*, 1936
h 11 cm, ⌀ 11 cm
United States, Millennium
Pictures Collection
(cat. no. 120)

89
Carlo Scarpa,
'Mezza filigrana' vase, 1934
h 17.5 cm
Union City, Odetto Lastra Collection
(*cf.* cat. no. 118)

90
Carlo Scarpa,
'Mezza filigrana' vase, 1934
h 18.5 cm
Union City, Odetto Lastra Collection
(cat. no. 118)

135

91
Carlo Scarpa, *'Sommerso'*
bubble cup, 1936
h 12 cm, l 30 cm
Private collection
(*cf.* cat. no. 116)

93
Carlo Scarpa, *Relief*
'corroso' vessels, 1936
h 16 cm (blue); h 17 cm (straw-yellow);
h 17.5 cm (green)
Treviso, private collection
(cat. no. 122)

94
Carlo Scarpa, *Relief*
'corroso' vase, 1936
h 11.5 cm
Lugano, private collection
(*cf.* cat. no. 122)

Carlo Scarpa,
'Corroso' vase, 1936
h 20 cm
United States, Millennium
Pictures Collection
(cat. no. 123)

Carlo Scarpa, *Chandelier*, 1936
h 110 cm, Ø 45 cm
Turin, Galleria Ecodiforme
(cat. no. 124)

99
Carlo Scarpa,
'Tessuto' bottle, 1940
h 31.5 cm
Turin, private collection
(*cf.* cat. no. 129)

100
Carlo Scarpa,
'Cinese' vase, 1940
h 26 cm
Treviso, private collection
(cat. no. 131)

101
Carlo Scarpa, *'Iridato' vessel,* 1940
h 8 cm, Ø 12.5 cm
Paris, Musée des Arts Décoratifs
(cat. no. 134)

Carlo Scarpa, *Vase with
trasparent 'murrina' inserts*, 1940
h 12.5 cm
Asti, private collection
(cat. no. 140)

104
Carlo Scarpa,
'Murrina' plate, 1940
l 24 cm
Zurich, Museum Bellerive
(*cf.* cat. no. 142)

105
Carlo Scarpa,
'Murrina' plate, 1940
l 35 cm
Rome, private collection
(cat. no. 143)

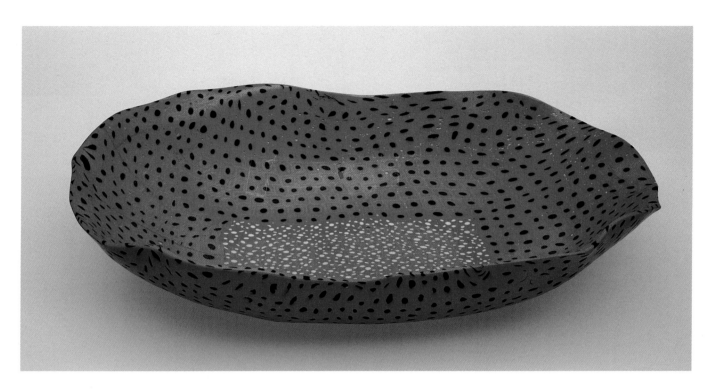

106
Carlo Scarpa,
'Murrina' plate, 1940
l 32 cm
Düsseldorf, Kunstmuseum
Düsseldorf, Glasmuseum Hentrich
(cat. no. 142)

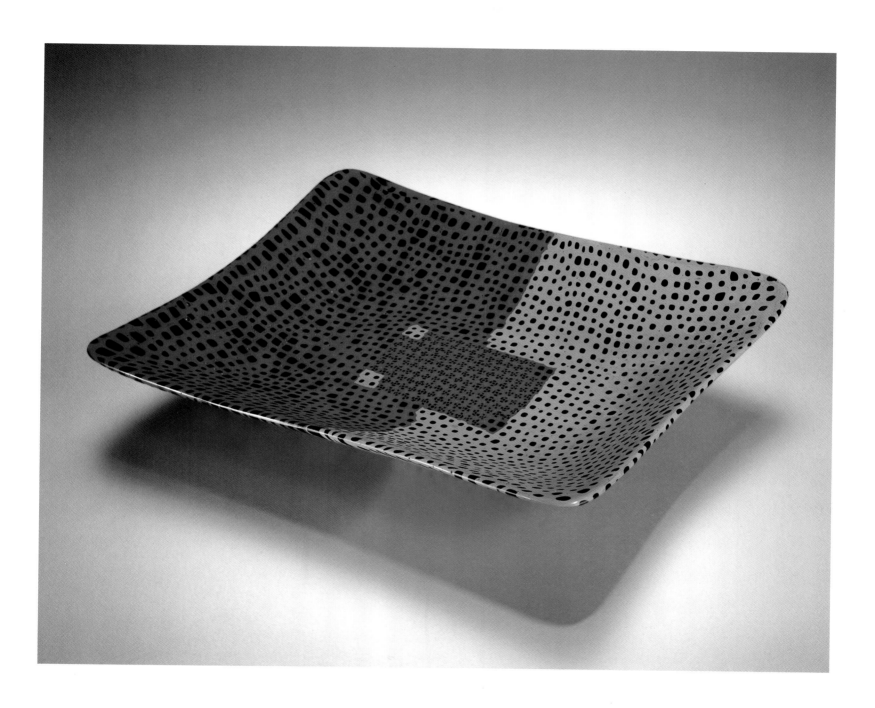

107
Carlo Scarpa,
Thread vase, 1942
h 18.5 cm
Treviso, private collection
(cat. no. 144)

108
Carlo Scarpa,
'Pennellate' vase, 1942
h 26.7 cm
Zurich, Museum Bellerive
(*cf.* cat. no. 145)

109
Carlo Scarpa,
'Pennellate' bowl, 1942
h 12.5 cm, ⌀ 20 cm
Union City, Odetto
Lastra Collection
(*cf.* cat. no. 145)

110
Carlo Scarpa,
'Pennellate' vases, 1942
h 18 cm; h 16 cm; h 19 cm
Milan, Galleria In. Arte
(*cf.* cat. no. 145)

111
Carlo Scarpa, *Owl*, 1943
h 38.5 cm
Padua, Università degli Studi,
Meeting Room
(cat. no. 148)

114
Fulvio Bianconi, *'Regional
costumes' figurine*, 1948
h 31 cm
Union City, Odetto
Lastra Collection
(*cf.* cat. no. 151)

115
Fulvio Bianconi, *'Regional
costumes' figurine
(La Veneziana)*, 1948
h 35 cm
Union City, Odetto
Lastra Collection
(*cf.* cat. no. 151)

116
Fulvio Bianconi, *Obelisk
with flame*, 1948
h 45 cm
Union City, Odetto
Lastra Collection
(cat. no. 154)

Following pages:

117
Fulvio Bianconi,
'Pezzato' vase, 1950
h 45 cm
New York, Barry
Friedman Collection
(*cf.* cat. no. 164)

118
Fulvio Bianconi,
'Pezzato' vase, 1950
h 13 cm
New York, Barry
Friedman Collection
(cat. no. 164)

119
Fulvio Bianconi,
'Pezzato' vase, 1950
h 20 cm
Union City, Odetto
Lastra Collection
(*cf.* cat. no. 164)

120
Fulvio Bianconi,
Banded vase, 1953
h 26 cm
Union City, Odetto
Lastra Collection
(cat. no. 170)

121
Fulvio Bianconi,
Cockerel, 1954
h 18 cm
Milan, Galleria In. Arte
(cat. no. 171)

122
Fulvio Bianconi,
'Informale' vase, 1968
h 42 cm
Union City, Odetto
Lastra Collection
(cat. no. 173)

123
Tyra Lundgren, *Leaf*, 1938
h 5.7 cm, l 30.2 cm
Union City, Odetto
Lastra Collection
(*cf.* cat. no. 174)

124
Tyra Lundgren, *Leaf*, 1938
h 13 cm, l 31 cm
Venice, Massimo
Nordio Collection
(cat. no. 174)

125
Tyra Lundgren, *Fish*, 1938
h 18 cm
Milan, Galleria In. Arte
(cat. no. 176)

126
Tyra Lundgren, *Fish*, 1938
h 10 cm
Turin, private collection
(*cf.* cat. no. 176)

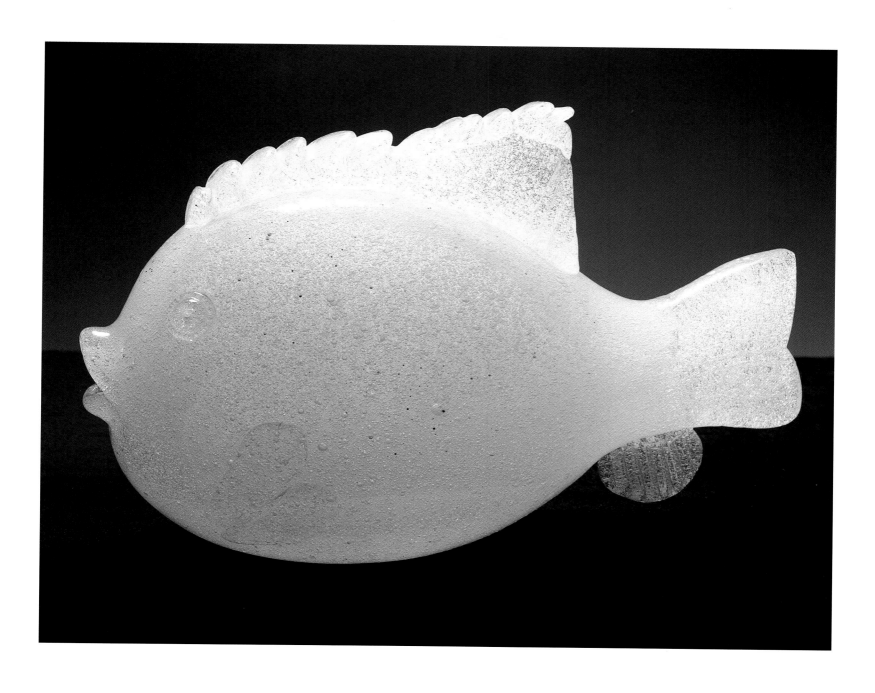

127
Ludovico Diaz de Santillana,
'Battuto' cup, 1960–61
h 14 cm, ∅ 51 cm
Turin, Galleria Ecodiforme
(*cf.* cat. no. 193)

128
Ludovico Diaz de Santillana,
'Battuto' goblets, 1960–61
h 28 cm; h 20 cm
Turin, Galleria Ecodiforme
(cat. no. 193)

Following pages:

129
Ludovico Diaz de Santillana,
'Battuto' cup, 1960–61
h 6.5 cm, ∅ 14 cm
Padua, private collection
(*cf.* cat. no. 193)

130
Ludovico Diaz de Santillana,
'Colletti' flasks, 1961
h 22 cm; h 37 cm; h 30 cm
Turin, Gerard Figliola Collection
(cat. no. 195)

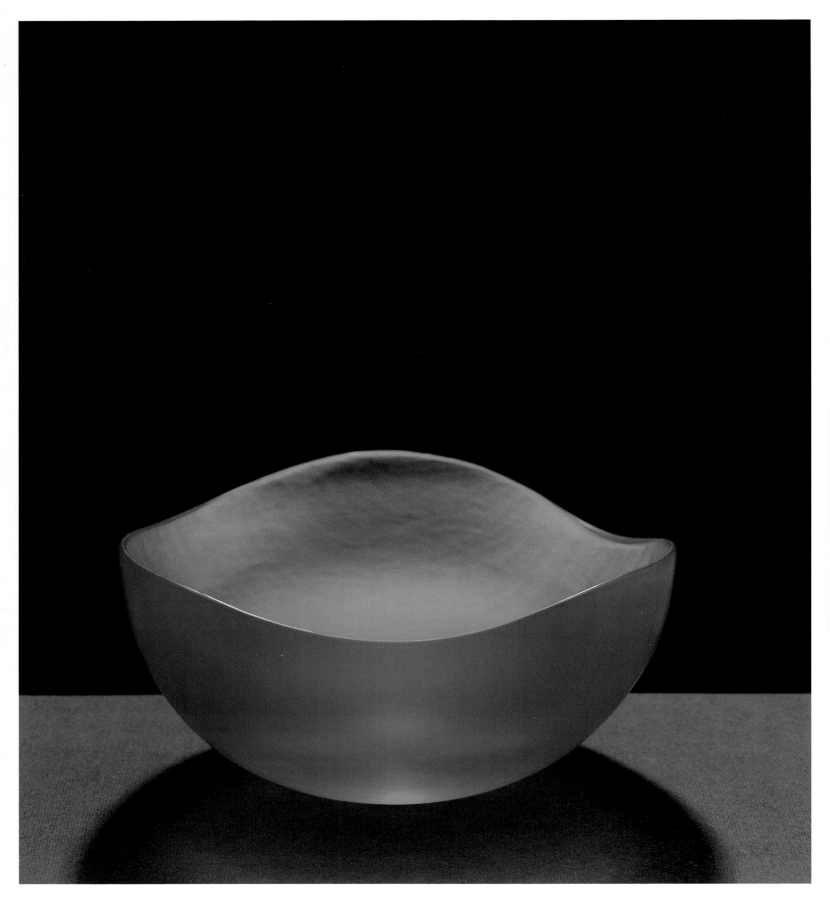

131
Ludovico Diaz de Santillana,
'Murrina' disc, 1962
⌀ 25 cm
Venice, Cassa di Risparmio
(cat. no. 197)

132
Ludovico
'Murrina
⌀ 23 cm
Milan, pr
(*cf.* cat. r

133
Ludovico Diaz de Santillana,
Tortoise, 1965
l 13 cm
Paris, private collection
(cat. no. 201)

134
Ludovico Diaz de Santillana,
Glassware for Pierre Cardin, 1969
h 12 cm, l 18 cm; h 24 cm, l 12 cm
Turin, Galleria Ecodiforme
(cat. no. 204)

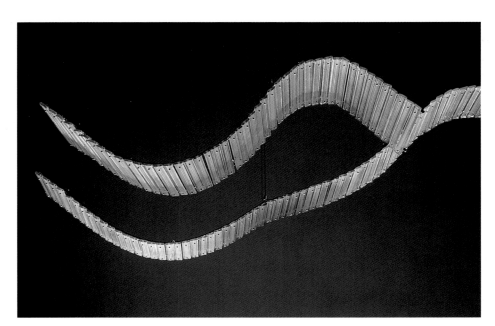

135
Ludovico Diaz de Santillana,
'Tappeto volante', 1984
l 300 cm
Bern, Städtlicher Berner Waisenhaus
(cat. no. 222)

136
Ludovico Diaz de Santillana,
Cube with layered silver-leaf,
c. 1987
h 22 cm
Lausanne, private collection
(cat. no. 224)

137
Ludovico Diaz de Santillana,
Tazebao, 1984
h 650 cm
Murano, Museo Venini
(cat. no. 223)

138
Massimo Vignelli,
'Spicchi' glassware, 1952
h 32 cm (jar); h 12,5 cm (glasses)
Padua, Maurizio Graziani Collection
(cat. no. 226)

139
Massimo Vignelli,
Suspension lamps, 1953–56
h 41 cm; h 34 cm
Udine, private collection
(cat. no. 227)

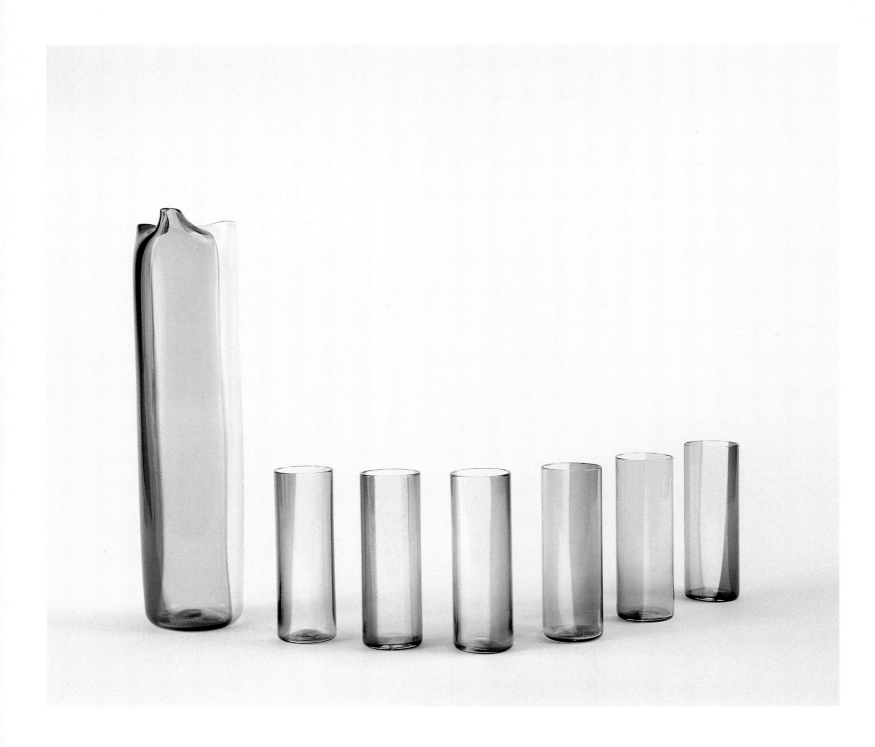

140
Toni Zuccheri, *'Giada'*
vase, 1964
h 30 cm
Milan, Galleria In. Arte
(cat. no. 233)

141
Toni Zuccheri, *Turkey*, 1964
h 45 cm
Turin, private collection
(cat. no. 235)

143
Riccardo Licata, *'Murrina'*
bowl, 1952–53
h 9 cm, Ø 12 cm
Union City, Odetto
Lastra Collection
(cat. no. 184)

144
Miroslav Hrstka,
Mirostre, 1968
h 35 cm
Murano, Museo Venini
(cat. no. 252)

145
Richard Marquis,
'Murrina' vases, 1970
h 11 cm; h 7 cm
Seattle, Richard
Marquis Collection
(cat. no. 253)

146
James Carpenter,
'Tessuto' vases, 1974
h 18 cm; h 9 cm; h 16 cm
New York, private collection
(cat. no. 255)

147
Laura Diaz de Santillana,
'Mimosa' disc, 1977
Ø 25 cm
Murano, Museo Vetrario
(cat. no. 262)

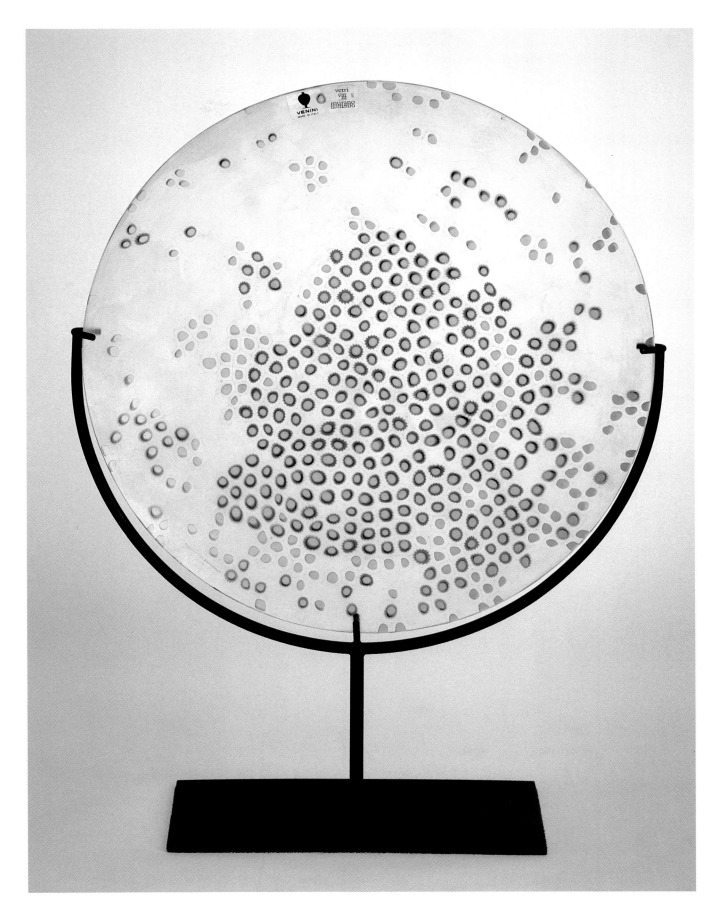

148
Laura Diaz de Santillana,
'Klee' vase, 1978
h 25 cm
Murano, Museo Vetrario
(cat. no. 263)

149
Alessandro Diaz de Santillana,
'Coccio' vase, 1984
h 16 cm
Venice, Alessandro Diaz
de Santillana Collection
(cat. no. 267)

150
Tina Aufiero, *'Alboino'*
vase, 1983
h 27 cm
Venice, Anna Venini Collection
(cat. no. 268)

151
Toots Zynsky, *'Folto' vases*, 1984
h 13 cm, ∅ 23 cm; h 31 cm,
∅ 23 cm; h 18 cm, ∅ 24 cm;
Venice, Laura Diaz
de Santillana Collection
(cat. no. 269)

151
Toots Zynsky, *'Folto' vases*, 1984
h 13 cm, ∅ 23 cm; h 31 cm,
∅ 23 cm; h 18 cm, ∅ 24 cm;
Venice, Laura Diaz
de Santillana Collection
(cat. no. 269)

152
Toots Zynsky, *'Chiacchera'
vases*, 1984
h 34 cm, ∅ 19 cm;
h 27 cm, ∅ 18 cm
Venice, Laura Diaz
de Santillana Collection
(cat. no. 270)

1. *'Veronese' vase*, 1921–25 (pl. 1)
h 32 cm
Venice, Anna Venini Collection

Free-blown vase in light-green glass, subsequently also blown in red, green, sapphire, straw-yellow, light violet and aquamarine; beaten foot, knop decorated with surface veining; large oval central body. The item remained a staple of production, becoming one of Venini's trademark pieces. (When Martinuzzi took over as art director from Zecchin in 1925, he used the latter's drawings to reinstate the piece in the firm's regular catalogue.)
This free-blown series created by Zecchin boasts a classical design in soft hues, free of the usual trammels associated with the Italian Novecento. The form itself derives from a vase containing a rose pictured in Veronese's *Annunciation* of 1578 (Accademia, Venice). Variants of the design include one with ribbing on the foot and body.

Catalogo blu no. 1633A fol. 6 (in one size only); *Catalogo rosso* no. 1333 (other sizes nos 1334, 1335, 1336, 1337); *Catalogo verde* no. 600 (other dimensions nos 600.0, 600.1, 600.2, 600.3, 600.4).
Exhibitions: Venice 1996; Zurich 1998.
Bibliography. Gli artisti di Venini…, 1996, p. 59 no. 1; *Venini. Glas…*, 1998, no. 1.
Carrà 1923, p. 67; Linzeler 1923ᵃ, p. 83; Papini 1923ᵃ, pp. 55, 57; *Trent'anni…*, 1954, p. 9; *Venini Murano…*, 1957, no. 10; *Vetri di Murano…*, 1960 p. 48 no. 3; Polak 1962, no. 51b; Mariacher 1967, p. 48; *Vetri di Murano…*, 1977, p. 6 no. 165; *Vetri Murano Oggi*, 1981, p. 17; *Vittorio Zecchin*, 1981, p. 37 no. 40; *Mille Anni…*, 1982, p. 255 no. 503; *Vetro di Murano…*, 1982, no. 101; *Mostra del vetro…*, 1984, pp. 70, 78 no. 70; Dorigato 1986, pp. 71, 72; *Murano, il vetro…*, 1986, p. 39; *Italienisches…*, 1987, p. 26 no. 7; Deboni 1989, pp. 14, 35 and no. 1; *Die Sammlung…*, 1989, p. 85 no. 203; *Venini…*, 1989, p. 59 no. 1; Tait 1991, pp. 13–14; *Vetri di Murano…*, 1991, pp. 14, 15 no. 2; *L'arte del vetro…*, 1992, pp. 227–28 no. 307; Barovier Mentasti 1992, p. 54; Cerutti, Dorigato 1992, p. 117 no. 15; Heiremans 1993, p. 238 no. 191; Deboni 1996, p. 261 no. 177; *Il Vetro Italiano…*, 1998, p. 161 no. 25, p. 162 no. 26.

2. *'Holbein' vase*, 1921–25 (pl. 2)
h 30 cm
Cologne, Museen der Stadt Köln, Museum für angewandte Kunst

Free-blown vase in straw-yellow glass with beaten foot, ribbed knop, and central body with applied handles having curled terminals.
Inspired by a piece featured in Hans Holbein's *Portrait of Georg Gistze* of 1530, now in the Staatliche Museen, Berlin.

Catalogo blu no. 1924 fol. 6; *Catalogo rosso* no. 1924; *Catalogo verde* no. 601.5.
Exhibitions: Venice 1996.
Bibliography. Gli artisti di Venini…, 1996, p. 59 no. 3.
Carrà 1923, p. 67; *Venini Murano…*, 1957, no. 1; Polak 1962, no. 51b; *Vetri di Murano…*, 1977, p. 6; *Vetri Murano Oggi*, 1981, p. 17; Barovier Mentasti 1992, p. 54; Cerutti, Dorigato 1992, p. 213.

3. *'Tintoretto' jug*, 1921–25 (pl. 3)
h 28 cm
Munich, Die Neue Sammlung, Staatliches Museum für angewandte Kunst, inv. 349/50

Free-blown jug in straw-yellow glass with ribbon handle, ring foot, and beaked spout.
This forms part of the set of blown-glass wares inspired by master paintings of the Italian Cinquecento. Others include the *Caravaggio* vase (*Catalogo verde* no. 601.0; Heiremans 1996, p. 24); the *Bordone* vase (Heiremans 1996, p. 24); and the *Tiziano* vase (*Catalogo blu* no. 1474 fol. 3; *Catalogo verde* no. 601.1).

Catalogo blu no. 3630 fol. 16; *Catalogo verde* no. 601.4.
Exhibitions: Venice 1996.
Bibliography. Gli artisti di Venini…, 1996, p. 59 no. 2.
Venini Murano…, 1957, no. 5; Kämpfer 1966, no. 203.

4. *Blown-glass vase*, 1922
h 30 cm
Location unknown

This vase opens the *Catalogo blu* of 1930, and was made in clear blown glass. The utter simplicity of line and the delicate 'ruff' collar were hallmarks of Zecchin's designs from 1921 to 1925.

Catalogo blu no. 1465 fol. 1; *Catalogo rosso* no. 1465.
Bibliography. Vetri di Murano…, 1977, no. 158 fig. 63.

5. *Amphora with angled handles*, 1922
h 31 cm
Venice, private collection

Free-blown amphora in transparent pale green glass with singular right-angled handles.

Catalogo blu no. 1878A fol. 5, (set) nos 1879, 1862 fol. 5; *Catalogo verde* (set) no. 601.6 (with specifications of colour range: red, green, sapphire, amethyst, straw-yellow, violet, aquamarine, pale green).
Bibliography. Linzeler 1923ᵃ, p. 83; Barovier Mentasti 1992, p. 52; *Gli artisti di Venini…*, 1996, p. 60 no. 6.

6. *Chalice*, 1922
h 20.1 cm
Vienna, Österreichisches Museum für angewandte Kunst, inv. GI 2554

Sleek chalice in pale green transparent glass, with long blown stem and widely flared bowl obtained using the open-mould process.

Bibliography. Vetri di Murano…, 1977, no. 161 fig. 62; *Vittorio Zecchin*, 1981, p. 37 no. 45; *Italienisches…*, 1987, p. 36 no. 17.

1

2

3

4

5

6

7. *'Rigadin retorto' vase*, 1922 (pl. 7)
h 28.8 cm, ⌀ 20 cm
Munich, Die Neue Sammlung, Staatliches
Museum für angewandte Kunst, inv. 488/90

Elemental flower vase with characteristic spiral
banding, a technique known in Venice as *rigadin
retorto* (twisted ribbing); body open-moulded.

Catalogo blu no. 1593A fol. 2 (shape).
Exhibitions: Venice 1996.
Bibliography. Gli artisti di Venini…, 1996, p. 62
no. 10.
Vittorio Zecchin, 1981, p. 37 no. 44.

8. *'Libellula' vase*, 1922–25 (pl. 4)
h 24 cm, ⌀ 37 cm
Gardone Riviera, Il Vittoriale degli Italiani,
Prioria, Stanza del Monco

Bowl in free-blown glass; applied flat foot with
beaten rim; widely splayed handles having curled
terminals.
The *Libellula* (Dragon-fly) vase was produced in
pale green, pale blue, and straw-yellow. In the
Catalogo blu it was incorrectly entered for
1925–30, coinciding therefore with Martinuzzi's
tenure as art director; properly catalogued as no.
1432A, it belongs to Zecchin's period.
Zecchin's *Libellula* was presented at the first
Mostra Internazionale delle Arti Decorative, held
in Monza in 1923.

Exhibitions: Gardone Riviera 1988; Venice 1996.
*Bibliography. Gabriele d'Annunzio e la Promozione
delle Arti*, 1988, no. 253b; *Gli artisti di Venini…*,
1996, p. 60 no. 4.
Carrà 1923, p. 67; *Catalogo Prima Mostra…*, 1923,
no. 15; Linzeler 1923[a], p. 84; Papini 1923[a], p. 55;
Papini 1923[b], p. 7; *Vetri di Murano…*, 1977, p. 19
no. 164; Barovier Mentasti 1982, p. 252 no. 253;
Mille Anni…, 1982, p. 255 no. 501; Deboni 1989,
no. 2; *Vetri di Murano*, 1989, p. 32; *Vetri di Murano…*, 1991, p. 17 no. 3; *L'arte del vetro…*, 1992,
pp. 183, 227, 229 no. 306; Heiremans 1993, p. 239;
Barovier, Barovier Mentasti, Dorigato 1995, p. 117
no. 15; Ricke 1995, p. 234 no. 375; *Venezia…*,
1995, p. 423 no. 330; *Italienisches…*, 1996, p. 12.

9. *Vase*, 1923 (pl. 5)
h 17.8 cm
Pavia, private collection

Vase in amethyst-coloured blown glass, iridised;
broad foot with beaten rim.
Owing to its shape, the piece associable with the
fruit-bowl category, which differs by the addition
of a lid bearing a fruit-shaped finial (in imitation of
sixteenth-century models).

Catalogo blu (fruit-bowl set) nos 1220, 1222, 1204,
1202, 1228, 1219, 1206, 1214, 1215, 1227, 1020A,
1018A, 1027A, 1032A, 1022, 1038A, 1014, 1015A,
1080, 1063A, 1054, 1021 fols 7–8; *Catalogo rosso*
(fruit-bowl set) nos 1022, 1080, 1083, 1084, 1085,
1086, 1087, 1088, 1089, 1090, 1091, 1092.
Exhibitions: Venice 1996.
Bibliography. Gli artisti di Venini…, 1996, p. 61
no. 7.
Linzeler 1923[a], p. 80.

10. *'Amphora' vase*, 1923 (pl. 6)
h 40.6 cm
Geneva, Musée Ariana, inv. V 123

Amphora-shaped vase in blown glass with welded
handles descending to lightly curling terminals on
body.
Although this model appeared in a display pho-
tographed at the 1923 Mostra Internazionale delle
Arti Decorative, held in Monza, it does not appear
in the official catalogue.

Catalogo blu no. 1695A fol. 6.
Bibliography. Linzeler 1922, p. 666; Linzeler 1923[a],
p. 83; Papini 1923[a], p. 57; Papini 1923[b], p. 9; *XXVI
Biennale…*, 1952; Deboni 1989, no. 3; Baumgartner
1995, p. 91 no. 142; Deboni 1996, p. 262 no. 178.

11. *Chalice*, 1923
h 32.5 cm
Location unknown

Elegant, tall chalice in blown glass composed of
long-stemmed foot with deep kick supporting a
welded bell-shaped bowl; a green-based version
exists at the Vittoriale on Lake Garda.

Catalogo blu nos 1489B, 1503B (taller variant)
fol. 3.
Exhibitions: Venice 1996.
Bibliography. Gli artisti di Venini…, 1996, no. 9.
Papini 1923[a], p. 56; Papini 1923[b], p. 8; Deboni
1989, p. 35 no. 5; *Verre de Venise…*, 1995, p. 92
no. 143.

12. *'Raindrop' vase*, 1923
h 18 cm, ⌀ 10 cm
Location unknown

Clear, wide-ribbed vase with ovoid body, made
with open-mould blown technique; flared mouth;
trailing darker gobs on lower section of body.

Catalogo blu no. 1938 fol. 5 (without ribbing).
Bibliography. 'Muranese Glass…', 1925, pp. 134–35;
Vittorio Zecchin, 1981, p. 37 no. 43; *Mille Anni…*,
1982, p. 255 no. 502; Deboni 1989, no. 4; Heiremans 1996, p. 23 no. 12.

13. *Chalice*, 1923
h 14 cm
Location unknown

Wide drinking vessel in blown glass with gently
ribbed outer surface; welded circular disk foot.

Catalogo blu no. 1462 fol. 3 (without ribbing).
Bibliography. Mille Anni…, 1982, p. 254 no. 500;
Vetro di Murano…, 1982, no. 100; *L'arte del
vetro…*, 1992, p. 227 no. 305; Barovier Mentasti
1992, p. 58 no. 49; Cerutti, Dorigato 1992, p. 203;
Gli artisti di Venini…, 1996, p. 60 no. 5; *Venini
Venezia…*, 1998, p. 63; *Il Vetro Italiano…*, 1998,
p. 163 no. 27.

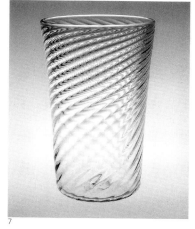
7

8

9

10

11

12

13

14. *Pumpkin-shaped vase*, 1925
h 26 cm
Acid-stamped: 'Venini Murano'
United States, Millennium Pictures Collection

Blown-glass vase with bowl in the form of a pump-kin; pale blue paste; long narrow neck with two ruffs towards base.
The piece is a great rarity.

Catalogo blu no. 1592B fol. 13.

15. *'Parigi' lamp*, 1925
Paris, Musée Nissim de Camondo

Large hanging light fixture in clear blown glass, notable for its elegant and sober line; long central shaft branches into eight bowls terminating in bell-shaped lamp-holders.
Exhibited in the national pavilion of the 1925 Exposition Internationale des Arts Décoratifs et Industriels in Paris; later donated by Paolo Venini to the Jeu de Paume pavilion in the Louvre, Paris. The piece went missing for several years, but subsequently re-emerged and is currently being restored ready to be reinstalled.

Exhibitions: Paris 1925.
Bibliography: Italie à l'Exposition..., 1925, s.p.

14

15

16. *Vase*, 1925–28 (pl. 8)
h 28 cm, ⌀ 28.8 cm
Zurich, Museum Bellerive, inv. 9204

Exquisite spherical hand-blown vase in straw-yellow glass.

Catalogo blu no. 3193 fol. 6.
Bibliography: Museum Bellerive..., 1995, p. 226 no. 392.

17. *Ansate vase*, 1925–28 (pl. 9)
h 46 cm, ⌀ 44 cm
Gardone Riviera, Il Vittoriale degli Italiani,
Prioria, Stanza del Lebbroso

Large amphora-shaped vase in aquamarine blown glass, with two striated ribbon handles.

Catalogo blu no. 1872 fol. 5 (model without handles).
Bibliography: Napoleone Martinuzzi..., 1992, p. 11.
Barovier Mentasti 1982, p. 258 no. 260; *Italianisches...*, 1987, p. 25 no. 6.

18. *'Doge' lamp*, 1925–30
h 120 cm
Venice, Palazzo Ducale

This forms part of a series of blown-glass hanging lights in light blue, straw-yellow, tea, and grey. The surface of the glass it very slightly ribbed, and the long shaft bearing the central bell-shaped element is punctuated by with glass orbs of varying sizes, some slightly compressed.
This pendant lamp enjoyed wide success and was remained in production for a long time; the *Catalogo blu* lists only two examples.

Catalogo blu nos 5008, 5007 fol. 119.
Bibliography: Marconi 1928–29, pp. 396–97, 399.

19. *Tall blue amphora*, 1925–31 (pl. 10)
h 74 cm
Padua, private collection

Amphora in thin blue blown glass; handles with curled lower terminals; broad applied foot; collar of neck emphasised with a spiral filament. Fashioned by the master glassmaker 'Fei' (alias Ferdinando Toso), the piece is a one-off sample that does not appear in the catalogues.

Exhibitions: Venice 1996.
Bibliography: Napoleone Martinuzzi..., 1992, p. 70 no. 10; *Gli artisti di Venini...*, 1996, p. 65 no. 15. Marconi 1928–29, p. 403.

20. *'Libellula' glass*, 1926
h 18 cm
Düsseldorf, Kunstmuseum Düsseldorf,
Glasmuseum Hentrich

Bowl in thin clear pale blue glass with wide, moderate ribbing; blown with open-mould technique; handles swing outward describing a wide arc; round foot. Martinuzzi's *Libellula* (Dragon-fly) piece was a revival of his forerunner Zecchin's, only slightly smaller and with this gentle ribbing.

Catalogo blu no. 3019 fol. 12; *Catalogo rosso* no. 1432 (Zecchin's model).
Exhibitions: Venice 1996.
Bibliography: Ricke 1995, p. 234 no. 375; *Gli artisti di Venini...*, 1996, p. 64 no. 13.

21. *Gazelle*, 1926–30
h 22.5 cm
Location unknown

The photograph, from the Venini archives, shows the corresponding model number from the *Catalogo blu*.
Unlike the joint Zecchin-Martinuzzi pieces of 1933, this one has straight legs.

Catalogo blu no. 2532 fol. 22.

22. *Birds and other animals*, 1926–30 (*cf.* pl. 11)
h 35 cm (pheasant); h 35 cm (bird on perch);
h 28 cm (swallow)
Location unknown

Bird figures in glass paste mounted on circular bases decorated with light ribbing and gold leaf inserts.
The *Catalogo blu* lists three variations only: nos 2531, 2527, 2525 (fol. 23); a fourth, that it isn't in the *Catalogo blu*, is documented in a photograph from the Venini archive.
Also listed in the *Catalogo blu* (fols 21–22) are other animal figures: a *Giraffe* (no. 2555), a *Camel* (no. 2540), a *Dove* (no. 2499), and a *Bear* (no. 2557). These animals figures from Martinuzzi's 'bestiary' are absent from the *Catalogo rosso* and *Catalogo verde*.

Catalogo blu nos 2527, 2531, 2525, fol. 23.
Bibliography: Paolucci 1930, p. 45; *Mostra di Vetri...*, 1931, p. 9; Deboni 1989, no. 22; *Napoleone Martinuzzi...*, 1992, p. 134 nos 86–87, p. 135 nos 88–89; *Gli artisti di Venini...*, 1996, p. 71 nos 31–32; *Venini Venezia...*, 1998, p. 65.

23. *Glass-drop chandelier*, 1926–30 (pl. 12)
h 103 cm, ⌀ 78 cm
Gardone Riviera, Il Vittoriale degli Italiani,
Prioria, Bagno Blu

Hanging light with transparent straw-yellow glass stem from which extend six S-shaped branches, each one terminating in a conical light-holder hung with a drop-pendant; similar pendants hang from the rim of the ceiling rosette, which is decorated with small leaves alternating with bulges.
The wall sconces in the same room match the chandelier, each one with three arms bearing large cup-shaped light-holders.
The chandelier design was repeated for another room, this time in amethyst glass.

Catalogo blu nos 2028, 2181 (sconce) fol. 109, no. 2050 (variant) fol. 109.

24. *Glass-drop chandelier*, 1926–30 (pl. 13)
h 76 cm, ⌀ 70 cm
Gardone Riviera, Il Vittoriale degli Italiani,
Prioria, Stanza Cicerin

Chandelier in transparent pale blue glass with six branches curving slightly upward to support dish-shaped candle-holders decorated with elegant crystal droplets, which are repeated around the rim of the ceiling rosette at the crown of the shaft.
The authorship of the design is still unclear, as the shape is similar to drawings made by Zecchin, who first met the house's owner, D'Annunzio, in Murano.

Catalogo blu no. 2025 fol. 107.

16

17

20

18

24

23

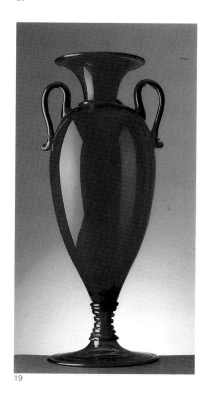

19

2532

21

2527   2531   1316   2526

22

25. *Globular amphora*, 1927
h 29 cm
Venice, private collection

Orb-shaped amphora in delicate clear blue glass, with two volutes applied to the neck under a gently lobed rim. Other examples were made in heavier glass, using the submerged technique.

Catalogo blu no. 3150 fol. 6.
Exhibitions: Venice 1996.
Bibliography. *Gli artisti di Venini…*, 1996, p. 65 no. 16.
Barovier Mentasti 1992, p. 58; *Napoleone Martinuzzi…*, 1992, p. 67 no. 5.

26. *Striated chalice-vase*, 1927
(pl. 15; *cf.* pl. 14)
h 24 cm, Ø 21 cm
Padua, private collection

Large conical vase in green-tinged blown glass wound with gentle, slightly oblique coils of ribbing; set on a welded disc foot.
The piece forms part of objects from Martinuzzi's early period of design, in which the influence of his precursor Zecchin can still be felt.
The vase was presented at the third Mostra Internazionale delle Arti Decorative, held in Monza in 1927.

Catalogo blu no. 3145 fol. 11.
Bibliography: *Impronte del soffio…*, 1987, no. 6; *Italienisches…*, 1987, p. 32 no. 13; Deboni 1989, p. 37 no. 6; *L'arte del vetro…*, 1992, p. 228 no. 310; Barovier Mentasti 1992, p. 57 no. 48; *Napoleone Martinuzzi…*, 1992, p. 66 no. 4; *Gli artisti di Venini…*, 1996, p. 64 no. 14.

27. *Duckling*, 1928 (pl. 16)
h 30 cm
Murano, Museo Vetrario

Duckling figure in blown crystal decorated with twisted *zanfirico* trails.
Exhibited at the 1928 Venice Biennale together with three animal figures of similar design, in crystal embedded with bubbles: *Pelican, Rabbit, Drake*.

Catalogo blu nos 2480 (*Drake*), 2481 (*Rabbit*), 2482 (*Pelican*) fol. 23.
Exhibitions: Venice 1996;
Bibliography: Dorigato 1986, p. 73; *Napoleone Martinuzzi…*, 1992, p. 39; Barovier, Barovier Mentasti, Dorigato 1995, p. 120 no. 21; *Il bestiario…*, 1996, p. 15 no. 2.
XVI Esposizione…, 1928, p. 98; Maraini 1928–29, p. 60; Dir. 1929, p. 31 and cover; *Mostra del vetro…*, 1984, p. 106 no. 148; de Guttry, Maino, Quesada 1985, p. 231 no. 6; *Napoleone Martinuzzi…*, 1992, p. 130 no. 80.

28. *Dish with horse design*, 1928
Location unknown

Elegant table platter in transparent, wafer-thin blown glass, decorated with trails of glass paste around the outer rim and for the horse pattern on the central disc.

Bibliography: Maraini 1928–29, p. 62; Dir. 1929, p. 31.

29. *Pumpkin*, 1928 (*cf.* pl. 20)
h 17 cm
Murano, Museo Vetrario

Squat, pumpkin-shaped piece in free-blown opaque red glass with heavy ribbing; green detailing and iridised finish.

Exhibitions: Venice 1996.
Bibliography: Dorigato 1986, p. 82; *Venini…*, 1989, pl. 9; *Napoleone Martinuzzi…*, 1992, pp. 13, 18, 20; *Gli artisti di Venini…*, 1996, p. 70 no. 28.
Papini 1927, p. 18; Papini 1930, pl. CXXXIX; Ponti 1929, p. 40; *Vetri di Murano…*, 1989, p. 18.

30. *Josephine Baker*, 1928–29
h 200 cm
Location unknown

Statue-tribute modelled after the black dancer Josephine Baker, in green *pulegoso* glass. Owing to its unusual height, the figure is constructed on a metal armature.
First presented at a large gathering of glassworkers at the Grand Hotel Excelsior at Lido in 1928, Martinuzzi's statue disappeared without trace after being put on show in a London gallery.
Another exemplar, almost identical, was put on display alongside selected Venini articles at the Salon d'Automne in Paris, 1929.
Being a one-off item, the piece has never appeared in the catalogues.

Bibliography: 'La statua in vetro…', 1928, p. 47; 'Venini, Ballerina…', 1928, p. 22; Deboni 1989, p. 19; *Napoleone Martinuzzi…*, 1992, p. 42; *Gli artisti di Venini…*, 1996, p. 17.

31. *Fruit-stand with fruit*, 1928–30 (pl. 18)
h 37 cm, Ø 37 cm
Gardone Riviera, Il Vittoriale degli Italiani, Prioria, Stanza della Musica

Fruit-stand in opalescent glass decorated with amethyst strands; contains fruit made in different types of glass: transparent glass with crackled, 'iced' surface; in cased glass, or veiled.
The novelty of the arrangement is underscored by its shrewd combination of classic Murano techniques, and not least the idea of transforming the whole into a form of light fitting.

Catalogo blu nos 2418, 2419, 2530, 2610, 2611 fol. 25 (for the fruit).
Bibliography: *L'arte del vetro…*, 1992, p. 237 no. 326; *Napoleone Martinuzzi…*, 1992, p. 16.
Paolucci 1930, pp. 44–45; Dorigato 1986, pp. 76–77; *Gabriele d'Annunzio e la Promozione delle Arti*, 1988; *Napoleone Martinuzzi…*, 1992, pp. 45, 122–23 nos 68–70.

32. *Boar*, 1928–30 (pl. 17)
h 35 cm
Asti, private collection

This *Boar* in white *pulegoso* has details in red glass paste.
Other versions were made entirely in glass paste.

Catalogo blu no. 2485 fol. 22.
Exhibitions: Venice 1996.
Bibliography: *Gli artisti di Venini…*, 1996, p. 72 no. 33; Deboni 1996, p. 269 no. 185.

25

28

26

27

29

31

32

33. *Fruit-stand*, 1928–30 (pl. 19)
h 16 cm, ∅ 21 cm
Gardone Riviera, Il Vittoriale degli Italiani,
Prioria, Stanza Cicerin

Broad-rimmed fruit-stand, blown in amethyst
glass; pronounced ribbing toward the base of the
bowl; raised beaten foot; open-mould blown.

Catalogo blu no. 1301 fol. 4.

34. *Large chandelier*,
1928–30 (pl. 21)
h 122 cm, ∅ 90 cm
Gardone Riviera, Il Vittoriale degli Italiani,
Prioria, Stanza del Mappamondo

Elaborate branched chandelier in the Rezzonico
style composed of three tiers of lamp-holders in
clear glass hung with pale blue drop pendants.
The crown of the shaft is decorated with a corona,
volutes, and further glass drops; the uppermost
bowl encloses a glass fruit.

Catalogo blu no. 2001 fol. 101.

35. *Large 'leaf' chandelier*,
1928–30 (pl. 24)
h 160 cm, ∅ 110 cm
Milan, private collection

Fourteen-light chandelier in pale green glass decorated with three orders of metal leaf-blades, the
first tier curving upward in an S-shape and hung
with pendant lamp-holders; the tall shaft is
crowned with a tier of leaves rising sharply upward.
The piece evinces an elegance and lightness characteristic of the period.

36. *Chandelier*, 1928–30 (pl. 22)
h 62 cm, ∅ 34 cm
Gardone Riviera, Il Vittoriale degli Italiani,
Prioria, Bagno delle Ospiti

Four-branched chandelier in transparent green
glass, with broad-rimmed lamp-holder disks decorated with glass pendants; long balustered shaft.

37. *Volute chandelier*,
1928–30 (pl. 25)
h 140 cm, ∅ 45 cm
Gardone Riviera, Il Vittoriale degli Italiani,
Casseretto, Gian Carlo Maroni's study

Ceiling light in transparent straw-yellow glass
with six S-curved branches; ribbed lamp-holder
dishes enhanced with amethyst trails; long shaft
with two torus knops; bowl sprouting volutes in
amethyst glass and droplets in straw-yellow.
Two three-branched wall sconces hanging in the
Maroni's study closely resemble the chandelier in
question.

33

34

35

36

37

30

38. *Cornucopia lamp*, 1928–30 (pl. 23)
h 80 cm, Ø 45 cm
Gardone Riviera, Il Vittoriale degli Italiani,
Prioria, Stanza Verde

Ceiling light with four cornucopia lamp-holders in
veiled ivory glass with gold-leaf inserts; original
lamps in gold ice-glass.
The Bergamo post-office building contains a wall-
mounted unit with seven arms bearing cornucopia
lamp-holders in turquoise veiled glass, outlined in
black and embellished with welded black leaves
on the central holder (datable to 1931–32).

Catalogo blu no. 5065 fol. 106 (similar).
Bibliography. Napoleone Martinuzzi…, 1992, p. 47.

39. *Toilet set*, 1929
Location unknown

Toilet set in pale lilac glass with ribbing picked out
in violet thread.

Catalogo blu no. 604 fol. 215.

40. *Foal*, 1929–30 (pl. 26; *cf.* pl. 27)
h 27 cm
Asti, private collection

Statuette of a foal in *lattimo* glass entirely overlaid with gold-leaf. A specimen in black glass
paste and gold-leaf was presented at the 1930
Venice Biennale (*cf. Catalogo blu* no. 2484 fol. 31;
XVII Esposizione Biennale…, 1930, p. 123) and at
the Milan Triennale of the same year (*cf. Il Vetro
Italiano…*, 1998, p. 170 no. 39).

Catalogo blu no. 2523 fol. 21; *Catalogo rosso* no.
10484.
Exhibitions: Venice 1996.
Bibliography. Vetri di Murano…, 1991, pp. 30–31;
Napoleone Martinuzzi…, 1992, p. 139 no. 94; *Gli
artisti di Venini…*, 1996, p. 74 no. 36
'Modelli di produzioni…', 1933, p. 558; *Vetri Mu-
rano Oggi*, 1981, no. 411; Deboni 1989, no. 24;
L'arte del vetro…, 1992, p. 234 no. 321;
Napoleone Martinuzzi…, 1992, p. 138 no. 92;
Barovier, Barovier Mentasti, Dorigato 1995, p. 124
no. 26; *Il Vetro Italiano…*, 1998, p. 170 no. 39.

41. *Elephant*, 1929–30 (pl. 29; *cf.* pl. 28)
h 19.5 cm
Padua, private collection

Elephant figure in *lattimo* glass with applied gold-
leaf.
Most of the elephants in the Venini production
tend to have a raised trunk.

Catalogo blu no. 2548A fol. 21, no. 2500 fol. 12
(variant).
Bibliography. Vetro di Murano…, 1982, no. 121;
Deboni 1989, no. 23; *Vetri di Murano…*, 1991,
pp. 24–25 no. 7; *L'arte del vetro…*, 1992, p. 234
no. 320; *Napoleone Martinuzzi…*, 1992,
pp. 144–45; *Il bestiario…*, 1996, no. 35; *Sculture…*, 1996, p. 9 no. 1.

42. *Bell-shaped table lamp*,
c. 1930 (pl. 30)
h 31.5 cm
Acid-stamped: 'Venini Murano'
Turin, Galleria Ecodiforme

Table light in tea-coloured cased *lattimo* glass finished in dark brown glass paste.

43. *Table glassware*,
c. 1930 (pl. 31)
h 13 cm, Ø 10 cm (water); h 11 cm, Ø 9 cm
(wine); h 12 cm, Ø 12 cm (champagne);
h 6 cm, Ø 6 cm (liqueur)
Gardone Riviera, Il Vittoriale degli Italiani,
Prioria, Office cucina

Set of glasses in grey blown glass composed of
circular foot, knop in coral-red glass paste, sur-
mounted by a conical bowl. Some have a double
cone separated by a coral knop.

44. *Amphora with five handles of grooved
ribbon*, 1930 (pl. 32; *cf.* pls 33, 34)
h 34 cm
Gardone Riviera, Il Vittoriale degli Italiani,
Prioria, Stanza della Zambracca

Glass amphora in green *pulegoso* with two sets of
five grooved ribbon handles at either side; inserts
of gold-leaf applied to mouth of bowl and handles.
Martinuzzi's *pulegoso* creations were first exhibited at the 1930 Monza Triennale.

Catalogo blu no. 3273 fol. 15, (set) nos 3218, 3221,
3874, 3259 fol. 15; *Catalogo rosso* (set) no. 3218.
Exhibitions: Venice 1996; Milan 1998.
*Bibliography. Gabriele d'Annunzio e la Promozione
delle Arti*, 1988, no. 388a; *Napoleone Martinuzzi…*, 1992, pp. 80–81; *Gli artisti di Venini…*,
1996, p. 67 no. 20.
Felice 1928, p. 30; Felice 1930, pl. 85; Felice
1930–31, p. 315; Lorenzetti 1931, p. 15 no. 22;
Vetri Murano Oggi, 1981, p. 30 no. 62; *Mille Anni…*, 1982, p. 265 no. 525; *Vetro di Murano…*,
1982, no. 119; Barovier Mentasti 1982, p. 266 no.
270; *Mostra del vetro…*, 1984, p. 107 no. 149; de
Guttry, Maino, Quesada 1985, no. 58; Dorigato
1986, p. 80; Deboni 1989, no. 14; *L'arte del
vetro…*, 1992, p. 239 no. 327; Barovier Mentasti
1992, p. 65 figs 52–53; Barovier, Barovier Mentasti, Dorigato 1995, p. 119 no. 20; *Il Vetro Italiano…*, 1998, p. 169 no. 38.

45. *Dachshund*, 1930 (pl. 35)
l 40 cm
Acid-stamped: 'Made in Italy'
Paris, private collection

Animal figure in coral-red glass paste with applied
details in gold-leaf; milk-white and black glass inserts for nose and eyes.

Catalogo blu no. 2439 fol. 21.
Exhibitions: Venice 1996.
*Bibliography. Barovier Mentasti 1992, p. 66 no. 54;
Gli artisti di Venini…*, 1996, p. 74 no. 37.

38

40

39

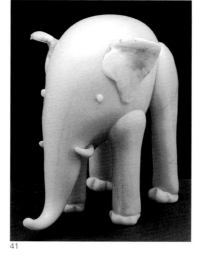
41

42

43

44

46. *Dolphins*, 1930 (pl. 38; *cf.* pl. 37)
h 35 cm each
Padua, private collection

Pair of dolphins in *lattimo* cased in crystal on stunted column bases in *lattimo*, with pedestal in malachite glass.

Exhibitions: Venice 1996.
Bibliography: Deboni 1989, p. 37; *Napoleone Martinuzzi…*, 1992, p. 132; Heiremans 1993, p. 242 no. 195; *Gli artisti di Venini…*, 1996, pp. 75–76 nos 40–41.

47. *Sea-horse*, 1930
h 18 cm
Piacenza, private collection

Rampant sea-horse statuette in crystal with gold-leaf, resting on a twisted column stump in gold-leaf crystal glass and *lattimo*.
The statuette is part of a table centrepiece comprising nine separate marine figures (*cf. Catalogo blu* nos 10309–10317 fol. 19).

Catalogo blu nos 10301–10308, 10318 fol. 20 (centrepiece with vegetal motifs and dolphins).
Bibliography: *Gli artisti di Venini…*, 1996, p. 75 no. 39.
Deboni 1989, p. 37; *Napoleone Martinuzzi…*, 1992, pp. 132–33 figs 82–85; Heiremans 1993, p. 242 no. 195; *Sculture…*, 1996, p. 26 no. 27.

48. *Malachite chalice*, 1930
Location unknown

Wide chalice in malachite with *all'antica* decoration.

Catalogo blu no. 3122 fol. 4.
Bibliography: Felice 1930, pl. 85; Barovier, Barovier Mentasti, Dorigato 1995, pp. 30–31.

49. *Vase with rostrate handle*, 1930
h 20 cm
Location unknown

Vase and rostrate handle in *pulegoso* glass. Presented at the 1928 Venice Biennale.

Catalogo blu no. 3226 fol. 15 (with two rostrate handles, among the *pulegoso* items of 1926–30).
Bibliography: Felice 1928, p. 30; *Vetri di Murano…*, 1991, pp. 34–35; *Napoleone Martinuzzi…*, 1992, p. 96; Barovier, Barovier Mentasti, Dorigato 1995, p. 124 no. 27.

50. *Banded vase*, 1930 (pl. 39)
h 32 cm
Venice, Anna Venini Collection

Vase with horizontal ribbing in *lattimo* cased in tea-coloured layer.

Catalogo blu no. 3294 fol. 15.
Bibliography: *Gli artisti di Venini…*, 1996, p. 65 no. 17.
Napoleone Martinuzzi…, 1992, p. 97 no. 39.

45

47

46

50

48

49

51. *Table lamp with aquarium*, 1930
h 25 cm
Location unknown
(Milan, Triennale, Archivio Fotografico)

Globular vase-lamp in clear *fumé* glass containing a marine plant supporting an orange sea-horse decorated with black glass threading. A variant containing a plant and fish also exists. The piece is designed to contain water, and typifies Martinuzzi's imaginative flair.
The aquarium vase series was presented at the 1930 Monza Triennale.

Catalogo blu nos 10806 (with fish), 10804 (with sea-horse) fol. 9.
Bibliography: Mostra di Vetri..., 1931, p. 11; *Mostra del vetro...*, 1984, p. 110 no. 161; *Vetri di Murano...*, 1991, pp. 38–39; *Napoleone Martinuzzi...*, 1992, pp. 68–69 figs 7–9; Heiremans 1993, p. 240 no. 193; *Gli artisti di Venini...*, 1996, p. 66 no. 19; Deboni 1996, pp. 266–67.

52. *Mermaid*, 1931 (pl. 36)
h 24.5 cm, l 29 cm
Piacenza, private collection

Mermaid figure in coral glass paste with gold-leaf applications. Holding both forks of her tail, the mermaid rises gracefully from the waves.

Exhibitions: Venice 1996.
Bibliography: Gli artisti di Venini..., 1996, p. 77 no. 43; *Venini Venezia...*, 1998, p. 64.

53. *Seven-branched sconce*, 1931–32
l 110 cm
Bergamo, Post-office building

Large wall-mounted light unit composed of cornucopia lamp-holders in black veiled glass tricked out with little black leaves applied to the central branch.

Bibliography: Napoleone Martinuzzi..., 1992, p. 48.

54. *Large cactus*, 1931–32
(pl. 42; *cf.* pls 40, 41)
h 225 cm
Bergamo, Post-office building

Cactus with four vertical trunks composed of glass corolla elements in green *pulegoso*; tips crowned with red glass and with gold leaf.
The first *pulegoso* plant was presented by Martinuzzi at the 1930 Triennale: an outsize thistle (*cf.* Reggiori 1929–30, p. 508; Nebbia 1930, p. 11). Four *pulegoso* cactus plants 2.5 metres high were submitted to the 1931 Rome Quadriennale (*cf.* *L'arte del vetro...*, 1992, p. 3)
One of Martinuzzi's plant creations, the *Grande Pianta fiorita* appeared at the 1931 Mostra del Fiore d'Arte in Florence (*cf.* Barovier Mentasti, 1982, p. 270 no. 276). The flowering version shown here was donated to the Pinacoteca Ambrosiana, Milan, by Paolo Venini in 1932 (*cf.* G. Galbiati, *Itinerario per il visitatore della Biblioteca Ambrosiana, della Pinacoteca e dei monumenti annessi*, Milan 1951); regrettably it was dismantled in 1989 and is no longer on exhibit.
The glass cactus plant enjoyed wide success in the Novecento (*cf.* Bossaglia 1975, p. 22).

Catalogo blu nos 2470, 2471, 2518, 2505, 2492, 2476, 2495, 2493, 2520, 2519, 2479, 2490 (smaller-sized cactus plants) fol. 17–18.
Bibliography: Felice 1930–31, p. 322; Polak 1962, p. 52; *Mostra del vetro...*, 1984, pp. 108–9 figs 152–53; *Murano, il vetro...*, 1986, p. 41; *L'arte del vetro...*, 1992, p. 236 nos 323–24; Barovier Mentasti 1992, p. 74 no. 63; *Napoleone Martinuzzi...*, 1992, pp. 124–26 nos 71–73; *Gli artisti di Venini...*, 1996, pp. 78–79 nos 45–48; Deboni 1996, p. 268 no. 184; *Venini Venezia...*, 1998, p. 64.

55. *Wall light*, 1931–32
h 55 cm
Bergamo, Post-office building

Wall-mounted light fitting in tea-coloured veiled glass with green detailing.

Bibliography: Napoleone Martinuzzi..., 1992, p. 48.

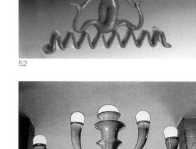

52

51

53

54

55

56. *Chandelier*, 1946–50 (pl. 43)
h 70 cm, ∅ 50 cm
Milan, Marco Arosio Collection

Large twelve-branched ceiling light in blown glass of various colours; central bowl in green blown glass; shaft with two spherical blown-glass knops in red and aquamarine.

Exhibitions: Zurich 1998.
Bibliography: Licitra Ponti 1990, p. 130; *Venini. Glas…*, 1998, no. 39.

57. *Welded bottle*, 1948–49
h 13.5 cm
Location unknown

Bottle in female form in welded layers of blown glass in two colours: red/blue, red/green with body in two-colour rods and long stopper in blown glass. Also made in: green opaline base with sapphire; pale blue base with amethyst; orange base with yellow; milk-white base with grey; sulphur base with grey; red opaline base with grey; apple-green opaline base with violet.

Catalogo verde no. 526.20, (set) nos 526.17 (h 33 cm, ∅ 7 cm); 526.18 (h 20 cm, ∅ 6 cm); 526.19 (h 33 cm, ∅ 12 cm).
Bibliography: Ponti 1959, p. 40bis; Deboni 1989, no. 88; *Italienisches…*, 1996, p. 132 no. 110.

58. *'Crinolina' bottle*, 1948–49
h 32 cm
Murano, Museo Venini

Blown-glass bottle made from two sapphire-red layers decorated with crinoline 'flounces' in white iridised glass. Stopper in red glass trimmed with flounce.

Catalogo rosso no. 3878, (set) no. 3873.
Bibliography: Ponti 1959, p. 40b; Deboni 1989, no. 87; *Gli artisti di Venini…*, 1996, p. 112 no. 129. *Mostra del vetro…*, 1984, p. 114 no. 174; Deboni 1989, no. 87; Licitra Ponti 1990, p. 131; Heiremans 1993, p. 256 no. 209.

59. *'Crinolina' vase*, 1950 (pl. 45)
h 13 cm, ∅ 12 cm
Turin, Galleria Ecodiforme

Small vase in *lattimo* glass decorated with three ruffled flounces in opaque turquoise and coral-red glass.

Bibliography: *Fragili e supremamente…*, 1997, p. 26.

60 . *Lamp in 'corroso' glass*,
c. 1950 (pl. 44)
h 38 cm
Turin, Galleria Ecodiforme

Table lamp in green corroded glass with large mushroom shade; decorated around the base with a ruffled band; this specimen is a very rare example of the design. The 'crinoline' decoration also occurs on bottles, and on a small *lattimo* vase.

61. *Cane glasses*, 1955 (pl. 46)
h 12 cm each
Turin, Galleria Ecodiforme

Pair of tall glasses composed of six different-coloured glass canes with rippled rim. These glasses form part of a tableware set comprising a jug and glasses in two different sizes.

Bibliography: Ponti 1959, p. 41; Cousins 1989, p. 95; *Fragili e supremamente…*, 1997, p. 26.

62. *Vetrate grosse*, 1966
h 350 cm, l 100 cm
Padua, Cassa di Risparmio

Mounted glazed screen composed of thick panes of glass containing bubbles and inserts of coloured glass paste embedded in crystal; metal armature Another glazed screen using the same glass panes – the only one of its kind – is in a private collection in New York (*cf.* fig. 62a)

Bibliography: Mariacher 1967, pp. 218–19; Licitra Ponti 1990, p. 230.

56

57   58

59

60

61

62a

62

63. *Casa Venini tableware set*, 1930
h 16 cm (jug); h 10.5 cm (wine), h 9.5 cm (water);
h 28 cm (bottle)
Boston, Francesca Hillyer Collection

Tableware set created for the personal use of the Venini family, designed by Paolo in pale green *rigadin* glass. In the early 1980s Ludovico Diaz de Santillana decided to put the set into production.

64. *Vase with bow-tie*, 1930–35
h 42.5 cm
Milan, private collection

Vase in transparent glass in the form of a male torso trimmed with a bow-tie; the piece was made by Paolo Venini for his friend Pietro Chiesa during the early years of the 'Labirinto' (Labyrinth) group. One-off piece.

Exhibitions: Venice 1996; Milan 1998.
Bibliography. *Gli artisti di Venini…*, 1996, p. 80 no. 50; *Il Vetro Italiano…*, 1998, p. 149 no. 2.

65. *Chinoiserie*, 1930–35
h 8 cm
Milan, private collection

One of a set of small objects in bubble glass with pale green exterior and red interior. These pieces were styled on designs by Maurice Marinot, whom Venini had met at the Salons des Artistes Décorateurs in Paris in 1921 and 1925, a distinct homage to the French master's art.
One-off pieces.

66. *Strip wall-light*, 1932–35
h 80 cm
Milan, former Stock Exchange building

Wall-mounted light fitting on a metal armature, composed of vertical strips of transparent glass. These lights were produced jointly with the architect Luigi Piccinato.

Catalogo blu no. 218 fol. 126.
Bibliography: 'Nuovi apparecchi…', 1929, p. 43.

67. *'Diamante' vase*, 1934–36
h 14 cm, l 32 cm
Acid-etched: 'Venini Murano'
Venice, Anna Venini Collection

Vase in solid transparent glass, whose name comes from the diamond faceting and four vertical nicks in the rim. The 'Diamante' (Diamond) set was produced in a very limited number, owing to the technical difficulties of execution, which entailed using *creccole* moulds. Other glasshouses on the island had meanwhile turned to imitating the technique, thereby impoverishing the object's unique characteristics and design. However, the table and standard lamps created using the *creccole* technique were very successful, and they are listed in the *Catalogo blu* as nos 507, 528, 502 (1938–42) fols 178, 178C.

Catalogo blu (set) no. 3631 fol. 37, nos 9035, 3631, 3638A, 3553, 3555, 3622, 3556, 3623, 3562, 3559, 3561, 3557 (1934–36) fol. 37, nos 3732, 3733, 3734, 3735, 3736 (1936) fol. 60; *Catalogo rosso* (set) nos 3553, 3556, 3559, 3561, 3562, 3622, 3732, 3733, 3736, 9034.

64

65

66

63

Bibliography: *XIX Esposizione…*, 1934; 'Una nuova "invenzione"…', 1936, pp. 22–23; 'Utili regali…', 1936, pp. 36–43; Deboni 1989, no. 44; *Gli artisti di Venini…*, 1996, p. 91 no. 80; *Italienisches…*, 1996, p. 58 no. 19; Heiremans 1997, p. 44 no. 41; *Il Vetro Italiano…*, 1998, p. 185 nos 75–76.

68. *'Murrine romane' vase*, 1936–38
h 12 cm, ∅ 18 cm
Location unknown

Vase composed of small inserts of transparent *murrina* with a central coloured dot. The pieces require great technical skill; the idea comes from Roman murrhine, whose weathered and slightly primitive look is gently pointed up by the new technique. Presented at the 1936 Venice Biennale and at the Milan Triennale of the same year.

Catalogo blu no. 4007 fol. 48, (set) nos 4008, 4004, 4010, 4006, 4007, 4009, 4005, 4003, 4000, 4002 fol. 48.

Bibliography: Dell'Oro 1936, p. 226; *XX Esposizione…*, 1936, p. 386; Barovier Mentasti 1992, p. 78 no. 98; Heiremans 1993, p. 246 no. 199; *Murano…*, 1994, p. 31 no. 13; Barovier, Barovier Mentasti, Dorigato 1995, p. 132 no. 41; *Venezia…*, 1995, p. 417 nos 376–77.

69. *Plastico E 42*
Location unknown

Large scale-model in transparent, individually milled glass pieces representing the project for the Esposizione Universale d'Arte, scheduled to be held in Rome in 1942. The model was put on a ship to be taken to the 1940 Expo in New York, but disappeared without trace on the outbreak of war. Notable characteristics were the range of delicate hues of the hand-made pieces.

70. *Obelisks*, 1948–50
h 33 cm, ∅ 10 cm
Venice, Anna Venini Collection

Pair of obelisks in transparent blue and crystal glass; the 'Obelisco' pieces were first proposed as items of interior design by Venini in 1936, exemplifying the intricate *diamante* technique, and were re-proposed at the 1954 Venice Biennale in a new version with embedded *zanfirico* canes. In the 1960s Ludovico Diaz de Santillana modified the traditional, transparent 'Obelisco' designs by Venini, accentuating the height and employing a sharper point.

Catalogo rosso nos 4261 (hexagonal), 4262 (octagonal), 4265–4267 (square), 4266–4268 (hexagonal), 4269 (octagonal), 4270 (twelve-sided), 4273 (octagonal), 4275 (square).
Exhibitions: Venice 1996.
Bibliography: *Gli artisti di Venini…*, 1996, p. 142 no. 201.
Mariacher 1967, p. 168b.

71. *Chess-board*, 1948–50
Location unknown

Large chess-board composed of transparent white and opaque black squares; chess-pieces in the form of little obelisks and balls containing coloured spirals. The present whereabouts of the board are unknown, but several of the chess-pieces have turned up in various private collections.

67

68

70

69

71

72. *Table lamp*, 1950
h 47 cm
Venice, Anna Venini Collection

Lamp in straw-yellow transparent glass, with an original metal support.

73. *Candle-holder*, 1950
h 22.5 cm
Acid-etched: 'Venini Italia'
Venice, Anna Venini Collection

Two-branched candle-holder in solid transparent glass, with broad circular foot outlined in blue glass; shaft made of two thick twisted canes of transparent glass that at a certain height separate and extend to a transparent blue candle-holder cup.

Catalogo blu no. 2385 fol. 252.

74. *Tableware for Ginette*, 1950 (pl. 57)
h 7 cm, ∅ 21,5 cm (cup);
h 15 cm, ∅ 20 cm (vase)
Venice, Anna Venini Collection;
Boston, Laura Venini Hillyer Collection

Large tableware set composed of drinking glass, goblets, jugs, bowls of various sizes and shapes; all articles made with *zanfirico* lace-threading, i.e., transparent glass and *lattimo* threads composing a delicate lace-like effect. Venini designed this superb collection of articles for his wife Ginette Gignous. One-off piece listed in the Venini production catalogues.

Exhibitions: Venice 1996.
Bibliography: *Gli artisti di Venini...*, 1996, p. 127 no. 169.

75. *Engraved bottles*, 1950 (pl. 47)
h 21.5 cm; h 19 cm; h 27 cm; h 40.5 cm;
h 31.5 cm; h 21.5 cm; h 29 cm
Venice, private collection

Varied set of bottles in composite glass having an engraved finish of delicate creases; colours ranging from blue, aquamarine, amethyst, tea, to yellow, and straw-yellow.
Designed after early snuffboxes of Chinese manufacture, the bottles are notable for their rounded shapes and economy of line.

Catalogo rosso nos 4585, 4586, 4587, 4588, 4589 (with veiled detailing), 4844, 4845 (with engraved detailing); *Catalogo verde* nos 722.18 (h 17 cm, ∅ 10 cm), 722.19 (h 35 cm, ∅ 10 cm), 722.20 (h 26 cm, ∅ 12 cm), 722.21 (h 23 cm, ∅ 10 cm), 722.22 (h 18 cm, ∅ 10 cm), 722.23 (h 18 cm, ∅ 10 cm), 722.24 (h 32 cm, ∅ 8 cm), combined colours: cornelian, prune, ocean-blue, putrid, violet.
Exhibitions: Venice 1996.
Bibliography: *Gli artisti di Venini...*, 1996, p. 127 no. 170.
Venini Murano..., 1957, nos 79, 84; Mariacher 1967, pp. 169, 50 no. 19; *La verrerie...*, 1988, p. 23 no. 5; *Venini Venezia...*, 1998, p. 75.

76. *'Ciclamino' vase*, 1952
h 25 cm
Venice, Anna Venini Collection

Vase in cased *lattimo* and cyclamen-coloured glass, whose shape is obtained a central waist-like constriction creating two bulging sections of unequal size.
The shape recurs often in the Venini production catalogues, with different designers. Carlo Scarpa proposed the same idea in *lattimo* (*cf.* Barovier 1997, p. 273), Venini also designed another version in twisted *zanfirico* spirals (*cf.* Ponti 1959, p. 38).

Catalogo blu no. 3576 fol. 30.
Bibliography: Heiremans 1996, p. 92 no. 102; *Il Vetro Italiano...*, 1998, p. 195 no. 93.

77. *Waisted vase*, 1952 (*cf.* pl. 50)
h 28 cm
Location unknown

Vase in opaline glass with a spherical lower section, central constriction and long neck with flared rim; the shape is reminiscent of a gourd.
Presented at the 1952 Venice Biennale.

Catalogo rosso no. 3655.
Bibliography: Ponti 1959, p. 36; Barovier, Barovier Mentasti, Dorigato 1995, p. 78.

78. *Trailed-spiral bottles*, 1952 (*cf.* pl. 48)
h 21.5 cm; h 27 cm; h 18.5 cm; h 20 cm
Location unknown

A series of bottles in transparent glass with opaque threads trailed around the surface in delicate spirals. The extraordinary appeal of these items lies in the attentive association of colours: transparent green with threads and stopper in glass paste in imitation of jade; soft grey with threads and stopper in coral-red; strong sky-blue with threads and stopper in aquamarine.
The practice of trailing coloured thread around the bottle is undoubtedly drawn from examples of Roman glass design.

Exhibitions: Venice 1996.
Bibliography: *Gli artisti di Venini...*, 1996, p. 141 no. 199.
Deboni 1989, no. 140.

79. *Long-necked bottles*, 1952
h 37.5 cm each
Acid-etched: 'Venini Murano Italia'
Venice, private collection

Distinctively shaped bottles with long necks and flared rim, one in *lattimo* glass cased in green, the other in blue. The design is unmistakably Venini's idea, as are nos 3655 and 3922 in the *Catalogo rosso*.
Presented at the 1952 Venice Biennale.

Catalogo rosso no. 3656; *Catalogo verde* nos 706.20, 706.21.
Exhibitions: Venice 1996.
Bibliography: *Gli artisti di Venini...*, 1996, p. 139, no. 196.
Mariacher 1954[a], no. 172; Gasparetto 1958, no. 189; Ponti 1959, p. 36; *Vetri di Murano...*, 1960, pl. XVII; Deboni 1989, no. 121.

72

73

74

75

77

76

80. *Cane bottle*, 1952–56 (pl. 52)
h 27.5 cm
Union City (USA), Odetto Lastra Collection

Free-blown transparent bottle with walls of narrow grey and aquamarine canes rising to a narrow neck; stopper in aquamarine glass.

Catalogo verde no. 526.11.
Bibliography: 'Rassegna Domus', 1956, p. 41; Ponti 1959, p. 41; *Vetri di Murano...*, 1960, pl. XXXVI; *Manualità...*, 1980, p. 71 no. 71; *Italienisches...*, 1987, pp. 60–61 nos 38–39; Deboni 1989, no. 125; *Gli artisti di Venini...*, 1996, p. 130 no. 197; *Venini Venezia...*, 1998, p. 74.

81. *Long-necked vase*, c. 1954
h 50 cm
Vaduz, Steinberg Foundation

Slender vase with flamboyantly elongated neck rising to a slightly splayed opening, walls of aquamarine decorated with *zanfirico* canes of amethyst and *lattimo*.
This striking object was created by Venini in partnership with his craftsmen; it was an experiment for the Swedish distributors of Venini products through the Nordiska Kompaniet based in Stockholm.
Not in catalogue.

Exhibitions: Venice 1996.
Bibliography: Gli artisti di Venini..., 1996, p. 131 no. 177.

82. *Bottle in 'zanfirico' mesh*, 1954 (pl. 51)
h 39 cm
Zurich, Museum Bellerive, inv. 1969-29

Bottle composed of dual layer of *lattimo* spirals running in opposite directions to form a dense mesh of *lattimo* threads.
Presented at the 1954 Milan Triennale.

Catalogo rosso no. 4584; *Catalogo verde* no. 526.4.
Exhibitions: Zurich 1998.
Bibliography: Museum Bellerive..., 1992, p. 31 no. 34; *Venini. Glas...*, 1998, p. 15.
Decima Triennale..., 1954, pl. XXXV; Ponti 1959, p. 41; *Gli artisti di Venini...*, 1996, p. 129 no. 175; *Il Vetro Italiano...*, 1998, p. 207 no. 128.

83. *'Murrina' vase*, 1954 (pl. 53)
h 31.7 cm
New York, Barry Friedman Collection

Tall vase with walls of tiny white and black *murrina* mosaic; walls taper upwards to a distinctive gently rippled rim.
Presented at the 1954 Venice Biennale.

Bibliography: Gasparetto 1954; *XXVII Esposizione...*, 1954, pp. 430–31 no. 172; Aloi 1955, p. 18; Ponti 1959, p. 39; Mariacher 1967, nos 170–71; Deboni 1989, nos 149–51; Barovier Mentasti 1992, p. 117 no. 106; Heiremans 1993, p. 278 no. 231; Barovier Mentasti 1994, no. 37; *Murano...*, 1994, p. 35; *Vetri veneziani...*, 1994, p. 59 no. 37; Barovier, Barovier Mentasti, Dorigato 1995, pp. 85, 178 no. 116; *Venezia...*, 1995, p. 433 no. 521; Heiremans 1996, p. 106 no. 125; *Italienisches...*, 1996, pp. 141–42 nos 121–22, pp. 144–45 nos 125–28, p. 147 no. 130; *Il Vetro Italiano...*, 1998, p. 205 no. 126.

78

79

80

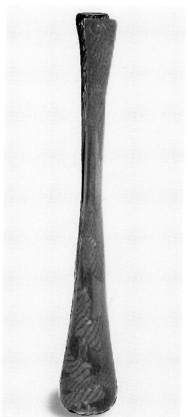

81

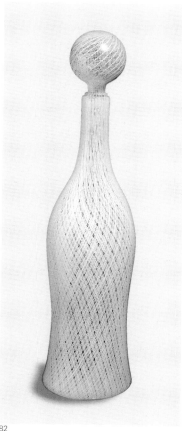

82

83

84. *Mosaic 'zanfirico' vase*, 1954
(pl. 54; *cf.* pls 49, 55, 56)
h 24.8 cm
New York, Barry Friedman Collection

Vase in anthracite glass with 'patch-work' decoration of criss-crossed strands of *lattimo*; body flares gently to an irregular-shaped rim; walls in transparent, ocean-blue, and anthracite.
Related to this series are several striking examples in which the pattern consists of a mosaic of textured canes (*cf. Gli artisti di Venini...*, 1996, p. 129 no. 174).
Presented at the 1954 Venice Biennale.

Catalogo rosso no. 4022.
Bibliography: XXVII Esposizione..., 1954, pp. 430–31 no. 173; 'Piccola rassegna...', 1955, p. 52; *Venini Murano...*, 1957, no. 62; *Italienisches...*, 1987, pp. 68–69 nos 45–46; *La verrerie...*, 1988, p. 123 no. 2; Deboni 1989, no. 128; *L'arte del vetro...*, 1992, p. 352 no. 360; Heiremans 1993, p. 279 no. 232; *Murano...*, 1994, p. 34 nos 17–18; Barovier, Barovier Mentasti, Dorigato 1995, p. 177 no. 115; *Gli artisti di Venini...*, 1996, p. 128 nos 171–72; Deboni 1996, p. 305 no. 221; Heiremans 1996, p. 122 no. 152; *Italienisches...*, 1996, pp. 136–38 nos 116–18, p. 140 no. 120; *Venini Venezia...*, 1998, p. 72; *Il Vetro Italiano...*, 1998, p. 207 no. 129.

85. *Mosaic 'zanfirico' vase*, 1954 (pl. 58)
h 39 cm
Milan, Galleria In. Arte

Vase in crystal with gently bellied central section in *zanfirico* canes with *lattimo* threads and diagonal brim. Two other colour combinations of this model exist: one transparent, the other in aquamarine glass.

Bibliography: XXVII Esposizione..., 1954, pp. 430–31 no. 173; 'Piccola rassegna...', 1955, p. 52; *Venini Murano...*, 1957, no. 62; *Italienisches...*, 1987, pp. 68–69 nos 45–46; *La verrerie...*, 1988, p. 123 no. 2; Deboni 1989, no. 128; *L'arte del vetro...*, 1992, p. 352 no. 360; Heiremans 1993, p. 279 no. 232; *Murano...*, 1994, p. 34 nos 17–18; Barovier, Barovier Mentasti, Dorigato 1995, p. 177 no. 115; *Gli artisti di Venini...*, 1996, p. 128 nos 171–72; Deboni 1996, p. 305 no. 221; Heiremans 1996, p. 122 no. 152; *Italienisches...*, 1996, pp. 136–38 nos 116–18, p. 140 no. 120; *Venini Venezia...*, 1998, p. 72; *Il Vetro Italiano...*, 1998, p. 207 no. 129.

86. *Velarium*
h 1300 cm, l 1600 cm
Venice, Palazzo Grassi

Large glazed roof section for the courtyard of Palazzo Grassi, Venice, composed of *ballotton* glass spheres; this large skylight was built to designs by Paolo Venini in 1954. It has since been replaced, and is in storage.

Exhibitions: Venice 1996.
Bibliography: Gli artisti di Venini..., 1996, p. 144 no. 205.

87. *'Murrina' bowl*, 1954 (pl. 59)
h 12.7 cm
Acid-etched: 'Venini Italia'
New York, Barry Friedman Collection

Small bowl in black and milk-white inserts of *murrina* glass. Venini used the same technique for one of his 'Canoa' pieces, an example of which belongs to a private collection in Milan. Owing to the fact that little documentation has survived, and to the fact that Ludovico Diaz de Santillana devotedly upheld the traditions established by his father-in-law, it is extremely difficult to discern which of the two men is the author of any given example of this type. That said, generally speaking the pieces by Paolo Venini are smaller, such as the 'Murrine del pavone' ('Murrina' Peacock) series; whereas in Ludovico's versions the birds' tails fan out in a wider circles.

Bibliography: Aloi 1955, p. 22; Ponti 1959, p. 39; Kämpfer 1966, no. 212; *La verrerie...*, 1988, p. 123 no. 3; Deboni 1989, no. 152; Ricke 1995, p. 236 no. 378; *Gli artisti di Venini...*, 1996, p. 129 no. 173; *Italienisches...*, 1996, p. 143 nos 123–24, p. 146 no. 129.

88. *Glazing for the 1957 Milan Triennale*, 1957
h 210 cm, l 120 cm
Venice, Carraro Collection

Glazed sections of glass panes mounted in metal frames. These flat sections of glazing are composed of an arrangement of interlocking geometrical segments assembled with a rich interplay of hues and transparency, and held in place by a metal support structure. The composition was created for the 1957 Milan Triennale. Venini designed another glazed section jointly with the architect Oscar Stonorov for the Metalworkers Union of Detroit.

Catalogo Commerciale Sezione 13/Vetrate.
Bibliography: Undicesima Triennale, 1957, pl. XLIb; *Venini vetrate*, 1957, pp. 47–50; Ponti 1959, pp. 31, 44; *Italienisches...*, 1996, p. 155; *Il Vetro Italiano...*, 1998, p. 212 no. 141.

89. *Hourglass*, 1955 (*cf.* pl. 60)
h 60 cm
Murano, Museo Venini

Sleek hourglass in green and sapphire blown glass, set in metal holders; the uprights are in coloured *zanfirico* twists; glass contains sand. A variant of this hourglass design is given in the *Catalogo rosso* nos 40905, 40906, 40907; and in the *Catalogo verde* nos 420.5, 420.6, 420.7, 420.8. Colours (*Catalogo verde*): red/green, green/sapphire, red/sapphire, amethyst/pale greenish blue, yellow/violet.

Catalogo rosso no. 4903, (set) nos 4900, 4901, 4902, 4904; *Catalogo verde* no. 420.0, (set) nos 420.1, 420.2, 420.3, 420.4, 420.9.
Bibliography: Deboni 1989 no. 132.
Vetri di Murano..., 1960, pl. XLIIa; Mariacher 1967, p. 169.

90. *'Ventaglio' sconce*, 1955
h 60 cm, l 55.5 cm
Venice, Anna Venini Collection

Fan-shaped wall light-fitting composed of mixed clear *mezza filigrana* and *lattimo* canes set at diagonals; the piece is still in production.

91. *'Canoa' platter*, 1955–59 (pl. 61)
l 25 cm
Milan, Galleria In. Arte

Canoe-shaped platter made of blue and black *murrina* tesserae.

Catalogo rosso nos 4883, 4884 (*murrina* inserts in two different sizes).
Exhibitions: Venice 1996.
Bibliography: Gli artisti di Venini..., 1996, p. 132 no. 180; Heiremans 1996, p. 145 no. 186; *Italienisches...*, 1996, p. 148 nos 131–32, pp. 156–57 nos 144–45; *Venini Venezia...*, 1998, p. 75.

92. *'Mezza filigrana' bottle*, *c.* 1956
h 35.5 cm
Acid-etched: 'Venini Murano Italia'
Toledo (USA), The Toledo Museum of Art, inv. 86.19

Bottle of spiralling *mezza filigrana* threads submerged in walls of crystal; elongated neck; conical stopper. Colours: milk-white threads/sulphur; coral threads/ sulphur.

Catalogo verde no. 526.13.

93. *Engraved bowl*, 1956
h 9 cm, ∅ 14 cm
Venice, Anna Venini Collection

Bowl in transparent glass with tea-coloured surface finished with lightly incised horizontal grooves. The bank group, Cassa di Risparmio of Venice, possesses a specimen of this series, in aquamarine glass, first exhibited at the 1956 Venice Biennale. The milled 'Velati' series come in a wide variety of forms, including bottles, bowls, vases, and candelabras; colours range from aquamarine, tea, straw-yellow, cornelian and pale violet, to putrid, prune, ocean-blu, and violet.

Catalogo rosso no. 4800, (set) from no. 4801 to no. 4830 (with engraved veiled detailing), from no. 4831 to no. 4843 (with engraved detailing); *Catalogo verde* (set) from no. 722.00 to no. 722.9, from no. 722.10 to no. 722.17, from no.722.25 to no. 722,29, composite colours: cornelian, prune, ocean-blue, putrid, violet.
Exhibitions: Venice 1996.
Bibliography: XXVIII Esposizione, 1956, p. 558; *Undicesima Triennale*, 1957, pl. XXXXIV; 'Per due sposi...', 1958, p. 27; Ponti 1959, p. 40; *Italienisches...*, 1987, pp. 82–90 nos 56–62; Barovier Mentasti 1992, no. 106; *Vetri veneziani...*, 1994, pp. 64–65 nos 42–43; *Gli artisti di Venini...*, 1996, p. 135 nos 187–89; *Il Vetro Italiano...*, 1998, p. 211 nos 139–40.

96

88

90

94. *Dual welded bottles*
with 'filigrana' band, 1956
h 33 cm; h 38 cm; h 35 cm
Location unknown

Set of welded bottles with a band of woven *mezza filigrana*; three oblong designs were made. Presented at the 1956 Venice Biennale.

Catalogo verde nos 526.5, 526.6, 526.7, colours: sapphire/turquoise band; green/red band; sky blue/sulphur band.
Bibliography. XXVIII *Esposizione*, 1956, p. 558; Ponti 1959, p. 40b; *Vetri di Murano…*, 1960, pl. XLIII; Deboni 1989, no. 133; Heiremans 1989, no. 204; Barovier, Barovier Mentasti, Dorigato 1995, pp. 88, 182 no. 123; Heiremans 1996, p. 131 no. 167.

95. *Pharmacist's jars*, 1958
h 17 cm; h 22 cm
Acid-etched: 'Venini Italia'
Venice, Anna Venini Collection

Two blown-glass vases in aquamarine and straw-yellow, with pointed stoppers. The design derives from antique pharmacy jars.

Catalogo rosso nos 4741/34, 4741/22, (set) nos 4740/44, 4740/35, 4740/28, 4742/45, 4742/35, 4743/40, 4743/32, 4743/28, 4744/33, 4744/22, 4745/35, 4745/25.
Bibliography. Ponti 1959, p. 40.

96. *Expo Light*, 1958
Tunis, Great Mosque

Large ceiling light assembly; created for the 1958 Brussels Expo, it was lodged in the main hall of the Italian Pavilion alongside some fine glazing installations. It was the first time geometrical components had been employed, their sizes and shapes determined by the number of pieces required. The light was subsequently purchased by the head of Tunisian government for installation in the city's main mosque.

Bibliography. Ponti 1959, p. 41.
Mariacher 1967, p. 204.

86

89

92

93

87

95

91

84

94

85

97. *Glass, crystal and silver*, 1932
Venice, formerly Istituto Statale d'Arte
(Venice, Biennale, Archivio Storico
delle Arti Contemporanee)

Group of stylish glass objects in diverse forms,
with foot or lip in fine silver.
First exhibited at the 1932 Venice Biennale. There
are no records of further examples of this set,
which now resides in the Istituto d'Arte in Venice,
albeit no longer comprising the entire set.

Bibliography: Barovier, Barovier Mentasti, Dorigato 1995, p. 35.

98. *Cased 'laguna' vase*, 1932–33
(pl. 62; *cf.* pl. 63)
h 28 cm
Milan, private collection

Spherical vase in *laguna* glass with applied silver-
leaf texturing.

99. *Twin-spouted vase*, 1933 (pl. 64)
h 16 cm, ∅ 20 cm
Padua, private collection

Vase composed of five layers of so-called *alba*
glass. The outer surface is flecked with gold-leaf.
The spouts are girdled with thick *lattimo* glass
tresses that terminate in a central handle.
The speciality of Buzzi's cased glasswork with
gold-leaf detailing is the use of four different
colours: *alba* (a gold-flecked blue), *alga* (greenish-
blue), *laguna* (pink), and *tramonto* (deep pink).
Taking over from Martinuzzi, Buzzi effected a thorough overhaul of the Venini production catalogue,
creating a new line of essential, elegant forms expressed in a refined range of hues. Buzzi's work
paved the way for the coming inventions of Carlo
Scarpa.

Bibliography: Deboni 1989, p. 45.

100. *Standard lamp*, 1933 (pl. 65)
h 170 cm
Turin, Galleria Ecodiforme

Standard uplighter with cased gold-flecked *lattimo* shade supported on a long shaft in transparent
glass terminating in a circular foot.

Catalogo blu no. 508 fol. 178.
Exhibitions: Zurich 1998
Bibliography: Venini. *Glas*…, 1998, no. 21.

101. *Four-light chandelier*,
1933 (pl. 66)
h 140 cm, l 120 cm
Turin, Galleria Ecodiforme

Large ceiling fixture hanging from two metal
shafts perpendicular to the glass/metal horizontal
bearing the four uplighters in tea-coloured *lattimo*
glass.

Catalogo blu no. 5212 fol. 132, n. 5214 (three-light
variant) fol. 130.

102. *'Mani' cup*, 1933 (*cf.* pls 67–71)
h 18.5 cm, ∅ 38 cm
Zurich, private collection

Wide cup in pink *laguna* glass supported by spread
hands in *lattimo* cased in straw-yellow layer with
applied gold-leaf. Very few of this model are
known to exist.

Catalogo blu no. 3416 fol. 27; *Catalogo rosso* no.
3416.
Bibliography: Papini 1933[a], p. 371 n. 23; *Vetri Murano Oggi*, 1981, p. 32 n. 110; *Vetro di Murano*…,
1982, no. 137; Deboni 1989, n. 34; *L'arte del
vetro*…, 1992, p. 240 no. 331.

103. *'Chiocciole' amphora*, 1933 (pl. 72)
h 13 cm
Acid-etched: 'Venini Murano'
Asti, private collection

The so-called 'snail' amphora is in pink *laguna*
glass composed of six separate layers, the outer of
which speckled with gold-leaf; raised applied foot.
Exhibited at the 1933 Milan Triennale.

Catalogo blu no. 3440 fol. 27, (set) no. 3443 fol. 27
(variant with horses); *Catalogo rosso* (set) nos
3440, 3443.
Exhibitions: Venice 1996.
Bibliography: Deboni 1989, no. 35; *Vetri di Murano*…, 1991, no. 17; *L'arte del vetro*…, 1992, no.
330; *Gli artisti di Venini*…, 1996, p. 80 no. 52.
Venezianisches…, 1981, no. 107; *Mille Anni*…,
1982, p. 266 no. 526; *Vetro di Murano*…, 1982, no.
128; *Museum Bellerive*…, 1995, p. 226 no. 393;
Heiremans 1996, p. 43 no. 40; *Il Vetro Italiano*…,
1998, p. 179 no. 56.

104. *'Alga' vase*, 1933 (pl. 73)
h 20 cm
Acid-etched: 'Venini Murano'
Turin, Galleria Ecodiforme

Small vase in *alga* (greenish-blue) glass encased
in five layers; surface layer flecked with gold-leaf;
base of neck decorated with gilt-crystal band;
cylindrical base in gilt-crystal.

Catalogo blu no. 3321 fol. 30.
Exhibitions: Venice 1996; Turin 1997.
Bibliography: *Gli artisti di Venini*…, 1996, p. 81
no. 54; *Fragili e supremamente*…, 1997, p. 12.
Barovier Mentasti 1982, p. 271 no. 277; *Mille An-
ni*…, 1982, p. 266 no. 527; Deboni 1989, no. 37;
Heiremans 1993, p. 241 no. 194.

105. *'Bugnato' vase*, 1933 (pl. 74)
h 18 cm
Acid-stamped: 'Venini Murano'
Piacenza, private collection

Small vase with flaring mouth and body punctuated with smooth, randomly arranged indentations;
vessel in pink *laguna* glass composed of five layers, the outer in gilt-crystal.
Specimens of this vase are extremely rare.

Catalogo blu no. 3431 fol. 27, (set) no. 3432 fol. 27;
Catalogo rosso (set) no. 3432.
Exhibitions: Venice 1996.
Bibliography: *Gli artisti di Venini*…, 1996, p. 82
no. 57.
Venini Venezia…, 1998, p. 65.

97

98

99

101

102

100

103

104

106. *Two ducks*, 1933 (*cf.* pl. 75)
h 27.5 cm; h 17.5 cm
Venice, private collection

Pair of duck figures in blown 'egg-shell' *lattimo* with gold-leaf, and applied details in *lattimo*; bases in *lattimo*; eye inserts in blue glass paste. Exhibited at the 1933 Milan Triennale

Catalogo blu nos 2580, 2596 fol. 24, (set) no. 2581 fol. 24 (variant); *Catalogo rosso* (set) nos 2580, 2581.
Exhibitions: Venice 1996.
Bibliography. Gli artisti di Venini..., 1996, p. 84 no. 61.
Papini 1933ᵃ, p. 371; *I Vetri d'arte...*, 1933, p. 379; *Vetro di Murano...*, 1982, no. 127; *Vetri di Murano...*, 1991, pp. 48–49; *Il bestiario...*, 1996, no. 42.

107. *Cockerel and hen*, 1933 (pl. 76)
h 21 cm; h 18 cm
Union City (USA), Odetto Lastra Collection

Two animal figures in *lattimo mezza filigrana* (diagonal canes in parallel) and crystal with base and crests of undulating lattimo; *lattimo* inserts for eyes and beaks; tail silhouetted in *lattimo*. A superb example is housed in the Museum Bellerive, Zurich (inv. 9612).
A copy of the *Hen* belongs to a private collection in Asti, made from *lattimo mezza filigrana* and crystal; the piece differs from the one shown in the *Catalogo blu* (no. 2591 fol. 24): its head is turned toward its tail. Caught in a more elegant pose here, the *Hen* was among the pieces presented at the 1933 Milan Triennale.

Catalogo blu nos 2590, 2591 fol. 24; *Catalogo rosso* (set) nos 2590, 2591.
Exhibitions: Venice 1996; Zurich 1998.
Bibliography. Gli artisti di Venini..., 1996, no. 63, *Venini. Glas...*, 1998, no. 26.
Museum Bellerive..., 1995, p. 227 no. 395; *Il bestiario...*, 1996, no. 41.

108. *Pear*, 1933 (pl. 79)
h 8 cm
Zurich, Museum Bellerive, inv. 9612

Fruit form in *mezza filigrana a reticello* (network of diagonal parallel canes) crystal with violet glass detailing. This article forms part of a group of vegetable forms: *cf. Catalogo blu* nos 2587 (*Pumpkin*), 2592 (*Apple*), 2593 (*Pepper*) fol. 25, which were presented at the 1933 Milan Triennale.

Catalogo blu no. 2586 fol. 25.
Exhibitions: Zurich 1998.
Bibliography: Museum Bellerive..., 1995, p. 227 no. 395; *Venini Venezia...*, 1998, no. 25.

109. *Crystal vase with relief decoration*, 1933
h 19 cm
Milan, Marco Arosio Collection

Vase composed of a thick layer of crystal glass with relief *ramage* decoration; plinth in *murrina* motes embedded in black glass paste.
Presented at the 1933 Milan Triennale.

Catalogo blu no. 3485 fol. 26, (set) nos 3490, 3496, 3486 fol. 26 (variants).
Bibliography: Papini 1933ᵃ, p. 370; 'La V Triennale...', 1933, s.p.; *I Vetri d'arte...*, 1933, p. 383; *Vetri di Murano...*, 1977, no. 65; *Il Vetro Italiano...*, 1998, p. 178 no. 55.

110. *Turquoise and black vase*, 1933
(pl. 77; *cf.* pl. 78)
h 36 cm
Tarzana (USA), Artur Liu Collection

Tall vase in *lattimo* cased in transparent aquamarine glass, with applied decoration in black threads; vessel body emblazoned with the silhouette of a leaping fawn; applied conical base outlined at top and bottom with black glass thread; broad, flared mouth with emphasised rim. A similar specimen (missing the silhouette) was presented at the 1932 Venice Biennale, together with other articles featured in the *Catalogo blu*: nos 3299, 3425, 3301, 3297, and 3308A, on fols 27–29.
Only three copies are known to exist (all in private collections), bearing the animal outline; though similar in type, they do not constitute a set: no. 3296, for example, belongs to a set in *lattimo* and gold-leaf, or among Buzzi's pieces in the *laguna* (green-lake) and *alba* (gold-flecked blue) colour category, also found in the *Catalogo blu* numbered 3318, 3315, 3314 fol. 29.

Catalogo blu no. 3296 fol. 29.
Exhibitions: Venice 1996.
Bibliography: Barovier, Barovier Mentasti, Dorigato 1995, p. 35; *Gli artisti di Venini...*, 1996, p. 80 no. 51.
Vetri di Murano..., 1991, pp. 46–47.

111. *Table lamp*, 1933 (pl. 80)
h 25 cm, Ø 30 cm
Treviso, private collection

Wide-bowled table lamp made of a thick wall of crystal, its interior acid-treated to give a satin finish; outer surface with leaves in relief; base in solid green glass in bands. These lamps belong to Buzzi's series included in the *Catalogo blu*, fol. 115.

Catalogo blu no. 9030 fol. 151, (set) no. 9029 fol. 151 (identical, without relief decoration).
Bibliography: Gli artisti di Venini..., 1996, p. 86 no. 64.
I Vetri d'arte..., 1933, p. 382.

105

106

108

107

109

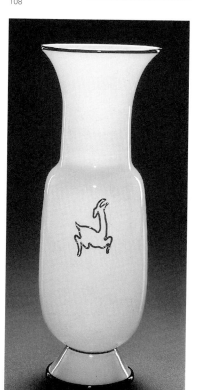
110

111

112. *Oval vase*, 1933 (*cf.* pl. 82)
h 16 cm
Treviso, private collection

Oval vase in blue *alba* glass in five layers, outer layer in crystal with gold-leaf; base and rim of mouth in gilt-crystal.

Catalogo blu no. 3298 fol. 29; *Catalogo rosso* no. 3629.
Exhibitions: Venice 1996.
Bibliography: *Gli artisti di Venini…*, 1996, p. 81 no. 55; *Venini. Glas…*, 1998, p. 65. Deboni 1989, no. 40; Barovier Mentasti 1992, p. 68 no. 57; *Gli artisti di Venini…*, 1996, p. 81 no. 53.

113. *'Egg-shell' vase*, 1933 (pl. 81)
h 35 cm
Acid-etched: 'Venini Murano'
Piacenza, private collection

Vase in *lattimo* 'egg-shell' glass with silver-leaf, lightly oxidised; applied foot; applied running-petal motif at base of neck.

Catalogo blu nos 3316, 3299 (variant) fol. 29 .
Exhibitions: Venice 1996.
Bibliography: *Gli artisti di Venini…*, 1996, p. 83 no. 59.

114. *'Tramonto' glass vase*, 1933
h 20 cm, l cm 23
United States, Millennium Pictures Collection

Vase composed of five layers in a deep pink termed *tramonto*; outer surface with gold-leaf inclusions; small base in *lattimo* glass.

Catalogo blu no. 3450 fol. 28.

112

113

114

115. *'Bollicine' vase*, 1932 (*cf.* pl. 95)
h 25 cm
Location unknown

Vase in white glass embedded with small bubbles obtained by adding potassium nitrate to the gather, which releases carbon dioxide upon firing. Exhibited at the 1952 Venice Biennale.

Catalogo blu no. 11005 fol. 33, (set) nos 11001, 11011, 11024, 11019, 11023, 11025, 11029, 11026, 11028, 11009, 11021, 11030, 11027, 11002, 11015, 11008, 11020, fols 33–34.
Bibliography: Ponti 1959, p. 35; Deboni 1989, no. 46; *The Venetians…*, 1989, p. 19; *Carlo Scarpa…*, 1991, pp. 65–66 nos 12–13; Heiremans 1993, p. 244 no. 197; *Museum Bellerive…*, 1995, p. 227; *Gli artisti di Venini…*, 1996, pp. 87–89 nos 68–70; *Italienisches…*, 1996, p. 61, no. 22; Barovier 1997, p. 204 no. 9.

116. *'Sommerso' bubble vase*, 1934
(pl. 84; *cf.* pls 83, 86, 91)
h 21 cm
Turin, private collection

Spherical vase in bubble glass, with submerged gilt-crystal in the mass trailed in a spiral pattern. On exhibit at the 1934 and 1952 Venice Biennales.

Catalogo blu no. 3539 fol. 35, (set) nos 3511, 3540, 3507, 3534, 3594, 3526, 3525, 3523, 3522, 3531, 3532, 3533, 3524, 3527, 3529, 3565, 3566, 3595, 3536, 3528, 3599, 3598, 3568, 3564, 3563, 3569, 3596, 3597, 3550, 3567, 3552, 3636, 3637, 3633, 3635, fols 35–36.
Bibliography: Motta 1934, p. 275; Aloi 1955, p. 12; Ponti 1959, p. 35; Dal Co, Mazzariol 1984, p. 185; *Mostra del vetro…*, 1984, p. 112; Deboni 1989, nos 47–48; *Carlo Scarpa…*, 1991, pp. 67–69; Barovier Mentasti 1992, p. 68 no. 56; Barovier, Barovier Mentasti, Dorigato 1995, p. 129 no. 36; *Museum Bellerive…*, 1995, p. 227 no. 396; *Venezia…*, 1995, p. 416; *Gli artisti di Venini…*, 1996, p. 88 pp. 90–91; Deboni 1996, p. 276 no. 192; *Italienisches…*, 1996, pp. 59–60 nos 20–21; Barovier 1997, p. 108 p. 205 no. 26; *Il Vetro Italiano…*, 1998, p. 184 no. 71.

117. *'Biennale' cup*, 1934
h 29 cm
Murano, Museo Venini

Blue cup in submerged glass with gold-leaf and tiny pockets of air; unusual base in clear solid glass, inscribed with the legend: 'XIX Biennale di Venezia'.

Exhibitions: Venice 1934 (XIX Biennale).
Bibliography: *XIX Esposizione…*, 1934, p. 227; Barovier, Barovier Mentasti, Dorigato 1995, p. 129 no. 37; *Venezia…*, 1995, p. 416 no. 371; Barovier 1997, p. 109.

118. *'Mezza filigrana' vase*, 1934
(pl. 90; *cf.* pls 87, 89)
h 18.5 cm
Union City (USA), Odetto Lastra Collection

Spherical vase in pale blue and crystal *mezza filigrana* (diagonal parallel canes).

Catalogo blu no. 3519 fol. 31, (set) nos 3538, 3541, 3542A, 3619, 3545, 3544, 3543, 3517, 3518, 3519, 3618, 3617, 3625, 3620, 3621, 3614, 3612, 3616, 3615, 3634, 3546, 3513 fols 31–32; *Catalogo verde* (set) nos 602.0 (h 35 cm), 602.1 (h 28 cm), 602.2 (h 36 cm), 602.3 (h 31 cm), 602.4 (h 14 cm), colours: milk-white, coral, black, turquoise, 602.5 (h 33 cm), 602.6 (h 27 cm), 602.7 (h 33 cm), 602.8 (h 6 cm), colours: *filigrana*, milk-white, coral, black, turquoise, 602.9 (h 7 cm), 602.10 (h 17 cm), 602.11 (h 10 cm), 602.12 (h 22 cm), 602.13 (h 22 cm), 602.14 (h 7 cm), 602.15 (h 15 cm), colours: milk-white, coral, black, turquoise, 602.16 (h 24 cm), 602.17 (h 9 cm), 602.18 (h 12 cm), colours: milk-white, coral, black, turquoise, wide *filigrana*.
Exhibitions: Venice 1996.
Bibliography: *Gli artisti di Venini…*, 1996, p. 86 no. 65.
Motta 1934, pp. 276–77; *XIX Esposizione…*, 1934, p. 227; Brusatin 1972, p. 28; Dal Co, Mazzariol 1984, p. 184 no. 229; Deboni 1989, no. 45; *Carlo Scarpa…*, 1991, p. 63 no. 11; *Vetri veneziani…*, 1994, p. 47 no. 22; Barovier, Barovier Mentasti, Dorigato 1995, p. 38; *Museum Bellerive…*, 1995, p. 228 no. 397; *Italienisches…*, 1996, p. 62 nos 23–24.

119. *'Soffiati' and 'Lattimi' wares*, 1936
h 25 cm
Location unknown

Vase in *lattimo* glass pinched at the neck to form a bi-conical vessel.
The group featured on folio 38 of the *Catalogo blu* is labelled 'SOFFIATI E LATTIMI 1936'. Various pieces of this set were produced, some in transparent glass, others in *lattimo*.

Catalogo blu no. 3586 fol. 38, (set) nos 3586, 3587, 3588, 3579, 3585, 3605, 3601, 3604, 3602, 3606 (spherical model proposed earlier by Buzzi, produced with varying techniques), 3608, 3609, 3509, 3610, 3611 fol. 38; *Catalogo rosso* (set) nos 3579, 3586, 3588, 3598, 3601, 3602, 3603, 3604, 3607; *Catalogo verde*: some forms reappear in different techniques, restyled by Ludovico Diaz de Santillana; note the shape of no. 3586 (fol. 38) of the *Catalogo blu*, which is reproposed in *zanfirico* in the *Catalogo verde* (no. 608.6).
Bibliography: Dell'Oro 1936, p. 226; Deboni 1989, no. 67; *Carlo Scarpa…*, 1991, p. 89; Barovier, Barovier Mentasti, Dorigato 1995, pp. 40, 132 no. 42; *Italienisches…*, 1996, p. 57 no. 18.

120. *'Corroso' goblet*, 1936 (pl. 88)
h 11 cm, ∅ 11 cm
Acid-etched: 'Venini ITALIA'
United States, Millennium Pictures Collection

Small goblet in transparent glass with corroded, iridised surface. Presented at the 1936 and 1952 Venice Biennales.

Catalogo blu no. 4113 fol. 40, (set) nos 4117, 4112, 4109, 4100, 4110, 4111 fol. 40; *Catalogo rosso* (set) nos 4109, 4110, 4111, 4112, 4115, 4117.
Bibliography: Gasparetto 1958, no. 57; Polak 1962, no. 51a; Dal Co, Mazzariol 1984, p. 184 no. 230; *Italienisches...*, 1987, p. 50 no. 30, p. 53 no. 31; *Carlo Scarpa...*, 1991, p. 71 no. 15; Heiremans 1993, p. 250 no. 203; *Italienisches...*, 1996, p. 68 nos 31–32, p. 69 no. 33; Barovier 1997, p. 120; *Venini Venezia...*, 1998, p. 67.

121. *Banded 'corroso' vase*, 1936 (pl. 92)
h 32 cm
Acid-etched: 'Venini Murano ITALIA'
United States, Millennium Pictures Collection

Vase in corroded glass lightly iridised in amber, wound with a thick welded band spiralling downward in relief.

Catalogo blu no. 4103 fol. 40; *Catalogo rosso* (set) no. 4103.
Exhibitions: Venice 1996; Brescia 1997.
Bibliography: Dal Co, Mazzariol 1984, p. 189 no. 230; *Carlo Scarpa...*, 1991, pp. 72–75 nos 16–17; *Vetri di Murano...*, 1991, pp. 60–61; *Gli artisti di Venini...*, 1996, p. 93 no. 83; Deboni 1996, no. 53; Barovier 1997, p. 121.

122. *Relief 'corroso' vessels*, 1936
(pl. 93; *cf.* pl. 94)
h 16 cm (blue); h 17 cm (straw-yellow);
h 17.5 cm (green)
Acid-etched: 'Venini Murano'
Treviso, private collection

Three little cone-shaped vessels in corroded glass of blue, straw-yellow, and green hue; welded irregular bases with relief stripe rising up the side of the bowl.
Presented at the 1936 Venice Biennale.

Catalogo blu no. 4105 fol. 40, (set) nos 4102, 4107, 4114, 4104 fol. 40; *Catalogo rosso* (set) nos 4102, 4104, 4105, 4107, 4108, 4105.
Exhibitions: Venice 1996; Brescia 1997.
Bibliography: *Gli artisti di Venini...*, 1996, p. 93 no. 82.
Dell'Oro 1936, pp. 225–29; G. P. 1936, pp. 28–29; *XX Esposizione...*, 1936, p. 388; Deboni 1989, no. 49; *Carlo Scarpa...*, 1991, p. 70 no. 15, p. 80 no. 20; Heiremans 1993, p. 250 no. 203; Barovier, Barovier Mentasti, Dorigato 1995, p. 133 no. 43; Heiremans 1996, p. 49 nos 48–49; *Italienisches...*, 1996, p. 67 no. 30; Barovier 1997, pp. 122–23, 210; *Il Vetro Italiano...*, 1998, p. 184 nos 72–73.

115

116

117

118

119

120

121

122

123. *'Corroso' vase*, 1936 (pl. 96)
h 20 cm
Acid-etched: 'Venini Murano'
United States, Millennium Pictures Collection

Vase in green glass with welded protuberances arranged at random; iridised and corroded finish.

Catalogo blu no. 4101 fol. 40, (set) nos 4110, 4100 fol. 40; *Catalogo rosso* (set) nos 4100, 4101.
Bibliography: Deboni 1989, no. 50; *Carlo Scarpa...*, 1991, pp. 76–79 nos 18–19; Heiremans 1993, p. 251 no. 204; *Gli artisti di Venini...*, 1996, p. 94 no. 84; *Italienisches...*, 1996, p. 66 no. 29; Barovier 1997, pp. 124–25, 211 nos 100, 101, 102.

124. *Chandelier*, 1936 (pl. 97)
h 110 cm, ∅ 45 cm
Turin, Galleria Ecodiforme

Cylindrical ceiling light composed of a tapering cascade of small crystal plates. The lower part is inset with a large sphere whose surface is made up of tiny crystal tesserae. The structure is supported on a metal frame fixed with decorative bosses visible all around the shade.

Catalogo blu no. 5284 fol. 164.
Exhibitions: Milan 1936 (VI Triennale).
Bibliography: Barovier 1997, p. 270 no. 10.

125. *'Puntini' wares*, 1937
h 13 cm; h 18 cm; h 9 cm
Location unknown

Transparent vessels of strongly iridised glass decorated with blobs of welded glass paste. Presented at the 1938 Venice Biennale.

Catalogo blu nos 3683, 3681, 3680 fol. 47, (set) nos 3679, 3700, 3682, 3684, 3701, 3678 fol. 47.
Bibliography: 'Una piccola collezione'..., 1938, p. 47.
Dell'Oro 1938, pp. 240–43; *Carlo Scarpa...*, 1991, pp. 84–85 no. 22; Heiremans 1993, p. 252 no. 205; Barovier, Barovier Mentasti, Dorigato 1995, p. 135 no. 45.

126. *'Variegato' cup*, 1938
h 8 cm, ∅ 15 cm
Location unknown

Wide cup in lightly iridised transparent glass with a jagged band in coloured glass gently spiralling to the base.

Catalogo blu no. 3719 fol. 48, (set) no. 3720 fol. 48.
Bibliography: Dell'Oro 1938, pp. 240–43; Heiremans 1993, p. 253 no. 206.

127. *Clocks and picture frames*, 1938–40
h 15 cm, l 15 cm each
Venice, Anna Venini Collection

A series of frames designed variously for clocks, mirror, or photographs; media techniques include corrosion, *murrina*, *filigrana*, and canes.

128. *Chandelier*, 1940 (pl. 98)
h 120 cm, ∅ 40 cm
Turin, Galleria Ecodiforme

Hanging light in clear glass and *lattimo* with two tiers of lamp-holders with clear-glass bowls. The upper section is richly embellished with volutes, with pendant drops hanging below. The piece is supported on a metal framework.

Catalogo blu no. 5315 fol. 181.
Bibliography: G. P. 1940, p. 58; Barovier 1997, p. 278 no. 34.

129. *'Tessuto' bottle*, 1940 (cf. pl. 99)
h 31.5 cm
New York, Oswaldo Costa Collection

Bottle composed of thin vertical canes of yellow, black, and clear glass. The surface is either milled or left smooth. The 'Tessuti' set is illustrated in the *Catalogo verde* with the forms chosen by Ludovico Diaz de Santillana in the 1970s. This does not exclude the existence of other forms realised in the *tessuto* technique (such as small bowls), but the preference remains for those that came from Carlo Scarpa's drawing-board.
Presented at the 1940 and 1952 Venice Biennales.

Catalogo blu no. 3900 fol. 58; *Catalogo rosso* no. 3900; *Catalogo verde* no. 524.2, (set) nos 524.0, 524.1, 524.2, 524.3, 524.4, 524.5, colours: two-colour turquoise/black, coral/black, sulphur/black, or mixed coral/black/turquoise/sulphur.
Bibliography: Mariacher 1954[a], no. 178; Gasparetto 1958, no. 163; Polak 1962, pl. 65a; Ponti 1959, p. 40; *Vetri di Murano...*, 1977, no. 175; *Venezianisches...*, 1981, no. 125; *Vetri Murano Oggi*, 1981, p. 39 no. 116; Barovier Mentasti 1982, p. 284 no. 291; *Mille Anni...*, 1982, pp. 55, 267 no. 529; *Vetro di Murano...*, 1982, no. 144; Dal Co, Mazzariol 1984, p. 316; *Glass in Miami*, 1984, p. 100 no. 566; *Murano il vetro...*, 1986, p. 170; Deboni 1989, no. 68; *Die Sammlung...*, 1989, p. 79 no. 192; *Carlo Scarpa...*, 1991, pp. 116–17 no. 38, pp. 120–23 nos 40–41; *L'arte del vetro...*, 1992, p. 253 no. 356; Heiremans 1993, p. 249 no. 202; Ricke 1995, p. 236 no. 379; *Gli artisti di Venini...*, 1996, p. 105 no. 115; Heiremans 1996, p. 64 no. 65; *Italienisches...*, 1996, pp. 74–75 nos 39–41; *Venini Venezia...*, 1998, p. 67.

130. *Two-colour 'tessuto' vase*, 1940
h 11 cm
Venice, private collection

Small vase with double 'weave' of yellow/black and red/black canes. The prototype is stamped with the letter 'E'. Owing to the high production costs, which entails blowing one casing inside another, this particular type of *tessuto* ware never went into production.

Catalogo blu no. 3918 fol. 55.
Exhibitions: Venice 1991; Venice 1996; Brescia 1997; Milan 1998.
Bibliography: P. 1940, p. 70; *Carlo Scarpa...*, 1991, pp. 118–19 no. 39; Barovier, Barovier Mentasti, Dorigato 1995, no. 58; *Gli artisti di Venini...*, 1996, p. 192 no. 114; Barovier 1997, p. 138; *Il Vetro Italiano...*, 1998, p. 192 no. 90.

123

125

127

124

129

128

126

130

131. *'Cinese' vase*, 1940 (pl. 100)
h 26 cm
Treviso, private collection

Taking its shape from Chinese porcelain, this vase is fashioned in opaque green glass; these forms are not given in the *Catalogo blu*, which leads one to think that despite the original design being one of Scarpa's, they were reintroduced in the 1960s by Ludovico Diaz de Santillana and Scarpa's son Tobia.

Catalogo rosso no. 8551, (set) nos 8552, 8553, 8554, 8555, 8556; *Catalogo verde* (set) nos 513.0, 513.1, 513.2, 513.3, 513.4, 513.5, colours: opaque, anthracite, antique red, antique green, amber, indigo, milk-white.
Exhibitions: Venice 1996.
Bibliography: *Gli artisti di Venini...*, 1996, p. 103 no. 108.
Glass in Miami, 1984, p. 101 no. 575; *Carlo Scarpa...*, 1991, pp. 114–15 no. 37.

132. *'Granulare' vessel*, 1940
h 13 cm, ⌀ 22 cm
United States, Millennium Pictures Collection

Small bowl in black glass with minute white counter-inserts; the 'Granulari' sets are missing from the Venini production catalogues (*Catalogo blu*, *Catalogo rosso*, *Catalogo verde*), given the limited issue of the objects produced.
These articles were presented at the 1940 Milan Triennale.

Bibliography: Deboni 1989, no. 64.
G. P. 1940, pp. 58–61; P. 1940, p. 70; *Carlo Scarpa...*, 1991, pp. 124–25 no. 42; *L'arte del vetro...*, 1992, p. 250 no. 353; *Gli artisti di Venini...*, 1996, p. 99 no. 96; Barovier 1997, p. 142.

133. *'Bugne lisce' vase*, 1940
h 24 cm
Treviso, private collection

Small vase in heavy, transparent pink glass with large welded knob-like prunts.
Presented at the 1940 Milan Triennale, and at the Venice Biennale of the same year.

Catalogo blu no. 3761 fol. 59.
Exhibitions: Brescia 1997.
Bibliography: Papini 1940, p. 219; Deboni 1989, p. 24; *Carlo Scarpa...*, 1991, pp. 82–83; Barovier, Barovier Mentasti, Dorigato 1995, p. 48; Barovier 1997, p. 216 no. 181.

134. *'Iridato' vessel*, 1940 (pl. 101)
h 8 cm, ⌀ 12.5 cm
Paris, Musée des Arts Décoratifs, inv. 37191

Small vessel in thin encased glass with a marked iridescent finish.
At the 1940 Venice Biennale and Milan Triennale, Scarpa presented a group of iridescent wares that stood out from previous models for the thickness of the glass, and the highly iridised surface, whence the set's name 'Iridati'.

Catalogo blu no. 3789 fol. 57, (set) nos 3728, 3729, 3971, 3776, 3758, 3730, 3783, 3983 fols 58–59.
Exhibitions: Venice 1996.
Bibliography: *Gli artisti di Venini...*, 1996, p. 109 no. 125.
Italienisches..., 1996, p. 82 no. 50; Barovier 1997, pp. 147, 279 no. 36.

135. *'Battuto' vase*, 1940 (cf. pls 85, 102)
h 33.5 cm
United States, Millennium Pictures Collection

Tall free-blown vessel in pale blue glass with a milled surface.

Catalogo blu no. 3791 fol. 57, (set) nos 3939A, 3940A, 3922, 3950, 3797, 3980, 3910, 3659 fols 56–57; *Catalogo rosso* (set) nos 3576, 3578, 3607, 3659, 3644.
Bibliography: G. P. 1940, pp. 58–61; P. 1940, p. 70; Ponti 1959, p. 31; *Vetri di Murano...*, 1960, pl. XVII; *La verrerie...*, 1988, p. 117 no. 3; Cousins 1989, p. 85; *Carlo Scarpa...*, 1991, pp. 86–101 nos 23–30; Barovier Mentasti 1992, p. 79 no. 69, p. 117 no. 106; Heiremans 1993, p. 247 no. 220; *Vetri veneziani...*, 1994, p. 68 no. 48; Deboni 1996, p. 277 no. 193; Heiremans 1996, p. 63 no. 63; *Italienisches...*, 1996, pp. 74–76 nos 42–43.

136. *Vase with incisions*, 1940
h 29 cm
United States, Millennium Pictures Collection

Aquamarine encased vase with deep-cut patterns and deep transparent base.
The 'Incisi' set in geometric or figurative shapes were one-off pieces that required extreme precision, for which the firm engaged the accomplished Bohemian engraver Franz Pelzel, resident on Murano. The piece was exhibited at the 1940 Milan Triennale.

Exhibitions: Venice 1996.
Bibliography: G. P. 1940, p. 59; P. 1940, p. 70; *Carlo Scarpa...*, 1991, p. 126 no. 43; *Gli artisti di Venini...*, 1996, p. 102 no. 106; Barovier 1997, pp. 153, 283 no. 45.

131

133

132

134

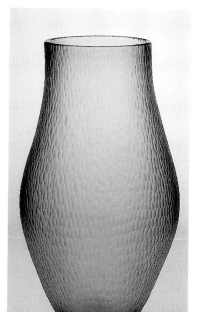

135

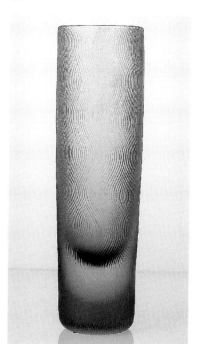

136

137. *Engraved overlaid vase with collar*, 1940
h 28 cm
United States, private collection

Vase in amethyst milled for satin effect and scored with horizontal bands. The body casings are joined at the neck with transparent glass and highlighted with a dark tea-coloured collar.
Exhibited at the 1940 Milan Triennale.

Catalogo blu no. 3755 fol. 58, (set) nos 3742, 3754, 3791, 3795 fols 57–58; *Catalogo rosso* (set) nos 3742, 3754, 3755, 3791, 3795.
Bibliography: Deboni 1989, no. 74; Barovier, Barovier Mentasti, Dorigato 1995, p. 142 no. 57; Barovier 1997, pp. 152, 281.

138. *Vase with applied details*, 1940
h 23 cm
Zülpich (Germany), Lösch Collection

Glass with iridised surface and two large welded relief patches in green and blue glass paste. Exhibited at the 1940 Milan Triennale.

Bibliography: Deboni 1989, no. 66; Heiremans 1996, p. 62 no. 62; Barovier 1997, pp. 163, 283.

139. *Patterned plate*, 1940
l 25 cm
United States, Millennium Pictures Collection

Plate in crystal glass with three alternating coloured bands and strongly iridised finish.

Catalogo rosso no. 4476, (set) nos 4477, 4478.
Bibliography: *Carlo Scarpa…*, 1991, pp. 162–63 no. 61; Barovier 1997, p. 162.

140. *Vase with transparent 'murrina' inserts*, 1940 (pl. 103)
h 12.5 cm
Asti, private collection

Small vase with spherical body made of irregular aquamarine *murrina* glass submerged in crystal.

Catalogo blu no. 3788 fol. 57; *Catalogo rosso* no. 3607.
Exhibitions: Venice 1996; Brescia 1997.
Bibliography: Deboni 1989, no. 65; *Gli artisti di Venini…*, 1996, p. 103 no. 109; Barovier 1997, pp. 171, 221.

141. *Black-and-red lacquered vase*, 1940
h 22.5 cm
Treviso, private collection

Blown-glass vase composed of layers of two different colours. The red section appears marvered because small glass spheres have been added to the incandescent mass.
Presented at the 1940 and 1952 Venice Biennales.

Exhibitions: Venice 1996.
Bibliography: G. P. 1940, pp. 58–61; XXII *Esposizione…*, 1940, p. 226; *L'arte del vetro…*, 1992, p. 251 no. 354; Barovier, Barovier Mentasti, Dorigato 1995, p. 140 no. 55; *Gli artisti di Venini…*, 1996, p. 100 no. 97; Barovier 1997, pp. 145, 216.

142. *'Murrina' plate*, 1940
(pl. 106; *cf.* pl. 104)
l 32 cm
Düsseldorf, Kunstmuseum Düsseldorf, Glasmuseum Hentrich

Square plate divided into two zones of *murrina*, one black and red, the other aquamarine and black; the two sections of *murrina* form an interlocking abstract pattern where they meet at the centre. The design marked the return of forgotten Murano techniques, unexpectedly re-employed after Paolo Venini's 'Murrine romane' wares of 1936, to great effect.

Catalogo rosso no. 4874.
Exhibitions: Venice 1996; Brescia 1997.
Bibliography: *Gli artisti di Venini…*, 1996, p. 104 no. 110; Barovier 1997, pp. 164–65.
Motta 1940, p. 244; P. 1940, p. 69; 'Alcuni elementi…', 1951, p. 29; Mariacher 1954ª, no. 178; Gasparetto 1958, no. 162; *Vetri Murano Oggi*, 1981, p. 39 no. 118; Barovier Mentasti 1982, p. 283 no. 290; *Mille Anni…*, 1982, p. 267 no. 531; *Murano, il vetro…*, 1986, p. 44; *Carlo Scarpa…*, 1991, pp. 130–42 nos 45–51; *L'arte del vetro…*, 1992, p. 251 no. 352; *Murano…*, 1994, pp. 26–29; Barovier, Barovier Mentasti, Dorigato 1995, no. 49; *Museum Bellerive…*, 1995, p. 228 no. 398; Deboni 1996, p. 281 no. 197; *Italienisches…*, 1996, pp. 71–73 nos 36–38; *Il Vetro Italiano…*, 1998, p. 196 no. 97.

143. *'Murrina' plate*, 1940 (pl. 105)
l 35 cm
Rome, private collection

One of Scarpa's finest *murrina* pieces from his last years at Venini & C., this oval plate features a yellow and red *murrina* section at the centre, surrounded by a wide border of red and black, the surface of the whole lathed to give a fine milled finish.

Exhibitions: Venice 1996.
Bibliography: *Gli artisti di Venini…*, 1996, p. 104 no. 110; Barovier 1997, pp. 164–65.
Motta 1940, p. 244; P. 1940, p. 70; 'Alcuni elementi…', 1951, p. 29; Mariacher 1954ª, no. 178; Gasparetto 1958, no. 162; *Vetri Murano Oggi*, 1981, p. 39 no. 118; Barovier Mentasti 1982, p. 283 no. 290; *Mille Anni…*, 1982, p. 267 no. 531; *Murano, il vetro…*, 1986, p. 44; *Carlo Scarpa…*, 1991, pp. 130–42 nos 45–51; *L'arte del vetro…*, 1992, p. 251 no. 352; *Murano…*, 1994, pp. 26–29; Barovier, Barovier Mentasti, Dorigato 1995, no. 49; *Museum Bellerive…*, 1995, p. 228 no. 398; Deboni 1996, p. 281 no. 197; *Italienisches…*, 1996, pp. 71–73 nos 36–38; *Il Vetro Italiano…*, 1998, p. 196 no. 97.

144. *Thread vase*, 1942 (pl. 107)
h 18.5 cm
Treviso, private collection

Round-bellied vase in thin blown glass embedded with bands of coloured rods in both body and neck. The so-called 'Variegati' wares form a set in which bands trailed in the transparent medium produce either a banded or variegated overall effect (*cf. Catalogo rosso*).
Exhibited at the 1942 Venice Biennale.

Catalogo rosso no. 4540, (set) nos 4561, 4562, 4563, 4564, 4565, 4566, 4567, 4568, 4569 (*variegato*).
Exhibitions: Venice 1996.
Bibliography: *Gli artisti di Venini…*, 1996, p. 107 no. 120.
XXIII *Esposizione…*, 1942, p. 260; *Vetri Murano Oggi*, 1981, p. 33 no. 117, p. 105 no. 412; Deboni 1989, nos 75, 80, 81, 86; *Carlo Scarpa…*, 1991, pp. 146–49 nos 53–54; Barovier, Barovier Mentasti, Dorigato 1995, p. 51 no. 73; Deboni 1996, p. 284 no. 200; Heiremans 1996, nos 67, 69; *Italienisches…*, 1996, p. 78 no. 44, pp. 80–81 nos 46–48; Barovier 1997, p. 176.

145. *'Pennellate' vase*, 1942
(*cf.* pls 108–10)
h 26.7 cm, ⌀ 15 cm
Zurich, Museum Bellerive

Conical vase in thin transparent glass decorated with coloured rods trailed through the vessel walls to create a 'brushstroke' effect. Presented at the 1942 Venice Biennale

Catalogo blu (set) nos 3644, 3788, 3901, 3779 fol. 47; *Catalogo rosso* no. 4541, (set) nos 3602, 3674.
Bibliography: Deboni 1989, no. 82; *Carlo Scarpa…*, 1991, p. 158 no. 59; Barovier Mentasti 1992, p. 76 no. 65; Barovier, Barovier Mentasti, Dorigato 1995, pp. 51, 150 no. 72; *Museum Bellerive…*, 1995, p. 229 nos 399–400; Deboni 1996, p. 283 no. 199; Heiremans 1996, no. 68; *Italienisches…*, 1996, p. 79 no. 45; *Venini Venezia…*, 1998, p. 67.

146. *'Macchie' dish*, 1942
⌀ 24 cm
Location unknown

Dish in clear glass with blue insert embedded on base, and applications of black glass in an abstract pattern. Strongly iridised finish.
Presented at the 1942 Venice Biennale.

Catalogo rosso no. 4475, (set) nos 4423, 4424, 4476, 4477, 4478.
Bibliography: *Italienisches…*, 1987, p. 59 nos 36–37; Deboni 1989, no. 76; *Carlo Scarpa…*, 1991, pp. 160–61; Barovier Mentasti 1992, p. 72 no. 61; *Gli artisti di Venini…*, 1996, no. 124; *Italienisches…*, 1996, p. 83 no. 51; Barovier 1997, p. 286.

147. *Shells*, 1942
Location unknown

Set of shells made with ranging techniques – in transparent glass, with thread decoration, iridised, with gentle ribbing – formed in an open mould. Presented at the 1942 Venice Biennale.

Catalogo rosso nos 4554, 4555, 4556, 4557, 4558, 4559.
Bibliography: Deboni 1989, nos 77–79; *Carlo Scarpa…*, 1991, pp. 154–55 no. 47; Barovier, Barovier Mentasti, Dorigato 1995, p. 52; *Gli artisti di Venini…*, 1996, p. 106 no. 117; *Italienisches…*, 1996, p. 82 no. 49; Barovier 1997, pp. 186–87, 286.

148. *Owl*, 1943 (pl. 111)
h 38.5 cm
Padua, Università degli Studi, Meeting Room

Iridised white glass speckled with gold-leaf. On 6 February 1943 the rector of University of Padua, Carlo Anti, invited the Murano-based glasshouses Barovier e Toso & Co., E. Ferro, S.A. Venini, and Seguso to design a set of animal figures for a centrepiece to designate the various departments of the University.
The design put forward by Carlo Scarpa for S.A. Venini was accepted by the sculptor Arturo Martini, the competition judge. The various figures created were: the *Bò* (Ox), *Bee and hive* (Political Science); *Swan and book* (Letters and Philosophy); *Snake and cup* (Pharmacy); *Beaver and cog* (Engineering); *Owl* (Physical Science and Mathematics); *Eagle and sword* (Jurisprudence); *Cockerel and skull* (Medicine and Surgery).

Exhibitions: Venice 1996; Brescia 1997.
Bibliography: *Carlo Scarpa…*, 1991, pp. 29–36; *Gli artisti di Venini…*, 1996, pp. 110–11 no. 128; Franzoia, in Barovier 1997, pp. 47–51.

149. *Engraved and milled vase*, 1942
h 35 cm
Location unknown

Vase in transparent glass incised with deep grooves and rectangular faceting. This vase of great rarity belonged to a set of one-off pieces presented at the 1940 and 1942 Venice Biennales. The glass-cutter was Eliseo Piano.

Exhibitions: Venice 1940 (XXII Biennale); Venice 1942 (XXIII Biennale); Venezia 1952 (XXVI Biennale).
Bibliography: Barovier 1997, p. 288 no. 61.

150. *Polyhedral waterfall-chandelier*, 1961
Turin, 'Italia '61', Italian Pavilion

This chandelier marks Carlo Scarpa's brief return of to the Venini furnaces in the 1960s.

Bibliography: *Vetri Murano Oggi*, 1981, p. 127 no. 239.

137

138

139

140

141

142

143

144

145

146

147

148

149

150

151. *Figurines from the Commedia dell'Arte*, 1948
(cf. pls 112–15)
h 40–45 cm
Chappaqua (USA), private collection

Figurines in *lattimo* glass with multicoloured glass-paste applications created by the master craftsman 'Boboli' (alias Arturo Biasutto). The pieces involve different techniques and colours: polychrome glass paste decorations on a *lattimo* base; multicoloured threads trailed over a *lattimo* base; *pezzato* mosaic sections with *lattimo* decorations. Bianconi's figurines were first presented at the 1948 Venice Biennale.

Catalogo rosso nos 2900 (*Giangurgolo*), 2901 (*Pantalone*), 2902 (*Peppe Nappa*), 2903 (*Meneghino*), 2904 (*Tartaglia*), 2905 (*Capitan Fracassa*), 2906 (*Arlecchino gymnast*), 2907 (*Rosaura*), 2908 (*Arlecchino*), 2009 (*Brighella*), 2910 (*Pulcinella*), 2911 (*Arlecchina*), 2983 (*Masked lady, female counterpart of Tartaglia*), 4521, 4522, 4523, 4524, 4525, 4526 (*Tiepolo*), 4850, 4851, 4852, 4853, 4854, 4855 (*Grotesques*), 4346 (*January*), 4347 (*February*), 4348 (*March*), 4349 (*April*), 4350 (*May*), 4351 (*June*), 4352 (*July*), 4353 (*August*), 4354 (*September*), 4355 (*October*), 4356 (*November*), 4357 (*December*), 2988, 2989, 2990, 2991, 2992, 2993, 2994, 2995, 2996, 2997, 2998, 2999 (*Regional costumes*), 4334 and 4335 (*1500s costumes*), 4336 and 4337 (*1700s costumes*), 4338 and 4339 (*Empire-style costumes*), 4340 and 4341 (*1850 costumes*), 2956, 2957, 2958 (*servants*: coloured women with bodies in *murrina*); *Catalogo verde* nos 402.0 (*Giangurgolo*), 402.1 (*Pantalone*), 402.2 (*Peppe Nappa*), 402.3 (*Meneghino*), 402.4 (*Tartaglia*), 402.5 (*Capitan Fracassa*), 402.6 (*Arlecchino*), 402.7 (*Rosaura*), 402.8 (*Arlecchino*), 402.9 (*Brighella*), 402.10 (*Pulcinella*), 402.11 (*Arlecchina*), 400.0, 400.1, 400.2, 400.3, 400.4, 400.5 (*Tiepolo* in *lattimo* with black detailing), 401.0, 401.1, 401.2, 401.3, 401.4, 401.5 (*Grotesques* in *lattimo*).

Bibliography: XXIV *Biennale…*, 1948, no. 93; Aloi 1955, p. 14; *Vetri Murano Oggi*, 1981, p. 113 no. 427; Barovier Mentasti 1982, p. 306 no. 321; *Mille Anni…*, 1982, p. 310 no. 647; *Die Fünfziger…*, 1984, no. 50; Dorigato 1986, p. 90; Deboni 1989, nos 95, 100; *L'arte del vetro…*, 1992, p. 252 no. 357; Barovier Mentasti 1992, p. 112 no. 99; Bossaglia 1993, nos 1–6, 9; *Gli artisti di Venini…*, 1996, p. 114 nos 133–34; Heiremans 1996, p. 72 nos 78–79; *Italienisches…*, 1996, pp. 94–96 nos 62–64; *Sculture…*, 1996, p. 36 nos 44–45, p. 37 no. 47; *Venini Venezia…*, 1998, p. 72.

152. *Musician*, 1948
Location unknown

Musician figure in *lattimo* with details in multicoloured glass paste, with characteristic musical instruments: harmonica, trumpet, toy-trumpet, cymbals, horn.
These pieces were first submitted at the 1948 Venice Biennale, together with the *Figurines from the Commedia dell'Arte*.

Catalogo rosso nos 2961, 2962, 2963, 2964, 2965, 2966 (drum) and 2967 (toy-trumpet) in the form of candle-holders.
Bibliography: XXIV *Biennale…*, 1948, s.p.; Bossaglia 1993, nos 4, 8.

153. *'Chagall'*, 1948
h 27 cm
Piacenza, private collection

Figure in clear iridised glass with applied details in black glass paste. Part of a set of imaginary figures (combinations of two different animals, or half-animal half-man). Although they date from the same period as the other figurines of 1948 (as shown in the *Catalogo rosso*), they differ in that instead of *lattimo* Bianconi used clear iridised glass. Now hard to come by, most exemplars are without trace; apparently they were less popular than their counterparts.

Catalogo rosso nos 2924, 2925, 2926, 2927, 2928.
Exhibitions: Venice 1996.
Bibliography: *Gli artisti di Venini…*, 1996, p. 117 no. 141.

154. *Obelisk with flame*, 1948 (pl. 116)
h 45 cm
Union City (USA), Odetto Lastra Collection

One of a set of obelisks: transparent glass containing flame in coral or *lattimo* glass; with octagonal base and faceted tip, in three dimensions: 40 cm, 30 cm, 25 cm; with circular base and rounded tip, in three dimensions: 44 cm, 30 cm, 20 cm; with square base and pointed tip, in three dimensions: 50 cm, 45 cm, 25 cm.
The *Catalogo rosso* on the pages with the obelisks with flame are some hand-written notes in pen regarding the production of a 'special' object with flame in *filigrana*.
Presented at the 1948 Venice Biennale and the 1951 Milan Triennale.

Catalogo rosso nos 2918, 2919, 2920 (octagonal base), 2897, 2898, 2899 (circular base), 2891, 2892, 2893 (square base); *Catalogo verde* with flame nos 455.0, 455.1, 455.2 (probably restyled by Ludovico Diaz de Santillana, keeping the idea of the obelisk containing a flame, but entirely reworking the shape), 455.3, 455.4, 455.5 (square base), 455.6, 455.7, 455.8 (round base).
Exhibitions: Venice 1996; Milan 1998.
Bibliography: *Gli artisti di Venini…*, 1996, p. 141 no. 200; *Il Vetro Italiano…*, 1998, p. 194 no. 92. Heiremans 1993, p. 259 no. 212; *Italienisches…*, 1996, p. 97 no. 65.

155. *Column*, 1948
h 40 cm
Switzerland, private collection

Glass column in transparent coral-red glass (variant in iridised transparent white). The base has four highly ornamented tiers, a fluted shaft, and Corinthian capital.
First presented at the 1948 Venice Biennale.

Catalogo rosso nos 9054, 9055.

151

152

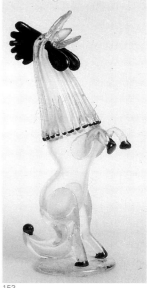

153

154

155

156. *Shells, cornucopias, hands, gloves*, 1948
Location unknown

Shell in *lattimo*; cornucopias in cased glass; leaves and base with gold-lear; hands in *lattimo* (variant with polychrome glass paste additions); gloves in *lattimo*.

Catalogo rosso nos 1154 (*Shell*), 2979 (*Cornucopia*), 2977 (*Hand with cornucopia*), 2978 (*Vase-holder hand*), 2982 (*Glove frayed*), 2969 (*Small hand*), 2917 (*Two small hands*).
Bibliography: Deboni 1989, no. 93; Heiremans 1993, p. 257 no. 210; *Gli artisti di Venini...*, 1996, p. 117 no. 142; *Italienisches...*, 1996, p. 92 no. 60.

157. *Moorish-figure candle-holder*, 1948
Location unknown

Part of a set of candle-holder figures in *lattimo* and black glass paste, seated or standing. The clothing for the standing figures is in ribbed *lattimo*, with the belt in opaque black glass; the seated ones are in *lattimo* with black thread details; in some case they hold up one or two candle-holders, or one placed on the head.

Catalogo rosso nos 2971, 2972, 2973, 2974, 2975, 2976.
Exhibitions: Zurich 1998.
Bibliography: *Venini. Glas...*, 1998, no. 10. Bossaglia 1993, no. 12.

158. *Coat-stand candelabra*, 1948
h 22 cm each
Milan, Galleria In. Arte

Pair of candelabra in *lattimo* with base and detailing in black glass paste. Presented at the 1948 Venice Biennale.

Catalcgo rosso no. 2913, (set) nos 2912, 2929, 2930, 2960, 2968.
Bibliography: Deboni 1989, no. 84; Bossaglia 1993, nos 8–14.

159. *'Fazzoletto' vase*, 1948
h 30 cm
Acid-stamped: 'Venini Murano Italia'
New York, Barry Friedman Collection

Vase in the form of a handkerchief in opaque glass cased in ivory and black submerged in the crystal. The rounded crests of the folds are particularly gracefully rendered; the entire form of the piece is evidence of the natural instinctive gesture of a skilled master glassmaker.
Fashioned from opaline glass by combining two or more colours, the design was prompted by Paolo Venini; thanks to Bianconi's gifts as an artist, the idea was developed with different techniques: simple *zanfirico*; *zanfirico a reticello*; or with glass canes in a variety of colours. Besides the original form, cblong variants were made with rounded points, others in smaller sizes.
Some time earlier Pietro Chiesa had created something similar for Gio Ponti's company Fontana Arte, styled as a stiff, stylised handkerchief; even Tyra Lundgren confessed to having had the idea of a glass composition in the form of a handkerchief. The Venini *Fazzoletto* has never gone out of production, and many version exist in museums around the world: the specimen in the Museum of

Modern Art in New York is displayed as exemplary of Italian design in the 1950s.
In his personal interpretation, Ludovico Diaz de Santillana made extensive use of glass canes to create a new series for the 1960s.

Catalogo rosso no. 2986 (original form), (set) nos 2987 (without peaks), 4215 (high, irregular peaks), 4216 (small and rounded, with low peaks), 4217 (round, without peaks), 4241 and 4274 (oblong, with rounded points), 4258 and 4258 special version (in vase form), 1156, 1157, 1158 (rounded, without peaks, on much smaller scale, probably devised for a *bonbonnière*); *Catalogo verde* (set) from no. 700.0 to no. 700.6 (original form in various sizes: 8 cm, 10 cm, 12 cm, 16 cm, 20 cm, 27 cm, 35 cm – in opaline glass, colours: red opaline with white, amethyst, tea, grey, aquamarine, orange, sulphur. Inside always white opaline, except for the sulphur/orange one); from no. 701.0 to no. 701.6 (original form, in various sizes – 8 cm, 10 cm, 12 cm, 16 cm, 20 cm, 27 cm, 35 cm – in *zanfirico*, colours: canes in milk-white, *zanfirico*, sapphire, cyclamen, and turquoise).
Bibliography: 'I vetri italiani...', 1951, p. 29; Ponti 1959, pp. 37–38; *Vetri di Murano...*, 1960, pl. XXXVIb; *Manualità...*, 1980, p. 71 no. 70; Barovier Mentasti 1982, p. 308 no. 323; *Mille Anni...*, 1982, p. 310 no. 649; *Design...*, 1984, pp. 47, 114 no. II–67; *Die Fünfziger...*, 1984, p. 52 no. 21; *Glass in Miami*, 1984, p. 101 no. 568; *Italienisches...*, 1987, p. 72 no. 49, p. 75 no. 50, p. 78 no. 53; Deboni 1989, no. 106; Barovier Mentasti 1992, p. 308 no. 323; Cerutti, Dorigato 1992, p. 214; Bossaglia 1993, nos 19, 21; Heiremans 1993, p. 260 no. 213; *Murano...*, 1994, p. 32; Ricke 1995, p. 237 no. 380; *Gli artisti di Venini...*, 1996, p. 113 nos 130–32; Deboni 1996, pp. 290–91 nos 206–7; Heiremans 1996, p. 77 no. 84; *Italienisches...*, 1996, p. 98 nos 66–67, p. 100 nos 69–70; *Venini Venezia...*, 1998, p. 68.

160. *'Ventaglio' vase*, 1949
h 20 cm
Badge: 'Venini Murano Italia'
Zülpich (Germany), Lösch Collection

Fan-shaped vase with circular base in transparent glass; body in black glass paste with *lattimo* thread; welded upper section composed of fine mesh of *zanfirico* canes. Created with Paolo Venini. Presented at the 1950 Venice Biennale.

Catalogo rosso no. 4327.
Bibliography: *XXV Biennale...*, 1950, p. 116; Deboni 1989, no. 91; *Vetri di Murano...*, 1991, pp. 94–95; Bossaglia 1993, no. 18; Heiremans 1996, p. 78 no. 85; *Italienisches...*, 1996, p. 99 no. 68.

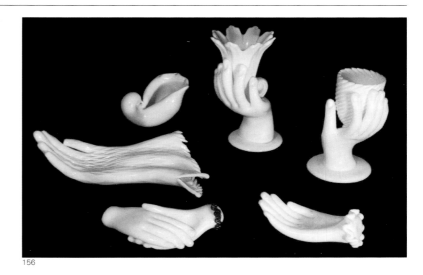
156

158

160

159

157

161. *'Pezzame' vessel*, 1949–50
h 30 cm
Milan, Galleria In. Arte

Vessel in transparent glass with *pezzame* (patch) inserts of polychrome glass patches.
Presented at the 1951 Milan Triennale.
In this volume distinctions have been made between the 'Pezzati', 'Pezzame', 'A colori', and 'Spicchi' sets listed in the *Catalogo rosso*; for this reason, we have illustrated only these as examples.

Catalogo rosso no. 4394, (set) nos 4392, 4393, 4396, 4397 (despite having all the characteristics of *pezzato* ware), 4398, 4399, 4400, 4402, 4403, 4404, 4406, 4407, 4408; *Catalogo verde* (set) nos 705.3, 705.4, 705.5, 705.6.
Bibliography: 'Sei vetri…', 1950, p. 39; 'I vetri italiani…', 1951, p. 29; Heiremans 1989, no. 185; Bossaglia 1993, no. 35.

162. *'Spicchi' vessels*, 1949–50
Location unknown

Glass vessels composed of broad vertical stripes of coloured glass.

Catalogo rosso nos 4890, 4891, (set) nos 4892, 4893, 4894, 4895, 4896, 4897, 4898; *Catalogo verde* (set) nos 703.0, 703.1, 703.2, 703.3, 703.4, 703.5.
Bibliography: XXVI Biennale…, 1952, p. 439 nos 499–504; Aloi 1955, p. 19; Ponti 1959, p. 42; *La verrerie…*, 1988, p. 93 no. 5; *The Venetians…*, 1989, no. 19; *Vetri di Murano*, 1989, p. 33; Bossaglia 1993, nos 30–32; Heiremans 1993, p. 261 no. 215, p. 274 no. 227; *Murano…*, 1994, p. 38 no. 23; Barovier, Barovier Mentasti, Dorigato 1995, p. 171 no. 105; *Venezia…*, 1995, p. 428 no. 494; Heiremans 1996, p. 110 nos 133–34; *Italienisches…*, 1996, p. 105 no. 76.

163. *'A colori' vase*, 1949–50
h 25 cm
New York, Barry Friedman Collection

Trapezoid vase in opaque glass with large mosaic inserts in red and pale blue.

Catalogo rosso no. 4318, (set) nos 4315, 4316, 4317, 4319, 4320, 4321, 4322, 4323, 4324, 4325, 4405, 4409, 4410, 4412; *Catalogo verde* (set) nos 705.5, 705.1, 705.2, 705.7.
Bibliography: Bossaglia 1993, no. 36.

164. *'Pezzato' vase*, 1950
(pl. 118; *cf.* pls 117, 119)
h 13 cm
Acid-etched: 'Venini Murano Italia'
New York, Barry Friedman Collection

Square vase composed of thin transparent mosaic patches (or on a *lattimo* base) applied by heating the patches separately and then joining them one by one to the vessel body. Three colour variants: 'Parigi' – red, sapphire, green, straw-yellow; 'Stoccolma' – grey, light pink, light violet, aquamarine; 'Istambul – crystal, grey, violet, yellow. Bianconi's vases using the *pezzato* technique were enthusiastically received at the 1951 Milan Triennale; the technique was reintroduced later using both transparent and opaque tesserae (*cf.* Bossaglia 1993, nos 53–54). In fact, an astonishing number pieces using this technique were made ex-production.

Catalogo rosso no. 4912, (set) nos 4910, 4911, 4913, 4914; *Catalogo verde* (set) from no. 704.0 to no. 704.5, colours: 'Stoccolma' (grey, pink, violet, aquamarine, straw-yellow) and 'Parigi' (red, sapphire, green, straw-yellow).
Bibliography: XXVI Biennale…, 1952, p. 439 nos 522–27; *Forme Nuove…*, 1954, no. 14; Aloi 1955, p. 20; *Venini Murano…*, 1957, no. 54; Ponti 1959, p. 42; Polak 1962, no. 64a; Mariacher 1967, p. 172; *Mille Anni…*, 1982, p. 310 no. 648; *Die Fünfziger…*, 1984, p. 49 no. 16; *Italienisches…*, 1987, p. 56 no. 35; *La verrerie…*, 1988, p. 93 nos 2–3; Deboni 1989, no. 107; Heiremans 1989, p. 177 no. 206; *The Venetians…*, 1989, no. 19; *Venini…*, 1990, nos 40–41; *L'arte del vetro…*, 1992, p. 254 no. 358; Barovier Mentasti 1992, p. 114 no. 103; Bossaglia 1993, nos 23–26, 68; Heiremans 1993, p. 264 no. 217, p. 268 no. 221; *Murano…*, 1994, pp. 36–37; Barovier, Barovier Mentasti, Dorigato 1995, p. 171 no. 104; Deboni 1996, pp. 298–99 nos 214–15; Heiremans 1996, p. 95 nos 106–8, p. 96 no.109; *Italienisches…*, 1996, pp. 106–7 nos 77–80, p. 109 no. 83, p. 112 no. 86; *Venini. Glas…*, 1998, no. 9; *Venini Venezia…*, 1998, p. 71.

165. *Mermaid*, 1950
h 28 cm
Acid-etched: 'Venini Murano'
Treviso, private collection

Little siren figure in crystal glass with trailed *fenicio* decoration in *lattimo* on her tail; iridised surface.
In Finland there is a version in iridised transparent material, a 'one-off' piece created by Paolo Venini for his friend Göran Schildt in memory of the cruises they took to Greece.
Presented at the 1950 Venice Biennale.

Catalogo rosso no. 4201, (set) nos 4202, 4203, 4204, 4205, 4206, 4207, 4208, 4209, 4210, 4211, 4212, 4213, 4420, 4421.
Bibliography: Gli artisti di Venini…, 1996, p. 123 no. 160.
Deboni 1989, no. 97; Bossaglia 1993, no. 44; Heiremans 1993, p. 270 no. 223; Deboni 1996, p. 294 no. 210; Heiremans 1996, pp. 85–86 nos 91–92, p. 87 no. 93; *Italienisches…*, 1996, pp. 110–11 nos 84–85; *Venini. Glas…*, 1998, no. 4.

166. *'Rete' vase*, 1950
h 47.5 cm
Location unknown

Vase in the form of a mermaid's tail in *fenicio* glass, or in tresses of glass thread.

Catalogo rosso no. 4228, (set) nos 4227, 4229, 4222, 4225, 4232.
Bibliography: Deboni 1989, no. 99; Gli artisti di Venini…, 1996, p. 122 no. 158; Heiremans 1996, p. 85 no. 90.

167. *Vases with stylised patterns*, 1950
h 30 cm (max), h 20 cm (min)
Location unknown

Set of vases in transparent glass with abstract patterns in coloured glass paste.
Presented at the 1950 Venice Biennale.

Catalogo rosso nos 4425, 4426, 4427, 4428, 4429, 4430, 4431, 4432.
Bibliography: La verrerie…, 1988, p. 93 no. 1; Heiremans 1993, p. 266 no. 219; *Italienisches…*, 1996, p. 104 no. 75.

168. *Patch vase*, 1950
h 27 cm
Acid-etched: 'Venini Murano'
Toledo (USA), The Toledo Museum of Art, inv. 54.49

Vase in transparent glass with inserts of abstract coloured patches.
Presented at the 1950 Venice Biennale, and the 1951 Milan Triennale. A copy is housed in the Brooklyn Museum, New York, a gift from the Italian government.

Catalogo rosso no. 4323, (set) nos 4320, 4321, 4322, 4324, 4325.
Bibliography: Arte decorativa…, 1950; *Vetri di Murano…*, 1960, pl. XXXVIIa; *Glass in Miami*, 1984, p. 101, no. 567; Deboni 1989, no. 116; Heiremans 1989, no. 199; Bossaglia 1993, nos 33–34; Heiremans 1993, p. 265 no. 218; *Venezia…*, 1995, p. 246 no. 464; Heiremans 1996, p. 84 no. 89; *Italienisches…*, 1996, pp. 102–3 nos 73–74; *Venini Venezia…*, 1998, p. 70.

169. *'Moore' vase*, 1951–52
h 33 cm
Zülpich (Germany), Lösch Collection

Vase in solid transparent green glass pierced through with three irregular holes.

Catalogo rosso no. 4395, (set) nos 4514, 4516, 4517, 4518, 4519, 4520, 4223, 4537, 4538, 4539.
Bibliography: Forme Nuove…, 1954, no. 15; Heiremans 1989, p. 173; *Museum Bellerive…*, 1992, p. 30 no. 31; Heiremans 1993, p. 271 no. 224; *Gli artisti di Venini…*, 1996, p. 121 no. 155; Deboni 1996, p. 301 no. 217; *Italienisches…*, 1996, pp. 114–15 nos 88–89.

170. *Banded vase*, 1953 (pl. 120)
h 26 cm
Union City (USA), Odetto Lastra Collection

Vase in clear glass with embedded bands of aquamarine, sapphire, black, and red glass.

Catalogo verde no. 523.1, (set) nos 523.0, 523.2, 523.3, 523.4, 523.5, band colours: 'Parigi' set in red, green, sapphire, straw-yellow; 'America' set in straw-yellow, yellow, black, green.
Exhibitions: Venice 1996.
Bibliography: Gli artisti di Venini…, 1996, p. 122 no. 156.
Gasparetto 1958, no. 190; *Vetri di Murano…*, 1991, pp. 100–101; Bossaglia 1993, no. 65; Heiremans 1993, p. 282 no. 235; *Italienisches…*, 1996, p. 116 no. 91; *Venini Venezia…*, 1998, p. 72.

171. *Cockerel*, 1954 (pl. 121)
h 18 cm
Milan, Galleria In. Arte

Cockerel figure in *lattimo* streaked with coloured threads. The series includes some animals made from black *fenicio* glass.

Exhibitions: Venice 1996.
Bibliography: Bossaglia 1993, nos 70–71; *Gli artisti di Venini…*, 1996, p. 117 no. 143. Aloi 1955, p. 16; *Il bestiario…*, 1996, pp. 95–96.

172. *Swallow*, 1954
h 10 cm
Maser, private collection

Swallow figure in *filigrana*, with details in black glass; belongs to the so-called 'Animali acquatici' (Aquatic animals) series.
Other examples were made in glass canes.

Catalogo verde no. 414.11, (set) nos 414.9, 414.10 (white and black *filigrana*), 414.12 (white *tessuto* with black decorations).
Bibliography: Venini Murano…, 1957, nos 27–29; Heiremans 1993, p. 280 no. 233; *Il bestiario…*, 1996, pp. 98–99 nos 91–92.

173. *'Informale' vase*, 1968 (pl. 122)
h 42 cm
Union City (USA), Odetto Lastra Collection

Mould-blown vase in aquamarine cased in crystal; the vase's shape vaguely resembles the female form; surface lightly corroded.

Catalogo verde no. 711.
Exhibitions: Venice 1996.
Bibliography: Gli artisti di Venini…, 1996, p. 157 no. 235.
Heiremans 1989, no. 222; Bossaglia 1993, no.100; Heiremans 1993, p. 293 no. 247; *Italienisches…*, 1996, p. 130 no. 108; *Venini Venezia…*, 1998, p. 79.

161

162

163

164

165

167

172

168

166

169

171

170

173

174. *Leaf*, 1938 (pl. 124; *cf.* pl. 123)
h 13 cm, l 31 cm
Acid-etched: 'Venini Murano'
Venice, Massimo Nordio Collection

Transparent glass streaked with amethyst trails; surface strongly iridised; elongated form with rim curling inward and rising to a pair of transparent leaves attached to the lip.

Catalogo blu (set) nos 2640, 2642, 2641, 2647, 2643, 2645, 2646, 2644, 2686, 2685, 2691, 2687, 2698, 2697, 2689, 2690, 2696, 2695, 2699, 2692, 2801, 2694A, 2688, 2693, 2700 fols 45–46; *Catalogo rosso* (set) nos 2644, 2645, 2647, 2685, 2688, 2691, 2693, 2694, 2695; *Catalogo verde* (set) nos 603.0, 603.1, 603.2, 603.3 (colours: *filigrana*, milk-white, black, turquoise or coral), 527.0, 527.1, 527.2 (hues: *tessuto*, red, tea, black, green).
Exhibitions: Venice 1996.
Bibliography. *Gli artisti di Venini…*, 1996, p. 98 no.94.
Polak 1962, p. 56 no. 65b; *Italienisches…*, 1987, p. 62 no. 40, p. 81 nos 54–55; Barovier Mentasti 1992, no. 67; *Gli artisti di Venini…*, 1996, p. 98; Deboni 1996, p. 273 no.189; *Italienisches…*, 1996, p. 85 no. 53.

175. *Doves*, 1938
h 18 cm; h 13 cm
Zülpich (Germany), Lösch Collection

Bird figures produced in blown glass with corroded surface.

Catalogo blu nos 2625, 2606 fol. 45, (set) nos 2601, 2624, 2630, 2629, 2628, 2664, 2667, 2666, 2665 fol. 45; *Catalogo rosso* (set) nos 2601, 2625, 2628, 2630.
Exhibitions: Venice 1996.
Bibliography. *Gli artisti di Venini…*, 1996, p. 96. 'Vetri…', 1938, p. 246; *Vetro di Murano…*, 1982, no.140; Deboni 1989, no. 56; *L'arte del vetro…*, 1992 p. 250 no. 351; Heiremans 1996, p. 56 no.58.

176. *Fish*, 1938 (pl. 125; *cf.* pl. 126)
h 18 cm
Milan, Galleria In. Arte

Green glass lightly submerged in crystal; surface iridised and corroded; large fin worked with gold-leaf.

Catalogo blu no. 2604 fol. 39, (set) nos 2603, 2634, 2631, 2636, 2638, 2633, 2632, 2681, 2679, 2679bis, 2683, 2680 fol. 45; *Catalogo rosso* (set) nos 2603, 2631, 2679.
Exhibitions: Venice 1996.
Bibliography. *Gli artisti di Venini…*, 1996, p. 96 no. 87.
XXI Esposizione…, 1938, p. 211; 'Vetri muranesi…', 1940, p. 32; Deboni 1989, no. 54; *L'arte del vetro…*, 1992, p. 250 no. 350; *Il bestiario…*, 1996, pp. 72–73 no. 59; Heiremans 1996, p. 55 no.56.

177. *'Calla' vase*, 1948
h 30 cm
Boston, Laura Venini Hillyer Collection

Tall vase in transparent glass veiled with strands of *lattimo* using the *fenicio* technique; gently tapering body rising to splayed mouth reminiscent of an arum lily. This may be the best-known example; *cf.* archive photo of the set presented at the 1948 Venice Biennale.

Catalogo rosso no. 3861, (set) nos 3862, 3863, 3864 (*'Calla' vase*).
Bibliography. Heiremans 1996, p. 75 no. 81; *Venini Venezia…*, 1998, no. 33.

178. *Snakes*, 1948
Location unknown

Coiled serpent figures with strongly iridised corroded finish; apparently a very limited production.

Catalogo rosso nos 2951, 2954, (set) nos 2951, 2954.

179. *Ducks*, 1938
l 50 cm each
Zülpich (Germany), Lösch Collection

Duck figures in heavy grey glass with strongly iridised finish.

Catalogo blu nos 2674, 2675bis fol. 51, (set) nos 2675A, 2672, 2673 fol. 51.
Exhibitions: Venice 1996.
Bibliography: *Gli artisti di Venini…*, 1996, p. 97 no. 91.
Il bestiario…, 1996, pp. 70–71 no. 58; *Venini Venezia…*, 1998, p. 65.

180. *Sparrows*, 1938
New York, Martin Cohen Collection

Sparrows in heavy tea-coloured glass with strongly iridised finish. Larger versions also exist, some with a corroded surface finish.

Catalogo blu nos 2626, 2635 fol. 51, (set) nos 2606, 2607, 2627, 2663, 2668, 2669, 2671 fol. 51; *Catalogo rosso* (set) nos 2626, 2627.
Exhibitions: Venice 1996.
Bibliography. *Gli artisti di Venini…*, 1996, p. 97 no. 90.
Vetro di Murano…, 1982, no.140; *Venezia…*, 1995, p. 413 no. 396; *Il bestiario…*, 1996, p. 69.

174

175

176

177

178

179

180

181. *Fish*, 1951
l 45 cm
Turin, Galleria Ecodiforme

Long fish form in blown glass with submerged tea-coloured layer; decorated on the surface with black and yellow filaments; eye insert of coral outlined with yellow filament. In 1951 Ken Scott was engaged by Macy's, New York, to set up a large window display to showcase Italian products. The display was created together with Ginette Venini, who arranged the glass fish amid classic Chioggia fishermen's baskets and nets. It was one of the first experiments in targeting Italian design for the American market.

Catalogo verde no. 422.0, (set) nos 422.1 (grey/sulphur-coral), 422.2 (tea/black-*fenicio*), 422.3 (tea/black), 422.4 (amethyst/tea-sulphur), 422.5 (crystal/grey-light blue), 422.6 (tea/orange), 422.7 (indigo), 422.8 (orange/black), 422.9 (orange/black), 422.10 (indigo/green *fenicio*), 422.11 (violet/coral), 422.12 (aquamarine/black), 422.13 (aquamarine/black *fenicio*), 423.14 (aquamarine/black *fenicio*), colours: the first indicated is the base colour, the second the main hue of the decoration.
Exhibitions: Venice 1996.
Bibliography: *Gli artisti di Venini...*, 1996, p. 126 no. 168.
'Venini 1963...', 1963, p. 41.

EUGÈNE BERMAN

182. *'Rovine' pieces*, 1951
Paris, Musée des Art Décoratifs; Venice, private collection; Rome, private collection

Table centrepiece composed of twelve pieces (seven obelisks and five goddesses) set in a sort of ruined underwater garden. The figurines are in strongly iridised crystal, with inclusions of gold powder. So delighted with the products he witnessed during a visit to the Venini glassworks, Eugène Berman in return proposed Paolo Venini this magnificent table centrepiece.
The few pieces still extant are scattered among various private collections.

Exhibitions: Venice 1996.
Bibliography: *Gli artisti di Venini...*, 1996, p. 125 nos 164–65, p. 126 no. 166.
Heiremans 1993, p. 269 no. 222; Heiremans 1996 p. 131 no. 109.

183. *Horn-shaped glasses*, 1954
h 20 cm; h 16 cm; h 21 cm
Milan, Fornasetti Collection

Drinking glasses in delicate straw-yellow blown glass styled like a hunting horn; Fornasetti's design bears all the hallmarks of his renowned humour and imagination. A devoted friend of Paolo Venini, upon the latter's death Fornasetti successfully campaigned for a *calle* in Venice be named in his honour.

Exhibitions: Venice 1996.
Bibliography: *Gli artisti di Venini...*, 1996, p. 134 no. 186.

RICCARDO LICATA

184. *'Murrina' bowl*, 1952–53 (pl. 143)
h 9 cm, Ø 12 cm
Union City (USA), Odetto Lastra Collection

Drinking bowl composed of patterned black and white *murrina* designed by the painter Riccardo Licata; welded band of transparent pale greenish-blue glass. These items were the fruit of a joint effort in which Licata designed the *murrina* and Paolo Venini the forms themselves. Versions include different combinations of welded bands, one of which with *murrina* inserts. Presented at the 1956 Venice Biennale.

Catalogo verde no. 518.2, (set) nos 518.0, 518.1, 518.2, 518.3, 518.4, 518.5, 518.6, colours: milk-white with assorted bands of *murrina* in two colours – violet/aquamarine, sapphire/green; sapphire/grey – with assorted *murrina* inserts, 518.2 and 518.4, a single colour – red, violet, pale greenish blue, sapphire – with assorted *murrina* inserts.
Bibliography: 'Arti decorative a Venezia', 1956, p. 65, nos 41–42; *Italienisches...*, 1987, p. 208, nos 169–70; Deboni 1989, nos 137–38; *L'arte del vetro...*, 1992, no. 362; Barovier Mentasti 1992, no. 98; Heiremans 1993, p. 281 no. 234; Barovier, Barovier Mentasti, Dorigato 1995, p. 182 no. 124; Ricke 1995, p. 237 no. 381; *Gli artisti di Venini...*, 1996, p. 133 no. 183, p. 134 nos 184–85.

185. *'Murrina' vase*, 1956
Location unknown

Vase in amethyst and sapphire glass decorated with a band of welded *murrina*.

Catalogo verde no. 518.5, (set) nos 518.0, 518.1, 518.2, 518.3, 518.4, 518.6.
Exhibitions: Venice 1956 (XXVIII Biennale); Venice 1996.
Bibliography: *XXVIII Esposizione...*, 1956, p. 552; 'Arti decorative alla Biennale', 1956, p. 37; *Italienisches...*, 1987, p. 208; Deboni 1989, nos 137–38; Heiremans 1993 p. 281 no. 234; *Murano. Fantasie di vetro*, 1994, p. 51 no. 40; Barovier, Barovier Mentasti, Dorigato 1995, p. 182 no. 124; *Gli artisti di Venini...*, 1996, p. 134 nos 184–85; Heiremans 1996, p. 133 nos 169–70.

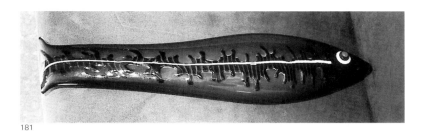

181

183

182

185

186. *'Occhi' vase*, 1960–61
Location unknown

Vase composed of eye-like crystal *murrina* inserts in a lattice of *lattimo*. Presented at the 1960 Milan Triennale and 1962 Venice Biennale.

Catalogo verde no. 520.1, (set) nos 520.0, 520.2, 520.3, 520.4, 520.5, 520.6, 520.7, 520.8, colours: crystal *murrina* 'eyes' in coral, milk-white, turquoise, tea, *murrina* crystal in coral, milk-white, turquoise, tea, sulphur; two-colour sets: crystal *murrina* 'eyes' in black/coral, black/milk-white, turquoise/milk-white.
Exhibitions: Venice 1996.
Bibliography: *Catalogo della XXXI Esposizione…*, 1962, p. 251; Warneke 1966, p. 75; *La verrerie…*, 1988, p. 11 no. 2; Deboni 1989, no. 165; *Vetri di Murano…*, 1991, pp. 96–97; *L'arte del vetro…*, 1992, no. 363; Barovier Mentasti 1992, nos 102, 114; *Gli artisti di Venini…*, 1996, pp. 150–51 nos 219–21; Deboni 1996, p. 308 no. 224; *Italienisches…*, 1996, p. 165 nos 153–54.

THOMAS STEARNS

187. *'Cappello del doge'*, 1962
h 13 cm
New York, private collection

Vase shaped like a doge's peaked cap in two double casing: base in yellow glass, band of crystal, band in antique green; surface iridised.

Exhibitions: Venice 1962 (XXXI Biennale); New York 1989; Venice 1996.
Bibliography: *Catalogo della XXXI Esposizione…*, 1962, p. 251; 'Nuovi vetri…', 1962, p. 38; Deboni 1989, no. 170; *The Venetians…*, 1989, p. 50 no. 52; *Vetri di Murano…*, 1991, pp. 104–5 no. 43; Barovier Mentasti 1992, no. 141; Barovier, Barovier Mentasti, Dorigato 1995, pp. 97, 199; *Venezia…*, 1995, p. 431 nos 567–68; *Gli artisti di Venini…*, 1996, p. 151 no. 223; Deboni 1996, p. 311 no. 227; Heiremans 1996, p. 159 no. 202; *Italienisches…*, 1996, p. 169 no. 158.

188. *'Facciate di Venezia'*, 1962
h 42 cm; h 39.5 cm
New York, Martin Cohen Collection

Vases constructed of glass rods applied in irregular patterns, in a range of brown hues; surface iridised.

Exhibitions: New York 1989; Venice 1996.
Bibliography: *Gli artisti di Venini…*, 1996, p. 152 no. 224.
Deboni 1989, no. 173; *The Venetians…*, 1989, no. 56; Barovier, Barovier Mentasti, Dorigato 1995, p. 97.

189. *Welded vase*, 1962
h 25 cm, ⌀ 10 cm
New York, Oswaldo Costa Collection

Small cylindrical vase with welded base in antique green glass and a band of crystal decorated with embedded threads of black glass; surface iridised.

Catalogo rosso no. 8632, (set) nos 8630, 8631, 8633, 8634; *Catalogo verde* no. 519.2, (set) nos 519.0, 519.1, 519.3, colours: vase green-straw-yellow with black threads; base antique red/pale blue with black threads; base anthracite/aquamarine with indigo threads; base anthracite/bright red with threads in antique red.
Bibliography: *Catalogo della XXXI Esposizione…*, 1962, p. 251; Deboni 1989, no. 171; Heiremans 1993, no. 244; *Gli artisti di Venini…*, 1996, p. 151 no. 222; Heiremans 1996, p. 162 nos 207–8; *Italienisches…*, 1996, pp. 167–68 nos 156–57; *Venini Venezia…*, 1998, p. 75.

GINETTE GIGNOUS

190. *'Piogge' vase*, 1965
h 26 cm; h 27 cm; h 30 cm; h 38 cm
New York, Oswaldo Costa Collection

Series of narrow vases made of long thin coloured rods submerged in walls of crystal. The design was thought up by Ginette, Paolo Venini's wife, who drew her idea from a printed fabric designed by the Finnish fashion designer Marimekko.

Catalogo verde nos 517.0, 517.1, 517.2, colours: 'estate' ('summer': *tessuto murrina* milk-white), 'primavera' ('spring': *tessuto murrina* milk-white/black).
Bibliography: *Gli artisti di Venini…*, 1996, p. 155 no. 232; *Italienisches…*, 1996, p. 175 no. 167.

186

187

188

189

190

191. *Polyhedron chandelier*, 1960
h 350 cm, ⌀ 230 cm
Rome, Farnesina, Ministery of Foreign Affairs,
International Meeting Room, Hall of Honour,
Main Foyer

Large light installations of hanging lamps and
wall-fittings composed of a cascade of small crystal polyhedrons; designed jointly with the architect Enrico Del Debbio.

Catalogo nero Sezione 3/Poliedri no. 3.8.

192. *'Canoa' dish*, 1960–61
l 60.5 cm
Venice, Anna Venini Collection

Canoe-shaped dish from the 'Battuti' series in
aquamarine glass, its entire surface lightly beat-
en. Produced in several colours: light green, pink,
light violet, yellow, tea, aquamarine. The other
forms were realised jointly with Tobia Scarpa.
Presented at the 1962 Venice Biennale.

Catalogo rosso nos 8500, 8501, 8502, 8503, 8504,
8505, 8506, 8507, 8508, 8509, 8510, 8511, 8512;
Catalogo verde no. 516.10.
Exhibitions: Venice 1996; Zurich 1998.
Bibliography. *Gli artisti di Venini...*, 1996, p. 145
no. 207; *Venini Glas...*, 1998, no. 54.
Gasparetto 1960, nos 54, 57; *Catalogo della XXXI
Esposizione...*, 1962, p. 251 no. 216; Deboni 1989,
nos 144–45; Heiremans 1993, no. 239.

193. *'Battuto' goblets*, 1960–61
(pl. 128; *cf.* pls 127, 129)
h 28 cm; h 20 cm
Turin, Galleria Ecodiforme

Goblets in amber-coloured glass, the entire surface having a light milled finish.
Exhibited together with the 'Battuti' series at the
1962 Venice Biennale, and the 1960 Milan Triennale.

Bibliography. *Catalogo della XXXI Esposizione...*,
1962, p. 251 no. 216; *Die Fünfziger...*, 1984, p. 51
no. 20; *Glass in Miami*, 1984, p. 101 nos 571–73;
Murano..., 1986, p. 170; Deboni 1989, no. 144;
The Venetians..., 1989, no. 15; *Venini...*, 1990,
p. 60; Heiremans 1993, p. 285 no. 239; Ricke 1995,
p. 238 no. 383; Heiremans 1996, p. 152 no. 192;
Italienisches..., 1996, p. 162 no. 150; *Il Vetro Italiano...*, 1998, p. 215 no. 152.

194. *Glass-drop lamps*, 1961
h 500 cm, ⌀ 250 cm each
Manchester, Airport Lobby

Large light fittings composed of crystal and grey
glass droplets; designed jointly with the architect
Stefan Buzas.

Catalogo nero Sezione 11/Gocce no. 11.1.
Bibliography. Mariacher 1967, p. 203; *Vetri Murano Oggi*, 1981, p. 128 no. 550.

195. *'Colletti' flasks*, 1961 (pl. 130)
h 22 cm; h 37 cm; h 30 cm
Turin, Gerard Figliola Collection

Flasks in thin blown glass with welded neck of
varying colours: light green with green neck;
straw-yellow with tea-coloured neck; aquamarine
with sapphire neck.

Catalogo verde nos 512.0, 512.1, 512.2, 512.3.
Bibliography. Mariacher 1967, p. 168a; *Glass in
Miami*, 1984, p. 102 no. 577; Dorigato 1986, p. 88;
Venini..., 1989, pl. 63; *Gli artisti di Venini...*,
1996, no. 233.

196. *Ceiling light*, 1962
l 750 cm (max), l 120 cm (min), h 120 cm
Montreal, Place des Arts, Auditorium

Ceiling-mounted light fitting with a cascade of
'fish-scale' crystal drops. Lengths vary from 750 to
120 centimetres; maximum height 120 centimetres.
Designed jointly with the architect Lebensold.

Catalogo nero Sezione 6/Pannelli no. 6.6.

197. *'Murrina' disc*, 1962 (pl. 131; *cf.* pl. 132)
⌀ 25 cm
Venice, Cassa di Risparmio, inv. 0005

Suspended roundel of flecked with motes of grey
anthracite. Employing the *murrina* technique Ludovico Diaz de Santillana devised a form of visual
divertimenti with this set of animals with bodies
in *murrina*, eggs, cylindrical boxes, all in submerged glass with *murrina* lids, and paper-
weights.

Exhibitions: Venice 1962 (XXXI Biennale); Venice
1996.
Bibliography. *Catalogo della XXXI Esposizione...*,
1962, p. 251; Deboni 1989, no. 157; *Vetri
veneziani del '900...*, 1994, no. 72; *Gli artisti di
Venini...*, 1996, no. 211.
Vetri Murano Oggi, 1981, p. 75 no. 345; *Vetro di
Murano...*, 1982, no. 222; *La verrerie...*, 1988,
p. 123 no. 4; Heiremans 1996, p. 166 no. 218; *Italienisches...*, 1996, pp. 158–61 nos 146–49,
p. 164 no. 152.

198. *'Cannette' vase*, 1963
h 33 cm
Tivoli, private collection

Tall vase in thin clear glass with the upper section
off wall embedded with rods to create a percolat-
ing effect descending from the rim; produced with
grey walls with coral rods; aquamarine walls with
indigo rods; amethyst walls with antique green
rods; straw-yellow walls with amber rods.

Catalogo verde nos 713.0, 713.1, 713.2, 713.3,
713.4, 713.5, 713.6, 713.7.
Bibliography. *Gli artisti di Venini...*, 1996, no. 234.

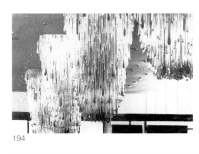
194

191

192

195

193

197

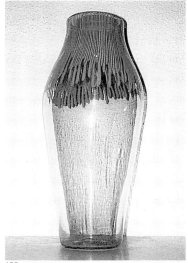
198

196

199. *'Petrolione'*, 1963–64
h 115 cm, ∅ 40 cm; h 83 cm, ∅ 40 cm
Venice, Anna Venini Collection

Tall table lamps in blown opaline glass, with upper section in white and the base grey; the variant has the base in amethyst opaline.

Exhibitions: Zurich 1998.
Bibliography: *Venini Glas...*, 1998, no.11.

200. *Ceiling light*, 1964
∅ 1300 cm
Ivrea, Olivetti, Headquarters

Large blown-glass ceiling luminaria composed of hexagonal modules of 40 centimetres. Overall diameter 13 metres. Design by Bernasconi & Fiocchi.

Catalogo nero Sezione 8/Moduli no. 8.2.

201. *Tortoise*, 1965 (pl. 133)
l 13 cm
Paris, private collection

Small tortoise figure in tea-coloured glass with *murrina* inserts of tea and blue.
A variant also exists in aquamarine; the one listed as no. 414.7 in the *Catalogo verde* comes with threads in tea, green, amber and milk-white.

Catalogo verde no. 414.8.
Exhibitions: Venice 1996.
Bibliography: *Gli artisti di Venini...*, 1996, no. 218.

202. *Furnishings for the Excelsior Bar*, 1967
Venice, Lido, Hotel Excelsior

Bar counter and tables for the bar in Hotel Excelsior at the Lido, Venice, fashioned in marbled *lattimo* and sapphire-coloured glass; cold-welded; other objects using the same technique were made, especially ashtrays.

Catalogo nero Sezione 6/Illuminazione no. 6.7.

203. *'Philips' cup*, 1968–70
h 18 cm
Badge: 'Venini Philips'
Location unknown

Rectangular chalice set on a tall cylindrical foot, with concentric rings trailed in blue, green, and red. Designed by Ludovico Diaz de Santillana for the Dutch company Philips at the end of the 1960s.

Bibliography: Deboni 1989, no. 175; *Vetri di Murano...*, 1991, pp. 110–11.

204. *Glassware for Pierre Cardin*,
1969 (pl. 134)
h 12 cm, l 18 cm; h 24 cm, l 12 cm
Turin, Galleria Ecodiforme

Square-section vases in solid clear glass, in crystal with indigo band, in cyclamen with turquoise band, in pale violet with orange band: h 12 cm, ∅ 12 × 12 cm; vase with six stackable receptacles: h 16 cm, ∅ 16 × 16 cm; mirrors in crystal with band in sulphur or orange, chrome-plated: h 30 cm, ∅ 30 × 30 cm, h 18 cm, ∅ 18 × 18 cm; ikebana vases in crystal with indigo or orange band, or in aquamarine with sulphur band: h 20 cm, ∅ 25 × 25 cm; h 12 cm, ∅ 18 × 18 cm; h 34 cm, ∅ 15 × 15 cm; h 13 cm, ∅ 12 × 12 cm; h 10 cm, ∅ 30 × 30 cm; h 40 cm, ∅ 18 × 18 cm.

This collection was presented at the fashion show staged at Maison Pierre Cardin in Paris, in 1969. Each item was carried in by one of the fashion models presenting Cardin's new line.

205. *'Grata' sconce*, 1970–75
h 20 cm
Venice, Anna Venini Collection

Wall-mounted light fittings realised in sphere of crystal with submerged *murrina*; colour range for the *murrina* inserts: grey crystal, or turquoise amethyst; chrome-plated armature.

Exhibitions: Zurich 1998.
Bibliography: *Venini Glas...*, 1998, no. 58.

206. *Chandelier-sculpture*, 1971
h 900 cm, l 250 cm
Singapore, Mandarin Hotel

Hanging light sculpture in a cascade of poured glass in metal moulds; mounted on a steel armature around a reinforced concrete pillar partly suspended from the ceiling, and partly emerging from the pool below; crystal with corroded finish; indirect illumination both upward and downward.

Catalogo nero Sezione 12/Mix no. 12.1

207. *Skylight*, 1971
l 90 cm (max), l 30 cm (min)
New York, Wall Street Branch,
Swiss Credit Bank

Foyer of the bank illuminated by a large ceiling panel made from *exprit* elements in crystal from 30 to 90 centimetres in diameter. Designed by Dietrich & Rosenbaum.

Catalogo nero Sezione 5/Exprit no. 5.1.

208. *High society*, 1975
Location unknown

Bottle and glasses in solid crystal with milled finish on most of the surface.
The ball-shaped stopper is not milled.

Bibliography: Mariacher 1967, p. 166; *Italian Re-evolution...*, 1982, p. 86 no. 2.

209. *'Murrina' egg*, 1975–78
h 12,5 cm
Venice, Anna Venini Collection

This piece forms part of a set of egg-shaped objects made with the *murrina* technique, or with coloured canes. Simple objects of a purely decorative function, the techniques used were however highly refined. They were highly successful, and the rod-based versions often appeared in Venini advertising.

Catalogo bianco nos 415.30, 415.31, 415.32 (*canne*), 415.21, 415.22, 415.23 (*filigrana*).
Bibliography: Deboni 1989, no. 174; Heiremans 1996, p. 175 no. 228.

210. *'Zanfirico Zeta'*, 1976
Location unknown

Blown-glass vessels worked free-hand with *zanfirico* canes.

Da Venini a Venini, 1978, nos 701.20, 701.21.

211. *'Zanfirico Emme'*, 1976
Location unknown

Blown-glass vessels worked free-hand with *zanfirico* canes.

Da Venini a Venini, 1978, nos 701.30, 701.31.

212. *'Mosche' pieces*, 1978
h 3.5 cm, ∅ 11; h 5 cm, ∅ 17 cm;
h 2.7 cm, ∅ 9 cm (three ashtrays);
h 3 cm, ∅ 17 cm (side-plate);
h 11 cm, ∅ 7.6 cm (each vase)
Location unknown

'Mosche' (Flies) set of three ashtrays, a side-plate, and a cylindrical container in crystal decorated with block *murrina* inserts.

213. *'Alabastro' lamps*, 1978
h 60 cm
Location unknown

Table-lamps with stand and shade made from imitation alabaster in green or brown tones. The peculiarity of this type of glass is that in order to achieve the patchy effect of the alabaster, the gob is dipped while still incandescent in a tub of tinted liquid. De Santillana made an entire set of lamps in this shape, but changed the stand and shade for mould-blown *rigadin* glass of transparent grey or white opaline.

214. *Jars with 'murrina' lids*, 1978
h 8 cm each
Venice, Anna Venini Collection

Little storage jars in orange, turquoise, green, milk-white, grey, and red, cased in a layer of crystal, with lids in crystal with cased *murrina* inserts.

215. *Large trilobate section ceiling fixture*, 1978
h 270 cm, ∅ 60 cm
Fulda (Germany), Schlosstheater

These large light fittings for the foyer of the Schlosstheater are composed of thousands of 'trilobate' elements suspended from metal chains. The installations covered a total of 400 m² of ceiling space, in colours ranging from tea to straw-yellow; each of the over 70,000 glass elements measuring 36 centimetres was fitted with a metal security device and sound-proofing.
Illumination with 2500 E27, 6W bulbs. Designed by Gerhard Weber & Partner.

Catalogo nero Sezione 1/Aste no. 1.1.
Bibliography: *Schlosstheater Fulda*, 1978.

216. *Ceiling light*, 1978
h 60 cm, ∅ 300 cm
Paris, Foire de Paris, Salon des Expositions de la Porte de Versailles

Recessed oval light fitting in hexagonal tubing of yellow glass. Designed jointly with the architect Bartal.

Catalogo nero Sezione 7/Tubi no. 7.4.

199

200

201

202

203

204

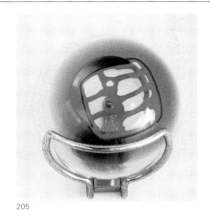
205

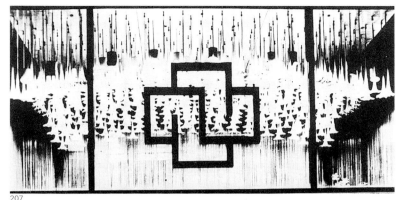
207

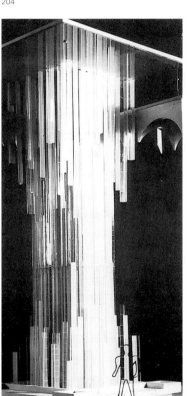
206

208

209

210

211

213

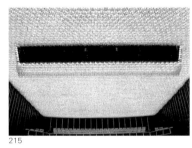
215

212

214

216

217. *Victor/Victoria sconces, c.* 1980
h 28 cm, ∅ 40 cm; h 20 cm, ∅ 30 cm
Venice, Anna Venini Collection

Wall-mounted light fitting; diffuser in white or black opaline, cube in transparent light pink or aquamarine glass; metal parts chrome-plated. The name of the light comes from the title of Blake Edwards' film *Victor/Victoria*.

Catalogo della nuova grafica Massimo Vignelli e Laura de Santillana nos 848.0, 848.01.

218. *'Tricorno' lamps*, 1982
h 206 cm, ∅ 30 cm each
Murano, Museo Venini

Floor-standing lamps; tricorn diffuser in opaline glass, hand-worked, available in white or black; shaft in striped white or black opaline; base in marble; metal parts lacquered.

Catalogo della nuova grafica Massimo Vignelli e Laura de Santillana no. 847.40.

219. *'Tessuto' lamps*, 1982
∅ 40 cm, ∅ 20 cm, ∅ 30 cm,
∅ 25 cm (table lamp); ∅ 40 cm
(suspended light); ∅ 40 cm (ceiling light)
Venice, Anna Venini Collection

Set comprising table, ceiling, and suspended lights in *tessuto* glass of crystal and *lattimo* worked freehand; metal parts lacquered white.

Catalogo della nuova grafica Massimo Vignelli e Laura de Santillana nos 819.0, 819.1, 819.2, 819.3, 819.12, 819.11, 819.18.

220. *Tolboi*, 1982
h 205 cm, ∅ 30 cm
Venice, Anna Venini Collection

Standard lamp: diffuser in white glass with crystal and coloured streaks; shaft in transparent glass with coloured core. Available colours: tea, sapphire, green. Base fixed with burnished brass; halogen lamp element.

Catalogo della nuova grafica Massimo Vignelli e Laura de Santillana no. 847.10.

221. *Fountain*, 1982
∅ 300 cm
Paris, Fourrures Georges V

Fountain in *alga* glass emerging from a small pond.

Catalogo nero Sezione 4/Alga no. 4.2

222. *'Tappeto volante'*, 1984 (pl. 135)
l 300 cm
Bern, Städtlicher Berner Waisenhaus

A new idea – a flying carpet – for creating overhead lighting installations, using floating 'ribbons' of glass: the elements are attached to a metal armature suspended from the ceiling on steel cables, and fitted with 20W halogen bulbs. The wave-like arrangement allows almost unlimited amplitudes and lengths. An example is housed in the Museo Venini on Murano.

Catalogo nero Sezione 10/Nastro no. 10.3.
Bibliography: Lumières..., 1985, p. 130 no. 64; *Gli artisti di Venini...*, 1996, p. 170 no. 264.

223. *Tazebao*, 1984 (pl. 137)
h 650 cm
Murano, Museo Venini

Large suspended light fitting composed of plates of crystal and blue; the installation is illuminated in the central section.

224. *Cube with layered silver-leaf*,
c. 1987 (pl. 136)
h 22 cm
Lausanne, private collection

Cube in dark grey solid glass sandwiched with alternating slivers of silver-leaf. A one-off piece created to commemorate two friends' 25 years of marriage.

225. *Cascade of striped rods*, 1983
l 320 cm (each rod);
l 600 cm (cascade)
Milan, Showroom Cassina

A cascade composed of striped rods of circular section, blown in crystal glass, and curved while hot. Each rod is 320 centimetres long; the overall size of the cascade is 600 centimetres. Design by Francesco Binfarè.

Catalogo nero Sezione 2/Canna no. 2.5.

217

218   220

219

221

222

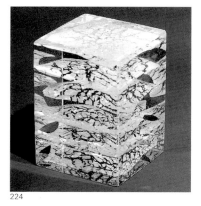
224

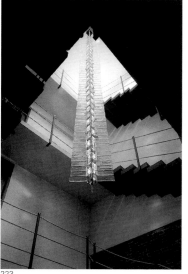
223

225

226. *'Spicchi' glassware*, 1952 (pl. 138)
h 32 cm (jar); h 12.5 cm (glasses)
Padua, Maurizio Graziani Collection

Tall cylindrical jar with irregular mouth; walls composed of wide vertical segments of glass in muted tones: straw-yellow, grey, pink, and crystal. Matching cylindrical glasses made with rods of the same colour. Examples housed in the Museum of Modern Art, New York.

Catalogo verde nos 333c (jar), 333.2 (glass).
Bibliography. Design Vignelli, 1981, p. 75; *La verrerie…*, 1988, p. 123 no. 1; Cousins 1989, p. 95; Deboni 1989, no. 113; *Gli artisti di Venini…*, 1996, p. 124 no. 162.

227. *Suspension lamps*, 1953–56 (pl. 139)
h 41 cm; h 34 cm
Udine, private collection

Ceiling light in *lattimo* glass with lower part of shade transparent with embedded streaks of blue, red, violet, green and blue. Weight distributed on suspended horizontal metal bar.

Bibliography. 'Vasi e lampade', 1956, pp. 45–48; Ponti 1959, p. 43; *Lumières…*, 1985, p. 128 no. 39; Barovier Mentasti 1992, pp. 101–2; *Gli artisti di Venini…*, 1996, pp. 16, 124.

228. *'Zaffiro 4000' table lamp*, 1956
h 34 cm, ∅ 27 cm
Venice, Anna Venini Collection

Table lamp in blown glass streaked with milk-white and amber rods; the piece won the 'Compasso d'Oro' design award in 1956.

Exhibitions: Milan 1998.
Bibliography. Il Vetro Italiano…, 1998, p. 217 no. 156.

229. *Articles in glass and silver*, 1963
h 24 cm; h 26 cm
Badged in diamond-point: 'Venini Murano'
Venice, Anna Venini Collection

Conceived jointly between Venini and Christofle Italia, these pieces are in composite engraved glass and silver-plate. Of the two jugs in question, one is in light blue submerged glass, and the other in glass submerged in a tea-coloured layer. Both are embellished with tiny incisions and machine-milled.

Exhibitions: Venice 1996.
Bibliography. Venini 1963…, 1963, pp. 41–47; 'Vetro e Metallo', 1963, s.p.; *Gli artisti di Venini…*, 1996, p. 148 no. 214.

230. *Neon*, c. 1980
h 15 cm
Venice, Anna Venini Collection

Letters of the alphabet composed in coloured cane submerged in crystal.
Intended for amusement, the letters were designed by Massimo Vignelli and Ludovico Diaz de Santillana in the Vignelli offices in New York. They were exhibited at a Macef trade fair, and each letter is presented in a black suede pouch.
Vignelli's collaboration with the Venini glasshouse included the redesign in 1982 of the firm's corporate identity, together with Laura Diaz de Santillana.

231. *'Groviglio' jar*, 1964
h 45 cm, ∅ 32 cm
Rome, Enrico Camponi Collection

Crystal vase with tangle of copper wire embedded in the base.

Catalogo verde no. 718.2, (set) nos 718.0, 718.1, 718.3, 718.4.
Bibliography. Barovier Mentasti 1992, no. 145; *Gli artisti di Venini…*, 1996, p. 153 no. 226; Heiremans 1996, p. 174 no. 227.

232. *'Crepuscolo' vase*, 1964
h 30 cm, ∅ 27 cm
London, Liliane Fawcett Collection

Noticeably rounded vase in which the dark solid part of the vessel fades up to transparency at the rim; the piece comes in aquamarine/indigo, amethyst/pale greenish blue, cyclamen/sapphire.

Catalogo verde no. 719.2, (set) nos 719.0, 719.1, 719.3, 719.4.
Bibliography. Heiremans 1993, p. 289 no. 243.

233. *'Giada' vase*, 1964 (pl. 140)
h 30 cm
Milan, Galleria In. Arte

Part of an assortment of glass objects designed in imitation of jade; made in opaque colours with inserts of antique-green copper, indigo, and brown.

Catalogo verde nos 720.0, 720.1, 720.2, 720.3, 720.4, 720.5, 720.6, 720.7.
Bibliography. Heiremans 1996, p. 179 no. 234.

234. *Ducks*, 1964
l 25 cm; l 35 cm
Venice, Anna Venini Collection

Ducks in solid glass in a variety of colours, submerged in crystal, with heads in brown and beaks in black glass.
The solid-glass duck figures of 1964 were created with the master glassblower Colelli, who travelled to Germany for a spell at the Rosenthal works; for this reason, or perhaps to simply effect a change of technique and design, Zuccheri later made a set of stylised *Ducks* in which the head and beak were elongated and in a single colour; in that instance the entire surface of the figure was milled, however.
There exist two small prototype vases made with the same cane technique used for the first set of *Ducks* without the milled finish; one of these is in the Oswaldo Costa Collection, New York; the other in the Anna Venini Collection, Venice.

Catalogo verde no. 413.0, (set) nos 513.1, 413.2, 413.3.
Exhibitions: Venice 1964 (XXXII Biennale).
Bibliography. Catalogo della XXXII Biennale…, 1964, p. 315; *Vetri Murano Oggi*, 1981, p. 72 nos 338–39; *Gli artisti di Venini…*, 1996, p. 154 no. 229; *Il bestiario…*, 1996, p. 118 no. 111.

226

227

229

228

230

231

234

232

233

235. *Turkey*, 1964 (pl. 141)
h 45 cm
Turin, private collection

Turkey figure with bronze armature made with the lost-wax process; body in blown *murrina lattimo* and crystal; head in *lattimo*; feet in bronze.

Catalogo verde no. 412.0.
Bibliography: Catalogo della XXXII Biennale..., 1964, p. 315 no. 344; Barovier, Barovier Mentasti, Dorigato 1995, p. 203 no. 156; *Il bestiario...*, 1996, p. 122 no. 113; Heiremans 1996, p. 176 no. 231.

236. *Guinea-fowl*, 1964
h 37 cm, l 27 cm
Venice, Cassa di Risparmio

Game-bird figurine in *murrina* flecked with anthracite grey, and head sculpted from black, white, and opaque red glass while hot; feet in fused bronze. For his 'bestiary', Zuccheri invented numerous animal figures in mixed coloured glass and bronze which, though omitted from the *Catalogo verde*, enjoyed much success. Notable items from the collection were the *Hoopoe*, the *Pheasant*, the *Owl*, the *Pigeons*, and the *Turtledove*.

Catalogo verde no. 412.1.
Bibliography: Catalogo della XXXII Biennale..., 1964, p. 314 no. 216; Mariacher 1967, p. 167; Mazzotti, Carta 1971, p. 157; *Vetro di Murano...*, 1982, nos 220–21; *Vetri veneziani del '900...*, 1994, p. 96 no. 79; *Gli artisti di Venini...*, 1996, p. 154 no. 228; *Il bestiario...*, 1996, p. 124 no. 115.

237. *Transparent bird figures*, 1966
Location unknown

Group of small bird figures in clear crystal tricked out with applied decorations in opaque glass; made in a variety of colours: crystal detailed with opaque red, orange, green, or turquoise.

Catalogo verde nos 414.0, 414.1, 414.2, 414.3, 414.4, 414.5, 414.6 (all l 20 cm).

238. *'Tronchi' series vase*, 1966
h 45 cm, Ø 11 cm
San Vito al Tagliamento, Toni Zuccheri Collection

Vase in opaque amber glass mould-blown in the form of a tree-trunk with relief ribbing; realised in various colours: opaque antique-red, antique-green, milk-white, amber, black, indigo, crystal ribbing.

Catalogo verde no. 714.0, (set) nos 714.1, 714.2, 714.3.
Bibliography: Heiremans 1993, p. 291 no. 245; *Gli artisti di Venini...*, 1996, p. 155 no. 230; Heiremans 1996, p. 184 no. 242; *Italienisches...*, 1996, p. 175 no. 166.

239. *'Scolpiti' series vase*, 1968
h 25 cm
New York, Oswaldo Costa Collection

Vase in *lattimo* submerged in crystal and decorated with deeply milled grooves exposing the underlying layer; comes in various versions: antiqued-red opaque, antique-green, milk-white, amber, black, indigo, with crystal grooves.

Catalogo verde no. 717.1, (set) nos 716.0, 716.1, 716.2, 716.3, 717.0, 717.2, 717.3 (milled), 717.4.
Bibliography: Catalogo della XXXIV Esposizione..., 1968, p. 173 no. 132; Cousins 1989, p. 85; Barovier, Barovier Mentasti, Dorigato 1995, p. 216 no. 177; *Venezia...*, 1995, p. 425 nos 618–19; *Gli artisti di Venini...*, 1996, p. 155 no. 231; Deboni 1996, p. 315 no. 231; Heiremans 1996, p. 183 nos 240–41; *Italienisches...*, 1996, p. 175 no. 165, p. 176 no. 168; *Venini Venezia...*, 1998, p. 76.

240. *'Murrina' jar*, 1979
New York, Oswaldo Costa Collection

Cylindrical jar in crystal, straw-yellow, green, and tea glass; surface milled and polished.
This little container was part of a set ordered by the jeweller Gio Caroli, but never went into production, which is why it is missing from the *Catalogo verde*.
Zuccheri's idea for the transparent 'Murrine' collection seems to have drawn inspiration from Paolo Venini's 'Murrine romane' creations of 1936.

Bibliography: Gli artisti di Venini..., 1996, p. 163 no. 250.

235

236

237

240

238

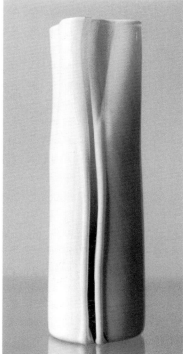
239

241. *Two vases in silver and glass*, 1965
h 40 cm, ∅ 40 cm; h 49 cm, ∅ 50 cm
Location unknown

Vases in silvered crystal; base in white or red lacquer; interior in aluminium.

TAPIO WIRKKALA

242. *'Bolle' vessels*, 1966
h 42 cm (max), h 15 cm (min)
Pavia, private collection

Set of vessels fashioned in transparent free-blown glass sections in two or three colours, welded at the seams; colours include grey, apple-green, tea, red, straw-yellow, sky-blue, and pale violet.

Catalogo verde nos 502.0, 502.1, 502.2, 502.3, 503.0, 503.1, 503.2, 503.4, 503.5, 503.6.
Exhibitions: Venice 1996.
Bibliography. Gli artisti di Venini..., 1996, p. 158 no. 238.
Mazzotti, Carta 1971, p. 155; *Venezianisches...*, 1981, p. 79; *Vetri Murano Oggi*, 1981, nos 512–16; *Barovier Mentasti* 1982, p. 307 no. 322; *Mille Anni...*, 1982, p. 311 no. 653; *Design...*, 1984, p. 115 no. II–74; *Glass in Miami*, 1984, p. 102 no. 585; *Tapio...*, 1987, p. 24 no. 25; *Venini...*, 1989, pls 48–49; *Venini Venezia...*, 1998, p. 77.

243. *'Coreani' vessels*, 1966
h 35 cm, ∅ 20 cm; h 13 cm, ∅ 20 cm
Venice, Anna Venini Collection

Set of vessels in blown glass in two colours: pale greenish blue and apple-green in a spiralling overlay.

Catalogo verde nos 500.0, 500.1, 500.2, 500.3, 500.4.
Exhibitions: Venice 1996.
Bibliography. Gli artisti di Venini..., 1996, p. 158 no. 237.
Tapio..., 1983, p. 28 no. 191; *Design...*, 1984, p. 115 no. II–73; *Glass in Miami*, 1984, p. 102 no. 583; *Tapio...*, 1987, p. 12 no. 13; *Venini...*, 1989, pls 93–94; *Venini Venezia...*, 1998, p. 76.

244. *'Pianissimo'*, 1966
h 20 cm
Venice, Anna Venini Collection

Vase in grey blown glass with welded turquoise band.
This highly refined piece of glasswork is technically very complex, and its success was limited; as a result, very few examples exist. Possible colours include grey, pale violet, violet, sky-blue.

Catalogo verde no. 504.0, (set) nos 504.1, 504.2, 504.3, 504.4, 504.5.
Exhibitions: Venice 1966 (XXXIII Biennale).
Bibliography. Gli artisti di Venini..., 1996, p. 159 no. 239.
Catalogo della XXXIII Esposizione..., 1966, p. 259; *Tapio...*, 1987, p. 29; *Venini...*, 1989, pl. 47.

245. *'Medusa' vase*, 1966
h 12 cm
Venice, Anna Venini Collection

Vase with spiralling filaments of embedded *mezza filigrana* in mauve or aquamarine glass; the thickness of the walls diminishes towards the top, where the rim splays out in a falling curve.
The vase was part of a set listed in the *Catalogo verde*, also available in *filigrana lattimo* threads submerged in walls of mauve or aquamarine.

Catalogo verde no. 501.1, (set) nos 501.0, 501.1, 501.2, 501.3, 501.4.
Bibliography. Catalogo della XXXIII Esposizione..., 1966, p. 249; *Gli artisti di Venini...*, 1996, p. 159 no. 240.3.
Tapio..., 1987, p. 29; *Cousins* 1989, p. 85; *Italienisches...*, 1996, p. 177 no. 169.

246. *'Ai lieti calici'*, 1966
h 11 cm, ∅ 35 cm
Venice, private collection

Blown-glass plate in the most delicate violet hue, with base in solid crystal enclosing a large air bubble.

Catalogo verde no. 510.0, (set) nos 510.1, 510.2, 510.3, 510.4, 510.5, 510.6.
Exhibitions: Venice 1966 (XXXIII Biennale).
Bibliography. Catalogo della XXXIII Esposizione..., 1966, p. 249 no. 239; *Vetri Murano Oggi*, 1981, p. 117 nos 519, 520, 521; *Tapio...*, 1987, p. 30; *Museum Bellerive...*, 1992, p. 32 no. 37; *Vetri veneziani del '900...*, 1994, p. 103 no. 88.

247. *'Gondolieri' series vases*, 1966–69
Location unknown

Free-blown vases in with welded base in solid glass; hat-rim aperture in grey, yellow, red, violet, or aquamarine.

Catalogo verde no. 507.2, (set) nos 507.0, 507.1, 507.3, 507.4, 507.5.
Bibliography. Tapio..., 1987, p. 30; *Museum Bellerive...*, 1992, p. 33 no. 38.

248. *Silmä*, 1966–69
h 20 cm
Location unknown

Vase in heavy black glass emblazoned with yellow *murrina* eye-motifs; made in variations with apple-green base and black and violet eye; with black base and yellow eye, or vice versa.

Catalogo verde no. 509.0, (set) nos 509.1, 509.2.
Bibliography. Tapio..., 1987, p. 30.

241

242

243

244

245

246

247

248

249. *'Tapio' dish*, 1969–70
⌀ 50 cm
Location unknown

Dish in pale grey glass with central boss-like insert in aquamarine; free-blown piece with welded central element. During this period Wirkkala explored the design through numerous variants of both type and decoration; examples were exhibited at the 1970 Venice Biennale.

Catalogo verde nos 511.50 (⌀ 50 cm), 511.40 (⌀ 40 cm), 511.30 (⌀ 30 cm): plates with *murrina* inserts in twelve different styles with rim in transparent colour and central element in *murrina*, identified with letters from 'A' to 'M'; *Catalogo nero* nos 529.0, 529.01; *Catalogo commerciale Venini* nos 529.2 (⌀ 50 cm): four plates with the centre moulded in blocks of three colours (from border to centre: grey, cyclamen, crystal; grey, cyclamen, pink; grey, cyclamen, aquamarine; straw-yellow, grey, pink), 530.0 (⌀ 50 cm): four plates with thick moulded centre in the following four hues: grey, cyclamen, pink, aquamarine; grey, cyclamen, straw-yellow, aquamarine; grey, cyclamen, pink, tea; straw-yellow, tea, cyclamen, black, 531.0 (⌀ 42 cm): four plates with outer rim in colour with suspended copper inclusions and coloured centre (aquamarine, straw-yellow, black centre; pale apple-green, straw-yellow, black centre; pale grey, pale violet, red centre; pale greenish blue, tea, straw-yellow centre), 532.0 (⌀ 40 cm): one plate in smoked opalescent glass with gold centre, designed by Sami Wirkkala.
Bibliography. Catalogo della XXXV Esposizione..., 1970, p. 134; *Vetri Murano Oggi*, 1981, p. 117 no. 509; *Tapio...*, 1987, p. 31; *Vetri veneziani del '900...*, 1994, p. 121 no. 109; *Gli artisti di Venini...*, 1996, p. 161 no. 243; *Italienisches...*, 1996, pp. 178–79 nos 170–71.
Vetri veneziani del '900..., 1994, pp. 116–17 nos 103–4.

250. *'Filigrane di Tapio' series cup*,
1972 (*cf.* pl. 142)
h 12.5 cm
Venice, Anna Venini Collection

Cup in free-blown glass with black *filigrana* cane trailed through a core of welded opaline.
Another example of free-blown glass with opaline *filigrana* trailed through the white core at the Kunstsammlungen der Veste at Coburg (inv. a.S. 4573/86: h 20 cm, ⌀ 23 cm), listed in the 1978 *Catalogo nero* as no. 534.1.
Wirkkala made two exceptionally fine glasses at the end of the 1960s in crystal and *lattimo* cross-threaded with crystal and pale violet. (*cf. Gli artisti di Venini...*, 1996, p. 159 no. 242; *Museum Bellerive...*, 1992, p. 33 no. 39).
The *murrina* techniques preferred by the Finnish designer were *incalmo* or welded casings, and *filigrana* (twisted threads); his passion was such that he soon perfected his expertise.

Catalogo nero 1978, no. 533.2, (set) nos 534.1, 534.0, 534.2, 537.1, 533.3, 537.0, 533.0, 533.1 (group of vases, cups and plates in black and white *filigrana*).
Bibliography. Vetri di Murano..., 1977, no. 73; Heiremans 1996, p. 193 no. 254.

251. *'Pavoni' vases*, 1972
h 31 cm, ⌀ 10 cm; h 20 cm, ⌀ 12 cm
Location unknown

Two free-blown vases with upper section in grey *filigrana* and lower in solid red: the 'peacock-tails' set includes various bottles in straw-yellow and apple-green patches, or straw-yellow with red patches (without *filigrana*); these correspond to nos 526.40, 526.41 (h 21 cm, ⌀ 9 cm; h 30 cm, ⌀ 8 cm); the series is very rare.

Bibliography. Tapio..., 1983, p. 12 no. 67; *Tapio...*, 1987, p. 33.

MIROSLAV HRSTKA

252. *Mirostre*, 1968 (pl. 144)
h 35 cm
Murano, Museo Venini

Vase in solid amethyst-coloured glass cut with deep spiralling grooves. Hrstka created this set of vases in unprecedented and unusual shapes; the series included versions in prune, brass, and bronze, with a sculpted surface; exhibited at the 1968 Venice Biennale.
Other items appearing the *Catalogo verde* are only known from drawings: *Mirosuno* nos 724.0, 724.1 (cornelian), 724.2 (putrid, sculpted surface); *Mirosdue*, nos 725.0, 725.1, 725.2, 725.3 (herb-green, brown, *acqua*, cyclamen, milled surface); *Hrstka*, nos 726.0, 726.1 (violet, cornelian, engraved surface).

Catalogo verde no. 727.0, (set) nos 727.1, 727.2.
Exhibitions: Venice 1996.
Bibliography. Gli artisti di Venini..., 1996, no. 236. Barovier Mentasti 1992, p. 161 no. 149; Barovier, Barovier Mentasti, Dorigato 1995, p. 216 no. 178; Deboni 1996, p. 319 no. 235; *Italienisches...*, 1996, pp. 172–74 nos 162–64.

RICHARD MARQUIS

253. *'Murrina' vases*, 1970 (pl. 145)
h 11 cm; h 7 cm
Seattle, Richard Marquis Collection

Group of small vases, two made from canes of yellow and grey, two in *murrina* with a stars-and-stripes motif after the American flag. Marquis decided to specialise in *murrina*, and nearly all of his designs are based on this technique. Regrettably, most of his production for Venini was destroyed in the factory fire in 1973.

Exhibitions: Venice 1996.
Bibliography. The Venetians..., 1989, no. 57; *Gli artisti di Venini...*, 1996, p. 162 no. 246; Oldknow 1997, p. 48 nos 14–15.

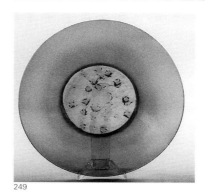
249

251

250

252

253

254. *Calabash*, 1972
∅ 30 cm; h 13 cm; h 21 cm;
h 18 cm; h 32 cm
Turin, Galleria Ecodiforme

Plate, cup, and three vases in opaque coloured *zanfirico* glass; plate in black/yellow/sulphur glass cased in black; vase in orange/yellow/green; vase in yellow/sulphur/green; cup in milk-white/yellow/green; vase in black/red/turquoise.

Exhibitions: Venice 1996.
Bibliography: *Vetri Murano Oggi*, 1981, nos 331–32; *Gli artisti di Venini…*, 1996, p. 163 no. 251.

255. *'Tessuto' vases*, 1974 (pl. 146)
h 18 cm; h 9 cm; h 16 cm
New York, private collection

Three vases of linear design made from woven canes submerged in crystal. The set was created jointly with Laura Diaz de Santillana, who designed their forms.

OVE THORSSEN – BIRGITTA CARLSSON

256. *'Merletti' vases*, 1972–74
h 24 cm; h 32 cm
Murano, Museo Venini

Set of vases made with a characteristic 'merletto' (lacework) of *lattimo* decoration cased in crystal. The floral decoration of *lattimo* strands is obtained through acid corrosion; each piece being worked is subjected to two phases of treatment, the first while the hot gather is still malleable, the second when cold, a practice of Nordic origin not often employed on Murano.

Catalogo nero nos 609.00, 609.01, 609.02, 609.03.
Exhibitions: Venice 1996.
Bibliography: *XXXVI Esposizione…*, 1972, p. 165; *Manualità…*, 1980, p. 72 no. 72; *Vetri Murano Oggi*, 1981, no. 334; *Venini…*, 1990, no. 65; *Gli artisti di Venini…*, 1996, p. 162 no. 247.

257. *'Piume' glassware*, 1974
h 36 cm, ∅ 21 cm (vase);
h 10 cm, ∅ 55 cm (dish)
Venice, Anna Venini Collection

'Feathers' vase and dish in indigo-coloured glass with grey submerged streaks. Also belonging to this 'family' is another vessel, not listed in the catalogue.

Catalogo nero nos 610.00, 610.01.
Bibliography: *Vetri Murano Oggi*, 1981, p. 72 no. 336.

258. *'Opulus' vases*, 1976
h 20 cm; h 32 cm
Venice, Anna Venini Collection

Two vases sporting aquamarine *rigadin retorto* ribbing; upper section with close spirals running counter to the more widely spaced ones below. Pieces were produced in combinations of crystal/grey, aquamarine/indigo, and amethyst/violet.

Catalogo nero nos 611.00, 611.01, 611.02.
Exhibitions: Venice 1996.
Bibliography: *Vetri Murano Oggi*, 1981, no. 333; *Gli artisti di Venini…*, 1996, p. 162 no. 248.

259. *'Optical' glassware*, 1976
h 12 cm (max); h 9 cm (min)
Venice, Anna Venini Collection

Matching glassware in clear glass with vertical *rigadin* ribbing; rims trimmed with aquamarine; colours include crystal with tea-coloured rim; crystal with aquamarine rim; crystal with green rim.

Catalogo nero nos 346.00 (glass), 346.01 (glass), 346.02 (glass), 346.04 (small cup), 345C (carafe).

LAURA DIAZ DE SANTILLANA

260. *'Numeri' disc*, 1975
∅ 25 cm
Corning (USA), The Corning Museum of Glass

Oval crystal 'numbers' disc fashioned from coloured *murrina* canes, inset with sequences of glass numerals, welded and milled. Awarded the 'New Glass '79' prize from the Corning Museum of Glass.

Catalogo nero no. 0048.824.
Exhibitions: Corning (New York) 1979.
Bibliography: *Mille Anni…*, 1982, p. 310 no. 652; *Glass in Miami*, 1984, p. 103 no. 599; Barovier Mentasti 1992, p. 158 no. 146; *Gli artisti di Venini…*, 1996, p. 164 no. 252.

261. *'Quattro stagioni' disc*, 1976
∅ 35 cm
Venice, Laura Diaz de Santillana Collection

One of the four discs bearing a central *murrina* tree emblem in a different colour, denoting the seasons of the year; milled surface. Entry won a prize at the 'New Glass '79 – Worldwide Survey' exhibition in 1979.
The same concept applies to the central *murrina* insert and surface milling for the four 'Pianeti' (Planets) dishes (∅ 35 cm) bearing symbols of the Moon, Star, Sun, Earth at their centre (*cf. Catalogo rosa* nos 0048.833, 0048.834, 0048.835, 0048.836).

Catalogo nero nos 0048.820 (*Spring*: green dish with tree insert in opaque green *murrina*), 0048.821 (*Autumn*: tea-coloured dish with dark tea-coloured *murrina* tree insert), 0048.822 (*Winter*: green dish with opaque green *murrina* tree insert), 0048.823 (*Summer*: red with orange *murrina* tree insert).
Exhibitions: Corning (New York) 1979; Venice 1981; Venice 1996.
Bibliography: *Vetri Murano Oggi*, 1981, p. 66 no. 347; Barovier Mentasti 1982, p. 309 no. 324; *Gli artisti di Venini…*, 1996, pp. 165–66 nos 251–54; *Venini Venezia…*, 1998, p. 79.

262. *'Mimosa' disc*, 1977 (pl. 147)
∅ 25 cm
Murano, Museo Vetrario

Disc in crystal made of welded yellow and grey *murrina* canes; surface milled. Also belonging to this series are the *murrina* creations *Glicine* (Wisteria), and *Geranio* (Geranium) (*cf. Catalogo rosa* nos 0048.828, 0048.829)

Catalogo nero no. 0048.827; *Catalogo rosa* no. 0048.827.
Exhibitions: Venice 1996.
Bibliography: *Vetri Murano Oggi*, 1981, no. 346; *Gli artisti di Venini…*, 1996, p. 166 no. 254.

254

255

256

257

259

260

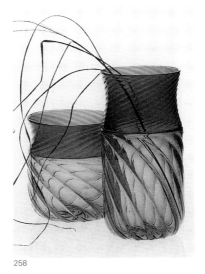
258

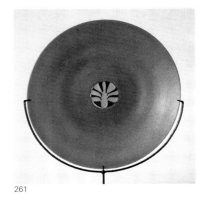
261

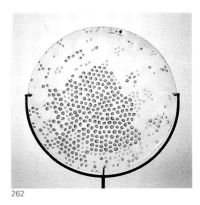
262

263. *'Klee' vase*, 1978 (pl. 148)
h 25 cm
Murano, Museo Vetrario

Vase with diagonal cane texturing in milk-white, grey, amethyst, straw-yellow, petrol, aquamarine, green; interior cased in *lattimo*.

Catalogo bianco no. 781.00.
Exhibitions: Venice 1981; Venice 1996.
Bibliography: *Vetri Murano Oggi*, 1981, no. 344; *Vetro di Murano...*, 1982, no. 219; *Gli artisti di Venini...*, 1996, p. 168 no. 257.

264. *'Biro' vases*, 1982
h 28 cm; h 40 cm; h 20 cm
Venice, Laura Diaz de Santillana Collection

Three widely splayed conical vases tapering to a sphere of solid crystal cased in crystal in a range of colour combinations: pewter/sulphur, turquoise/sapphire, green/cyclamen.

Catalogo bianco nos 783.00, 783.01, 783.02.
Exhibitions: Venice 1996.
Bibliography: *Gli artisti di Venini...*, 1996, p. 168 no. 258.

265. *'München' cup*, 1983
h 28 cm, Ø 40 cm
Venice, Anna Venini Collection

Large cup with bowl in transparent crystal resting on a base of solid beaten glass with an irregular shape, like a stone.

Catalogo bianco nos 555.00, 555.01, 555.02.
Exhibitions: Venice 1996.
Bibliography: *Gli artisti di Venini...*, 1996, p. 168 no. 259.

ALESSANDRO DIAZ DE SANTILLANA

266. *'Ustorio' lamp*, 1983
h 66 cm, Ø 21 cm
Venice, private collection

Halogen table lamp in glass and chrome-plated iron. The round dish of transparent milled *murrina* both diffuses and reflects the light back down towards the table worktop; the reflecting dish is on a swivel and can be oriented to adjust the amount of light reflected.

Catalogo azzurro no. 847.12

267. *'Coccio' vase*, 1984 (pl. 149)
h 16 cm
Venice, Alessandro Diaz de Santillana Collection

Small vase in *murrina* tesserae of transparent amber- and ivory-coloured glass.

Catalogo bianco no. 508.00.
Exhibitions: Venice 1996.
Bibliography: *Gli artisti di Venini...*, 1996, p. 169 no. 261.

TINA AUFIERO

268. *'Alboino' vase*, 1983 (pl. 150)
h 27 cm
Venice, Anna Venini Collection

Vase in solid amethyst-coloured glass, fitted with four full-height 'handles' in crystal.

Catalogo bianco no. 779.00, (set) no. 779.01 (*Rosmunda*, colours: sapphire/aquamarine, amethyst/red, apple-green/straw-yellow).
Exhibitions: Venice 1996.
Bibliography: *Gli artisti di Venini...*, 1996, p. 169 no. 260.

TOOTS ZYNSKY

269. *'Folto' vases*, 1984 (pl. 151)
h 13 cm, Ø 23 cm;
h 31 cm, Ø 23 cm;
h 18 cm, Ø 24 cm
Venice, Laura Diaz de Santillana Collection

Vase in opaque green glass decorated with web-like mesh of trailed orange thread; vase with body in opaque green and milk-white trimmed with pink mesh; vase in opaque blue with pink mesh.
Master glassblower Checco Ongaro.

Catalogo bianco nos 541.00 (green with orange mesh), 541.01 (green/milk-white with pink mesh), 541.02 (blue with pink mesh).
Exhibitions: Venice 1996.
Bibliography: *Gli artisti di Venini...*, 1996, p. 170 no. 262.

270. *'Chiacchera' vases*, 1984 (pl. 152)
h 34 cm, Ø 19 cm; h 27 cm, Ø 18 cm
Venice, Laura Diaz de Santillana Collection

Two wineskin-shaped vases in opaque blue and green glass, decorated with spiral trails; out-turned lip in contrasting colour.
Master glassblower Checco Ongaro.

Catalogo bianco nos 541.20 (green with black trails), 541.21 (blue with turquoise trails).
Exhibitions: Venice 1996.
Bibliography: *Museum Bellerive...*, 1992, p. 128 no. 189; *Gli artisti di Venini...*, 1996, p. 170 no. 263.

263

264

265

267

266

268

269

270

Historical Catalogues

General Note

*Three of the company's official
catalogues are reproduced here:*
Catalogo blu, *which covers production
for the early 1930s, but contains some
from 1921 onwards; published here
is the most complete version of that
catalogue and arranged by type;*
Catalogo rosso, *covering production
for the 1950s;*
Catalogo verde, *published in 1969,
covering all production from 1921,
with variant series.*

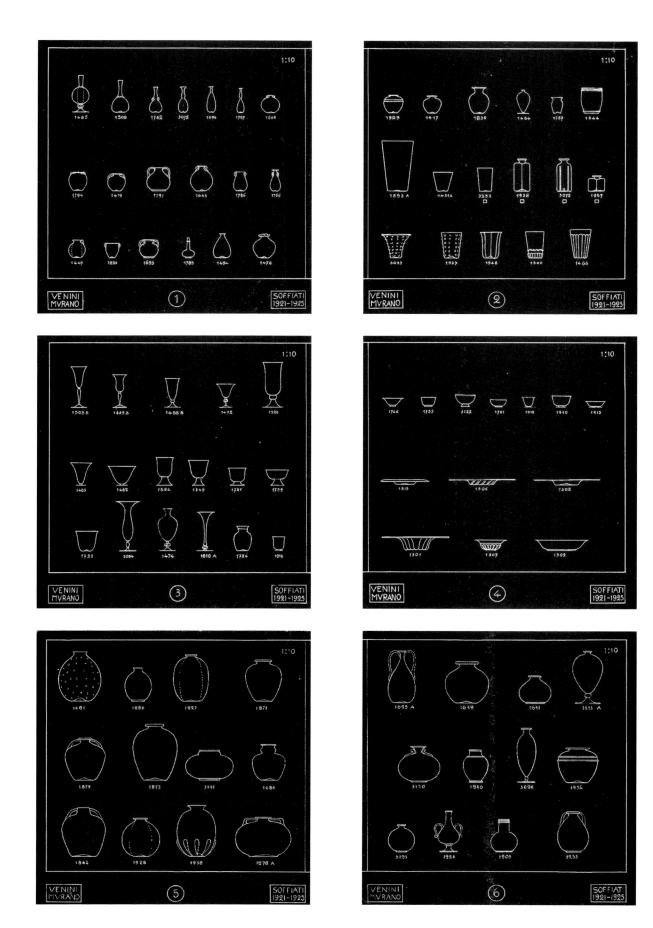

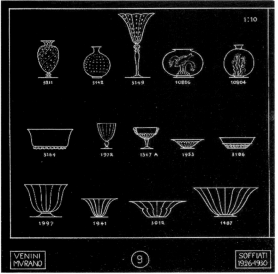

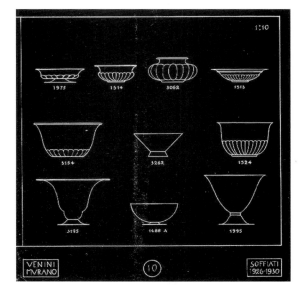

236

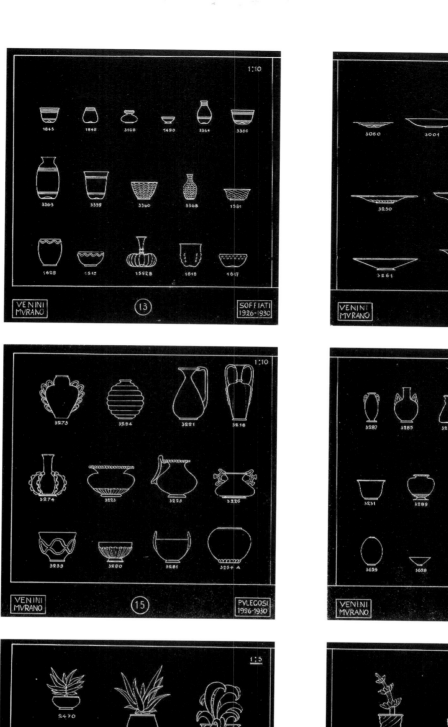

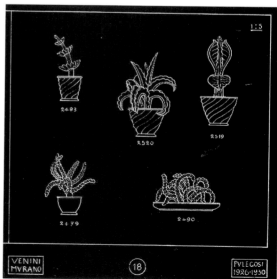

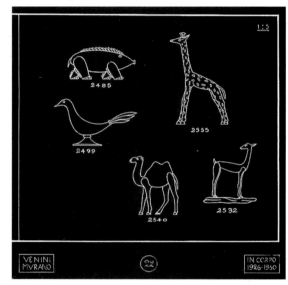

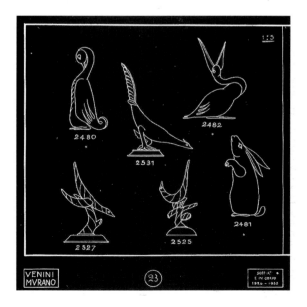

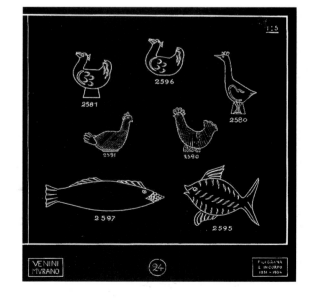

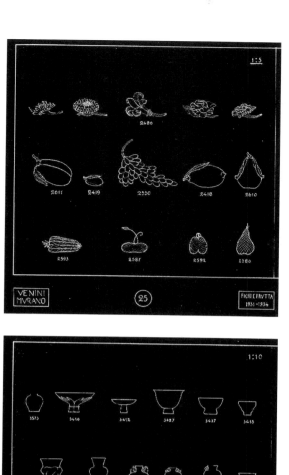

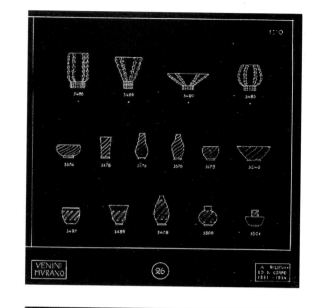

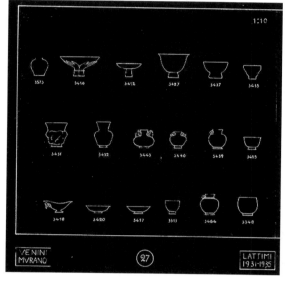

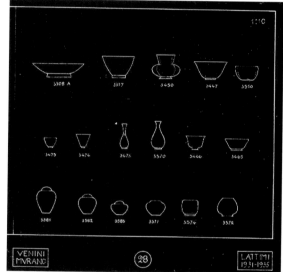

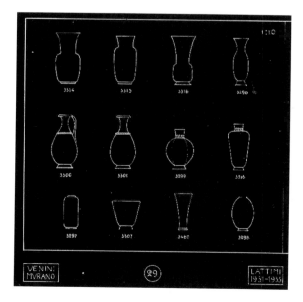

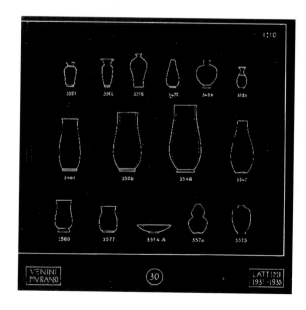

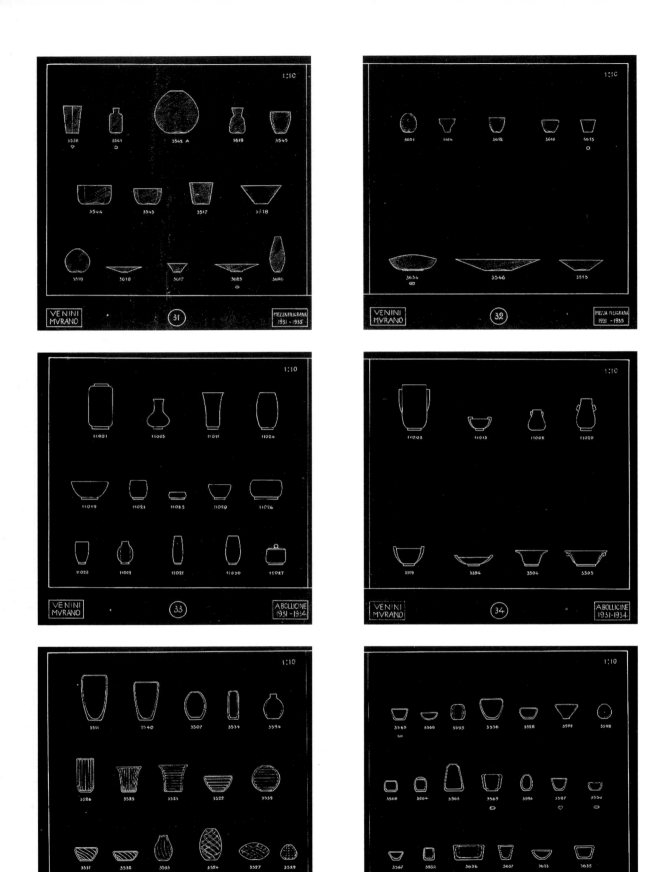

Catalogo blu, fols 37, 38, 39, 40, 41, 42

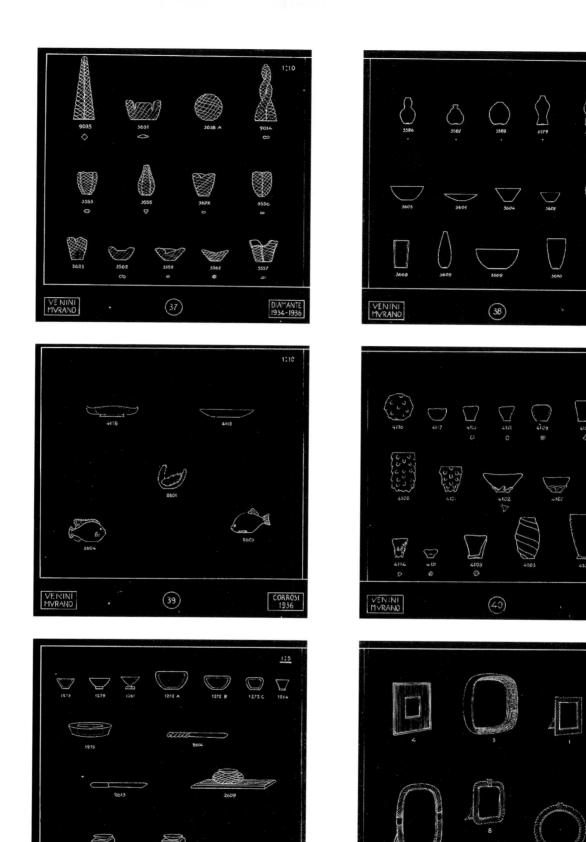

241

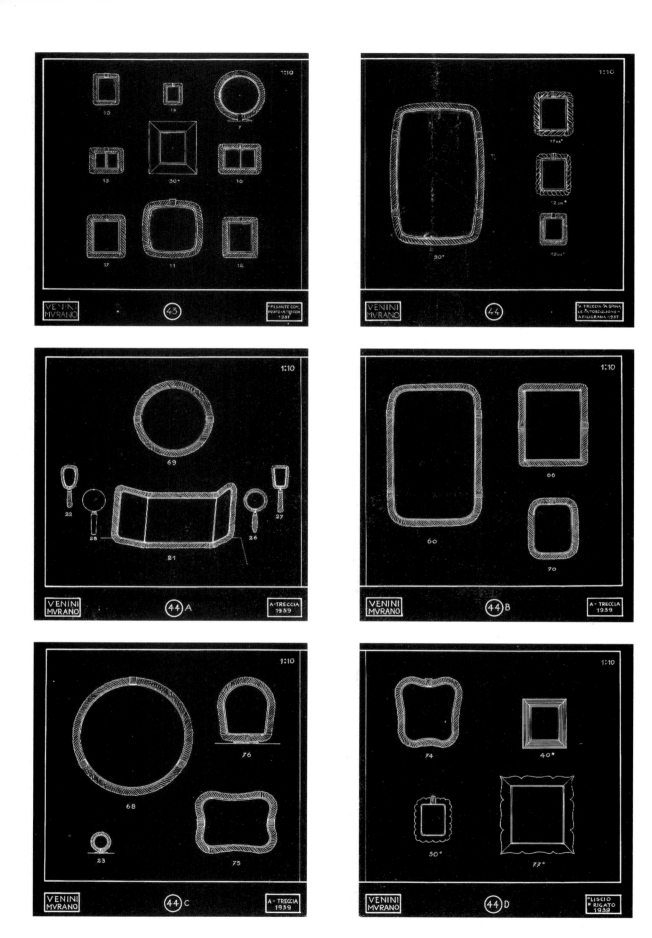

242

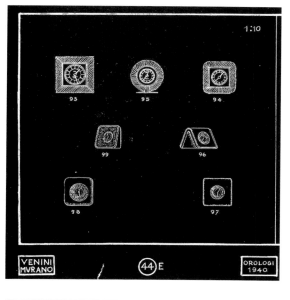

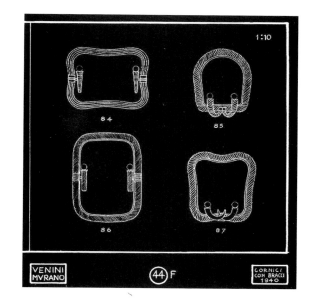

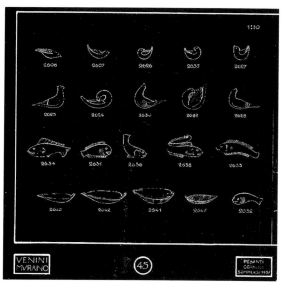

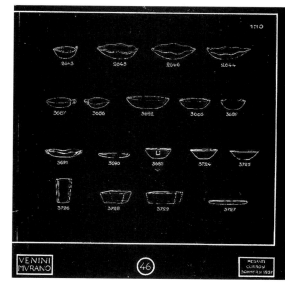

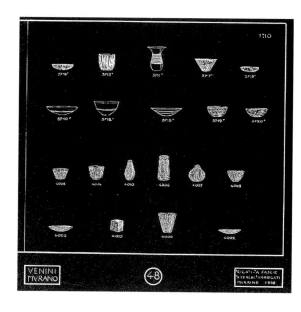

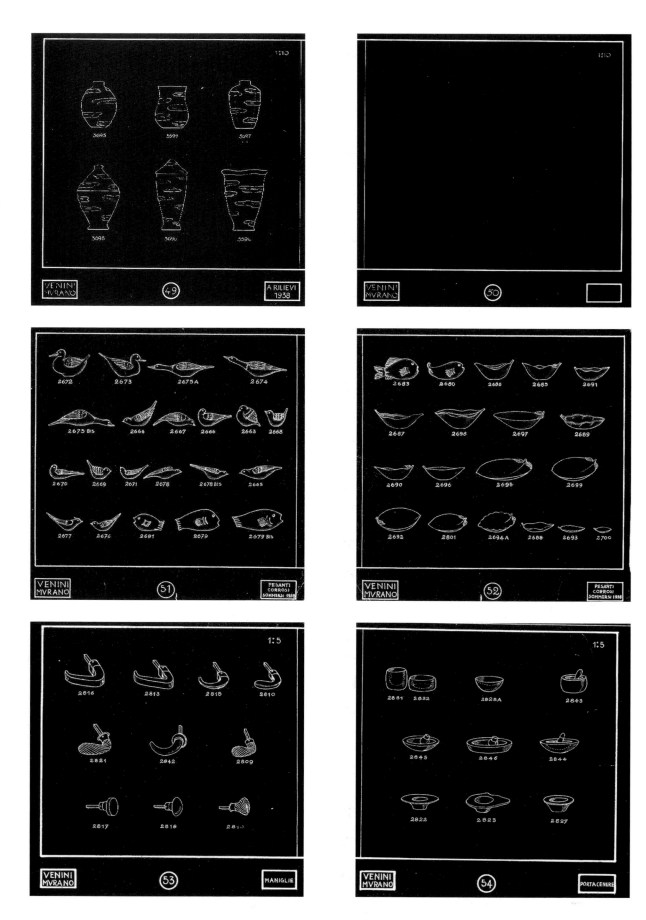

Catalogo blu, fols 49, 50, 51, 52, 53, 54

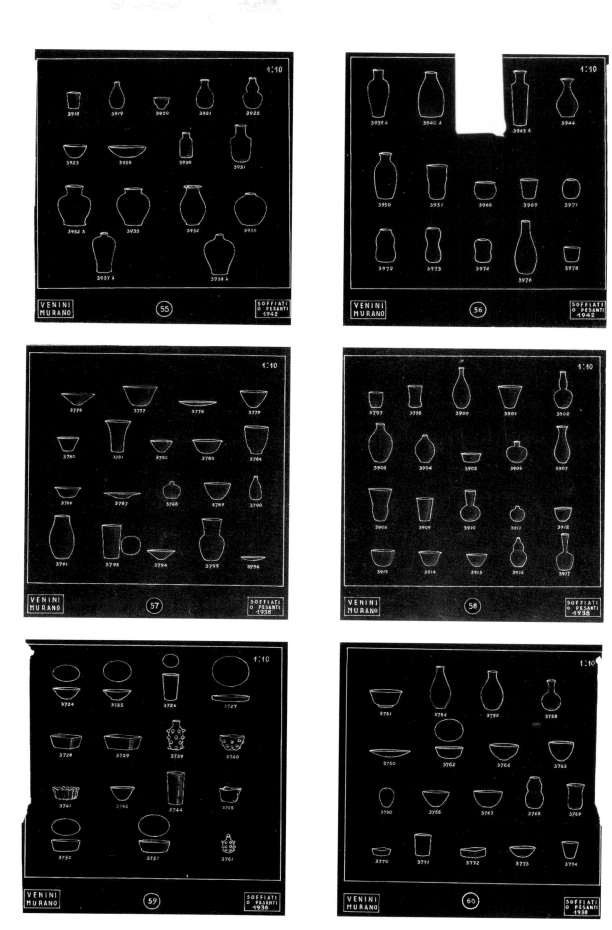

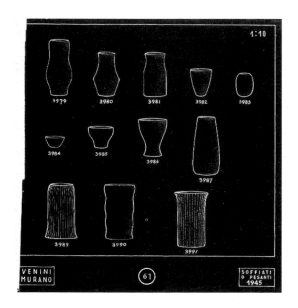

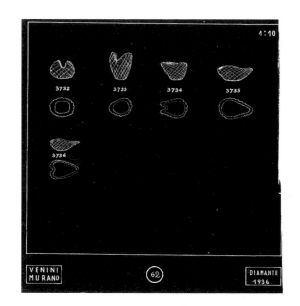

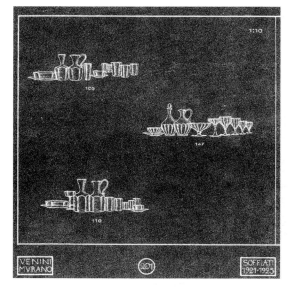

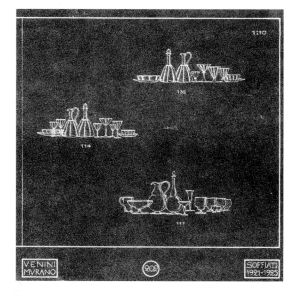

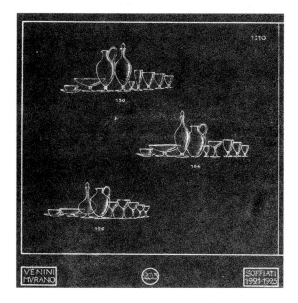

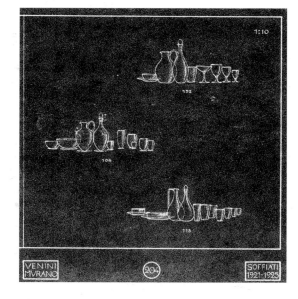

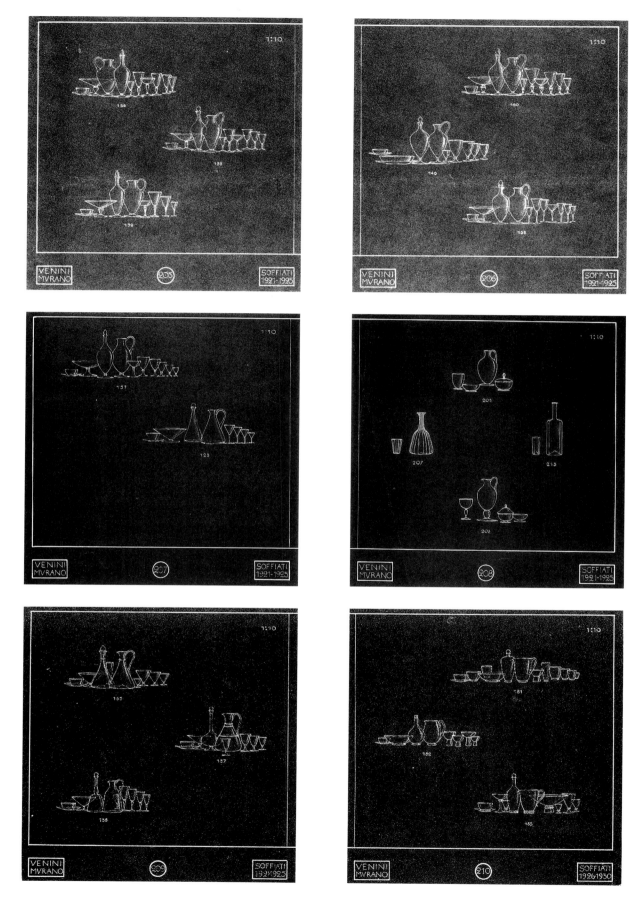

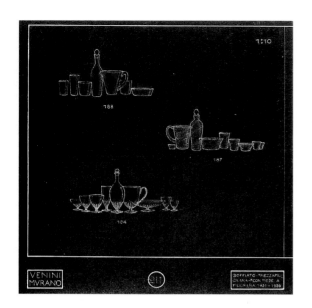

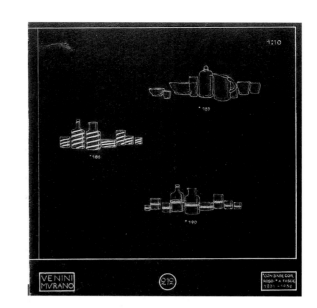

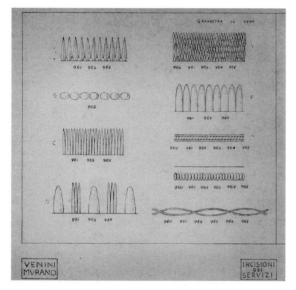

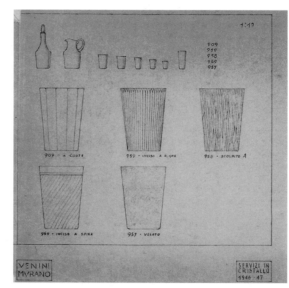

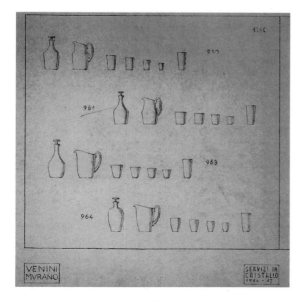

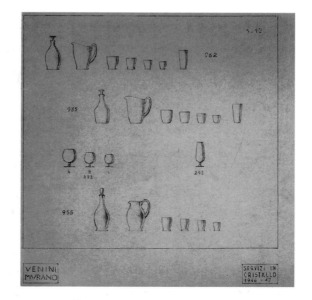

248

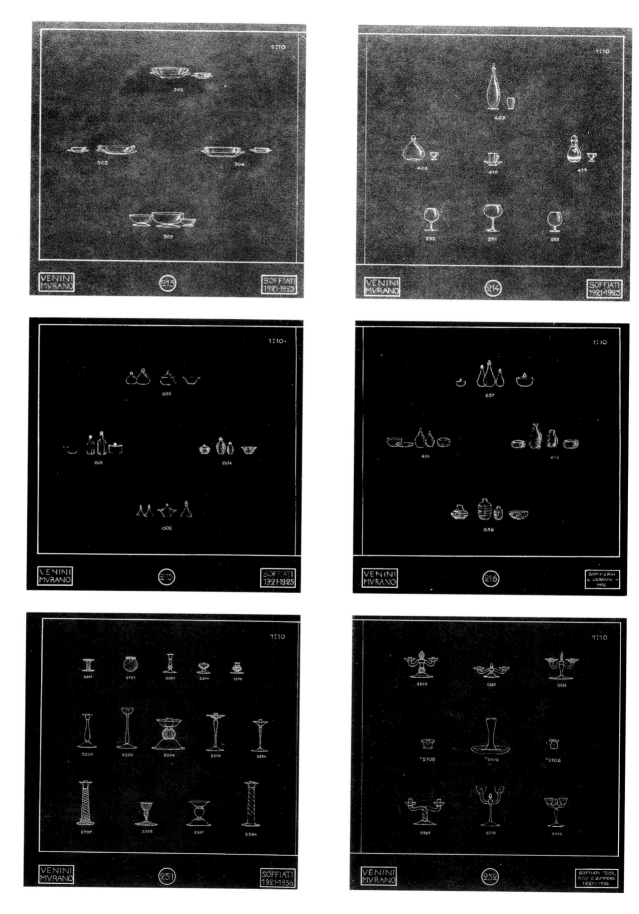

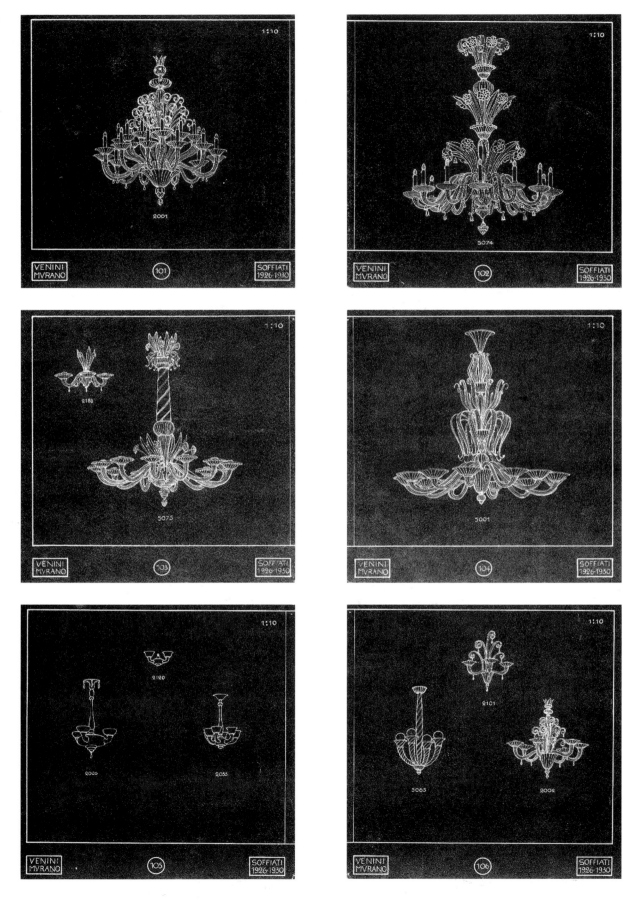

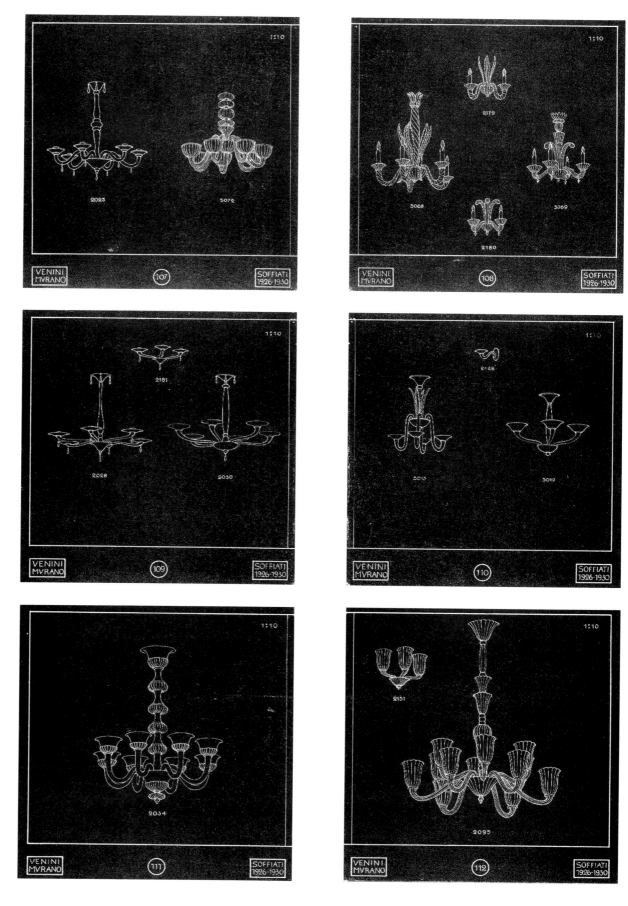

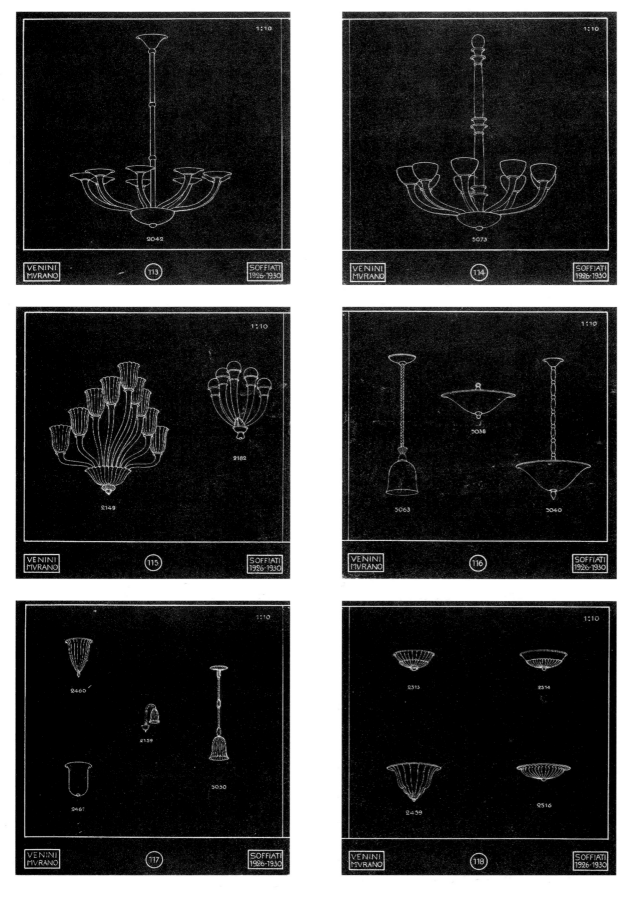

Catalogo blu, fols 113, 114, 115, 116, 117, 118

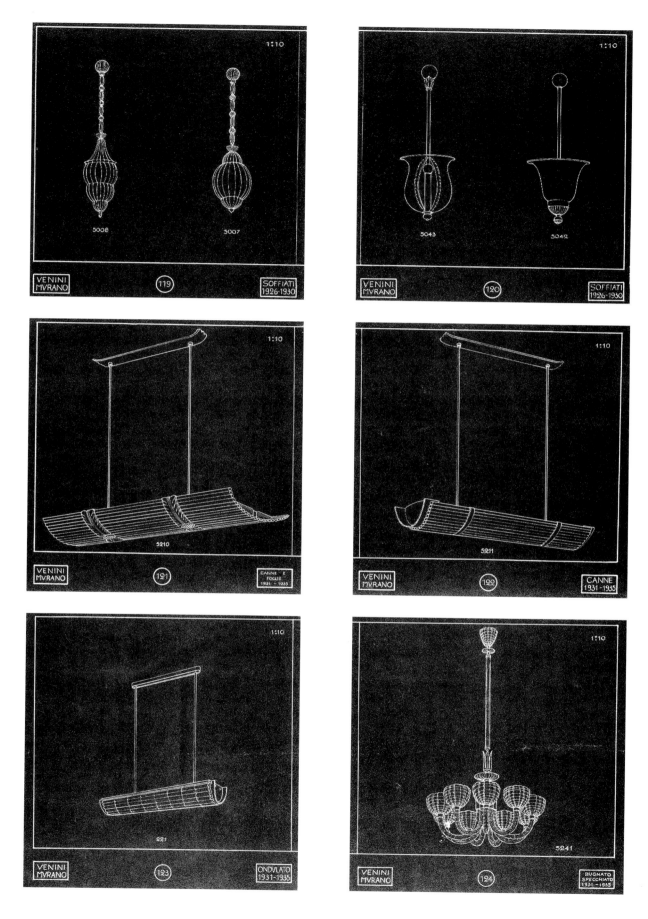

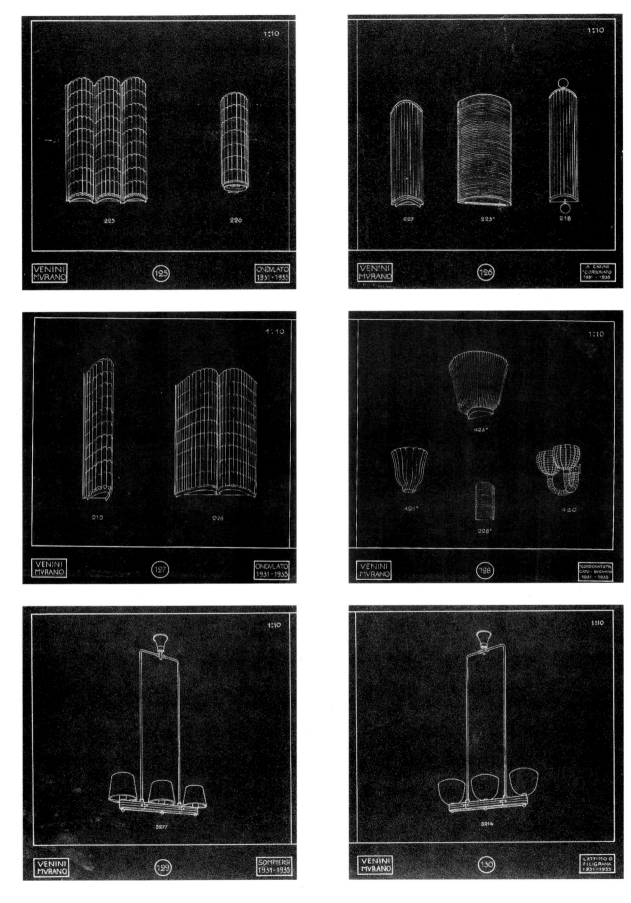

254

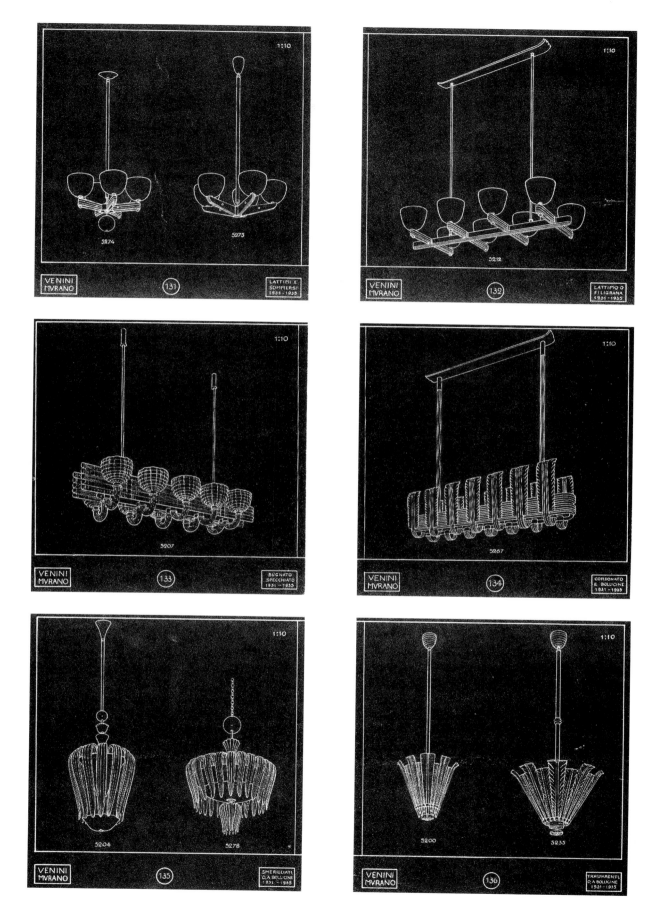

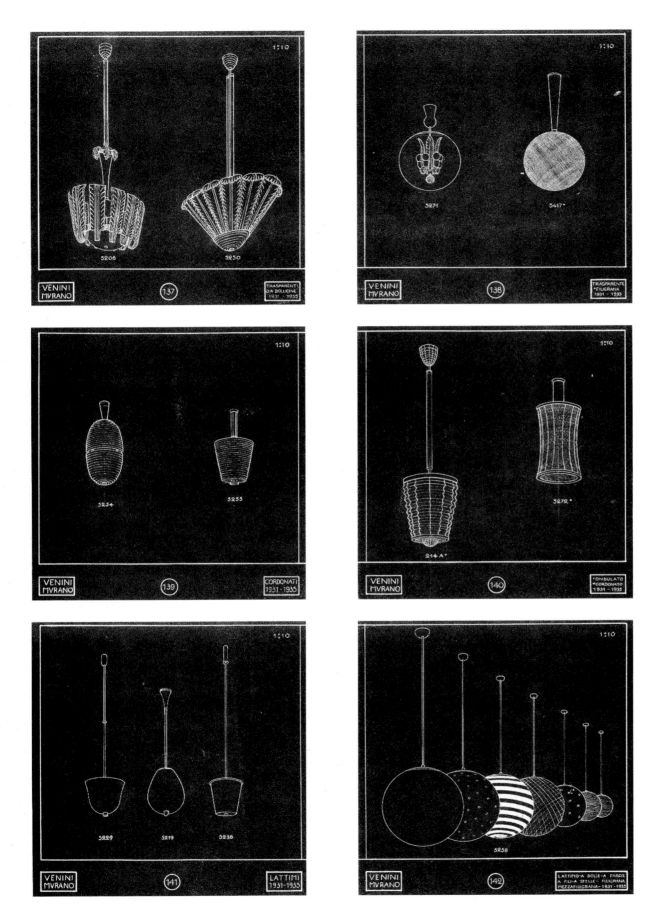

256

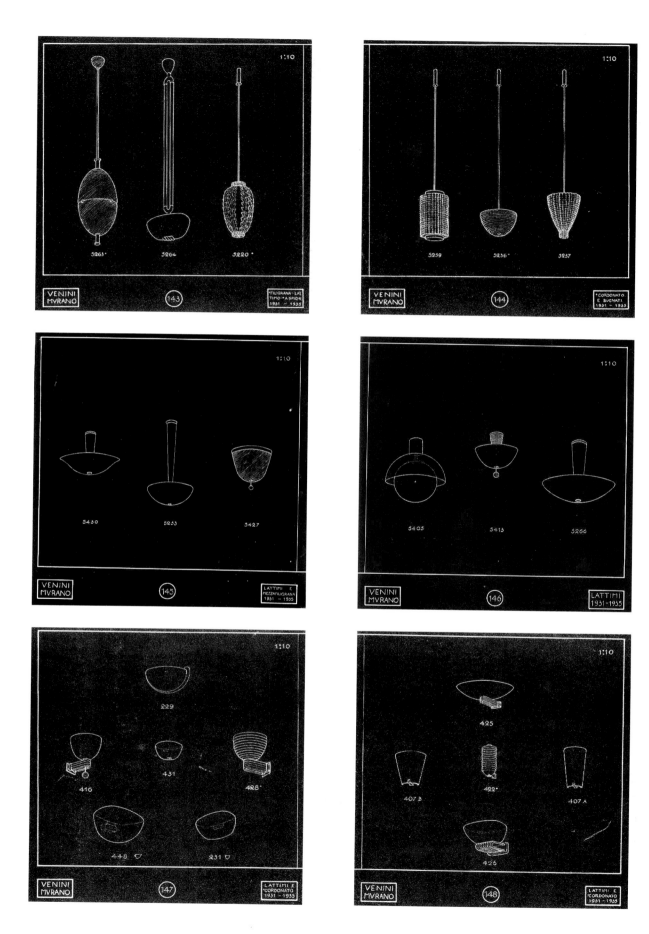

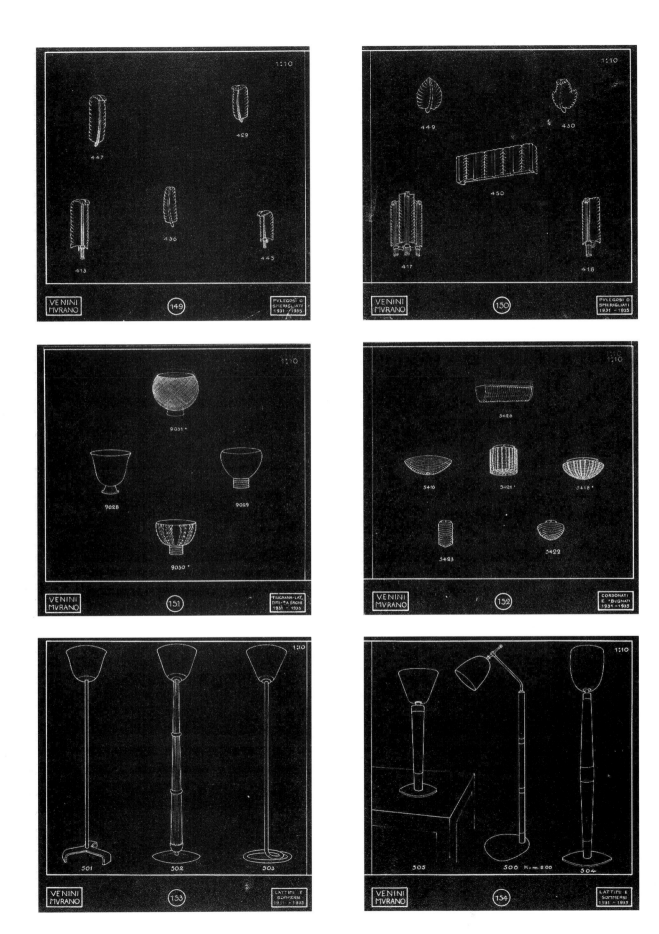

Catalogo blu, fols 149, 150, 151, 152, 153, 154

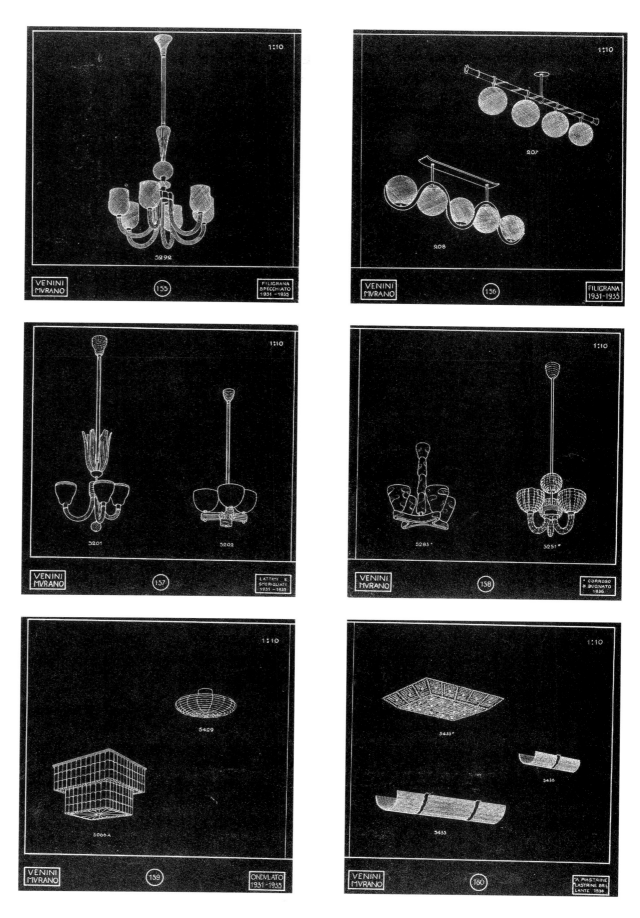

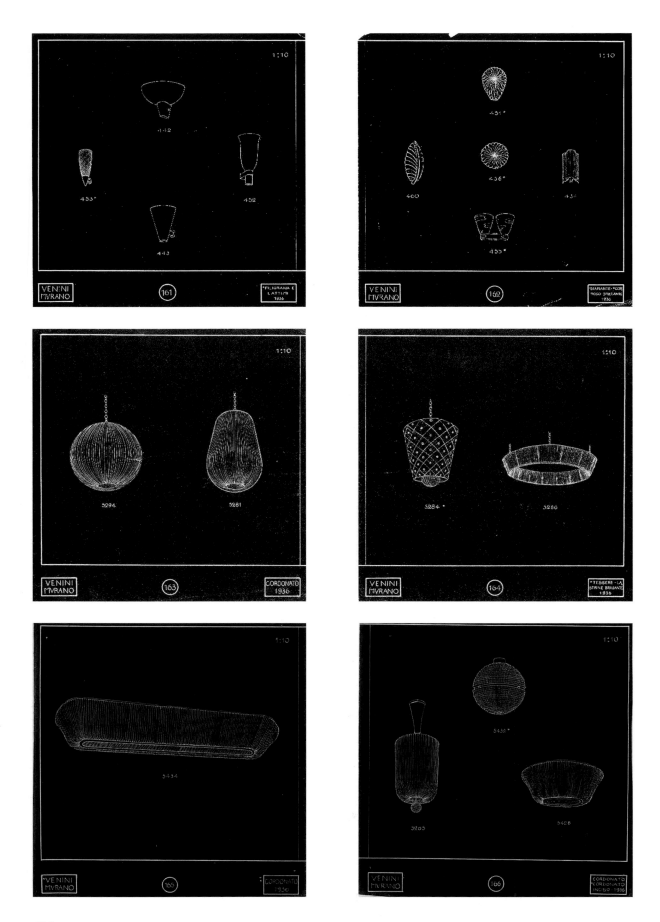

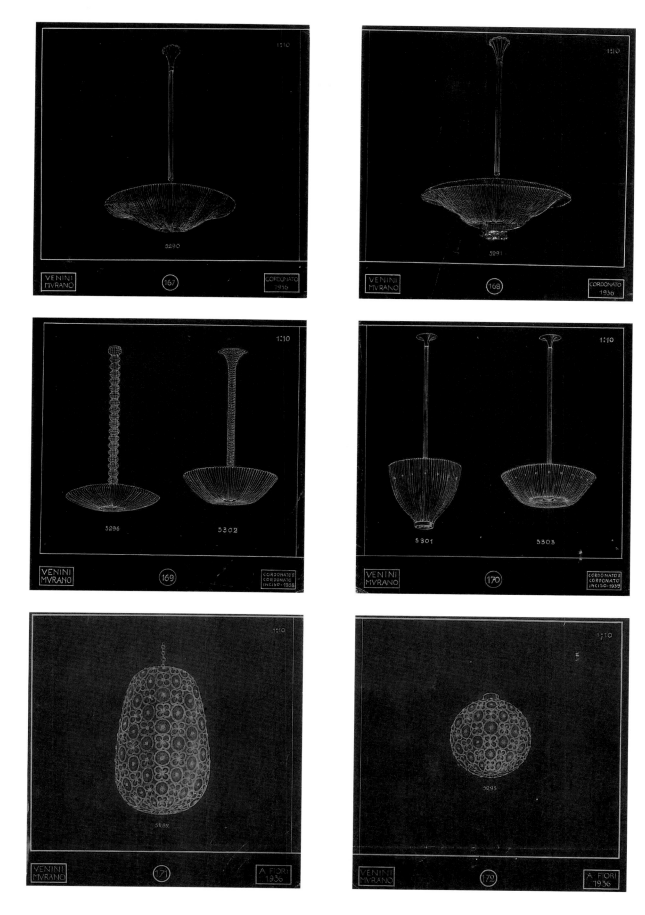

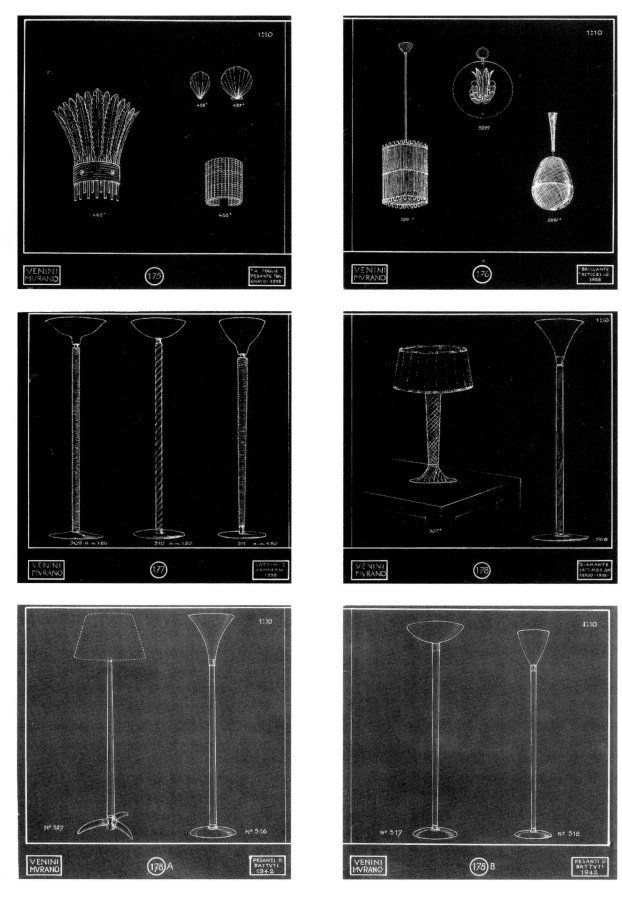

Catalogo blu, fols 175, 176, 177, 178, 178A, 178B

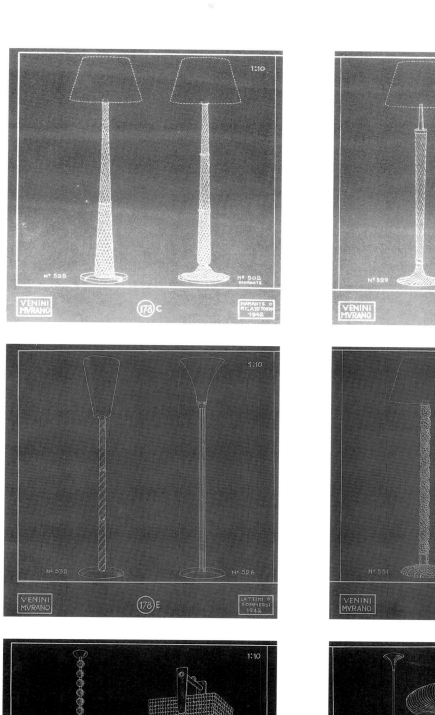

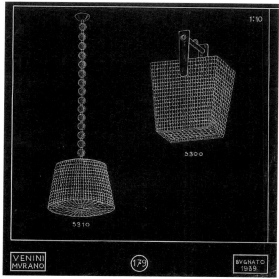

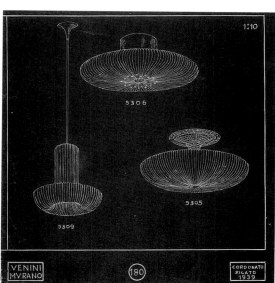

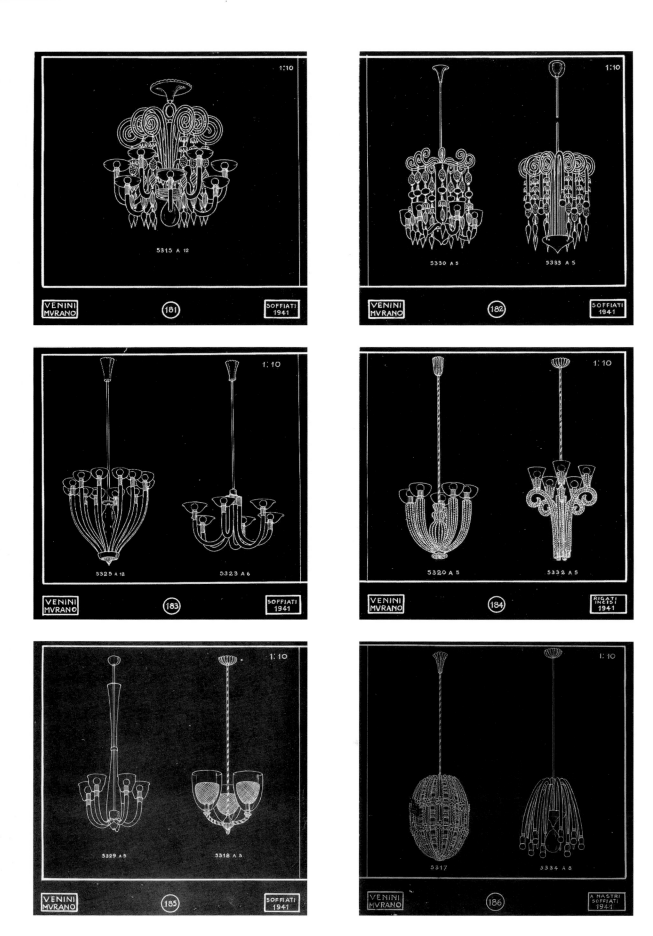

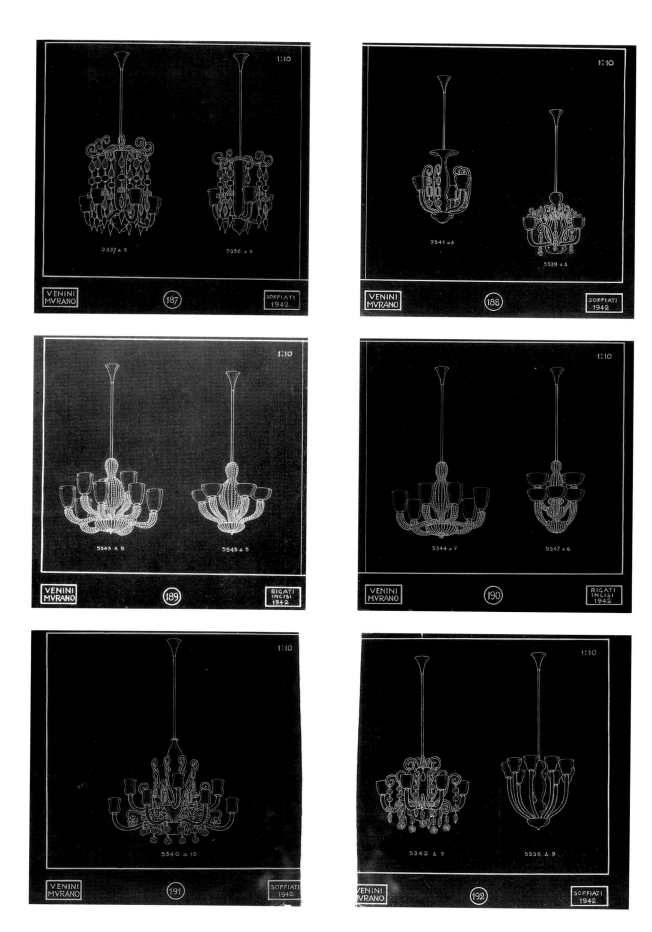

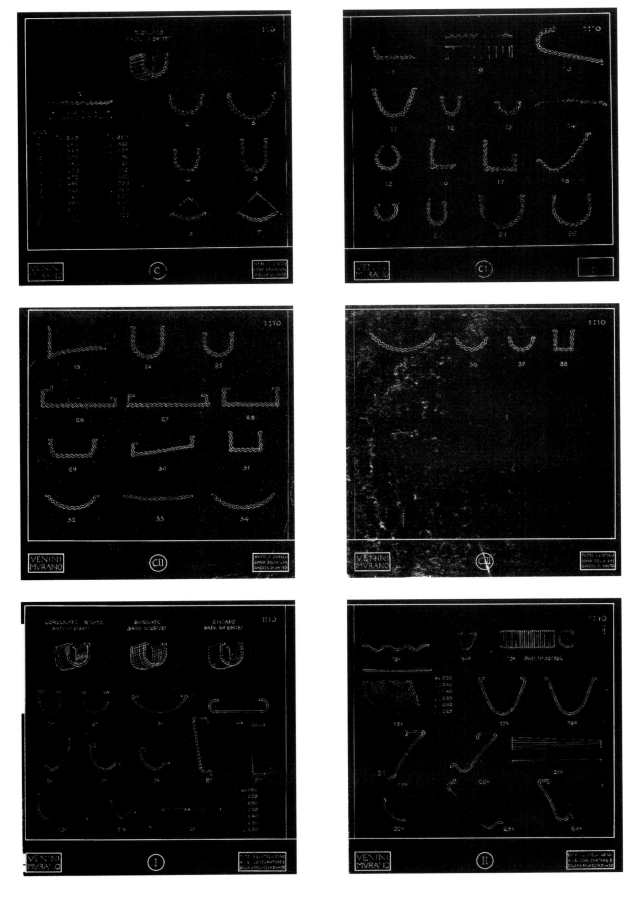

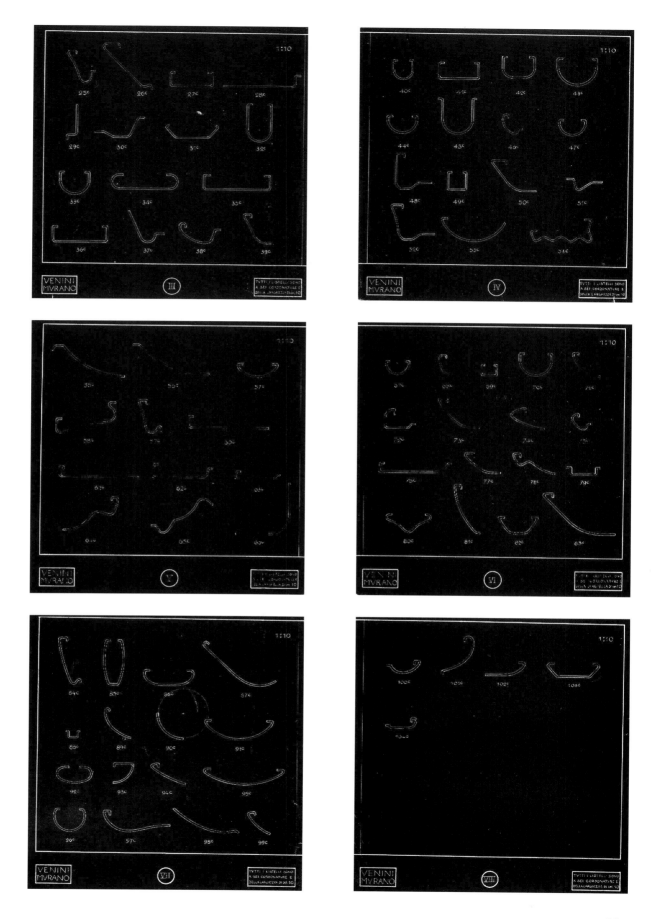

Catalogo blu, fols III, IV,
V, VI, VII, VIII

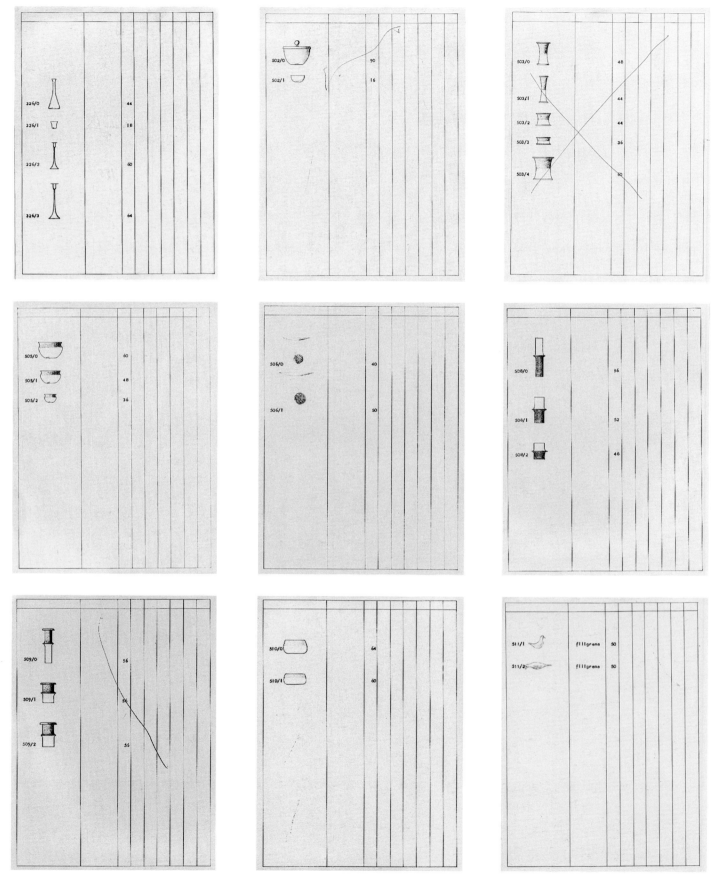

326/0		44	
326/1		18	
326/2		60	
326/3		64	

502/0		90
502/1		16

503/0		48
503/1		44
503/2		44
503/3		36
503/4		60

505/0		60
505/1		48
505/2		36

506/0		40
506/1		50

508/0		56
508/1		52
508/2		46

509/0		56
509/1		56
509/2		56

510/0		64
510/1		60

511/1		filigrana	50
511/2		filigrana	50

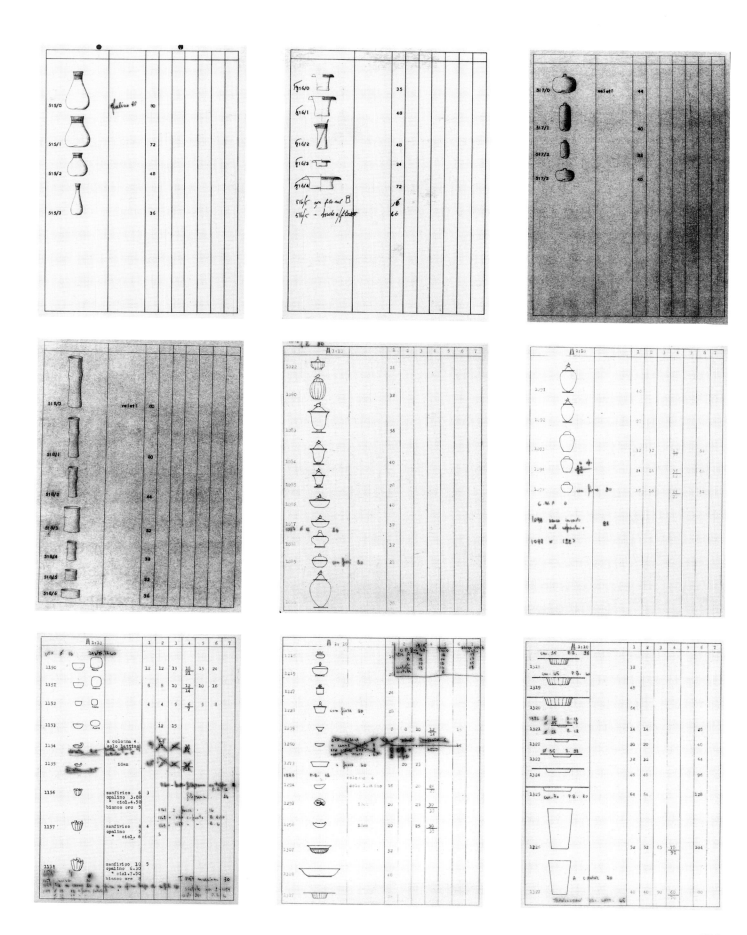

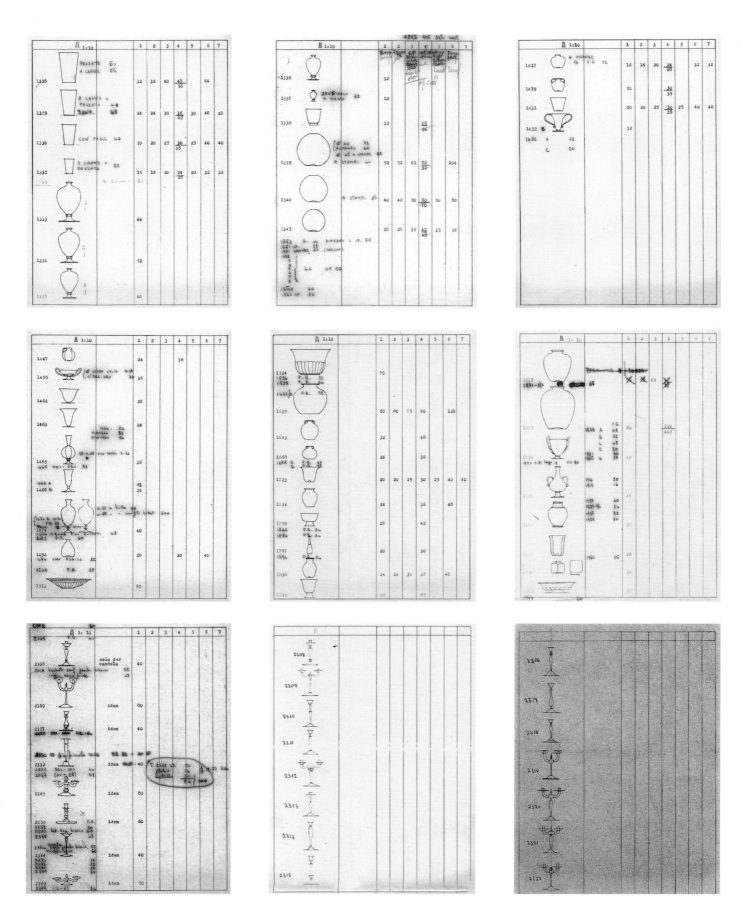

Catalogo rosso,
fols 19–27

270

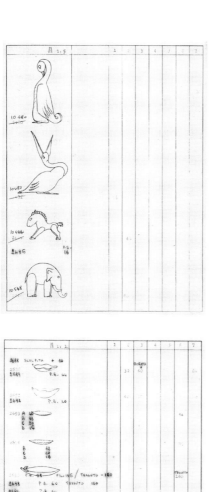

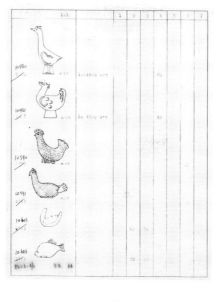

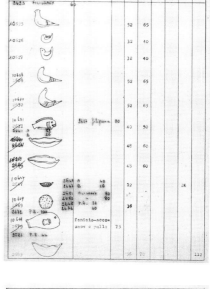

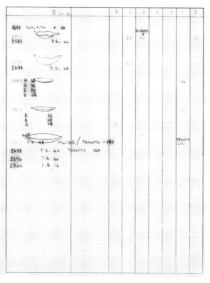

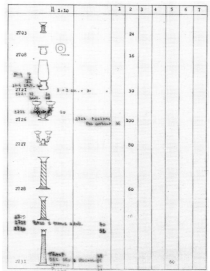

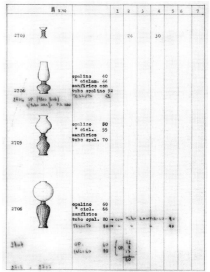

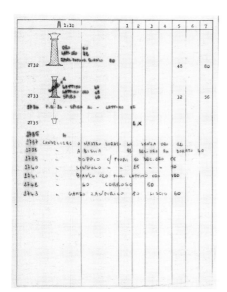

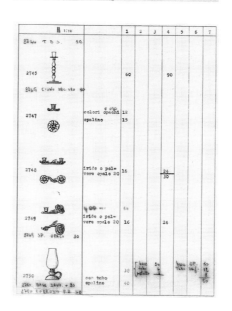

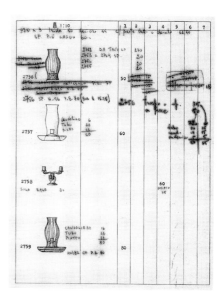

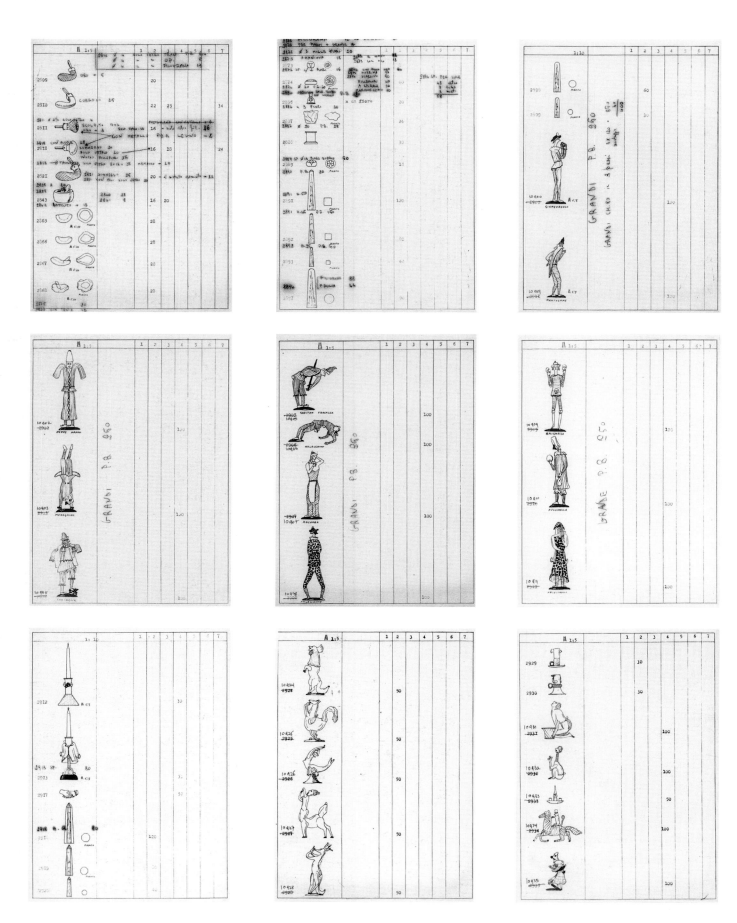

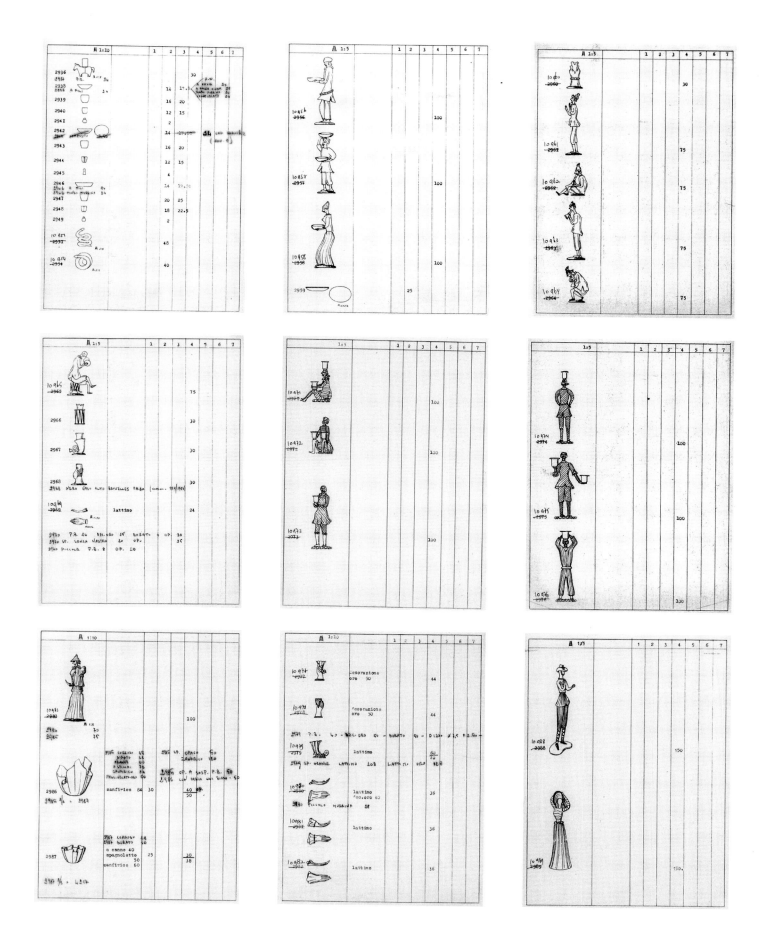

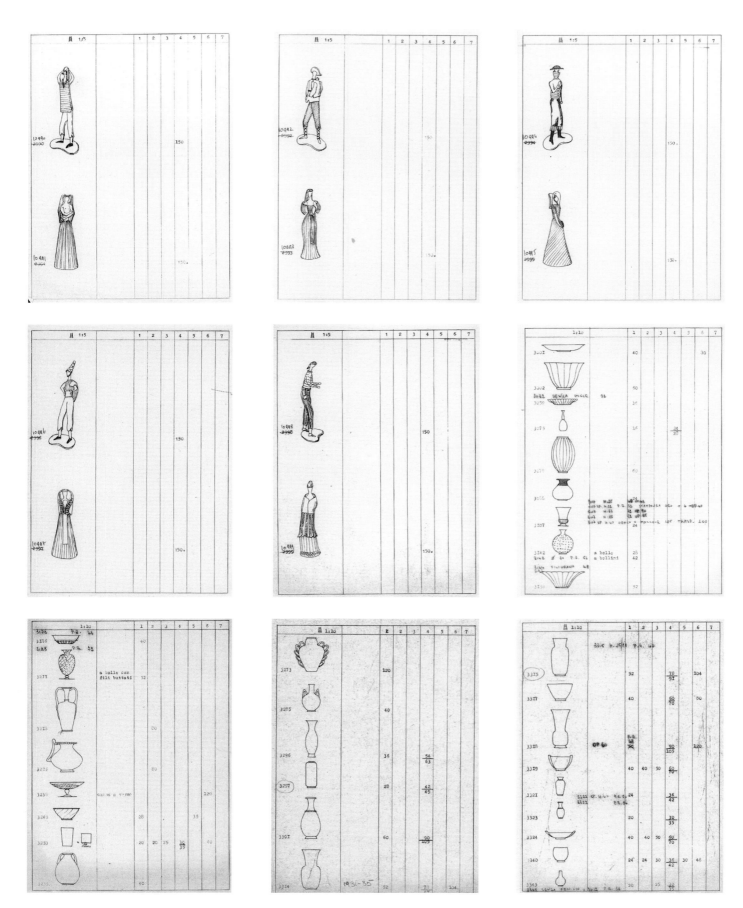

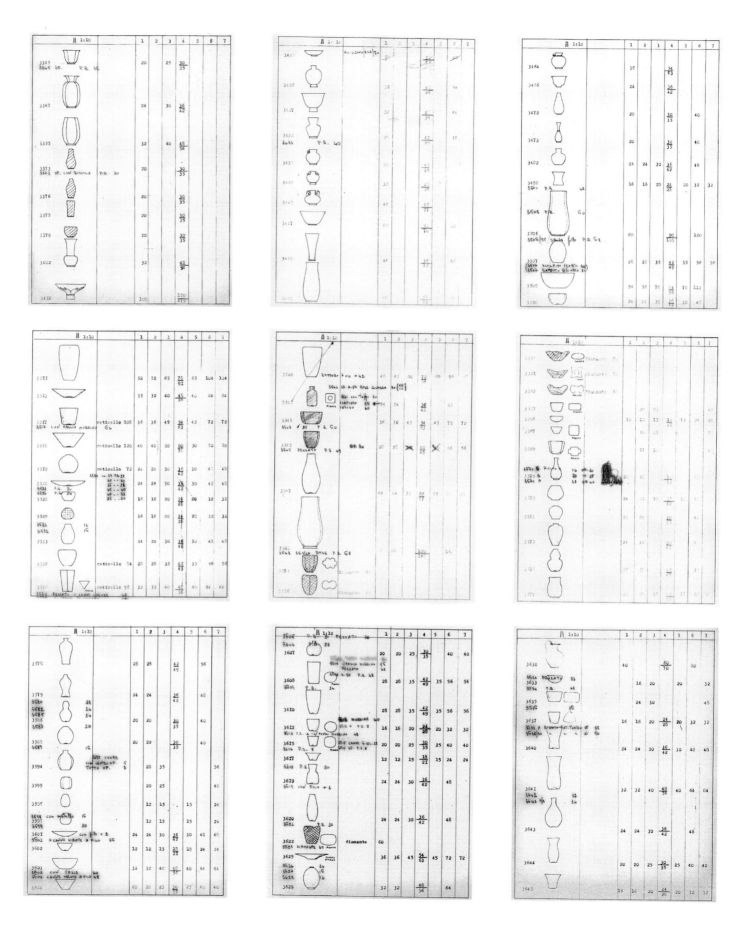

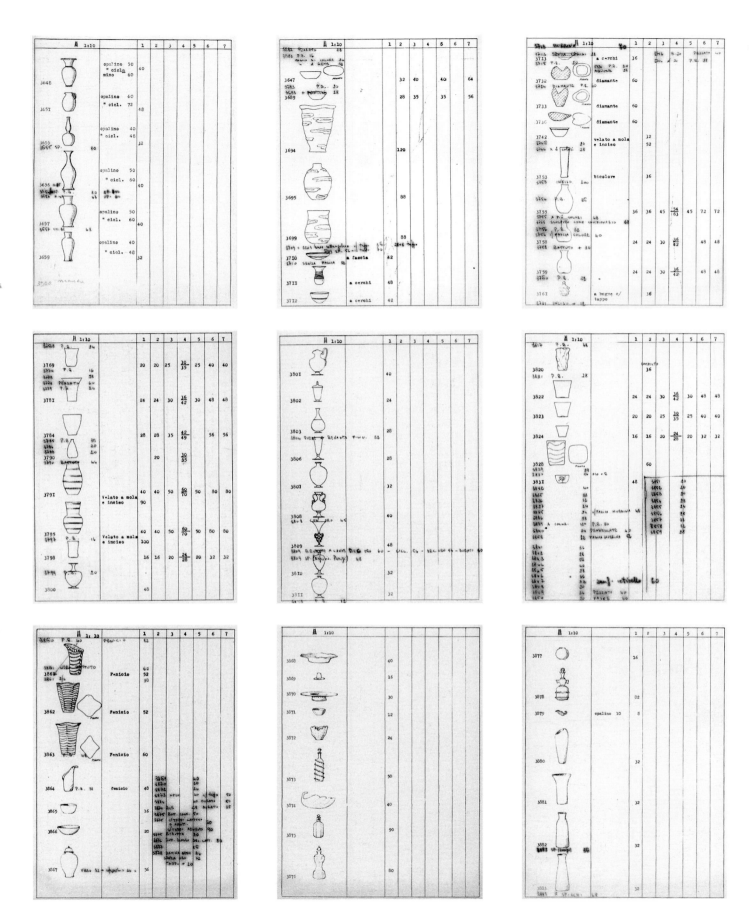

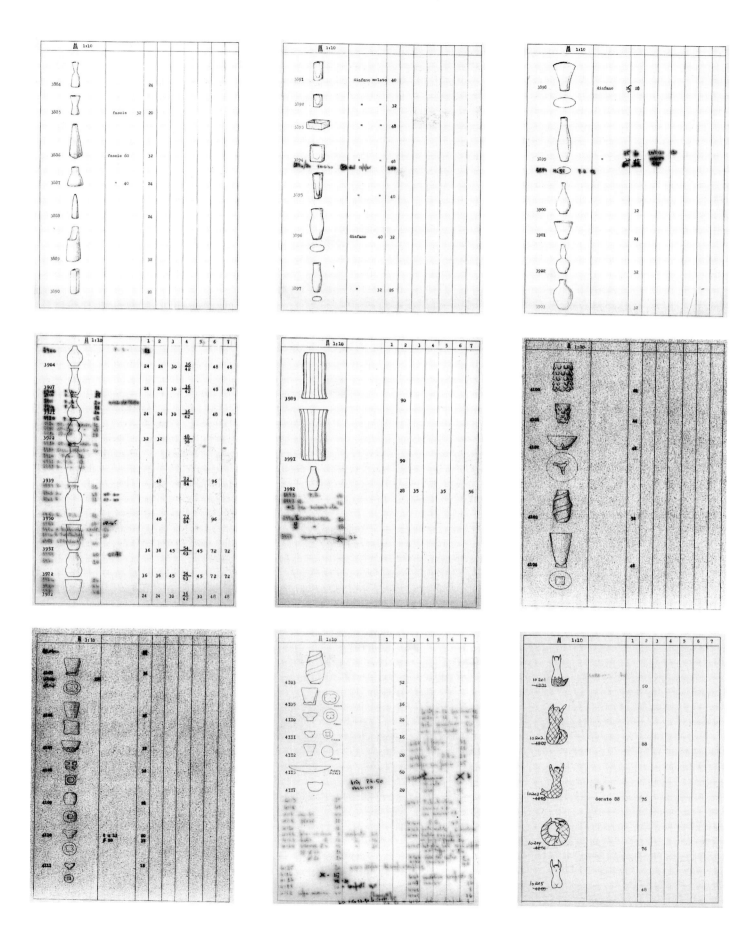

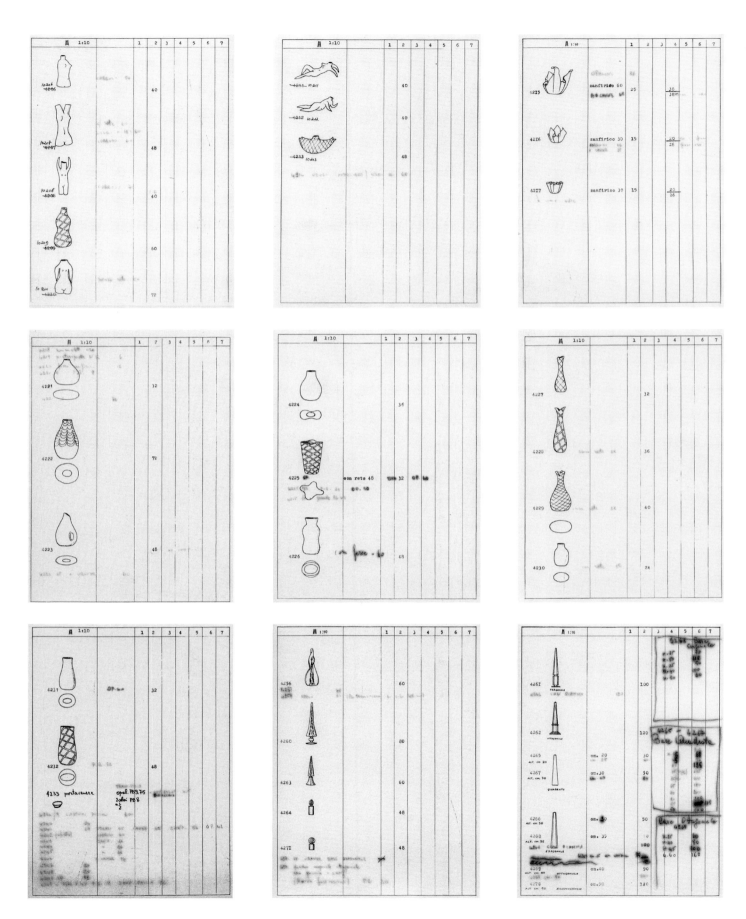

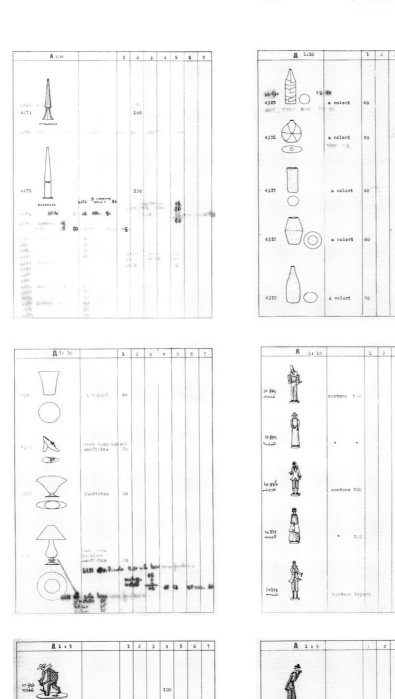

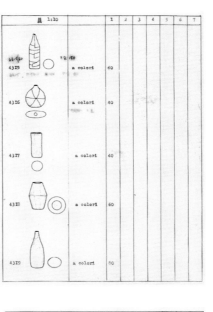

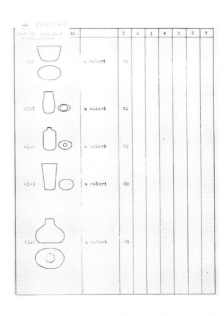

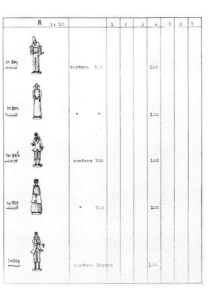

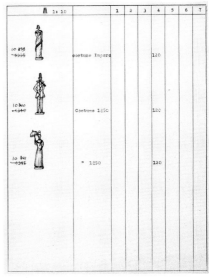

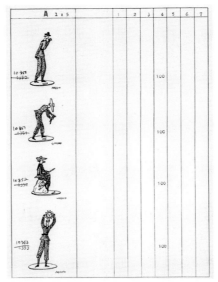

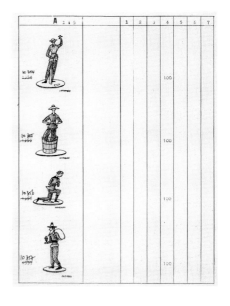

279

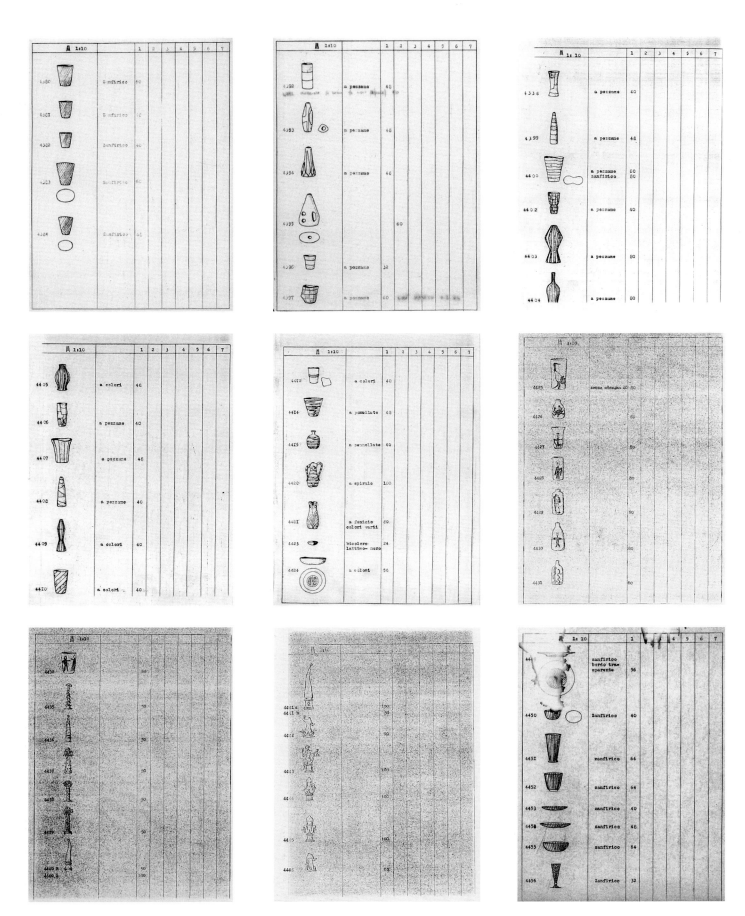

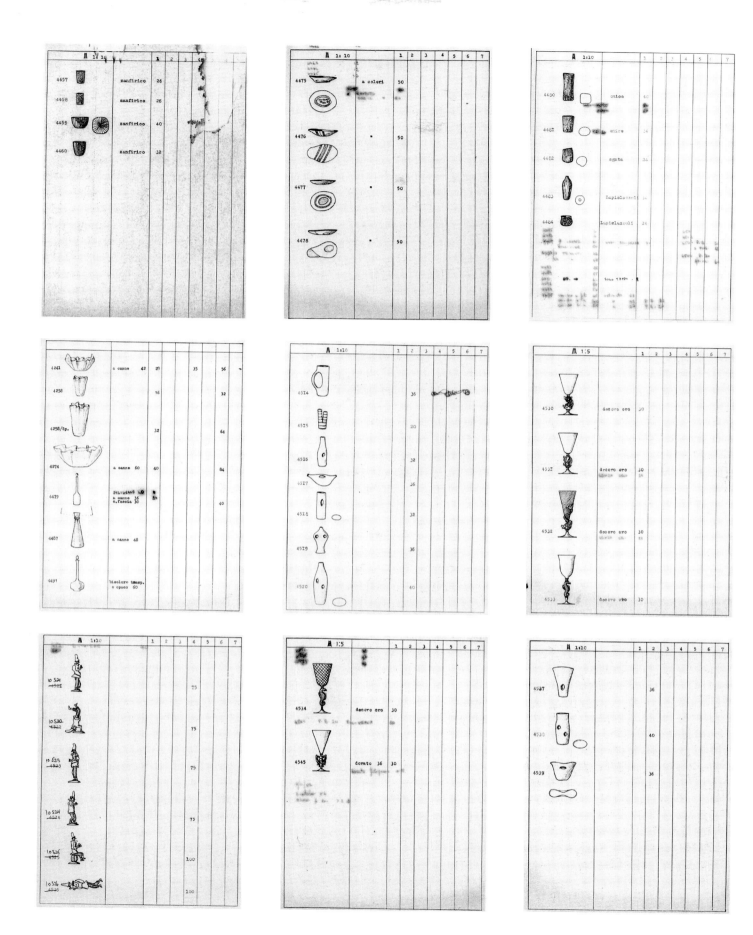

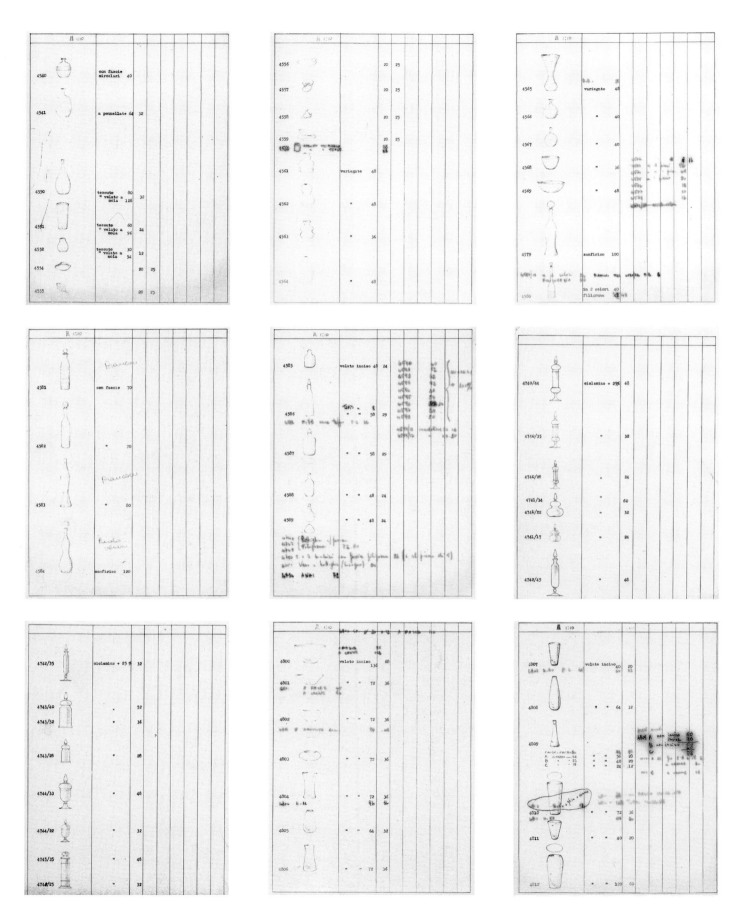

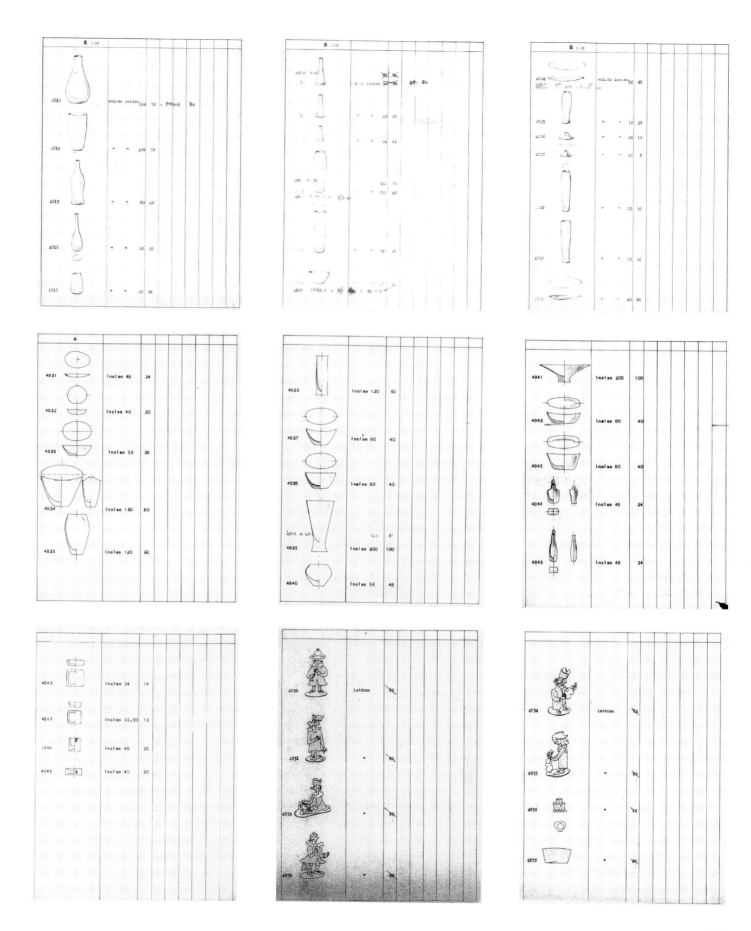

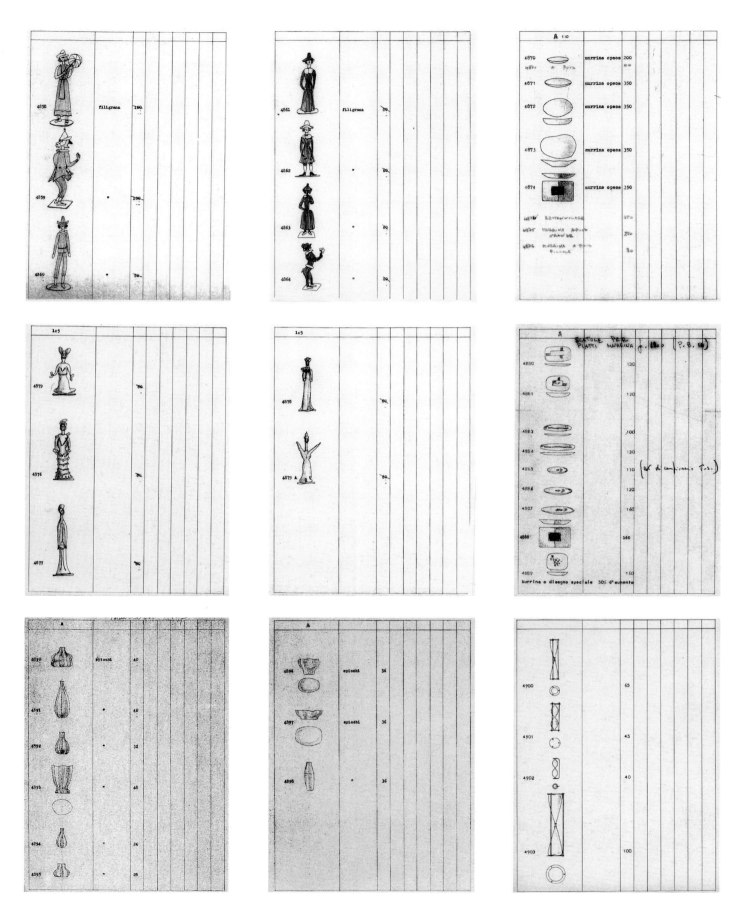

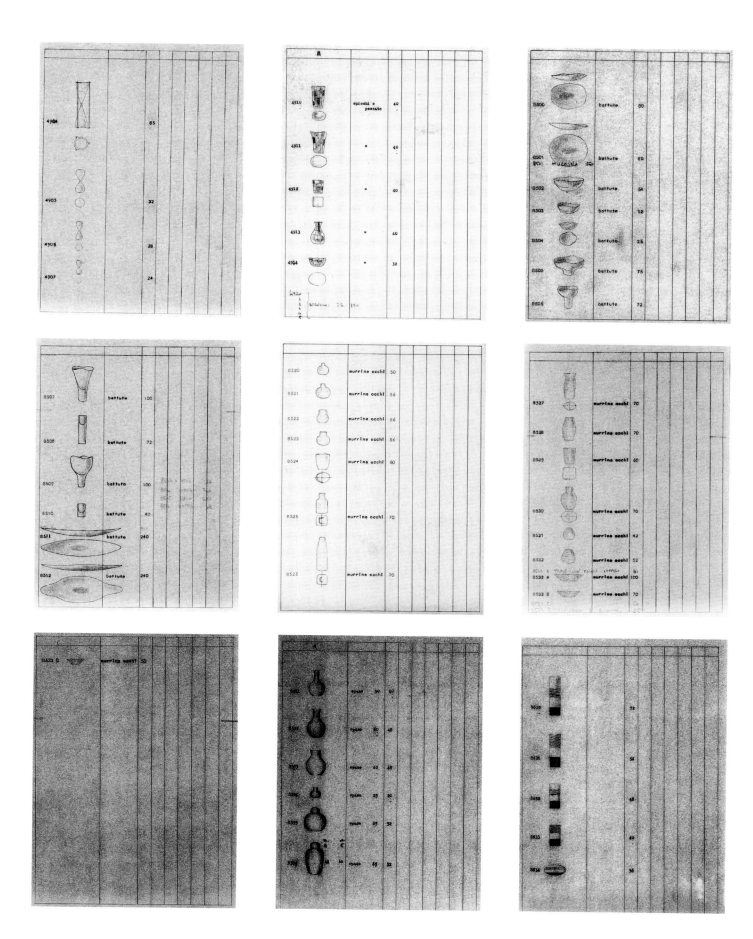

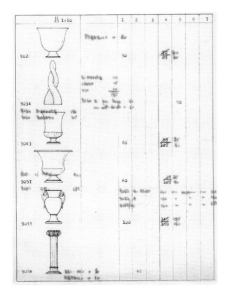

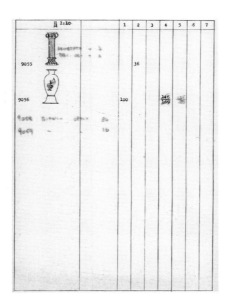

INDICE

Animali	414	15	Informali (vasi)	711	42
Anitre	413	15	Lampade da tavolo	850	48
Bagno (accessori)	200	3	Lapponi (vasi)	500	22
Battuti (vasi)	516	27	Lenti (fermacarte)	416	17
Bicchieri	310/324/327/328	8	Maniglie	210	4
Bicchieri	329/330/331/332	9	Maschere (figure)	402	14
Bicchieri	333/334/335/336	10	Meduse (vasi)	501	22
Bicchieri	337/338/339/340	11	Miros uno (vasi)	724	47
Bicchieri	3001/3002/3003/3004	12	Miros due (vasi)	725	47
Bicchieri	3005/3006/3007/3008	13	Miros tre (vasi)	727	47
Biglie	421	18	Ninfee (coppe)	715	43
Bigoli (vasi)	712	42	Obelischi	450/451	20
Bolle (vasi)	502/503	22	Obelischi	452/453/454/455	21
Bottiglie	526	31	Occhi (vasi)	520	28
Bottiglie	526	32	Opalini (vasi)	706	39
Bottiglie pesanti	721	45	Opalini (vasi)	706	40
Calici	510	24	Oro-argento (vasi)	525	30
Canne (vasi)	521	29	Palle murrina	416	16
Cannette (vasi)	713	42	Pesci	422	19
Cialde (fermacarte)	416	16	Pezzati (vasi)	704	38
Cinesi (vasi)	513	25	Pianissimo (vasi)	504	23
Classici	601	33	Piatti Wirkkala	511	24
Clessidre	420	18	Piogge (vasi)	517	26
Colletti (vasi)	512	25	Portaceneri	250	7
Coppe canne larghe	604	35	Portaceneri	726	47
Coralli (fermacarte)	416	17	Pressapapier	416	17
Coreani (vasi)	505	23	Scatole	101	1
Crepuscoli (vasi)	719	44	Scatole	101	2
Cubi incisi	421	19	Scolpiti (vasi)	717	43
Faraone	412	15	Silmà (vasi)	509	24
Fascia murrina (vasi)	518	28	Specchi	240/242	5
Fascie colorate (vasi)	523	30	Specchi	241/243	6
Fazzoletti	700/701/702	37	Spicchi (vasi)	703	38
Fermalibri	205	3	Tacchini	412	15
Fermaporte	416	17	Tessuti (vasi)	524	30
Filigrane (vasi)	602	34	Thomas (vasi)	519	28
Foglie in filigrana	603	35	Tiepolo (figure)	400	14
Foglie in tessuto	527	32	Tronchi (vasi)	714	43
Futilità (fermacarte)	416	17	Uova	415	16
Giade (vasi)	720	44	Variazioni (vasi)	705	38
Gondolieri (vasi)	507	23	Vasetti	100	1
Grotteschi (figurine)	401	14	Vasi a murrine	522	29
Grovigli (vasi)	718	44	Velati (vasi)	514/515	26
Incisi	722	45	Veronese (vasi)	600	33
Incisi (vasi)	722	46	Zanfirici (vasi)	607/608	36

VENINI

50 FOND. VETRAI - VENEZIA - MURANO

GRAFICHE RUGGERI - VENEZIA

LISTINO PREZZI 1969 — 1 VENINI

	H	Ø	Lit.
100.			
100.0	12	16	3.240
100.1	22	10	3.240
100.2	9	7	2.700
100.10	6	10	2.430
100.11	6	6	2.430

colori: pagliesco colletto thè, acquamare colletto zaffiro, verdognolo colletto verde, ametista colletto zaffiro.

	H	Ø	Lit.
100.12	10	11	2.970
100.13	12	17	4.860
100.14	24	10	4.050
100.15	12	11	3.240
100.16	18	14	4.860
100.17	27	13	5.400

colori: pagliesco colletto thè, acquamare colletto zaffiro, verdognolo colletto verde, ametista colletto zaffiro.

	H	Ø	Lit.
100.3	16	9	1.890
100.4	12	7	1.620
100.5	9	5	1.350
100.8	12	7	2.700
100.9	9	10	2.700

colori: verde mela filo zolfo, talpa filo corallo, adriatico filo antracite.

	H	Ø	Lit.
101.			
101.0	12	8.5 inciso	6.840
101.1	12	8.5	5.400
101.2	7	12 inciso	6.840
101.3	7	12	5.400

colori: talpa tappo giallo, ametista tappo viola, verdognolo tappo verde.

	H	Ø	Lit.
101.4	10	7	4.320
101.5	7	12	5.400

colori: opalino bianco, rosso, zolfo, acquamare, arancio, verde mela, con tappi molati con cerchio e murrina assortito.

	H	Ø	Lit.
101.6	12	16	6.480
101.7	24	17	8.100
101.8	13	14	6.480

colori: giallo tappo viola, verde tappo rosso, ametista tappo adriatico, bluino tappo verde.

	H	Ø	Lit.
101.9	14	9	4.320
101.10	12	7	3.780
101.11	10	6	3.240

colori: opalino celeste, acquamare, verde mela, zaffiro, bianco, ametista, viola, rosso con fiore cristallo decorato per tappo.

VENINI, 50 FOND. VETRAI, MURANO VENEZIA, ITALY, VENINI SHOWROOMS IN ROMA, MILANO, VENEZIA, PARIS, NEW YORK.

LISTINO PREZZI 1969 — 2 VENINI

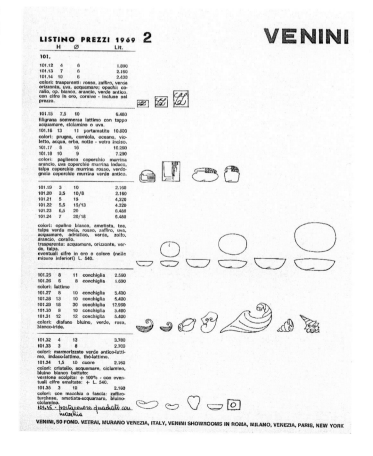

	H	Ø	Lit.
101.			
101.12	4	6	1.890
101.13	7	6	2.160
101.14	10	6	2.430

colori: trasparenti: rosso, zaffiro, verde orizzonte, uva, acquamare; opachi: corallo, op. bianco, arancio, verde antico. con cifre in oro, corsive - incluse nel prezzo.

	H	Ø	Lit.
101.15	7,5	10	6.480

filigrana sommersa lattimo con tappo acquamare, ciclamino o uva.

	H	Ø	Lit.
101.16	13	11 portamatite	10.800

colori: prugna, corniola, oceano, violetto, acqua, erba, notte - vetro inciso.

	H	Ø	Lit.
101.17	8	16	10.260
101.18	10	9	7.290

colori: pagliesco coperchio murrina arancio, uva coperchio murrina indaco, talpa coperchio murrina rosso, verdognolo coperchio murrina verde antico.

	H	Ø	Lit.
101.19	3	10	2.160
101.20	3,5	10/8	2.160
101.21	5	15	4.320
101.22	5,5	15/13	4.320
101.23	6,5	20	6.480
101.24	7	20/18	6.480

colori: opalino bianco, ametista, tea, talpa verde mela, rosso, zaffiro, uva, acquamare, adriatico, verde, zolfo, arancio, corallo. trasparente: acquamare, orizzonte, verde, talpa. eventuali cifre in oro o colore (nelle misure inferiori) L. 540.

	H	Ø	Lit.
101.25	8	11 conchiglia	2.560
101.26	6	8 conchiglia	1.690

colori: lattimo

	H	Ø	Lit.
101.27	8	10 conchiglia	5.400
101.28	13	10 conchiglia	5.400
101.29	13	30 conchiglia	12.960
101.30	8	10 conchiglia	5.400
101.31	12	12 conchiglia	5.400

colori: diafano bluino, verde, rosa, bianco-iride.

	H	Ø	Lit.
101.32	4	13	3.780
101.33	3	8	2.700

colori: marmorizzato verde antico-lattimo, indaco-lattimo, thè-lattimo.

	H	Ø	Lit.
101.34	1,5	10 cuore	2.160

colori: cristallo, acquamare, ciclamino, bluino bianco battuto: versione scolpita: + 100% - con eventuali cifre smaltate: + L. 540.

	H	Ø	Lit.
101.35	3	10	2.160

colori: con macchia o fascia: zaffiro-turchese, ametista-acquamare, bluino-ciclamino.

101.36 - portacenere quadrato con murrina

VENINI, 50 FOND. VETRAI, MURANO VENEZIA, ITALY, VENINI SHOWROOMS IN ROMA, MILANO, VENEZIA, PARIS, NEW YORK

VENINI

LISTINO PREZZI 1969 — 3

	H	Ø	Lit.
200.			
200.0	30		6.750
200.1	40		7.560
200.2	50		8.100
200.3	60		8.640
200.4	70		9.450
200.5	8	16	11.880
200.5	12	6	4.860
200.7	—	9	5.940
200.8	—	7	5.400
200.9	—	25	10.800
200.10	12	10	9.180
200.11	—	4,5	2.430

colori: macchia o anima opalino acquamare, lattimo, verde mela, ametista.
In filigrana (lattimo o turchese) prezzi
aumentati del 30%.

	H	Ø	Lit.
205.			
205.0	15x18	reggilibri	10.800

colori: cristallo con murrina rosso-lat-
timo o con triangoli rosso-verde-zaffiro-
giallo. metallo nichelato.

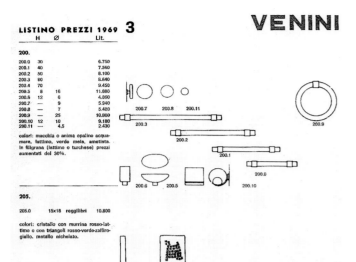

VENINI, 50 FOND. VETRAI, MURANO VENEZIA, ITALY, VENINI SHOWROOMS IN ROMA, MILANO, VENEZIA, PARIS, NEW YORK.

VENINI

LISTINO PREZZI 1969 — 4

	H	Ø	Lit.
210. maniglie			

210.0   Ø 8   la coppia   9.180
vetro ritorto rigadin - colori: cristallo,
ametista, acquamare.

210.1   Ø 8   la coppia   10.260
colori: cristallo con anelli corallo, turchese, zaffiro, zolfo o lattimo.

210.2   Ø 8   la coppia   11.340
colori: cristallo con fiore rosso, zolfo, zaffiro, verde mela o lattimo.

210.3   Ø 8   la coppia   9.180
colori: cristallo con macchia di opalino rosso, zaffiro, verde mela, lattimo.

210.4   Ø 8   la coppia   11.340
colori: cristallo con murrina millefiori.
metalli: nicheimat - salvo indicazioni
contrarie le maniglie saranno sempre
inviate in coppia.

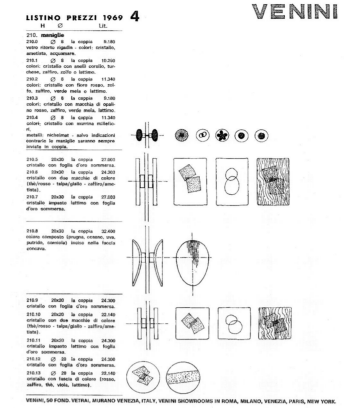

210.5   20x30   la coppia   27.000
cristallo con foglia d'oro sommersa.

210.6   20x30   la coppia   24.300
cristallo con due macchie di colore
(thè/rosso - talpa/giallo - zaffiro/ame-
tista).

210.7   20x30   la coppia   27.000
cristallo impasto lattimo con foglia
d'oro sommersa.

210.8   20x30   la coppia   32.400
colore composto (prugna, oceano, uva,
putrido, corniola) inciso nella faccia
concava.

210.9   20x20   la coppia   24.300
cristallo con foglia d'oro sommersa.

210.10   20x20   la coppia   22.140
cristallo con due macchie di colore
(thè/rosso - talpa/giallo - zaffiro/ame-
tista).

210.11   20x20   la coppia   24.300
cristallo impasto lattimo con foglia
d'oro sommersa.

210.12   Ø 20   la coppia   24.300
cristallo con foglia d'oro sommersa.

210.13   Ø 20   la coppia   22.140
cristallo con fascia di colore (rosso,
zaffiro, thè, viola, lattimo).

VENINI, 50 FOND. VETRAI, MURANO VENEZIA, ITALY, VENINI SHOWROOMS IN ROMA, MILANO, VENEZIA, PARIS, NEW YORK.

VENINI

LISTINO PREZZI 1969 — 5

	H	Ø		Lit.
240.				
240.0	60	42	specchio	32.400
240.1	42	38	specchio	27.000
240.2	30	24	specchio	22.950

colori: nastro opalino rosso, ametista
celeste, talpa, acquamare, bianco.

	H	Ø		Lit.
240.3	30	24	cornice f.	18.900
240.4	24	18	cornice f.	16.200
240.5	18	13	cornice f.	13.500

colori: nastro opalino rosso, ametista
celeste, talpa, acquamare, bianco.

	H	Ø		Lit.
240.6	35	35	specchio	32.400
240.7	45	35	specchio	32.400
240.8	50	40	specchio	37.800

colori: nastro opalino rosso, ametista
celeste, talpa, acquamare, bianco.

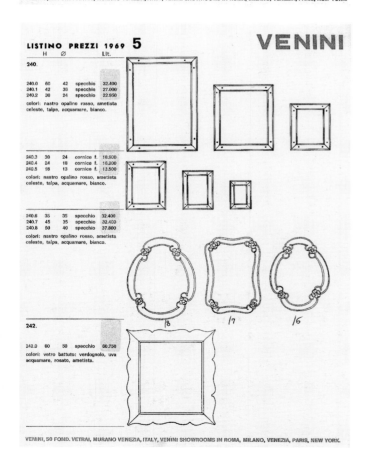

	H	Ø		Lit.
242.				
242.0	60	50	specchio	60.750

colori: vetro battuto: verdognolo, uva
acquamare, rosato, ametista.

VENINI, 50 FOND. VETRAI, MURANO VENEZIA, ITALY, VENINI SHOWROOMS IN ROMA, MILANO, VENEZIA, PARIS, NEW YORK.

VENINI

LISTINO PREZZI 1969 — 6

	H	Ø		Lit.
241.				
241.0	65	58	specchio	108.000
241.1	58	52	specchio	81.000

colori: murrina: millefiori, rosso antico, verde antico, indaco, ambra - nastri
opalino intonati a colore.

	H	Ø		Lit.
241.2	85	70	specchio	135.000

colori: murrina: millefiori, rosso antico, verde antico, indaco, ambra - nastri
opalino intonati a colore.

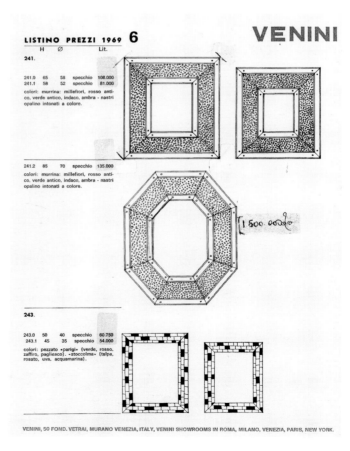

1 500.000/o

	H	Ø		Lit.
243.				
243.0	50	40	specchio	60.750
243.1	45	35	specchio	54.000

colori: pezzato «parigi» (verde, rosso,
zaffiro, pagliesco). «stoccolma» (talpa,
rosato, uva, acquamarina).

VENINI, 50 FOND. VETRAI, MURANO VENEZIA, ITALY, VENINI SHOWROOMS IN ROMA, MILANO, VENEZIA, PARIS, NEW YORK.

LISTINO PREZZI 1969 **7** VENINI

	H	Ø		Lit.
250.	portaceneri			
250.1	3	18x18		10.800
250.2	2,5	15x15		8.640
250.3	2	12x12		6.480

colori: cristallo macchia rosso, thè, zaffiro, nero, verde.

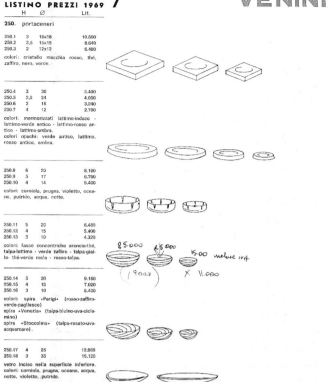

250.4	3	30		5.400
250.5	2,5	24		4.050
250.6	2	16		3.240
250.7	4	12		2.700

colori: marmorizzati lattimo-indaco - lattimo-verde antico - lattimo-rosso antico - lattimo-ambra.
colori opachi: verde antico, lattimo, rosso antico, ambra.

250.8	6	20		8.100
250.9	5	17		6.700
250.10	4	14		5.400

colori: corniola, prugna, violetto, oceano, putrido, acqua, notte.

250.11	5	20		6.480
250.12	4	15		5.400
250.13	3	10		4.320

colori: fasce concentriche arancio-thè, talpa-lattimo - verde zaffiro - talpa-giallo-thè-verde mela - rosso-talpa.

85.000   85.000   15.00 meluse IVA
(9000)   X 11.000

250.14	5	20		9.180
250.15	4	15		7.020
250.16	3	10		5.400

colori: spira «Parigi» (rosso-zaffiro-verde-pagliesco)
spira «Venezia» (talpa-bluino-uva-ciclamino)
spira «Stoccolma» (talpa-rosato-uva-acquamare).

250.17	4	25		12.960
250.18	3	35		15.120

vetro inciso nella superficie inferiore.
colori: corniola, prugna, oceano, acqua, notte, violetto, putrido.

LISTINO PREZZI 1969 **8** VENINI

	H	Ø		Lit.
310.				
310.1	10	8	1/6	4.860
310.2	14	7,5	1/6	5.400
310.3	12	5,5	1/6	4.320

colori: cristallo con pallina d'oro sommersa nella base.

324.				
324.0	4,5	11,5	1/6	2.025
324.1	6,5	7	1/6	1.690
324.2	8	8	1/6	2.025
324.3	9	9	1/6	2.295
324.C	20	18	1/1	5.130

colori: pagliesco filo thè - verdognolo filo verde.

327.				
327.1	10	4,5	1/6	1.890
327.2	12	5,5	1/6	1.755
327.3	13,5	6,5	1/6	2.025
327.C	23	11	1/1	4.590

colori: cristallo filo zaffiro, pagliesco filo corallo.

328.				
328.0	5	12	1/6	2.160
328.1	5,5	6	1/6	1.620
328.2	6,5	7	1/6	1.890
328.3	7	7,5	1/6	2.205
328.4	15	6,5	1/6	2.430
328.C	20	15	1/1	5.400

colori: cristallo filo lattimo - pagliesco filo thè - verdognolo filo verde antico.

LISTINO PREZZI 1969 **9** VENINI

	H	Ø		Lit.
329.				
329.0	5	12	1/6	2.160
329.1	6,5	6	1/6	1.620
329.2	8,5	7	1/6	1.890
329.3	9	7,5	1/6	2.025
329.4	15	5,5	1/6	2.430
329.C	24	15		5.900

colori: cristallo filo lattimo - pagliesco filo thè - verdognolo filo verde antico.

330.				
330.0	5	10	1/6	1.620
330.1	7	6,5	1/6	1.350
330.2	8	7	1/6	1.350
330.3	8,5	7,5	1/6	1.485
330.4	9	8	1/6	1.620
330.5	15	5	1/6	1.755
330.6	15	8	1/6	2.060
330.c	24	15		5.900

colori: cristallo filo lattimo, filo zaffiro, filo thè.

vino acqua

331.				
331.0	6	10	1/6	1.350
331.1	10,5	8,5	1/6	1.350
331.2	12	8,5	1/6	1.620
331.3	14	8,5	1/6	1.890
331.C	24	12,5		5.900

colori: cristallo filo lattimo, filo zaffiro, filo thè.

332.				
332.0	5	10	1/6	2.160
332.1	7	4,5	1/6	1.080
332.2	8,5	4,5	1/6	1.350
332.3	10	5	1/6	1.620
332.4	11	6	1/6	1.890
332.5	12,5	7	1/6	2.160
332.6	15	5,5	1/6	1.890
332.M	23	7,5		5.400
332.B	26	10		6.480
332.C	27	12		6.480

colori: talpa fascia lattimo, zaffiro fascia verde, verde fascia rosso, - cristallo fascia lattimo, fascia corallo, fascia arancio, fascia zolfo, fascia verde, fascia thè, fascia zaffiro.

LISTINO PREZZI 1969 **10** VENINI

	H	Ø		Lit.
333.				
333.1	8	6,5	1/6	1.620
333.2	12,5	7	1/6	1.890
333.3	12,5	4,5	1/6	1.620
333.4	15	6,5	1/6	2.430
333.C	30	10,5		7.560

Colori: «Stoccolma»: (viola, ciclamino, talpa, acquamare).

334.				
334.1	6	5,5	1/6	2.160
334.2	8	7,5	1/6	2.700
334.3	11	8,5	1/6	3.240
334.4	15	9	1/6	3.780
334.C	23	12		8.640
334.MP	16	13		7.560
334.MG	32	12		9.720

colori: canne sei colori (rosso, verde, zaffiro, pagliesco, viola, rosso) oppure talpa-giallo - zaffiro-verde - viola-acquamare - talpa-lattimo.

335.				
335.1	9	4,5	1/6	1.220
335.2	10,5	5	1/6	1.350
335.3	12	5,5	1/6	1.620
335.4	15	5	1/6	2.160
335.C	27	13		7.560

colori: spirale opaca lattimo, turchese, ambra.

336.				
336.1	7	6	1/6	2.160
336.2	9	6,5	1/6	2.700
336.3	10	7	1/6	3.240
336.4	15	7,5	1/6	3.780
336.C	25	12		8.640

colori: spirale trasparente verde, zaffiro, thè.

VENINI

LISTINO PREZZI 1969 11

	H	Ø		Lit.
337.				
337.1	7,5	8	1/6	2.430
337.2	8,5	9	1/6	2.700
337.C	26	14		7.560

colori: spirale «parigi» (rosso, verde, zaffiro, pagliesco) - spirale «america» (verde, giallo, nero, pagliesco).

	H	Ø		Lit.
338.				
338.1	8	9	1/6	3.240
338.2	10	10	1/6	4.320
338.C	20	15		8.100

colori: spirale «asia» (cristallo, viola, acquamare, talpa) - spirale «istambul» (cristallo, talpa, viola, giallo).

	H	Ø		Lit.
339.				
339.1	14	7	1/6	3.240

colore: cristallo filo lattimo - cristallo filo zaffiro.

	H	Ø		Lit.
340.				
340.1	7	6	1/6	2.700
340.2	8	7	1/6	2.970
340.3	9	7,5	1/6	3.240
340.C	22	11,5		8.100

colori: cristallo, pagliesco, verdognolo, oppure cristallo spire verde o zaffiro.

VENINI, 50 FOND. VETRAI, MURANO VENEZIA, ITALY, VENINI SHOWROOMS IN ROMA, MILANO, VENEZIA, PARIS, NEW YORK.

VENINI

LISTINO PREZZI 1969 12

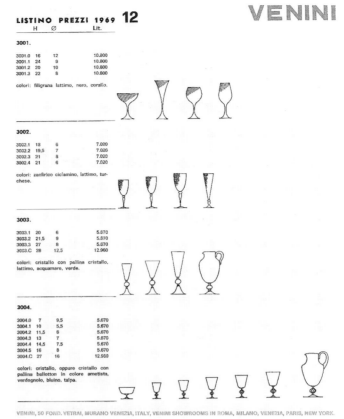

	H	Ø	Lit.
3001.			
3001.0	16	12	10.800
3001.1	24	9	10.800
3001.2	20	10	10.800
3001.3	22	8	10.800

colori: filigrana lattimo, nero, corallo.

	H	Ø	Lit.
3002.			
3002.1	18	6	7.020
3002.2	19,5	7	7.020
3002.3	21	8	7.020
3002.4	21	6	7.020

colori: zanfirico ciclamino, lattimo, turchese.

	H	Ø	Lit.
3003.			
3003.1	20	6	5.670
3003.2	21,5	9	5.670
3003.3	27	8	5.670
3003.C	28	12,5	12.960

colori: cristallo con pallina cristallo, lattimo, acquamare, verde.

	H	Ø	Lit.
3004.			
3004.0	7	9,5	5.670
3004.1	10	5,5	5.670
3004.2	11,5	6	5.670
3004.3	13	7	5.670
3004.4	14,5	7,5	5.670
3004.5	16	8	5.670
3004.C	27	16	12.960

colori: cristallo, oppure cristallo con pallina ballotton in colore ametista, verdognolo, bluino, talpa.

VENINI, 50 FOND. VETRAI, MURANO VENEZIA, ITALY, VENINI SHOWROOMS IN ROMA, MILANO, VENEZIA, PARIS, NEW YORK.

VENINI

LISTINO PREZZI 1969 13

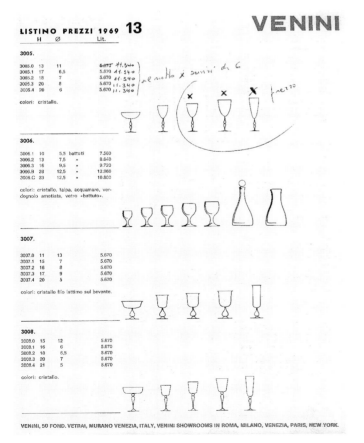

	H	Ø	Lit.
3005.			
3005.0	13	11	5.670 11.340
3005.1	17	6,5	5.670 11.340
3005.2	18	7	5.670 11.340
3005.3	20	8	5.670 11.340
3005.4	20	6	5.670 11.340

colori: cristallo.

(handwritten: al netto x serviri di 6 — prezzo)

	H	Ø		Lit.
3006.				
3006.1	10	5,5	battuti	7.560
3006.2	13	7,5	»	8.640
3006.3	16	9,5	»	9.720
3006.B	23	12,5	»	12.960
3006.C	23	12,5	»	10.800

colori: cristallo, talpa, acquamare, verdognolo ametista, vetro «battuto».

	H	Ø	Lit.
3007.			
3007.0	11	13	5.670
3007.1	15	7	5.670
3007.2	16	8	5.670
3007.3	17	9	5.670
3007.4	20	5	5.670

colori: cristallo filo lattimo sul bevante.

	H	Ø	Lit.
3008.			
3008.0	15	12	5.670
3008.1	16	6	5.670
3008.2	18	6,5	5.670
3008.3	20	7	5.670
3008.4	21	5	5.670

colori: cristallo.

VENINI, 50 FOND. VETRAI, MURANO VENEZIA, ITALY, VENINI SHOWROOMS IN ROMA, MILANO, VENEZIA, PARIS, NEW YORK.

VENINI

LISTINO PREZZI 1969 14

	H	Ø		Lit.
400.		tiepolo		
400.0	36			20.250
400.1	30			20.250
400.2	38			20.250
400.3	35			20.250
400.4	32			27.000
400.5	10			27.000

lattimo con particolari neri.

	H		Lit.
401.		grotteschi	
401.0	26		16.200
401.1	28		16.200
401.2	23		16.200
401.3	25		16.200
401.4	25		16.200
401.5	25		16.200

lattimo.

	H		Lit.
402.		maschere	
402.0	36	giangurgolo	27.000
402.1	36	pantalone	27.000
402.2	36	peppe nappa	27.000
402.3	36	meneghino	27.000
402.4	36	tartaglia	27.000
402.5	30	capitan fracassa	27.000
402.5	15	arlecchino	27.000
402.7	36	rosaura	27.000
402.8	36	arlecchino	27.000
402.9	36	brighella	27.000
402.10	36	pulcinella	27.000
402.11	36	arlecchina	27.000

lattimo con decorazioni multicolori.

VENINI, 50 FOND. VETRAI, MURANO VENEZIA, ITALY, VENINI SHOWROOMS IN ROMA, MILANO, VENEZIA, PARIS, NEW YORK.

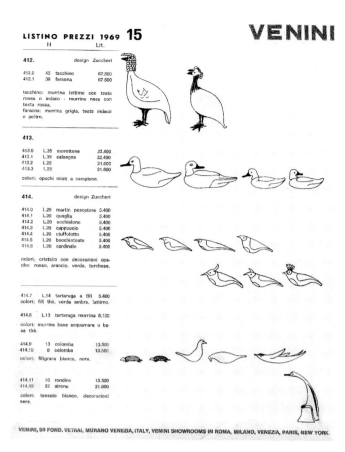

LISTINO PREZZI 1969 — 15 — VENINI

	H		Lit.
412.		design Zuccheri	
412.0	45	tacchino	67.500
412.1	38	faraona	67.500

tacchino: murrina lattimo con testa rossa o indaco · murrina nera con testa rossa.
faraona: murrina grigia, testa indaco o peltro.

413.			
413.0	L.35	morettone	32.400
413.1	L.35	salsegna	32.400
413.2	L.25		21.600
413.3	L.25		21.600

colori: opachi misti a campione.

414.		design Zuccheri	
414.0	L.20	martin pescatore	5.400
414.1	L.20	quaglia	5.400
414.2	L.20	occhialone	5.400
414.3	L.20	cappuccio	5.400
414.4	L.20	ciuffolotto	5.400
414.5	L.20	becchintesta	5.400
414.6	L.20	cardinale	5.400

colori: cristallo con decorazioni opache: rosso, arancio, verde, turchese.

| 414.7 | L.14 | tartaruga a fili | 5.400 |

colori: fili thè, verde ambra, lattimo.

| 414.8 | L.13 | tartaruga murrina | 8.100 |

colori: murrina base acquamare o base thè.

| 414.9 | 13 | colomba | 13.500 |
| 414.10 | 8 | colomba | 13.500 |

colori: filigrana bianca, nera.

| 414.11 | 10 | rondine | 13.500 |
| 414.12 | 32 | airone | 21.600 |

colori: tessuto bianco, decorazioni nere.

VENINI, 50 FOND. VETRAI, MURANO VENEZIA, ITALY, VENINI SHOWROOMS IN ROMA, MILANO, VENEZIA, PARIS, NEW YORK.

LISTINO PREZZI 1969 — 16 — VENINI

	H	Ø	Lit.
415.	uova		
415.0	12	8	10.800
415.1	9	6,5	7.560
415.2	7,5	5	4.320
415.3	4,5	3,5	3.240

cristallo con sfera d'oro

415.4	18	12	24.300
415.5	12	8	10.800
415.6	7	4,5	5.400
415.7	5	3,5	3.240

murrina rossa, verde mela, ambra, acquamare, lattimo, talpa.

| 415.8 | 15 | 7 | 14.040 |
| 415.9 | 12 | 8 | 12.960 |

uova «nembi» colori sfumati.

| 415.10 | 9 | 6 | 5.400 |
| 415.11 | 7 | 5 | 4.320 |

uova «spira».
colori: verde-arancio · zaffiro-ciclamino arancio-violetto.

| 415.12 | 12 | 8,5 | 10.260 |
| 415.13 | 9 | 6,5 | 11.880 |

uova «cirri».
colori: cristallo con motivo in spira acquamare · fili superficiali ametista o acquamare.

| 415.14 | 18 | 12 | 12.960 |
| 415.15 | 12 | 8 | 4.860 |

uova «marmorizzate», impasto di lattimo e nero, rosso antico, verde mela, indaco, thè.

415.16	12	8	7.560
415.17	9	6,5	5.400
415.18	7,5	5	4.320

uova «fiammate»: cristallo, fiamma corallo.

416.			
416.0	Ø	8	8.640
416.1	Ø	6	7.560

palle in murrina rosso, verde mela, ambra, acquamare, lattimo, talpa.

| 416.2 | Ø 10 | | 3.780 |

«claida»: spirale rosso-arancio · rosso-zaffiro · zolfo-zaffiro · zaffiro-verde.

| 416.3 | Ø 10 x 7 | | 4.050 |

«lente» · Sette combinazioni: zaffiro-nero · zolfo-nero · verde-nero · giallo-talpa · giallo-thé · rosso-verde · zaffiro-verde.

VENINI, 50 FOND. VETRAI, MURANO VENEZIA, ITALY, VENINI SHOWROOMS IN ROMA, MILANO, VENEZIA, PARIS, NEW YORK.

LISTINO PREZZI 1969 — 17 — VENINI

	H	Ø	Lit.
416.			
416.4	Ø 8		2.700

«futilità»
sette diverse decorazioni a colori fissi: esagono, collina, cima, onda, balaustra, griglia, stella.

416.5	7	13	pressepapier	4.050
416.6	5	10	pressepapier	2.700
416.7	5	5	pressepapier	1.890
416.7 B	2	6		1.890

«provenzali» —
Sei diverse combinazioni di colore:
Aix (zaffiro/lattimo) · Marseille (turchese/nero/zaffiro) · Tarascon (zolfo/nero/lattimo) · Arles (corallo) · Avignon (lattimo/rosso) · Camargue (nero/lattimo/arancio) · solo i colori di base.

| 416.8 | 5 | 8 | pressepapier | 4.050 |

«coralli»
cristallo con «coralli» in lattimo o corallo.

| 416.9 | 3 | 8 | pressepapier | 4.050 |

«arlecchino»
cristallo con pezzame «parigi» (verde/zaffiro/rosso/pagliesco).

| 416.10 | Ø 6 | | pressepapier | 2.240 |

palle in filigrana: nero, lattimo, corallo o turchese.

| 416.11 | 25 | 10,5 | | 10.800 |

palle in cristallo a spirali quadruple multicolori con base in legno tornito.

416.12	9	6	pressepapier	3.510
416.13	6	6	pressepapier	2.970
416.14	5	10	pressepapier	3.510
416.15	9	15	fermaporte	13.500

cristallo con «fiore» rosso, lattimo, zaffiro, zolfo, thé, viola, ciclamino, striati di lattimo.

| 416.16 | 9 | 15 | fermaporte | 13.500 |

varie esecuzioni:
— marmorizzato verde/lattimo · indaco/lattimo · rosso/lattimo · thé/lattimo · nero/lattimo.
— con palla oro.
— tipo «provenzale» vedi 416/5/6/7.
— tipo «millefiori» vari colori.

Basi

B/A		5	vetro	135
B/C		4	vetro	110
B/D		3	vetro	80
B/E	14	—	legno o vetro	1.485
B/F	17	—	legno o vetro	2.025
B/G	16	—	vetro	6.480
B/H	13	—	vetro	5.400
B/I	8	—	vetro	2.700

basi per appoggio di uova o biglie.

VENINI, 50 FOND. VETRAI, MURANO VENEZIA, ITALY, VENINI SHOWROOMS IN ROMA, MILANO, VENEZIA, PARIS, NEW YORK

LISTINO PREZZI 1969 — 18 — VENINI

	H	Ø	Lit.
420.	clessidre		
420.0	60	15	27.000
420.1	45	14	22.950
420.2	40	10	17.550
420.3	25	8	12.150
420.4	20	7	10.800

colori: rosso-verde · verde zaffiro · rosso-zaffiro · ametista-adriatico · giallo-viola · bacchette in zanfirico colorato.

420.5	22	8	8.640
420.6	18	6	7.560
420.7	13	5	6.480
420.8	20	10	9.720
420.9	22	10	12.150

colori: rosso-verde · verde-zaffiro · rosso-zaffiro · ametista-adriatico · giallo-viola · bacchette del 420.9 in zanfirico colorato.

421.	biglie		
421.0	20	11	15.660
421.1	16	9	13.500
421.2	13	13	12.150
421.3	9	9	9.720
421.4	6,5	6,5	8.100

colori: spire: rosso-nero-lattimo · verde-nero-lattimo · verde arancio. Si possono usare con o senza basi. I numeri 421.2, 421.3 e 421.4

421.5	14	7,5	zanfirico	10.800
421.6	13	7	macchia	9.720
421.7	14	7,5	zanfirico	10.800
421.8	15	5	spira	10.800

colori: zanfirico: lattimo, ciclamino, zaffiro; macchia: oceano, prugna, viola, putrido, corniola; spira: rosso-nero-lattimo · verde-nero-lattimo · verde-arancio.

VENINI, 50 FOND. VETRAI, MURANO VENEZIA, ITALY, VENINI SHOWROOMS IN ROMA, MILANO, VENEZIA, PARIS, NEW YORK.

VENINI

	H	Ø	Lit.
421.9	10	8	8.640
421.10	10	7	8.640
421.11	10	8	8.640
421.12	10	7	8.640

colori: cristallo con spira corallo, lattimo, nero, oppure con doppia spira co-
rallo-lattimo - turchese-lattimo - zolfo-
lattimo.

421.13	12x12x12	8.640
421.14	9x9x9	7.560
421.15	6x6x6	4.320
421.16	4,5x4,5x4,5	2.700
421.17	3x3x3	2.160
421.18		

colori: cristallo inciso con macchia in-
terna composta prugno, oceano, viola,
corniola o putrido.

422. pesci

	H	Ø	Lit.
422.0	45	thé/nero	17.280
422.1	40	talpa/zolfo - cor.	14.040
422.2	36	thé/fen. - nero	15.660
422.3	40	thé/nero	15.660
422.4	55	amet./thé - zolfo	14.580
422.5	30	crist./talpa - cel.	11.880
422.6	36	thé/arancio	12.960
422.7	32	orizzonte	11.340
422.8	34	arancio/nero	10.800
422.9	30	arancio/nero	11.880
422.10	38	orizz./fen. - ver.	12.960
422.11	20	viola/corallo	11.340
422.12	30	acquamare/nero	9.720
422.13	17	acquam./fen. - n.	7.560
423.14	15	acquam./fen. - n.	7.560

colori: il primo indicato è il colore di
base, il secondo il colore principale
della decorazione. I modelli 423.13 e
423.14 hanno base acquamare o corallo.

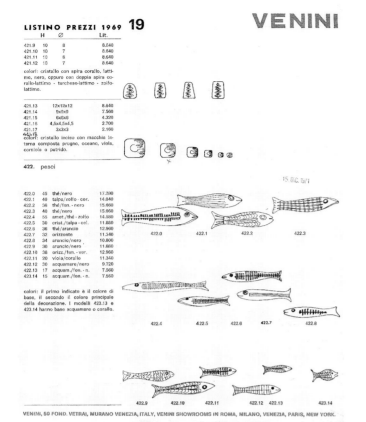

422.0   422.1   422.2   422.3

422.4   422.5   422.6   422.7   422.8

422.9   422.10   422.11   422.12   422.13   423.14

VENINI

450. obelischi

	H	Ø	Lit.
450.0	60	15	quadrato	33.750
450.1	50	12	»	27.000
450.2	40	8	»	22.680
450.3	35	7	»	18.360
450.4	25	6	»	10.800
450.5	20	5	»	8.100

colori: trasparenti acquamare, rosso,
zaffiro, verde, ametista, cristallo, giallo,
talpa.

450.6	50	12	esagono	31.860
450.7	40	9	»	27.000
450.8	25	7	»	13.500

colori: trasparenti acquamare, rosso,
zaffiro, verde, ametista, cristallo, giallo,
talpa.

450.9	50	12	ottagono	33.750
450.10	25	7	»	16.200

colori: trasparenti acquamare, rosso,
zaffiro, verde, ametista, cristallo, giallo,
talpa.

451.

	H	Ø	Lit.
451.0	40	10	esagono	27.000
451.1	30	10	»	21.600
451.2	45	10	triangolo	40.500
451.3	30	10	»	32.400

colori: cristallo con spirale rosso-nero
o verde-zolfo.

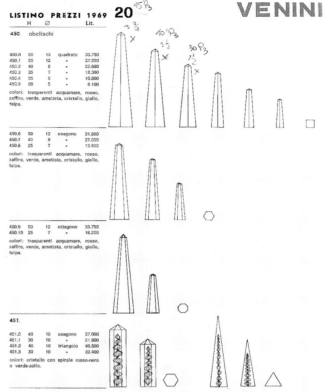

VENINI

	H	Ø	Lit.
452-453			
452.0	37	8	40.500
452.1	30	6	8.100
452.2	35	5,5	32.400
452.3	40	12	27.000
452.4	26	10	20.250

colori: trasparenti acquamare, rosso,
zaffiro, verde, ametista, cristallo, giallo,
talpa.

453.0	45	7,5	inciso	24.300
453.1	32	6,5	inciso	13.500

Stessi colori, vetro inciso.

454.

	H	Ø	Lit.
454.0	60	8	quadrato	33.750
454.1	45	6,5	»	24.300
454.2	35	5,5	»	16.200
454.3	45	8	tondo	27.000
454.4	30	6	»	18.200
454.5	25	5	»	8.100

colori: spirale multicolore.

455. fiammati

	H	Ø	Lit.
455.0	35	12	18.200
455.1	40	10	21.600
455.2	30	7	13.500

colori: cristallo con fiamma corallo o
lattimo.

455.3	40	8	quadrato	32.400
455.4	30	6	»	21.600
455.5	20	5	»	10.800
455.6	40	8	tondo	24.300
455.7	30	6	»	16.200
455.8	20	5	»	9.180

colori: cristallo con fiamma corallo o
lattimo.

VENINI

	H	Ø	Lit.
500. lapponi		design Wirkkala	
500.0	35	10	14.040
500.1	24	9	12.960
500.2	24	6	8.640
500.3	17	10	9.720
500.4	18	15	10.040

colori: base talpa; vetro rosso, viola,
acquamare, adriatico.

	H	Ø	Lit.
501. meduse		design Wirkkala	
501.0	32	20	24.300
501.1	16	16	18.900
501.2	14	30	24.300
501.3	12	26	21.600
501.4	11	20	18.900

colori: filigrana lattimo sommersa in
uva o acquamarina.

	H	Ø	Lit.
502. bolle		design Wirkkala	
502.0	17	20	10.800
502.1	19	19	10.800
502.2	21	12	10.800
502.3	15	17	10.800

colori: gamma di talpa, verde mela,
thé, rosso, pagliesco, celeste e uva,
come campioni.

	H	Ø	Lit.
503. bolle		design Wirkkala	
503.0	42	13	19.440
503.1	35	10	12.960
503.2	26	14	11.340

colori: gamma di talpa, verde mela,
thé, rosso, pagliesco, celeste e uva,
come campioni.

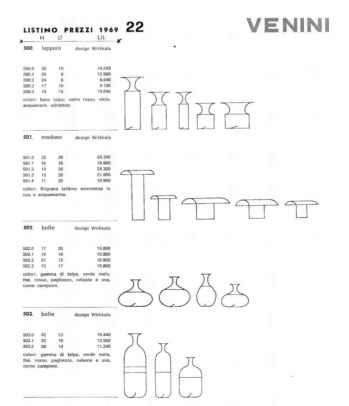

LISTINO PREZZI 1969 **23**   **VENINI**

	H	Ø	Lit.
504.	pianissimo		
504.0	21	12,5	13.500
504.1	22	12,5	14.040
504.2	18	14	12.960
504.3	10	12	9.720
504.4	6	30	7.560
504.5			

colori: gamma di talpa, uva, viola e celeste a campione.

	H	Ø	Lit.
505.	coreani	design Wirkkala	
505.0	35	20	16.200
505.1	14	20	12.960
505.2	22	15	12.960
505.3	27	10	11.340
505.4	11	35	16.200
505.5	14	30	16.200
505.6	32	12	12.960

colori: viola-verde mela e verde-verde mela.

	H	Ø	Lit.
507.	gondolieri	design Wirkkala	
507.0	20	30	18.360
507.1	13	28	18.360
507.2	8	30	16.200
507.3	10	30	16.200
507.4	14	20	14.560
507.5	8	22	12.960

colori: gamma di talpa, giallo, rosso, viola ed acquamare a campione.

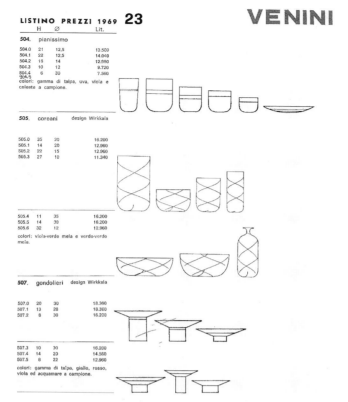

VENINI, 50 FOND. VETRAI, MURANO VENEZIA, ITALY, VENINI SHOWROOMS IN ROMA, MILANO, VENEZIA, PARIS, NEW YORK.

LISTINO PREZZI 1969 **24**   **VENINI**

	H	Ø	Lit.
509.	silmä	design Wirkkala	
509.1	—	40	piatto	19.440
509.2	—	30	piatto	16.200

colori: verde mela, occhio nero-viola; nero, occhio giallo.

	H	Ø	Lit.
510.	calici	design Wirkkala	
510.0	11	35	17.280
510.1	72	10	21.600
510.2	37	8	7.560
510.3	32	7	7.560
510.4	27	7	7.560
510.5	20	5	6.480
510.6	11	7	6.480

colori: acquamare o uva, chiarissimi. base piena.

			Lit.
511.		design Wirkkala	
511.50	—	50	40.500
511.40	—	40	26.350
511.30	—	30	19.440

Questi piatti sono realizzati in dodici diverse decorazioni con bordo in colore trasparente e motivo centrale in murrina identificato con lettere da «A» a «M».
Possono essere a richiesta muniti di metallo ad anello, verniciato nero, da muro per tutte le misure, o da tavolo per i 511.30.
costo Lit.   6.000

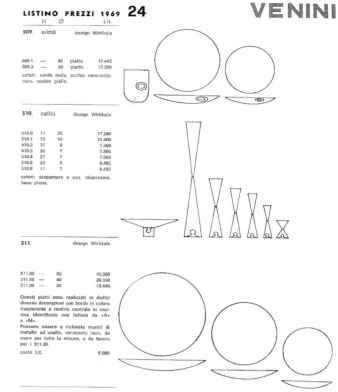

VENINI, 50 FOND. VETRAI, MURANO VENEZIA, ITALY, VENINI SHOWROOMS IN ROMA, MILANO, VENEZIA, PARIS, NEW YORK.

LISTINO PREZZI 1969 **25**   **VENINI**

	H	Ø	Lit.
512.	colletti		
512.0	37	22	21.600
512.1	30	24	19.440
512.2	22	20	12.960
512.3	30	12	9.720

colori: verdognolo collo verde, pagliesco collo thé, acquamare collo zaffiro.

	H	Ø		Lit.
512.4	18	20	ghiaccio	9.720
512.5	20	26	champagne	12.960
512.6	26	10	mixer	12.960
512.7	14	5	1/6	2.700
512.8	6	18	mandorle	6.480
512.9	12	40	frutta	19.440

colori: verdognolo collo verde, pagliesco collo thé, acquamare collo zaffiro.
Mescolatori in filigrana o zanfirico cm. 30 per 512.6   400

	H	Ø	Lit.
513.	cinesi		
513.0	24	15	13.500
513.1	27	18	16.200
513.2	24	20	16.200
513.3	22	21	17.550
513.4	30	18	17.550
513.5	10	10	6.750

colori: opachi: nero antracite, rosso antico, verde antico, ambra, indaco, lattimo.

VENINI, 50 FOND. VETRAI, MURANO VENEZIA, ITALY, VENINI SHOWROOMS IN ROMA, MILANO, VENEZIA, PARIS, NEW YORK.

VENINI

TRE VASI « CINESI ». DA SINISTRA A DESTRA: 513.2 · 513.0 · 513.4

VENINI, 50 FOND. VETRAI, MURANO VENEZIA, ITALY, VENINI SHOWROOMS IN ROMA, MILANO, VENEZIA, PARIS, NEW YORK

LISTINO PREZZI 1969 **26**   **VENINI**

	H	Ø	Lit.
514.	velati		

514.0	50	13	21.600
514.1	38	10	16.200
514.2	28	8	11.880
514.3	23	14	14.040
514.4	18	9	8.640
514.5	10	11	8.640
514.6	8	17	9.720

colori: acquamare, thé, rosso.

	H	Ø	Lit.
515.	velati		

515.0	20	24	11.880
515.1	30	13	10.800
515.2	18	9	8.640
515.3	14	17	10.800

colori: acquamare, thé, rosso.

	H	Ø	Lit.
517.	piogge		

517.0	38	12	24.300
517.1	30	11	18.900
517.2	22	10	16.200

colori: «estate» (tessuto murrina lattimo), «primavera» (tessuto murrina lattimo-nero).

VENINI, 50 FOND. VETRAI, MURANO VENEZIA, ITALY, VENINI SHOWROOMS IN ROMA, MILANO, VENEZIA, PARIS, NEW YORK.

LISTINO PREZZI 1969 **27**   **VENINI**

	H	Ø	Lit.
516.	battuti		

516.0	45	34	75.600
516.1	33	20	27.000
516.2	30	12	27.000
516.3	18	18	19.440
516.4	13	30	20.520

colori: verdognolo, rosato, uva, giallo,
thé, acquamare.

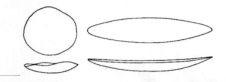

516.5	10	26	17.280
516.6	8	20	14.040
516.7	7	15	9.720
516.8	12	53	81.000

colori: verdognolo, rosato, uva, giallo,
thé, acquamare

516.9	5	35	21.900
516.10	5	80	64.800

colori: verdognolo, rosato, uva, giallo,
thé, acquamare.

VENINI, 50 FOND. VETRAI, MURANO VENEZIA, ITALY, VENINI SHOWROOMS IN ROMA, MILANO, VENEZIA, PARIS, NEW YORK.

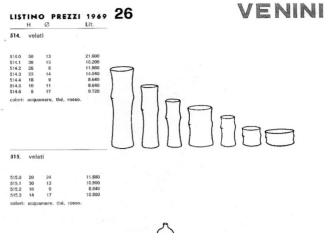

VENINI

GRUPPO DI VETRI BATTUTI. DA SINISTRA A DESTRA: 516.4 - 516.9 - 516.1

VENINI, 50 FOND. VETRAI, MURANO VENEZIA, ITALY, VENINI SHOWROOMS IN ROMA, MILANO, VENEZIA, PARIS, NEW YORK

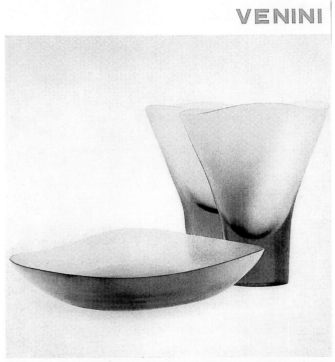

VENINI

GRUPPO DI VETRI BATTUTI. DA SINISTRA A DESTRA 516.8 - 516.0 - 516.0

VENINI, 50 FOND. VETRAI, MURANO VENEZIA, ITALY, VENINI SHOWROOMS IN ROMA, MILANO, VENEZIA, PARIS, NEW YORK

LISTINO PREZZI 1969 **28**   VENINI

518.

	H	Ø	Lit.
518.0	17	18	17.280
518.1	22	12	15.120
518.2	8	12	12.960
518.3	13	14	12.960
518.4	6	22	16.200
518.5	40	8	19.440
518.6	24	10	15.120

colori: lattimo con fascia murrina assortita, due colori (viola-acquamare - zaffiro-verde - zaffiro-talpa); con murrina assortita.
Coppe 518.2 e 518.4 un colore (rosso, viola, adriatico o zaffiro) con murrina assortita.

519. thomas   design Stearns

	H	Ø	Lit.
519.0	38	10	19.440
519.1	30	10	15.160
519.2	25	10	12.960
519.3	20	10	10.800

colori: vaso verde-pagliesco con fili neri; base rosso antico-bluino con fili neri; base antracite-acquamare con fili indaco; base antracite-rosso chiaro con fili rosso antico.

520. occhi

	H	Ø	Lit.
520.0	15	14	15.120
520.1	15	13	16.200
520.2	20	11	18.900
520.3	34	10	18.900
520.4	27	11	18.900
520.5	16	12	16.200

colori: murrina a «occhio» cristallo, in corallo, lattimo, turchese, thé.

	H	Ø	Lit.
520.6	7	28	27.000
520.7	6	22	16.800
520.8	5	16	13.500

colori: murrina a «occhio» cristallo, in corallo, lattimo, turchese, thé, zolfo.
Bicolori: murrina a «occhio» cristallo in nero-corallo, nero-lattimo, turchese-lattimo.

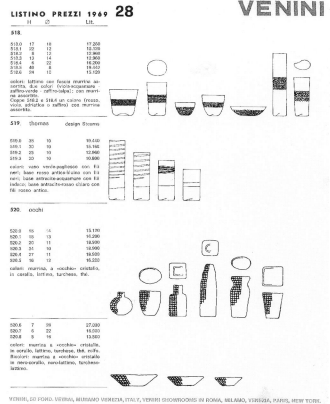

VENINI

GRUPPO DI VETRI A «OCCHI». DA SINISTRA A DESTRA: 520.1 - 520.3 - 520.2

LISTINO PREZZI 1969 **29**   VENINI

521.

	H	Ø	Lit.
521.0	30	20	16.200
521.1	23	17	13.500
521.2	16	13	9.720
521.3	11	11	6.480

colori: canne a sette colori oppure canne alternate rosso-zaffiro, rosso-verde o verde-zaffiro.

521.0-1-4

522. vasi a murrine

	H	Ø	Lit.
522.0	22	6	16.200
522.1	12	12	13.500
522.2	18	15	18.900

colori: murrina B (mezzaluna): zolfo-nero - lattimo-nero.

	H	Ø	Lit.
522.3	12	12	10.800
522.4	22	11	18.900
522.5	24	14	18.900
522.6	26	11	21.600

colori: murrina C (dame): turchese-lattimo, nero-lattimo, nero-zolfo, nero-turchese.

	H	Ø	Lit.
522.7	25	11	24.300
522.8	13	13	10.800
522.9	21	13	24.300
522.10	30	14	32.400

colori: murrina A (faraona): talpa o rosso trasparente, turchese, corallo o nero opachi.

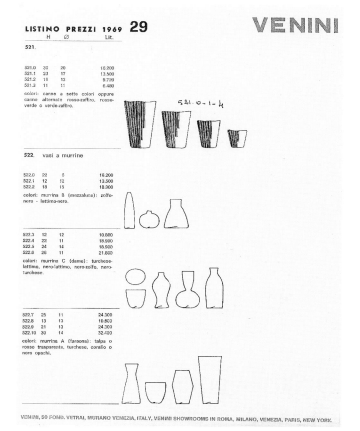

LISTINO PREZZI 1969 **30**   VENINI

523.

	H	Ø	Lit.
523.0	46	20	21.600
523.1	27	32	20.500
523.2	38	16	16.200

colori: fascie «parigi» (rosso, verde, zaffiro, pagliesco).
fascie «pagliesco» (pagliesco, giallo, nero, verde).

	H	Ø	Lit.
523.3	20	16	9.450
523.4	11	25	10.800
523.5	34	28	20.250

colori: fascie «parigi» (rosso, verde, zaffiro, pagliesco).
fascie «america» (pagliesco, giallo, nero, verde).

524. tessuti

	H	Ø	Lit.
524.0	11	12	10.800
524.1	17	9	13.500
524.2	34	14	21.600
524.3	12	10	10.800
524.4	24	14	16.200
524.5	16	16	16.200

colori: bicolore: turchese-nero - corallo-nero - zolfo-nero.
oppure: corallo - nero - turchese - zolfo.

525. oro/argento

	H	Ø		Lit.
525.0	7	13	oro	3.780
			argento	3.240
525.1	18	10	oro	3.780
			argento	3.240
525.2	8	9	oro	3.780
			argento	3.240
525.3	12	13	oro	3.780
			argento	3.240
525.4	24	6	obelis. oro	12.960
525.5	28	14	oro	7.560
			argento	6.480
525.6	22	23	oro	7.560
			argento	6.480

cristallo con oro e cristallo con argento.

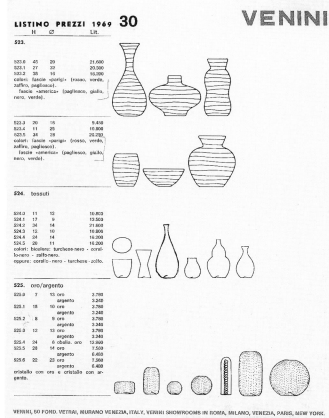

LISTINO PREZZI 1969 · 31 · VENINI

526.	bottiglie	H	Ø	Lit.
526.0		35	7	11.340
526.1		42	11	16.200

colori: filigrana lattimo, nero, corallo, turchese.

526.2	52	13	34.400
526.3	37	3	17.280
526.4	52	12	27.000

colori: zanfirico, lattimo, ciclamino, turchese.

526.5	35	8	21.600
526.6	38	8	21.600
526.7	30	8	21.600

colori: zaffiro fascia filigrana turchese, verde fascia filigrana rossa, celeste fascia filigrana zolfo.

526.8	50	10	21.600
526.9	48	10	21.600
526.10	48	9	21.600
526.11	32	8	13.500

colori: canne verticali talpa-giallo - verde-zaffiro - lattimo-talpa - zaffiro-rosso, - verdemela-ciclamino.

526.12	36	7	13.500
526.13	48	8	16.900

colori: filigrana corallo-zolfo e lattimo-zolfo.

526.14	40	8	18.900

colori 3 fasce orizzontali: verde, due fasce zolfo e una viola - zaffiro, fasce celeste e una viola - talpa, due fasce zolfo e una lattimo.

526.15	46	8	18.900

due fasce: verde fascia zolfo - talpa fascia lattimo, zaffiro fascia op. rosso.

526.16	30	11	6.480

una fascia: verde fascia opalino rosso, zaffiro fascia turchese, rosso fascia opalino verde.

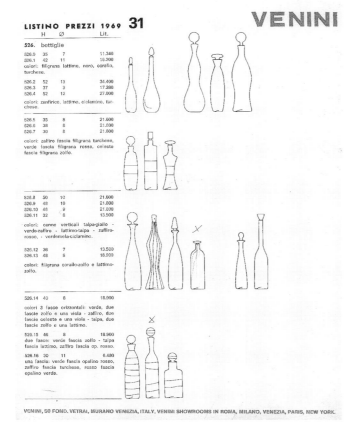

VENINI, 50 FOND. VETRAI, MURANO VENEZIA, ITALY, VENINI SHOWROOMS IN ROMA, MILANO, VENEZIA, PARIS, NEW YORK.

LISTINO PREZZI 1969 · 32 · VENINI

	H	Ø	Lit.
526.17	33	7	12.960
526.18	20	6	8.100
526.19	30	12	16.200

colori: base opalino verde-zaffiro - base opalino celeste-ametista - base arancio e giallo base lattimo-talpa - base zolfo-talpa - base opalino rosso e talpa - base opalino verde mela e viola.

526.20	36	8	16.200

colori: talpa-giallo - thé-verde mela - ametista-celeste.

527.	foglie in tessuto	H	Ø	Lit.
527.0		40		43.200
527.1		40		21.600
527.2		35		27.000

colori: tono rosso, tono thé, tono nero, tono verde.

VENINI, 50 FOND. VETRAI, MURANO VENEZIA, ITALY, VENINI SHOWROOMS IN ROMA, MILANO, VENEZIA, PARIS, NEW YORK.

VENINI

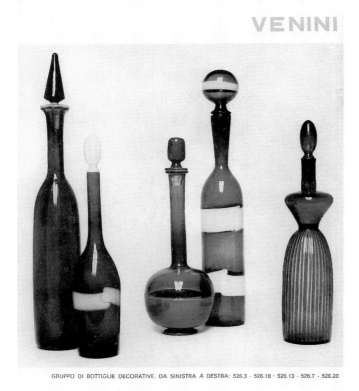

GRUPPO DI BOTTIGLIE DECORATIVE. DA SINISTRA A DESTRA: 526.3 - 526.18 - 526.13 - 526.7 - 526.20

VENINI, 50 FOND. VETRAI, MURANO VENEZIA, ITALY, VENINI SHOWROOMS IN ROMA, MILANO, VENEZIA, PARIS, NEW YORK.

LISTINO PREZZI 1969 · 33 · VENINI

600.	veronese	H	Ø	Lit.
600.0		40	25	17.280
600.1		35	20	14.040
600.2		30	17	10.800
600.3		25	13	8.640
600.4		12	6	3.240

colori: rosso, verde, zaffiro, ametista, pagliesco, uva, acquamare, verdognolo.

601.

601.0	25	16	caravaggio	8.640
601.1	34	14		10.800
601.2	34	14		12.960
601.3	28	11	tiziano	8.640

colori: rosso, verde, zaffiro, ametista, pagliesco, uva, acquamare, verdognolo.

601.4	25	16	tintoretto	10.800
601.5	32	15	holbein	11.880
601.6	13	13		6.480

colori: rosso, verde, zaffiro, ametista, pagliesco, uva, acquamare, verdognolo.

601.7	25	13	10.800
601.8	18	12	5.400
601.9	20	8	5.400
601.10	25	8	6.480
601.11	20	10	6.480
601.12	20	8	4.320

colori: rosso, verde, zaffiro, ametista, pagliesco, uva, acquamare, verdognolo.

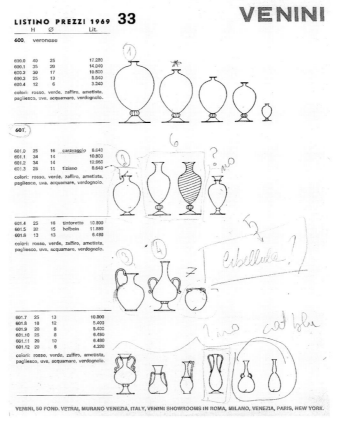

VENINI, 50 FOND. VETRAI, MURANO VENEZIA, ITALY, VENINI SHOWROOMS IN ROMA, MILANO, VENEZIA, PARIS, NEW YORK.

LISTINO PREZZI 1969 34   VENINI

602. filigrane

	H	Ø	Lit.
602.0	35	21	21.600
602.1	28	20	21.600
602.2	36	17	21.600
602.3	31	15	17.280
602.4	14	15	10.800

colori: filigrana lattimo, corallo, nero o turchese.

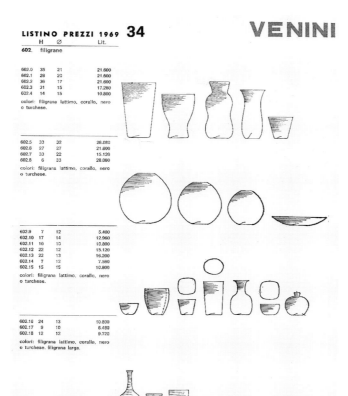

	H	Ø	Lit.
602.5	33	32	26.080
602.6	27	27	21.600
602.7	33	22	15.120
602.8	6	33	28.080

colori: filigrana lattimo, corallo, nero o turchese.

	H	Ø	Lit.
602.9	7	12	5.400
602.10	17	14	12.960
602.11	10	10	10.800
602.12	22	12	15.120
602.13	22	13	16.200
602.14	7	12	7.560
602.15	15	15	10.800

colori: filigrana lattimo, corallo, nero o turchese.

	H	Ø	Lit.
602.16	24	13	10.800
602.17	9	10	6.480
602.18	12	12	9.720

colori: filigrana lattimo, corallo, nero o turchese. filigrana larga.

LISTINO PREZZI 1969 35   VENINI

603. foglie in filigrana

	H	Ø	Lit.
603.0	Ø	25-20	9.720
603.1	Ø	27-25	21.600
603.2	Ø	25-20	10.800
603.3	Ø	20-14	17.280

colori: filigrana lattimo, nero, turchese o corallo.

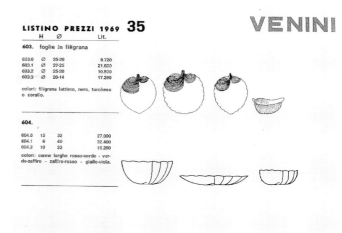

604.

	H	Ø	Lit.
604.0	15	32	27.000
604.1	6	40	32.400
604.2	10	22	16.200

colori: canne larghe rosso-verde - verde-zaffiro - zaffiro-rosso - giallo-viola.

LISTINO PREZZI 1969 36   VENINI

607. zanfirici

	H	Ø	Lit.
607.0	20	12	14.850
607.1	20	24	14.850
607.2	20	14	12.960
607.3	30	8	12.960
607.4	12	22/17	19.440
607.5	16	10	10.800

colori: zanfirico M: lattimo, nero, corallo, turchese.

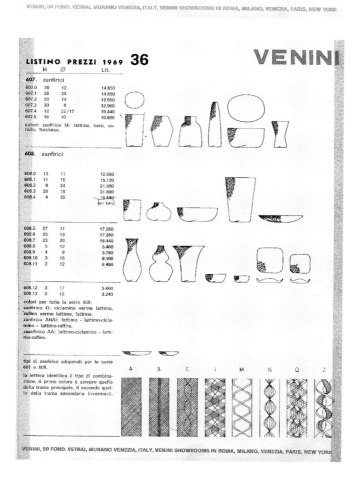

608. zanfirici

	H	Ø	Lit.
608.0	13	11	12.960
608.1	11	15	15.120
608.2	9	24	21.600
608.3	26	18	21.600
608.4	4	30	19.440
608.5	27	11	17.280
608.6	23	13	17.280
608.7	23	20	19.440
608.8	5	12	5.400
608.9	4	9	3.780
608.10	3	16	8.100
608.11	2	12	6.480
608.12	3	17	5.400
608.13	2	12	3.240

colori per tutta la serie 608:
zanfirico O; ciclamino verme lattimo, zaffiro verme lattimo, lattimo.
zanfirico ANAI: lattimo - lattimo-ciclamino - lattimo-zaffiro.
zaanfirico AA: lattimo-ciclamino - lattimo-zaffiro.

tipi di zanfirico adoperati per le serie 607 e 608.

la lettera identifica il tipo di combinazione, il primo colore è sempre quello della trama principale, il secondo quello della trama secondaria («verme»).

A   B   C   I   M   N   Q   Z

LISTINO PREZZI 1969 37   VENINI

700. fazzoletti

	H	Ø	Lit.
700.0	35	25	10.800
700.1	27	27	8.100
700.2	20	18	6.750

colori: opalino rosso, bianco, ametista, thé, talpa, acquamare, aranzio, zolfo. Interno sempre opalino bianco salvo che per lo zolfo e arancio.

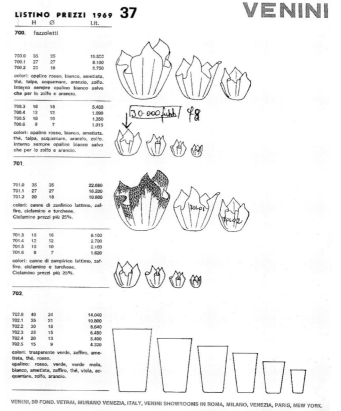

	H	Ø	Lit.
700.3	16	16	5.400
700.4	12	12	1.890
700.5	10	10	1.350
700.6	8	7	1.015

colori: opalino rosso, bianco, ametista, thé, talpa, acquamare, aranzio, zolfo. Interno sempre opalino bianco salvo che per lo zolfo e arancio.

701.

	H	Ø	Lit.
701.0	35	35	22.680
701.1	27	27	16.200
701.2	20	18	10.800

colori: canne di zanfirico lattimo, zaffiro, ciclamino e turchese. Ciclamino prezzi più 25%.

	H	Ø	Lit.
701.3	16	16	8.100
701.4	12	12	2.700
701.5	10	10	2.160
701.6	8	7	1.620

colori: canne di zampirico lattimo, zaffiro, ciclamino e turchese. Ciclamino prezzi più 25%.

702.

	H	Ø	Lit.
702.0	40	24	14.040
702.1	35	21	10.800
702.2	30	18	8.640
702.3	25	15	6.480
702.4	20	13	5.400
702.5	15	9	4.320

colori: trasparente verde, zaffiro, ametista, thé, rosso.
opalino: rosso, verde, verde mela, bianco, ametista, zaffiro, thé, viola, acquamare, zolfo, arancio.

VENINI

703. spicchi

H	Ø	Lit.
703.0	20	20	10.800
703.1	36	14	10.800
703.2	27	20	12.960
703.3	20	10	8.640
703.4	13	13	7.500
703.5	13	18	9.720

colori: «stoccolma» (talpa, rosato, uva, acquamarina), «parigi» (rosso, zaffiro, verde, pagliesco).

704. pezzati

	H	Ø	Lit.
704.0	35	13	21.600
704.1	21	15	10.800
704.2	28	9	12.960
704.3	20	12	10.800
704.4	12	10	10.800
704.5	25	15	10.800

colori: «stoccolma» (talpa, rosato, uva, acquamarina), «parigi» (rosso, zaffiro, verde, pagliesco).

705. variazioni

	H	Ø	Lit.
705.0	35	10	16.200
705.1	20	20	10.800
705.2	25	16	16.200
705.3	30	8	12.960
705.4	24	18	16.200

colore: pezzame opalino rosso e zaffiro, ed opalino zaffiro e verde alternati.

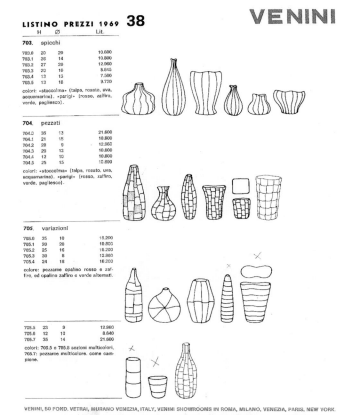

	H	Ø	Lit.
705.5	23	9	12.960
705.6	12	10	8.640
705.7	35	14	21.600

colori: 705.5 e 705.6 sezioni multicolori, 705.7: pezzame multicolore, come campione.

VENINI

706. opalini

	H	Ø	Lit.
706.0	37	18	16.200
706.1	65	34	64.800
706.2	55	21	21.600
706.3	45	18	20.250

colori opalini: bianco, ametista, thé, talpa, verde mela, rosso, zaffiro, acquamare, viola, adriatico, verde.

Per tutti i vasi in opalino il colore ciclamino (su richiesta) comporta un aumento sui prezzi del 25%

	H	Ø	Lit.
706.4	60	26	54.000
706.5	60	18	27.000
706.6	50	15	21.600
706.7	52	24	20.250
706.8	30	15	10.800

colori opalini: bianco, ametista, thé, talpa, verde mela, rosso, zaffiro, acquamare, viola, adriatico, verde.

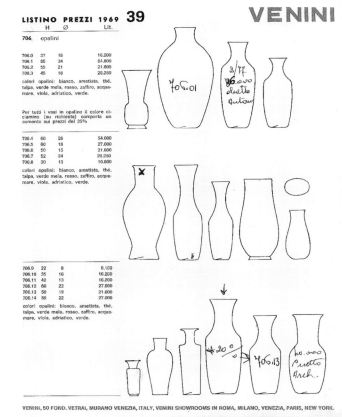

	H	Ø	Lit.
706.9	22	8	8.100
706.10	35	16	16.200
706.11	42	13	16.200
706.12	60	22	27.000
706.13	50	19	21.600
706.14	50	22	27.000

colori opalini: bianco, ametista, thé, talpa, verde mela, rosso, zaffiro, acquamare, viola, adriatico, verde.

VENINI

	H	Ø	Lit.
706.15	30	16	13.500
706.16	30	11	10.800
706.17	24	14	10.800
706.18	27	13	10.800
706.19	25	11	9.450
706.20	38	14	13.500
706.21	60	22	27.000

colori opalini: bianco, ametista, thé, talpa, verde mela, rosso zaffiro, acquamare, viola, adriatico, verde.

	H	Ø	Lit.
706.22	36	17	17.550
706.23	35	17	17.550
706.24	32	18	13.500
706.25	30	20	10.800
706.26	20	15	8.100
706.27	16	15	9.180

colori opalini: bianco, ametista, thé, talpa, verde mela, rosso zaffiro, acquamare, viola, adriatico, verde.

	H	Ø	Lit.
706.28	28	12	10.800
706.29	20	11	8.100
706.30	13	13	5.400
706.31	40	30	33.750
706.32	25	18	12.960
706.33	18	14	8.100

colori opalini: bianco, ametista, thé, talpa, verde mela, rosso, zaffiro, acquamare, viola, adriatico, verde.

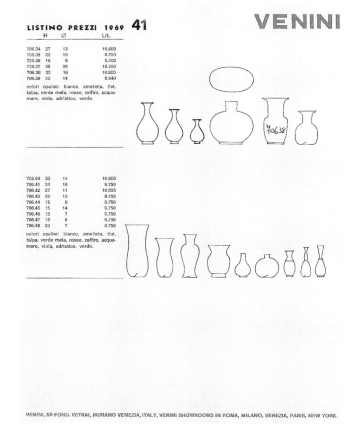

VENINI

	H	Ø	Lit.
706.34	27	13	10.800
706.35	22	10	6.750
706.36	16	8	5.400
706.37	28	26	16.200
706.38	30	16	10.800
706.39	22	14	8.640

colori opalini: bianco, ametista, thé, talpa, verde mela, rosso, zaffiro, acquamare, viola, adriatico, verde.

	H	Ø	Lit.
706.40	33	14	10.800
706.41	24	10	6.750
706.42	27	11	10.800
706.43	20	13	9.450
706.44	15	9	6.750
706.45	15	14	6.750
706.46	18	7	6.750
706.47	19	6	6.750
706.48	20	7	6.750

colori opalini: bianco, ametista, thé, talpa, verde mela, rosso, zaffiro, acquamare, viola, adriatico, verde.

LISTINO PREZZI 1969 42 **VENINI**

	H	Ø		Lit.
711.	informali		design Bianconi	
711.0	46	27		32.400
711.1	38	24		28.350
711.2	24	26		24.300

colori: verdino, cristallo, giallino.

	H	Ø		Lit.
712.	bigoli		design Bianconi	
712.0	26	7		8.640
712.1	24	7		7.500
712.2	18	7		6.480

colori: fili lattimo, arancio o nero su cristallo.

	H	Ø		Lit.
713.	cannette			
713.0	26	24		27.000
713.1	18	16		16.200
713.2	33	15		21.600
713.3	14	14		13.500
713.4	30	19		21.600

colori: talpa cannette corallo - acquamare cannette indaco - ametista cannette verde antico - paglierino cannette ambra.

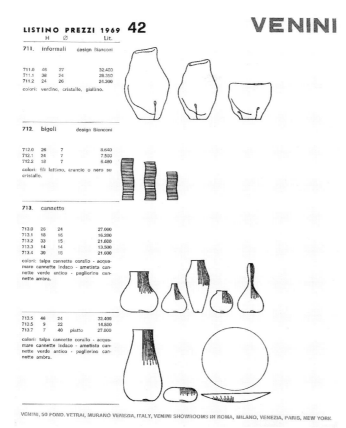

	H	Ø		Lit.
713.5	46	24		32.400
713.6	9	22		14.850
713.7	7	40	piatto	27.000

colori: talpa cannette corallo - acquamare cannette indaco - ametista cannette verde antico - paglierino cannette ambra.

VENINI, 50 FOND. VETRAI, MURANO VENEZIA, ITALY, VENINI SHOWROOMS IN ROMA, MILANO, VENEZIA, PARIS, NEW YORK.

LISTINO PREZZI 1969 43 **VENINI**

	H	Ø		Lit.
714.	tronchi		design Zuccheri	
714.0	45	11		11.340
714.1	37	10		9.720
714.2	33	11		8.100
714.3	32	7		6.480

colori opachi: rosso antico, verde antico, lattimo, ambra, nero, indaco. venature cristallo.

	H	Ø		Lit.
716.			design Zuccheri	
716.0	26	10		10.800
716.1	22	8		9.720
716.2	20	14		8.100
716.3	13	11		6.480

colori opachi: rosso antico, verde antico, lattimo, ambra, nero, indaco. fessure cristallo.

	H	Ø		Lit.
715.	ninfee		design Zuccheri	
715.0	18	65		10.800
715.1	18	55		9.720
715.2	15	45		8.100
715.3	20	35		6.480
715.4	12	25		4.320

colori opachi: rosso antico, verde antico, lattimo, ambra, nero, indaco. venature cristallo.

	H	Ø		Lit.
717.	scolpiti		design Zuccheri	
717.0	40	13		21.600
717.1	25	7	molato	14.300
717.2	22	27	molato	16.900
717.3	35	9	molato	18.900
717.4	50	15		32.400

colori opachi: rosso antico, verde antico, lattimo, ambra, nero, indaco. fessure ed occhi in cristallo.

VENINI, 50 FOND. VETRAI, MURANO VENEZIA, ITALY, VENINI SHOWROOMS IN ROMA, MILANO, VENEZIA, PARIS, NEW YORK.

LISTINO PREZZI 1969 44 **VENINI**

	H	Ø	Lit.
718.	grovigli	design Zuccheri	
718.0	12	28	16.200
718.1	11	35	20.250
718.2	45	32	40.500
718.3	15	15	13.500
718.4	15	15	16.200

colori: cristallo con fili sommersi di rame.

	H	Ø	Lit.
719.	crepuscoli	design Zuccheri	
719.0	15	16	10.800
719.1	13	15	10.800
719.2	30	27	21.600
719.3	30	23	16.200
719.4	14	15	10.800

colori: acquamare-indaco - ametista-adriatico - ciclamino-zaffiro.

	H	Ø	Lit.
720.	giade	design Zuccheri	
720.0	19	14	6.480
720.1	25	11	7.560
720.2	17	11	5.400
720.3	30	9	8.640
720.4	40	13	13.500
720.5	23	13	9.450
720.6	18	17	10.800
720.7	11	17	12.150

colori opachi con inclusioni di rame: rosso antico, verde antico, indaco, marrone.

VENINI, 50 FOND. VETRAI, MURANO VENEZIA, ITALY, VENINI SHOWROOMS IN ROMA, MILANO, VENEZIA, PARIS, NEW YORK.

VENINI

GRUPPO DI VASI « INCISI ». DA SINISTRA A DESTRA: 722.16 - 722.17 - 722.8 - 722.8

VENINI, 50 FOND. VETRAI, MURANO VENEZIA, ITALY, VENINI SHOWROOMS IN ROMA, MILANO, VENEZIA, PARIS, NEW YORK

VENINI

721.

	H	Ø		Lit.
721.0	35	17		18.900
721.1	22	10		9.720
721.2	40	20		18.900
721.3	26	14		9.720
721.4	13	14		6.480
721.5	6	13		5.400

colori: composti corniola, prugna, oceano, putrido, violetto.

altri colori su richiesta

722. incisi

	H	Ø		Lit.
722.0	50	26	incisi	54.000
722.1	40	22	»	43.200
722.2	35	18	»	28.080
722.3	48	12	»	32.400
722.4	40	25	»	32.400

colori: composti corniola, prugna, oceano, putrido, violetto.

722.5	24	28	incisi	43.200
722.6	45	22	»	38.880
722.7	43	12	»	21.600
722.8	40	14	»	21.600
722.9	32	10	»	16.200

colori: composti corniola, prugna, oceano, putrido, violetto.

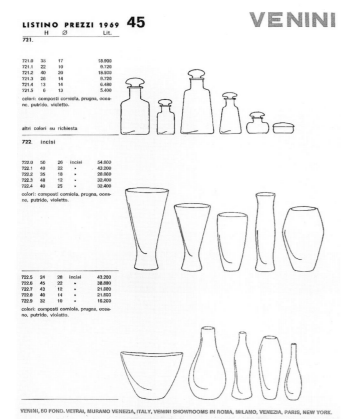

VENINI

	H	Ø		Lit.
722.10	30	15	incisi	19.440
722.11	20	10	incisi	10.800
722.12	32	10	incisi	17.280
722.13	25	13	incisi	19.440
722.14	15	28	incisi	36.720
722.15	10	20	incisi	12.960

colori: composti; corniola, prugna, oceano, putrido, violetto.

722.16	20	25	incisi	25.920
722.17	10	18	incisi	19.440

colori: composti: corniola, prugna oceano, putrido, violetto.

722.18	17	10	incisi	12.960
722.19	35	10	incisi	15.860
722.20	26	12	incisi	15.660
722.21	23	10	incisi	12.960
722.22	18	10	incisi	12.960
722.23	18	10	incisi	12.960
722.24	32	8	incisi	12.960

colori: composti; corniola, prugna, oceano, putrido, violetto.

722.25	15	30	36.720
722.26	43	13	32.400
722.27	26	15/10	17.280
722.28	9	18	16.200
722.29	32	15	32.400

colori: composti: corniola, prugna, oceano, putrido, violetto.

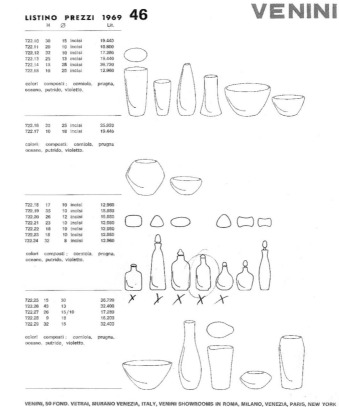

VENINI

DUE VASI A « FASCIE ». DA SINISTRA A DESTRA: 723.0 - 723.5

VENINI

724. Miros uno   design Hrstka

	H	Ø	Lit.
724.0	32	9	48.600
724.1	11	22	48.600
724.2	20	16	48.600

colori: 724.0: oceano; 724.1: corniola; 724.2: putrido; superficie scolpita.

725. Miros due   design Hrstka

	H	Ø	Lit.
725.0	30	16	32.400
725.1	24	12	21.600
725.2	15	13	21.600
725.3	9	21	24.300

colori: erba, bruno, acqua, ciclamino. Superficie molata.

726.   design Hrstka

	H	Ø	Lit.
726.0	15	27	27.000
726.1	9	18	19.250

colori: violetto, corniola. Superfici con incisioni.

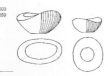

727. Miros tre   design Hrstka

	H	Ø	Lit.
727.0	35	15	67.500
727.1	22	13	40.500
727.2	14	18	48.600

colori: prugna, ottone, bronzo. Superficie scolpita.

LISTINO PREZZI 1969 **48**   **VENINI**

	H	Ø	Lit.
850.	lampade da tavolo		

	H	Ø	Lit.
850.0	31	12	10.800
850.1	29	15	13.500
850.2	45	18	16.200
850.3	48	11	10.260
850.4	50	15	16.200

colori: basi in opalino rosso, bianco, zaffiro, thé, verde mela, verde, ametrista, viola, zolfo, arancio. Globo sempre in opalino bianco. Metalli, ottone lucido.

	H	Ø	Lit.
850.5	28	12	10.800

colori: base trasparente rosso, verde, thé, giallo, ametista. Tubo cristallo sabbiato.

	H	Ø	Lit.
850.6	45	9	10.800

colori base composta: prugna, oceano, corniola, violetto, putrido, bronzo, erba, notte, ottone. Tubo cristallo sabbiato.

	H	Ø	Lit.
850.7	38	12	10.800

colori: base con fiore zolfo, rosso, lattimo, zaffiro o verde. Tubo cristallo sabbiato.

	H	Ø	Lit.
850.8	42	11	12.960

colori: fascia murrina zolfo, arancio o rosso su base lattimo. Tubo cristallo sabbiato.
Metallo ottone lucido.

VENINI, 50 FOND. VETRAI, MURANO VENEZIA, ITALY, VENINI SHOWROOMS IN ROMA, MILANO, VENEZIA, PARIS, NEW YORK.

Appendix

The master glassmaker Ermete Toso
at work

Work in progress

Chronology

1921

Paolo Venini and Giacomo Cappellin found the glassworks Vetri Soffiati Muranesi Cappellin Venini & C., with Vittorio Zecchin as art director. During this period, master craftsmen working at the factory include Ceno Barovier, Nane Patare (Giovanni Seguso), Rafael Ferro, Malvino Pavanello, and Attilio Moratto.

1922

The first Venini shop is opened to the public in Venice, in piazzetta dei Leoncini.
Subsequently, a new Venini store opens in Paris.

1923

Giacomo Cappellin converts his shop in via Montenapoleone, Milan, to an exclusive outlet for Venini glassware.

1925

Giacomo Cappellin and Paolo Venini go their separate ways: the new glassworks set up by Paolo is called Vetri Soffiati Muranesi Venini & C., with Napoleone Martinuzzi appointed art director.

1926

The shop in via Condotti, Rome, is inaugurated.
Napoleone Martinuzzi creates a series of installations to adorn the Vittoriale, the villa of Gabriele D'Annunzio on Lake Garda: vast chests of fruit supported on luminous columns.

1927

Martinuzzi continues his work at the Vittoriale villa, and begins using *pulegoso* glass for his new creations.
Meanwhile the 'Labirinto' (Labyrinth) group is established, composed of Tomaso Buzzi, Pietro Chiesa, Emilio Lancia, Michele Marelli, Giovanni Ponti, Paolo Venini, and Countess Carla Visconti di Modrone, formed with the aim of promoting the decorative arts.

1928

Napoleone Martinuzzi creates a life-size glass statue of the black dancer Josephine Baker from St Louis, made entirely of *pulegoso* glass. The statue is presented on the occasion of the glass expo held in the Hotel Excelsior on the Venice Lido.

1929

The glassworks takes the name Venini & C.

1930

Reintroduction of *filigrana* and *lattimo* glass; new production sees glasses for many embassies around the world.

1931

Continuing as art director of production is Napoleone Martinuzzi.
New contracts include artistic lighting installations for the Bergamo post-office building, designed with the architect Angiolo Mazzoni. The building still houses the sizeable *Cactus* composition (h 2.5 m). Mazzoni's collaboration with the state postal and railways divisions continues intensely over this period (the two were merged into a single department in 1924). Venini & C. created lighting installations for the main post-office buildings in the towns of Trent, Palermo, Pola, Forlì, Savona, Gorizia, and Ferrara. Correspondingly, many mainline railway stations (Reggio Emilia, Ferrara, Siena, Trent) are fitted out with Venini lighting systems.

1932

Tomaso Buzzi is the new art director.
Carlo Scarpa begins occasional contract work the glassworks.

1933

New forms and colours are introduced: objects and animal figures to designs by Tomaso Buzzi. The new collections are 'Alga' (Alga), 'Laguna' (Lagoon), 'Tramonto' (Sunset), 'Sera' (Evening), 'Alba' (Dawn).

1934

Carlo Scarpa joins the design team.

1936

Paolo Venini inaugurates the series of 'Murrine romane' pieces.
At the Milan Triennale Venini meets the Swedish ceramist Tyra Lundgren and invites her to Murano.

1938

Tyra Lundgren on the Venini design team.
Carlo Scarpa's collaboration continues.

1941

The onset of war halts production at the glassworks.

1943

Venini & C. wins a design competition for a *Centrepiece* for the University of Padua; each faculty is represented by a glass animal figure designed by Carlo Scarpa.

1943–45

The factory manufactures light-bulbs and medicine flasks.

1946–47

A series of bottles and glasses designed by Gio Ponti for the APEM, withheld from production until 1956. First 'Uova a battuto' ('Battuto' eggs) series for the perfumiers Ulrich.

1948

Fulvio Bianconi joins the design team.

1949

Paolo Venini and Fulvio Bianconi design a group of vases using the *zanfirico* and *fenicio* techniques.
New items in the catalogue include the *Fazzoletto* (Handkerchief) vase, which enters the permanent collection of the Museum of Modern Art, New York.
Anna Venini, the second born, begins to work alongside her mother Ginette overseeing production control.
In Paris a new glass store, Arcet, is inaugurated.

1950

Fulvio Bianconi creates the 'Pezzati' series, in which the colour range is created together with Ginette Venini.
Other trademark Venini designs enter the MoMA's permanent collection.

1951

The American architect Eugène Berman designs a group of glass figures entitled 'Rovine' (Ruins).
Meanwhile, Ken Scott authors the 'Pesci' (Fish) series for the windows of Macy's department store in New York. Frank Lloyd Wright pays a visit to the Venini glassworks, accompanied by Carlo Scarpa, Mario de Luigi, and Oscar Stonorov.

1953

The painter Riccardo Licata begins his collaboration at the Venini glassworks.

1954

Massimo Vignelli joins the Venini design team.
Also on the team is Piero Fornasetti.
The inner court of Palazzo Grassi in Venice is given a glazed skylight of *ballotton* spheres.

1955

Lyn Tissot joins Venini & C.: his glassware is put on show at Bonniers, New York.
New stores open: Forum in Naples, Soland in Zurich, Altamira in New York.

1956

The '4000' series of lamps by Massimo Vignelli received special mention for the 'Compasso d'oro' prize.

1957

Bianconi's 'Grotteschi' (Grotesques) series are produced alongside Vignelli's 'Spicchi' (Slices), and exhibited at the MoMA in New York.
Oscar Stonorov's glazing installations are

made for the United Automobile Workers head offices in Detroit.

1958

Paolo Venini and the architect Ignazio Gardella conceive the first of the composite polyhedron lamps, on exhibit at the Salon d'Honneur of the Brussels Expo, together with four installations by Paolo Venini.
The new Olivetti showroom in New York is designed by Belgioioso, Peressutti, and Rogers; the Venini hanging light fittings are composed of multicoloured layers (by Paolo Venini).

1959

Window for the church of San Domenico, Siena, after cartoons by the painter Bruno Saetti.
Glass tubes for television sets. Necklaces in silver, glass and *murrina* with Grete Kormoso.
After Paolo Venini's death, his wife Ginette and son-in-law Ludovico Diaz de Santillana, together with the son of Carlo Scarpa, Tobia, continue the company founder's work.

1960

The arrival at Venini & C. of the Philadelphia-born textile designer Thomas Stearns marks the dawn of close interchange with American artists.
Rome: new projects include polyhedron lamps designed in tandem with the architect Del Debbio for the Ministry of Foreign Affairs, at the Farnesina.

1961

For the main foyer of the Teatro Comunale dell'Opera in Florence, a lighting installation composed of grouped glass canes encasing a crystal core.
For the main lounge airport of Manchester, huge composite lighting fittings of glass drops.

1962

Gio Ponti, with Toni Zuccheri and Ludovico Diaz de Santillana invent the 'Vetrate grosse' series.
International conference on glass manufacture held in the United States.

1963

Massimo Vignelli designs a collection of articles in glass and silver for Christofle.

1964

Toni Zuccheri ideates his renowned 'Bestiaro' (Bestiary) series.
Tapio Wirkkala joins the Venini design team.

1965

Ginette Venini introduces her 'pioggia' glasswork.

1966

Lucio Fontana and Ignazio Gardella work with Venini on the design of the foyer of the Hotel Excelsior on the Lido, Venice.

Gio Ponti designs a set of 'Vetrate grosse' installations for the offices for the bank Cassa di Risparmio of Padua.

1968

Dale Chihuly arrives from the United States for a stage at the Venini glassworks; he stays for two years.

1969

Venini & C. make an unusual foray into the world of fashion: Pierre Cardin commissions a set of glassware inspired by his lines of haute couture, designed by Ludovico Diaz de Santillana.

Richard Marquis comes from America to study glass techniques at the Venini factory, and soon became one of the principal experts in the creation of *murrina* glass.

1970

Ludovico Diaz de Santillana presents his '952 Patchwork' light fittings composed of coloured tiles drawn by hand.

1971

Like the previous American trainees who enrolled at Venini & C., the architect James Carpenter is fresh out of the Rhode Island School of Design. Carpenter goes on to participate in the American Studio Glass co-operative, which creates various items of glassware included in the Venini catalogue. Other arrivals to Venini & C. include Ove Thorssen and his wife Birgitta Carlsson. Among major projects for the year is the huge lighting installation 'waterfall' for the Mandarin Hotel, Singapore.

1972

More newcomers from America: Michael Nourot and John Milner. Also new on the design team is Marvin Lipofsky, professor at the University of California, Berkeley.

1973

The American Dan Dailey arrives.

A terrific fire in October this year destroys the Venini office and museum; fortunately the flames stop short of the furnaces themselves.

1974

The American William Pringle arrives. Reconstruction work on the Venini offices is terminated; the furnaces resume work as usual.

1975–76

Fresh out of the School of Visual Arts, New York, the daughter of Ludovico and Anna Venini, Laura Diaz de Santillana joins the staff of Venini & C.

1977–78

Another American, Benjamin Moore, comes to Venini & C.

For the Schlosstheater in Fulda, Germany, Venini creates customised *trilobi* lamps, plus a vast skylight made of solid glass canes.

1979

New designs by Laura Diaz de Santillana are added to production.

1980

Launch of 'Glicine' (Wisteria) and 'Klee' creations by Laura Diaz de Santillana.

1982

New 'multicolour' identity applied to the Venini trademark, to designs by Massimo Vignelli and Laura Diaz de Santillana.

Laura designs her 'Biro' vases series, and the 'Sigul' lamps.

1983

Glazing designed by Laura and Ludovico Diaz de Santillana are nominated for the 'Compasso d'Oro' design award.

1984

New designs by Laura and Alessandro Diaz de Santillana enter the catalogue.

1985

New designs by Alessandro Diaz de Santillana introduced include his 'Scozzesi' (Scottish) series.

1986

Family business is sold.

Designers for Venini

Franco Albini
(Robbiate, Como 1905 – Milan 1977)
Graduated from Milan Politecnico (Science University) in 1929, specialising in Planning and Design. Takes part in the Rationalists movement pivoting on the magazine *Casabella*. Designed several lamps for Venini together with Ludovico Diaz de Santillana. Among his major restoration projects in Genoa are the Palazzo Bianco and Palazzo Rosso, and the San Lorenzo cathedral treasury.

Tina Aufiero
(New York 1959)
Attends the Rhode Island School of Design in Providence. Since 1981 she has taught at the New York Experimental Workshop. Came to work for Venini in 1982–83 and designed the *'Alboino'* vase. She is an active contributor at the Pilchuck Glass School.

Eugène Berman
(St Petersburg 1899 – Rome 1972)
After studying at the Académie Ranson in Paris with Édouard Vuillard he moved to the United States. In 1958 he moved to Rome. In 1951 he designed for Venini & C. a group of figures in clear glass called 'Rovine' (Ruins).

Fulvio Bianconi
(Padua 1915 – Milan 1996)
Bianconi attended the Istituto d'Arte and the Accademia in Venice. Graphic designer, cartoonist, and designer in the field of glass, his contact with glass occurred very early. His work with Venini began in 1947, and generated the striking set of stylised figures typical of the Commedia dell'Arte, the *Pagliacci* based on the frescoes of Tiepolo in Ca' Rezzonico.
Other key works include the 'Sirene' (Mermaids) series with their elegant tails in *fenicio* glass, and the brightly coloured 'Pezzati' set.
He returned to work for Venini in 1967 creating the acclaimed *Informale* vase, which marks a break with the established formulas of the period.

Tomaso Buzzi
(Sondrio 1900 – Rapallo 1981)
In 1923 Buzzi graduated from the Milan Politecnico (Science University) in Architec-

ture, and taught at the Faculty of Architecture from 1930 to 1954.
In conjunction with Paolo Venini, Gio Ponti, Pietro Chiesa, and Michele Marelli, he founded the 'Labirinto' group to promote modern decorative arts at the Milan Triennale.
A regular contributor to *Domus*, in 1932–33 he replaced Napoleone Martinuzzi as art director at Venini & C.
For Venini he designed a much-admired collection of delicately coloured pieces obtained through the subtle application of gold leaf and *filigrana*.

Giacomo Cappellin
(Venice 1887 – Paris 1968)
Cappellin began his career in the antiques business, first in Venice and then in Milan. Together with Paolo Venini and Andrea Rioda in 1921 he founded the company entitled Vetri Soffiati Muranesi Cappellin Venini & C. Owing to differences of opinion, in 1925 the company disbanded. A new company Maestri Vetrai Muranesi Cappellin & C. folded in 1932. At the end of the 1930s he moved to Paris, where he opened a workshop producing perfume bottles.

Birgitta Carlsson
(Stockholm 1943)
Trained at the National College of Art, Craft and Design Department in Stockholm. From 1971 to 1974 she and her husband Ove Thorssen worked on and off at Venini & C., where they created the highly unusual new 'Merletti' (Lacework) and 'Opulus' series.

James Carpenter
(1949)
After graduating from Rhode Island School of Design in 1972, Carpenter repeated up his first visit to the Venini glassworks in Murano 1971 on several other occasions to delve alongside Ludovico Diaz de Santillana into new techniques for the production of large-scale sections of glazing. He also designed a series of glass objects, including the *Calabash* made from coloured canes, still in production.

Dale Chihuly
(Tacoma 1941)
Chihuly graduated in Interior Design in 1965 from the University of Washington; after

taking a Master's in Science at Wisconsin University in 1967, he completed his studies at the Rhode Island School of Design in 1968.
Awarded a Fullbright scholarship that year, he joined Venini as a student, an experience that largely determined his career. In 1970 he returned the United States and the next year founded a new school, the Pilchuck Glass School.
Chihuly's achievements stem from a thorough knowledge of glass techniques learned from the masters of Murano, and particularly for having adopted the island's teamwork 'piazza' system of gaffer and apprentices.
His work received international acclaim, and examples of his art can be seen in many museums around the world. He remains one of the greatest living masters of the art of glassmaking.

Alessandro Diaz de Santillana
(Paris 1959)
After schooling in Classics he entered the Venini workforce. He has had various one-man shows, and has taken part in group exhibitions, notably the travelling show 'The Glass Skin', which started from the Hokkaido Museum of Modern Art in Sapporo (Japan), and ended at the Coburg Museum. From the outset he contributed to the biennial 'Aperto Vetro' program. From 1997 to 1999 he was a visiting lecturer at the University of California, San Diego, teaching sculpture in glass.

Laura Diaz de Santillana
(Venice 1955)
After schooling in the Classics she went to New York to attend the School of Visual Arts from 1975 to 1977. Her work with Venini began in 1979 alongside her father Ludovico. In 1979 she took part in the travelling exhibition that began at the Corning Museum of Glass and moved to the Toledo Museum of Art, then to the Metropolitan Museum of Art, New York, to the Victoria & Albert in London, and lastly to the Musée des Arts Décoratifs, Paris.
Since 1979 Laura Diaz de Santillana has staged numerous one-man exhibitions in Europe and the United States. Recently her works were exhibited in Japan.
Today Laura continues her work as an independent designer, and her creations are

produced by Venini, Rosenthal, Arcade, Steuben, and Salviati.

Ludovico Diaz de Santillana
(Rome 1931 – Terranuova Bracciolini 1989)
After graduating from the Venice Scuola di Architettura, de Santillana became an assistant teacher to Ignazio Gardella.
In 1953 he married Anna Venini, daughter of Paolo, and in 1959 he assumed the leadership of Venini & C. until 1985, when he continued his role at the helm of the new company, Eos.
Among the works for which he is famous are the 'Canoe', the 'Colletti', the transparent 'Murrine' series, and not least the huge lighting installations in which he applied his extensive experience in architecture. His last creation, *Tappeto volante* (Flying Carpet), was received with great enthusiasm; the work was a modern tribute to the component system used by his predecessor Paolo Venini in the 1930s.
Working with Laura Diaz de Santillana, in the 1980s he created the new type of glazing composed of platters, mostly in *murrina* glass.
A large abstract sculpture of his in glass stands in Singapore.

Piero Fornasetti
(Milan 1913 – 1988)
Fornasetti attended the Brera Academy, Milan, and later the Scuola Superiore d'Arte Applicata.
For Venini he created a series entitled 'Corni da caccia' (Hunting horns).

Ignazio Gardella
(Milan 1905 – 1999)
Gardella graduated in Architecture and became one of the country's leading figures in the field.
At Venini & C. he worked alongside Ludovico Diaz de Santillana on the lighting for the Olivetti outlet in Düsseldorf; on the restyling of the main bar at the Hotel Excelsior on the Venice Lido; the lighting installation for the Residence Gritti in Venice (in league with the architect Menghi); and for the lighting of the Hotel Cavalieri Hilton, Rome.

Ginette Gignous
(Stresa 1891 – Venice 1982)
She is the daughter of Eugenio Gignous, a

painter and member of the Milan-based Scapigliatura movement of artists and writers, and of Matilde Ferri.
In 1923 she married Paolo Venini in Milan, but moved directly to Murano, to the Palazzo Da Mula.
Her participation in the Venini firm began a little later towards the 1940s, but assisted in all the factory business. Together with her son-in-law Ludovico Diaz de Santillana, in 1959 she moved closer to production upon the death of her husband Paolo. Her principal occupation was the choice of colours. One of her inventions led to the design of 'pioggia' (raindrops) glass that derived from a house built by Alvar Aalto for Marimekko.

Miroslav Hrstka
(Prague 1933 – 1983)
Hrstka studied under Libensky at the School of Decorative Arts in Prague, and was enrolled as a designer at the Borske Sklo glassworks. He came to Murano to work for Venini & C., where he devised a series of glasswares with deep incisions. In 1968 he took part in the 34th Venice Biennale.

Giovanni Leone
(Catania 1929)
Leone graduated from the Istituto Universitario di Architettura of Venice in 1956. He took part in the CIAM in 1954. Close to Ludovico Diaz de Santillana since their university days, the two friends worked together on the lighting installations for the Central Palace Hotel in Catania; for the banking offices of the Banca Popolare di Santa Venera they installed sections of glazing, and likewise for the church of Sant'Euplio and for Villa Cerami.

Riccardo Licata
(Turin 1929)
Licata attended the Accademia in Venice; since 1957 he is a resident professor at the École des Beaux-Art in Paris. His skills as a painter, graphic artist and designer brought him to Venini & C., where in 1956 he created a series of objects embedded with highly distinctive *murrina* details.

Tyra Lundgren
(Stockholm 1897 – 1979)
Lundgren studied the decorative arts in her hometown, rapidly earning acclaim for her ceramics which, while predominantly a hand-crafted creation, enabled her to enter the international field while enjoying great esteem in Sweden, Finland, Italy, and France.
Her first meeting with Paolo Venini took place at the 1936 Milan Triennale. He offered her the chance to design a collection of objects in glass. In 1938 she designed for the firm a set of animal figures and vases in *fenicio* glass, subsequently exhibited at the 1948 Venice Biennale.

Richard Marquis
(Bumble Bee, Arizona 1945)
Marquis graduated from Berkeley University but before completing his studies he received a Fullbright grant and came to the Venini works in 1969, where he learned the traditional techniques of working *murrina* glass, *zanfirico*, and *reticello*, and designed objects inspired by those of Carlo Scarpa before him, with an accent on *murrina* decorative details.
Marquis was one of the founders of the Pilchuck Glass School, together with Dale Chihuly. Today he lives and works in Seattle, and is widely regarded as one of the greatest living masters of glass; his work is found in museums around the world.

Napoleone Martinuzzi
(Murano 1892 – Venice 1977)
Martinuzzi studied at the Accademia in Venice, and though he attended courses on the Nude a factor determining his career was his experience in Rome studying under Angelo Zanelli, where he worked in an atelier and contributed to the creation of the national monument, the Altare della Patria. Among the works on exhibit at the 1911 Expo, those of Klimt and Ivan Mestrovich seized his imagination.
From 1926 to 1927, upon careful reflection, Martinuzzi made a decisive choice for his later artistic enquiry: he entered the Venini factory and fathered one of the most important lines of glass production this century. From this moment on his dual talents as sculptor and creator of objects and sculptures in glass were closely interwoven. Ever faithful to the canons of Novecento Neoclassicism, he explored these through his glass creations for Venini. Of particular importance were the articles in *pulegoso* glass, and the collection he designed for the Vittoriale manor on Lake Garda, home of Gabriele D'Annunzio, a close friend.
In 1932 he left Venini & C. and founded a new company with Francesco Zecchin, Zecchin & Martinuzzi.

Roberto Menghi
(Milan 1920)
Graduated from the faculty of Architecture of Milan Politecnico (Science University) in 1944, Menghi is widely known as an architect, industrial designer, and teacher. Among his numerous works of architecture are private homes in Italy and the United States, and commissions for the C.I.G.A. (Compagnia Italiana Grandi Alberghi) hotel chain, for the Gulf Oil Company, the Milan Chamber of Commerce, the Touring Club Italiano, Pirelli, and for Techint. He has designed furniture for Arflex and Zanotta, appliances for Siemens, kitchen equipment for Merloni, glass wares for Venini, glasses for Bormioli, and lighting for Fontana Arte.
He taught at the University of Venice (1953–57; 1986–87) and at the faculty of Architecture at Milan Politecnico (1964–71). His designs in plastic were presented at the Milan exhibition entitled 'Mostra Internazionale per le Materie Plastiche' (1956); several other works are on show at the Museum of Modern Art (MoMA), New York.

Giovanni (Gio) Ponti
(Milan 1891 – 1979)
Ponti graduated in Architecture in Milan in 1921. He founded the renowned design magazine *Domus* in 1928.
The partnership between Gio Ponti and Paolo Venini was already under way in the 1920s, when the 'Labirinto' group, formed in Milan around Carla Visconti di Modrone, initiated the marriage of the art industry with the architects Buzzi, Lancia, Marelli, and Ponti for the Triennales of Monza and Milan. Ponti never ceased to admire the distinct, modern expression of the Venini glassworks, and his perennial involvement with production bore three landmark designs: the objects in glass and silver for Venini and Christofle in 1928 (16th Venice Biennale); lamps, glasses, and bottles (including his 'Donne-bottiglie' and the 'Bottiglie "morandiane"') in the years 1946–50; and lastly the 'Vetrate grosse' pieces of 1966.

Carlo Scarpa
(Venice 1906 – Sendai, Japan 1978)
Scarpa studied at the Accademia in Venice, and in 1926 taught at the Architecture Faculty of the university there. An architect of international renown, Scarpa's first incursion into the world of glass came in 1927, when he was engaged to work for the Maestri Vetrai Muranesi Cappellin & C. In 1931 he passed over to the glassworks of Paolo Venini. Though he took Martinuzzi's place as artistic advisor, his role went far beyond that of mere designer, spending long hours at the furnaces alongside the factory's craftsmen. Belonging to these early years at Venini's were the 'Filigrana' glassware and the 'Sommersi', which would be exhibited at the 1934 Venice Biennale. At both the Venice and Milan exhibitions of 1936 there appeared new 'Murrina' pieces invented in tandem with Paolo Venini, and the *lattimo* wares. At the 1938 Biennale new entries included the opaline, two-colour, 'Pennellati', the 'Variegati', and the 'Martellati' wares, followed closely by the heavy vases in composite wheel-ground pieces A significant factor of Scarpa's considerable output was the technical challenge that makes them difficult to emulate today, such as the engraved glassware of 1940, and the 'Vetri velati', the 'Granulari', and 'Tessuti'.
Scarpa's collaboration with Venini lasted until 1947.

Tobia Scarpa
(Venice 1935)
Son of Carlo and now a well-known architect, he has carried out important research work in the application of glass in building. In 1958 he associated himself with Venini & C. and currently works as an interior designer with his wife Afra.

Kenneth George Scott
(Fort Wayne, Indiana 1918)
Scott studied design at the Parsons School in New York, and painting at the Moses Soyer Art School.
In 1951 for the exhibition 'Made in Italy' at Macy's department store on Manhattan he construed a set of fish in composed glass manufactured by Venini & C. and displayed in Venetian fishermen's baskets and fishing nets.

Thomas Stearns
(Philadelphia 1936)
Stearns graduated from the Cranbrook Academy of Art. In 1959 he came to Italy, and alongside the master craftsman Checco Ongaro he designed a collection of exquisite 'Soffiati' that were exhibited at the 1962 Venice Biennale. Once back in the United States, Stearns dedicated himself to exploring the application of plastics in art.

Ove Thorssen
(Stockholm 1945)
Swedish designer who trained at the National College of Art, Craft and Design Department in Stockholm. for Venini & C. he and his wife Birgitta Carlsson designed the 'Merletti' (Lacework) and 'Opulus' series. Currently teaches at the Department of Design and Craft at the University of Göteborg.

Lyn Charles Tissot
In 1955 he designed a collection of glassware fot Venini & C. that were put on display at Bonniers in New York.

Franco Venini
(Milan 1905 – Venice 1948)
Younger brother of Paolo, he later graduated from the Bocconi college for Business studies. He moved to Venice to follow his brother's firm as a research chemist, creating the unusual and quite inimitable blends of colour that typify Venini production.

Paolo Venini
(Milan 1895 – Venice 1959)
A few months after the death of Paolo Venini, Gio Ponti wrote this dedication in the magazine *Domus*: 'Venini moved from his native Milan to Venice in 1921, and in his first concern on Murano he was associated with Giacomo Cappellin. [...] The establishment of this glassworks largely marked the start of the "modern history" of Murano glass. The two founders then took off on their separate ways. What Venini must be credited with is the remarkably unobtrusive way he managed to reconnect this "art" with the evolving world of art of his day, without misrepresenting it, and instead highlighting the very characteristics intrinsic to it; and without either rigid theorising but with acute intuition, working on his craftsmen and with the artists, all together.
Venini brought Murano glass to new frontiers – such as the new windows (1957) and the outstanding light designs (1958) – and in line with his competitors (with blown glass and freehand lathing) by introducing production in series, such as the sets of lamps (1956), an idea entirely his own.
Glass pieces issuing from his factory – a thoroughly Italian concern with business contacts all over the world – are found in the Victoria and Albert Museum in London; in the Louvre, Paris; in the Museum of Modern Art, New York; at the Corning Museum of Glass, Corning.
Venini's work appeared at all the Milan Triennales and Venice Biennales; he also held his own exhibitions all over Europe and in the United States.
Paolo Venini died in Venice on 22 July 1959' (G. Ponti, 'Venini', in *Domus*, 361, December 1959, p. 33).

Massimo Vignelli
(Milan 1931)
Vignelli attended the Brera Academy in Milan, and graduated in Architecture from the University of Venice. He worked for Venini & C. from the 1950s onwards; for around thirty years now ha has lived in New York, where he and his wife Elena Valle founded a graphics and design studio.

Tapio Wirkkala
(Hanko 1915 – Helsinki 1985)
Wirkkala studied at the Helsinki school of arts and crafts, of which he was the director from 1951 to 1954.
He worked for the Venini glassworks from 1964 to 1980.

Vittorio Zecchin
(Murano 1878 – Venice 1947)
After attending the Accademia in Venice, Zecchin attentively followed the pulse of cultural changes taking place in Venice at the time, and was particularly taken with the output of Jan Toorop and Klimt, which he had witnessed at the 1905 and 1910 Venice Biennales. He was an active contributor to the exhibitions held in Ca' Pesaro. In 1916 he set up a tapestry workshop in a defunct convent on Murano. From 1921 to 1925 he was artistic advisor to the firm Vetri Soffiati Muranesi Cappellin Venini & C., where he created articles in blown glass of extraordinary delicacy modelled on works by sixteenth-century master glassblowers. After Cappellin and Venini went their separate ways, Zecchin continued in his capacity as artistic advisor to Maestri Vetrai Muranesi Cappellin & C.
Zecchin's activities as an artist were not limited to glass alone; he also designed artefacts in wood, silver, pottery, and explored tapestry, embroidery, and mosaics.

Toni Zuccheri
(Venice 1937)
Zuccheri graduated in Architecture. In 1964 he joined the team of designers at Venini & C., where his fascination for animal forms led him to create a 'bestiary' and other objects based on trunks and flowers; for Venini he also produced vases with metal inserts embedded in the glass.
Particularly adept at the application of colours, Zecchin had a profound knowledge of techniques of glassworking, and ideated some splendid collections.

Toots Zynsky
(Boston 1951)
Zynsky studied at the Rhode Island School of Design in the United States. In the early 1980s she designed a series of objects involving the new technique of *fili gettati*, her own invention, which received such wide acclaim that they are now to be found in many museums around the globe.

Glossary

Glass Types

'A fili' glass

This form of decoration, meaning literally 'threaded', is obtained by trailing glass filaments in a variety of colours onto the surface of the freshly blown form; a subsequent process of 'marvering' and further blowing can cause the filaments to be absorbed into the vessel's wall, ensuring a smooth, even surface.

'Alga' and 'laguna' glass

A type of glass used by Tomaso Buzzi for his designs of the early 1930s. Composed of a layer of *lattimo* glass encased in a coloured overlay – pink for the 'Laguna', and green for the 'Alga' series – and heightened with flecks of gold leaf. The same procedure is used to obtain the delicate hues characteristic of the *alba* (gold-flecked blue) and *tramonto* (deep pink).

'Battuto' glass

The surface of this type of glassware is textured with tiny dents of varying depth, arranged at random, producing a 'distressed' surface in imitation of the hammering technique common to metalwork. The technique was revived by Venini & C. after its reappearance in France in the 1900s, and was applied by Carlo Scarpa to designs and later by his son Tobia and by Ludovico Diaz de Santillana, giving rise to the 'Battuto' series of wares that enjoyed widespread popularity.

'Calcedonio' glass

A dark glass of reddish translucent medium streaked with coloured veins, in imitation of agate, a variety of chalcedony. This complex technique originated in Murano around the mid-fifteenth century, and involves adding various metal compounds to the molten mass, each in a pre-set sequence and moment. The secret formula for the procedure disappeared some time between the end of the eighteenth and early nineteenth centuries, until it was rediscovered by the nineteenth-century glassmaker Lorenzo Radi.

'Corroso' glass

This method of surface 'weathering' is achieved by dipping the vessel in hydrofluoric acid after being treated with a resin that can be chipped away when dry, leaving selected parts exposed to the corrosive action of the acid. The masked parts remain unaltered and smooth as a result.
This modern technique was first explored by Venini in 1933 with the 'Corrosi' series.

'Diamante' glass

So-called diamond glass is a thick clear material that is blown twice encased in a half-mould of metal strips laid in criss-cross fashion to yield the characteristic faceting that distinguishes semi-precious stones and gems.

'Fenicio' glass

Named after a technique known to the ancient Phœnicians and Egyptians, this type of decoration is obtained while the glass is still hot by trailing on strands of molten glass, which are then combed with a special tool into running festoons.
When reheated and hand-blown again, these patterns are assimilated into the vessel wall, leaving an even, smooth surface. Though the technique was first used in Murano at the end of the sixteenth or early seventeenth century, it is not clear what term was used to designate it at the time. The modern term *fenicio* was adopted in the later nineteenth century.
Fenicio glass was introduced at Venini & C. by Tomaso Buzzi and the Swedish designer Tyra Lundgren.

'Filigrana' and 'mezza filigrana'

Invented in Murano before the sixteenth century, this sophisticated technique involves pulling crystal rods shot with *lattimo* or coloured threads in ribbons or spirals through the walls of the vessel. One practice, known as the *reticello* technique, produces a delicate network of threads within the body of the glass; whereas *filigrana a retortoli* produces spiralling patterns, also known as *zanfirico* (from the name of the Venetian antiques dealer Antonio Sanquirico, who commissioned numerous copies of antique glass pieces exemplifying this technique in the first half of the nineteenth century).
The variant of the *mezza filigrana* technique involves pulling plain canes of glass diagonally through the molten batch.

'Incamiciato' glass

Cased or *incamiciato* glass is achieved by casing several *levade* or layers of different colours; or inserting between two layers a film of metal (more often gold and silver), or rods of colour and *filigrana* to obtain the separate casings with composite colours. The technique of casing was practised in ancient times, and came back into widespread use in the nineteenth century, becoming enormously popular in the 1930s.

'Lattimo' glass

A milky opaque form of glass invented in Murano around the mid-fifteenth century, at first in imitation of the early porcelain wares very popular throughout Europe at the time, and whose methods of production were a trade secret. The material has a characteristic milky consistency obtained from micro-crystals of calcium fluoride and sodium.

'Murrina' glass

Murrina is glass that contains vari-coloured tesserae inserted into the molten mass, often without any pattern, and fused together in the furnace; a common variant of the *murrina* technique is known as *millefiori*.

'Pennellate' glass

This form of surface decoration involves trailing irregular strands of coloured glass around the free-blown vessel; these are pulled by means of putting clear hot glass over the coloured stands while the gather is still hot, giving the effect of brush-strokes.

'Pezzato' glass

Production involves two separate phases: first flat thin canes of coloured glass are allowed to cool and then cut into small rectangles; second, they are reheated and layered onto the bowl or vessel being fashioned.

'Pulegoso' glass

The Murano word *puleghe* (air-bubbles) prompted the name for this type of semi-opaque or translucent glass with irregularly spaced bubbles in the vitreous mass that produce a scabby finish due to surface bursting.
The *pulegoso* effect is obtained by purposely introducing foreign matter into the mass while molten (sodium bicarbonate or petrol), which burns off under intense heat, leaving gas-pockets of varying dimensions. The inventor of this technique was Napoleone Martinuzzi, while art director of the Venini works from 1925 to around 1932.

'Sommerso' glass

Submerged or *sommerso* glass results in a thick-walled vessel made up of several layers of matter overlaid and enriched with a variety of decorative techniques, such as gold-leaf, air bubbles, iridising, and veiling. It is achieved by dipping the gather successively into each of the molten batches to be added to the mass.
The first submerged glassware for Venini & C. was designed by Carlo Scarpa in the second half of the 1930s.

'Tessuto' glass

The term derives from the Italian for 'fabric' or 'weave', and entails a variation of the glass-cane technique, here used in alternating colours to form numerous thin vertical strips. On occasion, a finer finish is achieved by treating the surface on a wheel-lathe.
Dreamed up by Carlo Scarpa for Venini & C. towards the end of the 1930s, the technique would be used extensively by Paolo Venini for his glazing installations.

Glassmaking Tecniques

'A mano volante'

This term aptly describes the method of freehand glassblowing typical of the Murano master glass craftsmen, by which the hot gather, is drawn from the melting pot with a hollow metal tube (blowpipe), and skilfully inflated by blowing down the tube, keeping the glass malleable with heat from the furnace, while it is being worked and modelled by various glassmaking tools that have been in use for centuries – termed locally as the *tagiante* (grozing iron), *borselli* (pincers), and *paciofi* (clappers) – until the gather has reached its near-definitive shape. At this point the paraison, or ready wad of formed glass, still relatively pliant, is flipped and transferred to a solid metal rod called a pontil, where it undergoes the final shaping with other manual tools; once done, the piece of glass is knocked off clean from the pontil and placed into a kiln (a reheating process known as *ara* or *tempera* or *muffola*) designed to allow it to cool

gradually to avoid cracking through sudden contraction.

'A murrine'

This technique involves glass canes incorporating numerous coloured threads; the canes are cut into slices 5–10 millimetres long, which are laid on a cold metal tray in designs of varying complexity; the arrangement is then heated and fused, and the resulting glass can then be blown or drawn at will, producing an article entirely in *murrina*.

The classic *millefiori* paperweight is created with pearls of *murrina* submerged into a body of clear glass.

'A pennellate e fili'

Trailed spirals or bands of glass thread are two classic forms of decoration used at Venini & C. by Carlo Scarpa in the late 1930s and early '40s. The former technique entailed trailing threads of varying colours onto the vessel wall, which were then absorbed into the medium with a secondary blowing and subsequent marvering.

The 'brushwork' trails were created by applying patches of coloured crystal glass at various points on the surface of the incandescent, still-pliant mass and drawing them through the glass to create an effect similar to brush strokes.

'A stampo'

Wads of hot glass can also be fashioned with the auxiliary of a mould, made either of wood or of metal, which lends the required shape to a vase or lighting element. With this method, the glass is blown inside the mould while being rotated to impress the desired form on the wad, whereas the 'fixed-mould' system allowed faceted or uneven forms, not rotatted. Mould-blown

glass can require a fair quantity of material, and so several gathers are taken in sequence until the required mass is obtained. Each new gather must be purged of air bubbles or other defects before being introduced into the mould; this is done by rolling the paraison on a platform known as a *bronzin*, the process itself denoted as *marmorizzar* or 'marvering'.

Once the batches have been transformed into a *pea*, i.e., a pear-shaped paraison, it is put in the mould and blown until it assumes the form of the mould, whence it is transferred to the *ara* or annealing furnace and then to the *moleria*, the cold-work department, equipped with diamond saws, drills, and special abrasive discs and wheels.

'Alla ruota'

The practice of grinding and lathing semifinished free-blown pieces takes various forms: surfaces can be engraved with patterns, or lightly abraded to produce a satin finish that is papery to the touch. The technique of *vetro battuto*, introduced by Venini with the 'Battuti' series, involves the entire surface of the vessel being ground on the wheel to bring out numerous tiny, irregular markings running in the same direction.

'Applicazioni a caldo'

The term refers to the system of hot-application during freehand work on the still-incandescent piece being fashioned. Decorative glass elements of varying kinds may be applied at this stage, by which such details as a coloured profile may be added to emphasise the border or lip of the article. Alternatively, spiral threads may be trailed around the body, or in multiple layers, to provide relief decoration. It is essential that

the vessel and applied decoration be kept at the same temperature to ensure the additions take properly, and do not risk detachment. The application of spiral threads and 'brushwork' are two forms of embellishment taken up at Venini & C. by Carlo Scarpa in the late 1930s early '40s.

'Incalmo'

A challenging but classic practice on Murano, the *incalmo* technique consists in welding two blown vessels while still hot, usually of different colours, and of equal circumference, so that the colours play off each other within the same vessel.

Exhibitions

1922
Paris, Salon d'Automne.
Venice, XIII Biennale d'Arte.
1923
Monza, Villa Reale, 'Prima Mostra Internazionale delle Arti Decorative'.
Florence, 'Prima Esposizione Nazionale delle Piccole Industrie e dell'Artigianato' (first prize).
1924
Venice, XIV Biennale d'Arte.
1925
Paris, Salon des Artistes Décorateurs ('Grand Prix').
Monza, II Biennale delle Arti Decorative.
Rome, III Biennale d'Arte.
1926
Paris, Salon d'Automne.
Florence, 'Mostra Artigianato E.N.A.P.I' (first prize).
Venice, XV Biennale d'Arte.
Rome, 'Mostra Nazionale d'Arte Marinara'.
1927
Monza, III Biennale delle Arti Decorative.
Geneva, Musée des Arts appliquées (one-man exhibition).
Vienna, Kunstindustrie Museum (one-man exhibition).
1928
Venice, XVI Biennale d'Arte.
Turin, 'Esposizione Nazionale e Internazionale delle Arti e delle Piccole Industrie' ('Grand Prix').
1929
Paris, Salon d'Automne.
Barcelona, Palacio de Artes Industriales y Aplicadas ('Grand Prix').
1930
Venice, XVII Biennale d'Arte ('Grand Prix')
Monza, IV Triennale ('Gran Premio d'Arte').
London, Nelson Bernard Gallery (one-man exhibition)
1931
Rome, I Quadriennale.
Amsterdam, Exhibition of Decorative Arts.
Florence, Palazzo Vecchio, 'Mostra del Fiore d'Arte'.
Athens, 'Exhibition of Art and Work in Italy'.
Padua, 'Arte Sacra e Moderna' (second prize).
1932
Venice, XVIII Biennale d'Arte.
Cagliari, Permanent Exhibition.
1933
Milan, V Triennale ('Grand Prix').
Rome, Castel Sant'Angelo, 'Mostra dell'Arte del Vetro'.

Stuttgart, Landesgewerbe Museum.
Rome, 'Arte Decorativa Navale'.
1934
Venice, XIX Biennale d'Arte.
Paris, Salon des Artistes Décorateurs.
Turin, 'Mostra della Nuova Torino'.
Florence, Palazzo Vecchio, 'Mostra del Giardino'.
1935
Rome, II Quadriennale.
Florence, V Mostra Nazionale dell'Artigianato.
Paris, 'Mostra E.N.A.P.I.' and exhibition at the Jeu de Paume.
Brussels,'Crafts Exhibition' ('Grand Prix').
Rome, 'Seconda Mostra Mariana'.
Florence, 'V Fiera Nazionale dell'Artigianato'.
Rome, Premio della Reale Accademia d'Italia.
Venice, Istituto Veneto del Lavoro.
1936
Venice, XX Biennale d'Arte.
Milan, VI Triennale.
Vienna, 'Crafts Exhibition'.
1937
Paris, Exposition Internationale d'Art (first prize).
Berlin, 'International Exhibition of 19th Century and Contemporary Art'.
São Paulo (Brazil), Expo, Italian Pavilion.
1938
Venice, XXI Biennale d'Arte.
Stockholm, Nordiska Kompaniet.
Helsinki, Artek.
Naples, 39 Mostra d'Oltremare.
1939
Rome, III Quadriennale.
1940
Milan, VII Triennale.
Venice, XXII Biennale d'Arte (special room for Paolo Venini).
1941
Leipzig, 'Arts & Crafts Gala Expo'.
Dresden, Grassi Museum (one-man exhibition).
1942
Venice, XXIII Biennale d'Arte.
1943
Leipzig, 'Arts & Crafts Gala Expo'.
Stockholm, Nationalmuseum.
Hamburg, 'Italian Design for the Future'.
1947
Milan, VIII Triennale (second prize).
1948
Venice, XXIV Biennale d'Arte.

Locarno, 'Mostra dell'Artigianato Veneto'.
1949
Stockholm, Nordiska Kompaniet.
1950
Venice, XXV Biennale d'Arte (Award of Honour).
Stockholm, Nordiska Kompaniet (one-man exhibition)
New York, 'Italian Arts & Crafts Exhibition'.
Milan, Galleria 'Il Naviglio' (one-man exhibition of Fulvio Bianconi).
Chicago, The Art Institute of Chicago, 'Italy at Work'.
1951
Milan, IX Triennale ('Grand Prix').
Helsinki, Artek (one-man exhibition).
1952
Venice, XXVI Biennale d'Arte.
Munich, Die Neue Sammlung, Staatliches Museum für angewandte Kunst.
Munich, American House, European Exhibition.
Santiago, 'Italian Arts & Crafts Exhibition'.
Toronto, Eaton, 'Seven Seas'.
Vienna, 'Italian Fair'.
Stockholm, Nordiska Kompaniet.
Frankfurt, 'Arts & Crafts Gala Expo'.
Cologne, 'Arts & Crafts Gala Expo'.
Paris, Musée des Art Décoratifs.
1953
London, Liberty; Copenhagen, Illums Boligus; Brussels, Palais des Beaux-Arts (one-man exhibitions).
Helsinki, Artek.
Oslo, 'Crafts Exhibition'.
Venice, Palazzo Vendramin Calergi.
Frankfurt, 'Arts & Crafts Gala Expo'.
Stockholm, Nordiska Kompaniet (exhibitions of Venini and Orrefors)
Hamburg, Museum für Kunst und Gewerbe Hamburg.
1954
Venice, XXVII Biennale d'Arte.
Milan, X Triennale.
1955
Stockholm, Nordiska Kompaniet (one-man exhibition).
Helsinki, Artek (one-man exhibition).
New York, Jensen, 'Design Exhibition'.
London, National Crafts Department.
New York, Bonniers.
1956
Venice, XXVIII Biennale d'Arte.
New York, Chattanooga, San Diego, Worchester, Toledo, Toronto (travelling exhibition sponsored by Jensen).

Paris, Exposition des Arts Décoratifs.
Tokyo, Department Store Takashimaya, Art Gallery, 'Italian Exhibition'.
Zurich, Soland (one-man exhibition).
Manchester, 'Modern Italian Design'.
Liverpool, 'Modern Italian Design'.
1957
Milan, XI Triennale.
Hamburg; Hanover; Baden Baden; Düsseldorf; Frankfurt; Linz (Venini and Orrefors exhibit together).
Hanover, 'Arts & Crafts Gala Expo'.
Karlsruhe, Landesgewerbe Museum.
Toronto, 'Italian Exhibition'.
Vienna, Österreichisches Museum für angewandte Kunst.
Long Beach, Municipal Art Center; Minneapolis, Walker Art Center; Columbia, Columbia Museum of Art (exhibitions sponsored by Jensen).
1958
Venice, XXIX Biennale d'Arte.
Vienna, Österreichisches Museum für angewandte Kunst.
Stockholm, Nordiska Kompaniet.
1959
Paris, Salon des Artistes Décorateurs.
Helsinki, Artek (one-man exhibition).
Corning, The Corning Museum of Glass, 'Glass '59'.
Munich, Die Neue Sammlung, Staatliches Museum für angewandte Kunst.
1960
Milan, XII Triennale ('Grand Prix').
Venice, XXX Biennale d'Arte.
Dallas, Neiman Marcus.
Verona, Palazzo della Gran Guardia.
Essen, 'A.I.D Award'.
1961
Turin, 'Italia '61'.
Paris, Christofle.
Madrid, Casón del Buen Retiro.
Lisbona, 'Vidras de Murano'.
1962
Venice, XXXI Biennale d'Arte.
Florence, 'Mostra del Regalo'.
1963
Munich; Cologne; Hamburg; Frankfurt; Berlin (travelling exhibition with Orrefors and Baccarat).
Helsinki, Artek.
1964
Milan, XIII Triennale.
Venice, XXXII Biennale d'Arte.
London, 'Italian Lighting Fixtures Exhibition'.
Paris, Institut du Commerce Extérieur.

Helsinki, Artek (one-man exhibition).

1965
Munich, 'Italian Crafts Expo'.
Montreal, E.N.A.P.I.
Stockholm, E.N.A.P.I.
New York, The Museum of Modern Art.

1966
Venice, XXXIII Biennale d'Arte.
Milan, XIV Triennale.
Bremen, 'Glas aus Murano'.

1967
Stuttgart, National Institute of Foreign Trade.

1968
Milan, XIV Triennale.
Venice, XXXIV Biennale d'Arte
Munich, 'International Crafts Expo'.
Montreal, Italian Pavilion.

1970
Venice, XXXV Biennale d'Arte.

1972
Venice, XXXVI Biennale d'Arte.
Vicenza, Accademia Olimpica, Sala Domus Conastabilis.

1973
Milan, XV Triennale.

1977–78
Monza, Villa Reale (one-man exhibition).

1979
Corning, The Corning Museum of Glass, 'New Glass '79 – Worldwide Survey' ('Grand Prix').
São Paulo (Brazil), NDI, 'MOMA Design'.

1981
Venice, Palazzo Grassi, 'Vetri Murano Oggi'.
Washington, Renwick Gallery.

1982
Tokyo, 'Vetro di Murano: ieri e oggi'.
Montreal, Musée des Arts Décoratifs.
Helsinki, Artek, 'Un Hommage à Venini'.
Venice, Palazzo Ducale; Museo Correr, 'Mille Anni di Arte del Vetro a Venezia'.
La Jolla (California), Museum of Contemporary Art, 'Italian Re-evolution. Design in Italian Society in the Eighties'.

1983
Philadelphia, Philadelphia Museum of Art, 'Design since 1945'.

1984
New York, Heller Gallery, 'Venini. The Spirit of the Moment'.
New York, Fifty-50, 'Venini and the Murano Renaissance: Italian Art Glass of the 1940s and 50s'.
Turin, Palazzo Nervi, 'Mostra del vetro italiano 1920-1940'.
Munich, Museum Villa Stuck, 'Die Fünfziger Stilkonturen eines Jahrzehnts'.

1985
Paris, Gerard Laubie Galerie.
Paris, Beaubourg, 'Lumières, je pense à vous'.

1988
Gardone Riviera, Villa Alba, 'Gabriele d'Annunzio e la Promozione delle Arti'.

1989
New York, Muriel Karasik Gallery, 'The Venetians. Modern Glass 1919-1990'.

1991
Venice, Galleria Marina Barovier, 'Carlo Scarpa. I vestri di Murano 1927-1947'.

1996
Venice, Fondazione Giorgio Cini, 'Gli artisti di Venini. Per una storia del vetro d'arte veneziano'.

1997
Brescia, Palazzo Martinengo, 'Carlo Scarpa. I vetri di un architetto'.
Turin, Palazzo Nervi, 'Fragili e supremamente inutili'.

1998
Milan, Castello Sforzesco, 'Il Vetro Italiano a Milano 1906-1968. Tra creatività e progettazione'.
Zurich, Museum Bellerive, 'Venini. Glas aus Murano'.

Bibliography

1922

R. Linzeler, 'Les Verreries de Cappellin Venini', in *Art et Décoration*, pp. 666–68.
XII Esposizione Internazionale d'Arte della città di Venezia 1922. Catalogo, Venice.

1923

C. Carrà, *L'arte decorativa contemporanea alla prima Biennale Internazionale di Monza*, Milan.
Catalogo della Prima Mostra Internazionale delle Arti Decorative (Villa Reale, Monza), Milan-Rome.
A. Francini, 'Le nostre arti decorative a Venezia', in *Le Arti Decorative*, March, p. 19.
R. Linzeler, 'Les Verreries de Cappellin Venini', in *Art et Décoration*, March, pp. 79–84 [cit. Linzeler 1923a].
R. Linzeler, 'I vetri soffiati muranesi di Cappellin e Venini', in *Arte Pura e Decorativa*, no. 3 [cit. Linzeler 1923b].
R. Papini, *Le Arti a Monza nel MCMXXIII*, Bergamo [cit. Papini 1923a].
R. Papini, 'La Mostra delle Arti Decorative a Monza. III Le arti della terra', in *Emporium*, LVIII, 343, July, pp. 3–21 [cit. Papini 1923b].
'La premiazione alla mostra d'arte decorativa di Monza. Gran Diploma d'Onore', in *Emporium*, LVIII, 346, October, p. 255.

1924

U. Nebbia, 'La XIV Biennale Veneziana. Un po' d'arte decorativa', in *Emporium*, LIX, 354, June, p. 370.
XIV Esposizione Internazionale d'Arte della città di Venezia 1924. Catalogo, Venice.

1925

Italie à l'Exposition Internationale des Arts Décoratifs et Industriels moderns, Paris.
'Muranese Glass by Cappellin and Venini', in *The Studio Year Book of Decorative Art*, Paris.
U. Nebbia, 'L'Italia alla Esposizione Internazionale di Parigi di Arti Decorative e Industriali Moderne', in *Emporium*, LXII, 367, July, p. 17.
R. Papini, 'Le Arti a Monza nel 1925. II Dalle ceramiche ai cartelloni', in *Emporium*, October, pp. 223–43.

1926

'Decorative Art 1926', in *The Studio Yearbook of Decorative Art*, XXI, London.
P. Du Colombier, 'Le Salon d'Automne', in *Art et Décoration*, November, pp. 185–90.
Salon d'Automne. Catalogue des Ouvrages de peinture, sculpture, dessin, architecture e art décoratif, Paris.
'I vetri di Murano e la Vetri Soffiati muranesi Venini & C.', in *Le Tre Venezie*, August, pp. 43–44.
XV Esposizione Internazionale d'Arte della città di Venezia 1926. Catalogo, Venice.

1927

Catalogo ufficiale della Terza Mostra Internazionale delle Arti Decorative (Villa Reale, Monza), Milan.
G. Dell' Oro, 'I Veneti alla III Biennale delle Arti Decorative a Monza', in *Le Tre Venezie*, III, 8, August, pp. 41–43.
E. Z., 'I vetrai Veneziani a Lipsia', in *Le Tre Venezie*, III, March, p. 61.
G. Marangoni, *Enciclopedia delle moderne arti decorative italiane. III Le arti del fuoco: ceramica – vetri – vetrate*, Milan, pp. 103–20.
'Muranese Glass designed by Martinuzzi and executed by Venini and Co.', in *The Studio Year Book of Decorative Art*, London.
R. Papini, 'Le arti a Monza nel 1927. 1 Gli italiani', in *Emporium*, July, pp. 14–32.
The Studio Year Book of Decorative Art, edited by C.G. Holme, S.B. Wainwright, London.

1928

Casabella, June.
G. Damerini, 'Il nuovo assetto e l'avvenire dell'arte Italiana', in *Le Tre Venezie*, IV, 5, May, pp. 15–20.
'Gli espositori alla casa degli architetti all'Esposizione di Torino', in *Domus*, September, p. 18.
C.A. Felice, 'Le arti decorative. Vetri di Orrefors e di Murano, argenti di Fegarotti, la scuola d'arte di Padova', in *Domus*, July, pp. 29–33.
'Filigrane di Murano. Un'arte che riappare in forme nuove', in *Domus*, January, p. 29.
G. D. O. [G. Dell'Oro], 'Le piccole industrie venete all'esposizione di Torino', in *Le Tre Venezie*, IV, 7, July, pp. 45–47.
'Lampade e Paralumi', in *Domus*, XII, December, p. 77.
'Notiziario', in *Domus*, IV, April, p. 50.
'Le piccole industrie alla mostra di Torino', in *Le Tre Venezie*, IV, 8, August, p. 41.
'La statua in vetro di Napoleone Martinuzzi', in *Le Tre Venezie*, IV, 12, December, p. 47.
'Venini, Balleriana o Josephine Baker?', in *Domus*, X, October, p. 22.

XVI Esposizione Internazionale d'Arte della città di Venezia 1928. Catalogo, Venice

1928–29

A. Maraini, 'L'Architettura e le Arti Decorative alla XVI Biennale Veneziana', in *Architettura e Arti Decorative*, I, VIII, pp. 49–65.
P. Marconi, 'La rinascita delle Arti Applicate e la recente produzione dei Vetri di Murano', in *Architettura e Arti Decorative*, I, VIII, pp. 394–404.

1929

'Le arti dell'arredamento alla XVI Biennale di Venezia', in *Casabella*, May.
Dir., 'Vetri di Murano', in *Domus*, February, pp. 31–33 and cover.
Exposición Internacional de Barcelona 1929, exhibition catalogue edited by R. Targett, Milan-Rome.
International Exhibition of Glass and Rugs, exhibition catalogue edited by C.R. Richards, Portland (Maine).
'Napoleone Martinuzzi, Nuovi vetri "pulegosi"', in *Domus*, September, pp. 30–31.
'Nuovi apparecchi d'illuminazione editi da Venini', in *Domus*, December, p. 43.
'Le piccole industrie italiane alla Fiera di Lipsia', in *Domus*, June, pp. 36–37.
G. Ponti, 'Formazione di alcuni caratteri stilistici contemporanei', in *Domus*, December, p. 40.

1929–30

A.F. Reggiori, 'La Triennale di Monza', in *Architettura e Arti Decorative*, I, X, pp. 481–526.

1930

'Alla triennale di Monza', in *Domus*, July, pp. 34–41.
C.A. Felice, *Arte decorativa 1930 all'Esposizione di Monza*, Milan.
'Napoleone Martinuzzi vaso in vetro soffiato', in *Domus*, August (cover).
U. Nebbia, 'I Veneti alle Arti Decorative di Monza', in *Le Tre Venezie*, June, pp. 10–16.
E. Paolucci, 'Le ultime creazioni di Venini', in *Casabella*, III, October, pp. 44–45.
R. Papini, *Le arti d'oggi. Architettura e arti decorative in Europa*, Milan-Rome, Figg. 564–77.
XVII Esposizione Biennale Internazionale d'Arte 1930, exhibition catalogue edited by U. Nebbia, Venice.

1930–31

C.A. Felice, 'I vetri alla Triennale di Monza', in *Dedalo*, October, pp. 312–26.

1931

G. Lorenzetti, *Vetri di Murano*, Rome.
Mostra di Vetri, Ceramiche e Merletti d'Arte Moderna Italiana, exhibition catalogue (Staedelyk Museum, Amsterdam), Amsterdam.
'I muranesi alla mostra del fiore d'arte in palazzo Vecchio a Firenze', in *Domus*, July, p. 53.
'Produzione dell'Enapi', in *Domus*, November, pp. 78–81.

1932

P. Chiesa, 'Vetri incisi a Venezia', in *Domus*, August, pp. 477–79, 513 [cit. Chiesa 1932a].
P. Chiesa, 'Il vetro alla Biennale veneziana', in *Domus*, July, pp. 416–21 [cit. Chiesa 1932b].
U. Nebbia, 'L'Arte decorativa alla Biennale', in *Le Tre Venezie*, May, pp. 305–9.
'Il padiglione di Porto Marghera alla Fiera di Padova', in *Le Tre Venezie*, June, p. 392.
XVIII Esposizione Biennale Internazionale d'Arte 1932. Catalogo, Venice.

1933

'Bianco e nero', in *Domus*, November, p. 600.
'La Casa Media', in *Le Tre Venezie*, July, pp. 526–35.
'Modelli di produzioni artigiane di ceramiche, vetri, cuoi moderni', in *Domus*, October, pp. 558–59.
R. Papini, 'La Quinta Triennale a Milano', in *Emporium*, December, pp. 331–84 [cit. Papini 1933a].
R. Papini, 'La Triennale milanese delle arti', in *L'illustrazione italiana*, Milan, 4 June, pp. 850–76 [cit. Papini 1933b].
G. Piva, 'Artisti e artigiani veneti alla Triennale', in *Le Tre Venezie*, July, pp. 522–25.
'La V Triennale di Milano', in *La Rivista illustrata del Popolo d'Italia*, special number, August, s.p.
'I vetri d'arte italiani alla Triennale', in *Domus*, May, pp. 236–39.
'I vetri d'arte italiani alla Triennale', in *Domus*, July, pp. 379–83.

1934

I. Hald, 'Italiensk Glass', in *Form*.
E. Motta, L'Arte Decorativa', in *Le Tre Venezie*, May, pp. 275–78.
T. Lundgren, 'Den Italienska Konstindustrien', in *Form*.
R. Papini, 'L'arte decorativa', in *Le Tre Venezie*, May, pp. 275–78 [cit. Papini 1934a].

R. Papini, 'Vetri di Paolo Venini', in *Le Tre Venezie*, May, p. 279 [cit. Papini 1934b].

'Suggerimenti', in *Domus*, September, pp. 34–35.

XIX Esposizione Biennale Internazionale d'Arte 1934. Catalogo, Venice.

1936

G. Dell'Oro, 'L'Arte Decorativa alla XX Biennale', in *Le Tre Venezie*, July, pp. 225–29.

G. P. [G. Ponti], 'Considerazioni sui vetri di Venini', in *Domus*, July, pp. 28–33.

'Una nuova "invenzione" vetraria muranese. Il cristallo diamante', in *Domus*, February, pp. 22–23.

R. Pancini, 'La VI Triennale d'arti decorative a Monza', in *Emporium*, LXXII, November.

'Utili regali per Natale che Vi consigliamo', in *Domus*, 108, December, pp. 36–43.

XX Esposizione Biennale Internazionale d'Arte 1936-XIV. Catalogo, Venice.

1937

T. Lundgren, 'Den Internationella Triennalen i Milano 1936', in *Form*.

1938

G. Dell'Oro, 'L'Arte decorativa alla XXI Biennale', in *Le Tre Venezie*, June, pp. 240–43.

Exposición Italiana de Arte Decorativa, exhibition catalogue, Buenos Aires.

I. Hald, 'Italiensk Glass', in *Form*.

'Una piccola collezione di paralumi', in *Domus*, May, pp. 32–33.

'Regali per la signora giovane', in *Domus*, December, pp. 28–29.

'Vetri di Venini', in *Le Tre Venezie*, June, pp. 246–47.

XXI Esposizione Biennale Internazionale d'Arte 1938-XVI. Catalogo, Venice.

1940

G. P. [G. Ponti], 'Venini o della castigatezza', in *Domus*, June, pp. 58–61.

T. Lundgren, 'Paolo Venini in Murano', in *Form*.

E. Motta, 'Vetri e merletti', in *Le Tre Venezie*, XVI, May, pp. 240–44.

P., 'Nuovi vetri muranesi', in *Domus*, October, pp. 69–71.

R. Papini, 'Le arti a Milano nell'anno XVIII', in *Emporium*, May, pp. 211–19.

'Tipi: maniglie di Venini', in *Domus*, August, p. 56.

'Vetri muranesi di Tyra Lundgren', in *Domus*, January, pp. 32–35.

XXII Esposizione Biennale Internazionale d'Arte 1940-XVIII. Catalogo, Venice.

1941

C.A. Felice, 'Contro la produzione fittizia', in *Domus*, January, pp. 54–55.

'Vetri e ceramiche', in *Domus*, January, pp. 54–55.

1942

XXIII Esposizione Biennale Internazionale d'Arte 1942-XX. Catalogo, Venice.

1943

T. Lundgren, 'Uttsallningen i Rohsska museet och Nationalmuseam-Det Moderna Italienka Glaset', in *Form*, pp. 108–10.

1944

'Venini', in *AD*, no. 162.

'Venini', in *Art et Décoration*, November.

1948

'Murano alla Biennale di Venezia', in *Domus*.

'Vetri e gioielli d'arte', in *Domus*, IV, pp. 40–41.

XXIV Biennale di Venezia. Catalogo, Venice.

1949

Les Arts Décoratifs Vénitiens à la Biennale di Venezia, in *L'Œil*, January.

G. Hennum, 'Innenfor et Glashus', in *Magasinet*, October.

1950

A. Gasparetto, 'Arte decorativa alla Biennale', in *Domus*, October, pp. 38–41.

"Seconda Mostra selettiva nazionale dell'artigianato artistico", Milan.

'Sei vetri di Fulvio Bianconi', in *Domus*, February, pp. 44–45.

E. Steenberg, 'Glasdirigent med Muranoorkester', in *Form*, pp. 202–3.

"Terza Mostra selettiva dell'artigianato artistico", exhibition catalogue, Milan.

XXV Biennale di Venezia. Catalogo, Venice.

1951

'Alcuni elementi di illuminazione', in *Domus*, September, p. 29.

L'Art du verre, exhibition catalogue (Musée des Arts Décoratifs, Paris), Paris.

'Decorative Art', in *The Studio Year Book 1950-51*, London.

G. Galbiati, *Itinerario per il visitatore della Biblioteca Ambrosiana della Pinacoteca e dei monumenti annessi*, Milan.

Nona Triennale di Milano, exhibition catalogue edited by A. Pica, Milan.

'I vetri italiani alla Triennale', in *Domus*, October, pp. 27–37.

1952

'Murano alla Biennale', in *Domus*, November.

XXVI Biennale di Venezia, Catalogo, Venice.

1953

G. Mariacher, 'La mostra Storica del vetro di Murano alla XXVI Biennale', in *Arte Veneta*, VII.

'Vaso con molatura a fiamma', in *Domus*, December.

1954

'Arti decorative alla Biennale', in *Domus*, October.

Decima Triennale di Milano, exhibition catalogue, Milan.

'Decorative Art', in *The Studio Year Book 1953-54*, London.

'Forme italiane a Zurigo', in *Domus*, September.

Forme Nuove in Italia, exhibition catalogue (Kunstgewerbe Museum, Zurich), Zurich.

A. Gasparetto, 'Antico e moderno nella Vetreria di Murano', in *Sele Arte*, no. 6.

G. Mariacher, *L'arte del vetro*, Milan [cit. Mariacher 1954a].

G. Mariacher, 'I vetri della raccolta Maglione presso il museo vetrario di Murano', in *Giornale Economico*, May [cit. Mariacher 1954b].

'Il nuovo negozio Olivetti a New York: lampade di Venini', in *Domus*, September.

'Trent'anni di Triennale', in *Domus*, November. pp. 9–20.

Venetians Glaas, exhibition catalogue (Gemeentemuseum, The Hague), The Hague.

XXVII Esposizione Biennale Internazionale d'Arte, Venice.

1955

R. Aloi, *Esempi. Vetri di Murano Oggi*, Milan.

Glaskunst aus Murano, exhibition catalogue (Kunstgewerbe Museum, Basel), Basel.

'Le nuove lampade di Venini con Massimo Vignelli', in *Domus*, December.

'Piccola rassegna di Venini', in *Domus*, April, p. 52.

'Premi alla qualità italiana Lampade', in *Stile industria*, December, pp. 6–14.

'Regali di Natale', in *Domus*, December.

E. Steenberg, B. Simmingskold, 'Venini', in *Glas*.

'Vasi di Murrine di Paolo Venini', in *Domus*, December.

1956

'Arti decorative a Venezia', in *Domus*, November, p. 65.

'Arti decorative alla Biennale', in *Domus*, October, p. 37.

B. Clow, 'Venetian Glass', in *Craft Horizons*, August, pp. 41–43.

G. Mariacher, 'Venetian Glass, Lamps and Chandeliers', in *The Connoisseur*, December, pp. 168–73.

'Nuovi vasi e bottiglie', in *Domus*, December, p. 65.

'Rassegna Domus', in *Domus*, December.

'Vasi e lampade', in *Domus*, January, pp. 45–48.

XXVIII Esposizione Biennale Internazionale d'Arte, Venice.

1957

A. Gasparetto, 'Dieci Secoli di Vetreria Muranese', in *Ateneo Veneto*, no. 2.

Glas der Gegenwart, exhibition catalogue edited by P.W. Meiste (Museum für Kunsthandwerk, Frankfurt), Frankfurt.

Undicesima Triennale, exhibition catalogue, Milan.

'Venini in Europa', in *Domus*, July.

Venini Murano Glas, exhibition catalogue (Kestner Museum, Hanover), Hanover.

'Venini vetrate', in *Domus*, August, pp. 47–50.

1958

A. Gasparetto, *Il vetro di Murano dalle origini ad oggi*, Venice.

'Per due sposi a Milano', in *Domus*, 347, October, pp. 23–28.

M. Schildt, 'Paolo Venini i fokus', in *Form*, October, pp. 270–73.

'A Venini Chandelier', in *International Lighting Review*, 6, June, pp. 194–95.

O. Verff, 'Portrait des Monats: Paolo Venini', in *Die Schaulade*, September, p. 638.

XXIX Esposizione Biennale Internazionale d'Arte, Venice.

1959

Corning Glass 1959-New Glass a Worldwide Survey, Corning.

K. Ekholm, 'Paolo Venini, lank mellan syd och nord', in *Form*, July, p. 428.

Glass 1959, exhibition catalogue, (Carnegie Institute, Pittsburgh), Pittsburgh.

'In Memoriam, Paolo Venini', in *Die Schaulade*, September, p. 800.

G. Ponti, 'Venini', in *Domus*, 361, December, pp. 31–46.

'Venini-Italienischer Glasmacher Kunst', in *Die Schaulade*, vol. 64, no. 10, October.

1960

A. Gasparetto, 'Ricordo di Venini', in *Ateneo Veneto*, vol. 144, no. 1, pp. 71–74.

Vetri di Murano 1860-1960, exhibition catalogue edited by A. Gasparetto (Palazzo della Gran Guardia, Verona), Venice.

XXX Esposizione Biennale Internazionale d'Arte, Venice.

1961

P. Carluccio, P.C. Santini, 'Italia '61', in *Comunità*, June.

Domus, December.

1962

Catalogo della XXXI Esposizione Biennale Internazionale d'Arte-Venezia, Venice.

A. Gasparetto, 'Le arti decorative venete alla XXXI Biennale di Venezia', in *Giornale Economico*, August, pp. 936–41.

'Nuovi vetri di Venini', in *Domus*, January, pp. 38–39.

A. Polak, *Modern Glass*, London.

1963

J. Banti Pereira, *Ikebana: fiori viventi*, Milan.

'Dalla "haute couture" ai vetri soffiati', in *La Nazione*, 11 October, p. 18.

Domus, May.

'Venini 1963: vetro e argento', in *Domus*, July, pp. 41–47.

'Vetro e Metallo', in *Abitare*, June, s.p.

1964

Catalogo della XXXII Biennale Internazionale d'Arte-Venezia, Venice.

H. Dirr, 'Venini Heute', in *Die Schaulade*, August, pp. 1052–54.

S. Viola, 'I ricordi di un artista del vetro', in *Novità*.

1965

Domus, February.

G. Perocco, *Artisti del primo Novecento italiano*, Turin.

1966

Catalogo della XXXIII Esposizione Biennale Internazionale d'Arte-Venezia, Venice.

M. Causa, *L'arte del vetro. Dal Rinascimento ai nostri giorni*, Milan.

F. Kämpfer, *Viertausend Jahre Glas*, Dresden.

G. Ponti, 'Le vetrate grosse alla Ponti, da Venini', in *Domus*, March, pp. 25–29.

Vittorio Zecchin, exhibition catalogue edited by G. Perocco (Galleria Bevilacqua La Masa, Venice), Venice.

A. Warneke, *Kultur in Glas und Porzellan*, Hamburg.

1967

Domus, December.

G. Mariacher, *I Vetri di Murano*, Milan.

1968

Catalogo della XXXIV Esposizione Biennale Internazionale d'Arte-Venezia, Venice.

1970

Catalogo della XXXV Esposizione Biennale Internazionale d'Arte-Venezia, Venice.

1971

G. Mazzotti, T. Carta, *Artigianato veneto*, Rome.

1972

M. Brusatin, 'Carlo Scarpa architetto veneziano', in *Controspazio*, March-April, pp. 2–85.

G. Perocco, *Le origini dell'arte moderna a Venezia*, Treviso.

XXXVI Esposizione Biennale Internazionale d'Arte-Venezia, Venice.

1974

L'Art Déco, Geneva.

Carlo Scarpa, exhibition catalogue (Accademia Olimpica, Vicenza), Vicenza.

1975

R. Barovier Mentasti, 'Tre opere di Vittorio Zecchin al Vittoriale', in *Notizie da Palazzo Albani*, VI, no. 2.

R. Bossaglia, *Il "Déco" italiano. Fisionomia dello stile 1925 in Italia*, Milan.

'Venezianische Glaskunst in Frauenauer Museum', in *Bayerwald Bote*, June.

1976

R. Barovier Mentasti, 'I vetri smaltati veneziani tra '800 e '900', in *Rivista della Stazione Sperimentale del vetro*, VI.

M. Greenhalgh, 'Donatello in Perspective: the Chellini Madonna', in *History Today*, XXVI, XI, November, pp. 734–42.

1977

R. Barovier Mentasti, 'La vetreria veneziana moderna dal 1895 al 1920', in *Journal of Glass Studies*, XIX.

H. Newman, *An Illustrated Dictionary of Glass*, London.

Vetri di Murano del '900, exhibition catalogue edited by R. Barovier Mentasti, Venice.

1978

Schlosstheater Fulda, illustrated brochure, Fulda.

1979

A. Gasparetto, 'Una grande mostra storica del vetro veneziano a Londra', in *Arte Veneta*, XXVII.

G. Hennum, 'Innenfor et Glasshus', in *Magasinet*, October.

S. Tagliapietra, *La magnifica comunità di Murano 1900-1925*, in S. Tagliapietra, *Cronache muranesi*, Verona.

1980

Arti decorative 1890-1940, auction catalogue, Finarte, Milan.

A. Branzi, M. De Lucchi, *Il design italiano degli anni '50*, Milan.

Ph. Garner, *Contemporary Decorative Art from 1940 to the Present*, New York.

Manualità-Città dell'artigianato, exhibition catalogue, Milan.

Massara Hotel, brochure illustrativa del progetto di illuminazione, Lyon.

1981

'Creative Venini Glass at Renwick Gallery', in *Southern Antiques*, September.

Design Vignelli, edited by E. Ambasz, New York.

From the 1920's Venini Glass Makes a Special Statement, in *The New York Pennsylvania Collector*, September.

D. MacNeil, 'The Noble Tradition of Murano revived by a Milanese Lawyer', in *House and garden*, November, pp. 178–79.

C. Pauly, 'Lo shopping: Venini', in *AD* (supplement).

'Sites exhibits Venini Glass', in *Collectors News*, November.

T. Wirkkala, exhibition catalogue, Moscow.

Venezianisches Glas 19. bis 20. Jahrhundert aus den Glasmuseum Murano, exhibition catalogue edited by A. Dorigato, R. Barovier Mentasti (Kunstgewerbe Museum Schloss Kopenick), Berlin.

Vetri Murano Oggi, exhibition catalogue edited by R. Barovier Mentasti, A. Dorigato, G. Romanelli (Palazzo Grassi, Venice), Venice.

Vittorio Zecchin, exhibition catalogue edited by G. Perocco (Museo d'Arte Moderna Ca' Pesaro, Venice), Milan.

1982

D. Baroni, 'L'arte nell'industria', in *Interni*, November, pp. 54–56.

R. Barovier Mentasti, *Il vetro veneziano. Dal Medioevo al '900*, Milan.

P.V. Gardner, 'Maestri di Murano: a saluto to Venini', in *American Craft*, April–May.

V. Gregotti, *Il disegno del prodotto industriale*, Milan.

Important Art and Crafts, Art Nouveau and Art Déco, auction catalogue, Christie's, New York.

Italian Re-evolution. Design in Italian Society in the Eighties, exhibition catalogue edited by P. Sartogo (Museum of Contemporary Art, La Jolla), Milan.

Mille Anni di Arte del Vetro a Venezia, exhibition catalogue edited by R. Barovier Mentasti, A. Dorigato, A. Gasparetto, T. Toninato (Palazzo Ducale, Venice), Venice.

Vetri '900 manifesti mobili di Giò Ponti, auction catalogue, Galleria Salamon Agustoni Algranti, Milan.

Vetro di Murano: ieri e oggi, exhibition catalogue edited by G. Romanelli, A. Dorigato, Tokyo.

1983

A. Dorigato, *Murano-Il vetro a tavola ieri e oggi*, exhibition catalogue, Venice.

Intérieurs 50, immeuble Pierre Cardin, Brussels.

'Italian Re-evolution una giornata made in Italy', in *Casa Vogue*, January.

Tapio Wirkkala, exhibition catalogue (Musée des Arts Décoratifs, Paris), Paris.

'Venini', in *Modo*, March.

1984

Arti decorative del '900, auction catalogue, Finarte, Milan.

S.K. Chambers, 'Reviews: Venini the Spirit of the Moment', in *New York Magazine*, nos 19–20, summer–autumn.

F. Dal Co, G. Mazzariol, *Carlo Scarpa. Opera completa*, Milan.

Design since 1945, exhibition catalogue edited by K.B. Hiesinger (Philadelphia Museum of Art, Philadelphia), Wisbech.

Die Fünfziger Stilkonturen eines Jahrzehnts, exhibition catalogue edited by G. Fahr Beker-Sterner (Museum Villa Stuck, Munich), Munich.

Glass in Miami, exhibition catalogue edited by J. Baratte (Center for the Fine Arts, Miami), Miami.

M.E. Haus, 'Italian Glass Goes Blue Chip', in *Art and Auction*, April.

Mostra del vetro Italiano 1920-1940, exhibition catalogue edited by S. Asti, Turin.

'Venini', in *Abitare*, June.

Venini and the Murano Renaissance. Italian Glass of the 1940s and 50s, exhibition catalogue edited by M. Isacson, New York.

'I vetri di Venini in mostra negli Stati Uniti', in *Abitare*, November.

'Vetri sulla Laguna', in *Abitare*, July–August.

1985

Arts Décoratifs du XX siècle, auction catalogue, Sotheby's, Munich.

A. Botti Monti, 'Italiani a New York', in *Casa Vogue*, June.

'Una calle per Paolo Venini', in *Casa Vogue*, September.

E. Cibot, 'Murano aujourd'hui', in *La Revue de la Céramique et du Verre*, September–October.

Decorative Arts, auction catalogue, Sotheby's, London.

I. de Guttry, M.P. Maino, M. Quesada, *Le arti minori d'autore in Italia dal 1900 al 1930*, Rome-Bari.

Lumières, je pense à vous, exhibition catalogue edited by J.F. Grunfeld, M.L. Jousset (Centre Georges Pompidou, Paris), Paris.

T. Periainen, *Tapio Wirkkala*, Helsinki.

'Venini', in *Neues Glas*, February.

Verriers à Rouen, exhibition catalogue, Rouen.

Les vitraux de Venini à la Galerie Gerard Laubie à Paris, June (press release).

1986

Decorative Arts from 1880 to the present day, auction catalogue, Christie's, London.

A. Dorigato, *Il Museo vetrario di Murano*, Milan.

Murano, il vetro e la sua gente, Treviso.

1987

Impronte del soffio. Tradizione e nuovi percorsi a Murano, exhibition catalogue edited by B. Nerozzi. Venice.

Italienisches Glas 1950-60, exhibition catalogue edited by W. Neuwirth (Museum Carolinum Augusteum, Salzburg), Vienna.

'Museo vetrario di Murano. Vetri moderni e contemporanei - Vetri del '900. Doni al Museo 1950-1987', in *Giornale del Museo*, edited by A. Dorigato, Venice.

Tapio Wirkkala. Venini, exhibition catalogue (Finnish Glass Museum, Riihimäki), Riihimäki.

'Venini', in *Metropolis*, September.

E. Westerdahl, 'Fargsprakande Venini Glasny auktionsfavorit', in *Antike Auktion*, Stockholm, pp. 59–63.

1988

R. Barovier Mentasti, *Il vetro veneziano*, Milan.

'Due aste: a Ginevra da Christie e a Milano da Finarte', in *Antiquariato*, January.

Gabriele d'Annunzio e la Promozione delle Arti, exhibition catalogue edited by R. Bossaglia, M. Quesada (Villa Alba, Gardone Riviera), Milan-Rome.

La verrerie européenne des années '50, exhibition catalogue edited by D. Baldouy Maternati, Marseilles.

1989

A Concise History of Glass. The Chrysler Museum of Norfolk, edited by N.O. Merril, Princeton.

M. Cousins, *20th Century Glass*, London.

F. Deboni, *I vetri Venini*, Turin.

Die Sammlung Wolfang Kermer, exhibition catalogue edited by A. Hannes (Glasmuseum Frauenau, Frauenau), Zurich.

'Exclusivit Venini-glas Klassiker for glasalskare', in *Femina*, June, pp. 82–83.

M. Heiremans, *Murano Glas 1945-1970*, Antwerp.

The Robert Mapplethorpe Collection, auction catalogue, Christie's, New York.

G. Sarpellon, *Salviati il suo vetro e i suoi uomini*, Venice.

S. Tagliapietra, 'Ludovico Diaz de Santillana', in *Giornale Economico*, pp. 29–32.

The Venetians. Modern Glass 1919-1990, exhibition catalogue (Muriel Karasik Gallery, New York), New York.

Venini, Murano 1921, edited by G. Romanelli, P. Mauriès, E. Loupari, A. Belgioioso, Milan.

Vetri di Murano, exhibition catalogue edited by A. Dorigato, R. Barovier Mentasti (Kunstindustrimuseet, Oslo), Venice.

1990

Arti decorative del Secolo XX, auction catalogue, Sotheby's, Milan.

S. Jones, 'Venini and Italian Art Glass', in *Antiques and Collecting*, December.

C. Laks, 'Collectionner le verre italien des années 50', in *La Revue de la Céramique et du Verre*, July–August.

L. Licitra Ponti, *Gio Ponti. L'opera*, Milan.

P. Martinuzzi, *Napoleone Martinuzzi*, Venice.

G. Sarpellon, *Miniature di vetro: Murrine 1838-1924*, Venice.

Twentieth Century Decorative Arts, auction catalogue, Christie's, Geneva.

Venetian Glass 1910-1960. An Important Private Collection, auction catalogue, Sotheby's, Geneva.

'Venini and Italian Art Glass', in *Antiques and Collecting*, December.

1991

Arti decorative del Secolo XX, auction catalogue, Sotheby's, Milan.

Carlo Scarpa. I vetri di Murano 1927-1947, edited by M. Barovier, Venice.

D'Annunzio e Venezia, Conference proceedings edited by E. Mariano, Rome.

O. Drahotova, *L'arte del vetro in Europa*, La Spezia.

English and Continental Glass from 1500-1960, auction catalogue, Sotheby's, London.

'Meesterstukken uit Murano', in *Glass und Keramiek*, April-May-June.

H. Tait, *Cinquemila anni di vetro*, Milan.

Vetri di Murano del '900. 50 capolavori, exhibition catalogue edited by M. Cocchi (Galleria In. Arte, Milan), Milan.

1992

L'arte del vetro. Silice e fuoco: vetri del XIX e XX secolo, exhibition catalogue edited by M. Quesada (Palazzo delle Esposizioni, Rome), Venice.

R. Barovier Mentasti, *Vetro veneziano 1890-1990*, Venice.

C. Cerutti, A. Dorigato, *Il vetro dal Rinascimento al Novecento*, Novara.

R. Colombo, 'Antiche forme rivisitate per una Murano vestita di nuovo', in *Antiquariato*, April.

Museum Bellerive Zürich, Glas, vol. I, Zurich.

Napoleone Martinuzzi vetraio del Novecento, edited by M. Barovier, R. Barovier Mentasti, Venice.

Treasure from the Corning Museum of Glass, exhibition catalogue, Yokohama.

'Venini', in *Maison et Jardin*, April.

Vetri artistici Murano 1910-1960, auction catalogue, Finarte, Milan.

1993

R. Bossaglia, *I vetri di Fulvio Bianconi*, documents and appendix edited by M. Cocchi, Turin.

A. Dorigato et al., *Art of Barovier Glassmaker in Murano 1866-1972*, Venice.

M. Heiremans, *Art Glass from Murano, 1910-1970*, Stuttgart.

Importanti Vetri Venini nella collezione di Madame Ruth Hine, edited by F. Semenzato, Milan.

'Miniature per creare uno zoo di fantasia', in *Antiquariato*, January.

F. Perego, 'Il vate Artigianato', in *L'E-spresso*, September, p. 103.

1994

L. Berndt, 'Murano's Opinion', in *Glass*, V, 56.

'Corroso, bulicante, pulegoso, gli strani nomi del vetro della riscossa', in *Antiquariato*, January.

Ettore Sottsass, exhibition catalogue (Centre George Pompidou, Paris), Paris.

S. Humair, 'Venise : la verrerie de Venini', in *Maison et Jardin*, April.

Murano. Fantasie di vetro, exhibition catalogue edited by M. Barovier (Galleria Marina Barovier, Venice), Venice.

Vetri di Murano del '900, auction catalogue.

Vetri veneziani del '900. La collezione della Cassa di Risparmio di Venezia. Biennali 1930–1970, edited by R. Barovier Mentasti, Venice.

1995

M. Barovier, R. Barovier Mentasti, A. Dorigato, *Il vetro di Murano alle Biennali, 1895–1972*, Milan.

E. Baumgartner, *Verre de Venise et "Façon de Venise"*, exhibition catalogue (Musée Ariana, Geneva), vol. II, Geneva.

Museum Bellerive Zürich, Glas, vol. II, Zurich.

H. Ricke, *Glaskunst Reflex der Jahrhunderte*, Munich, New York.

Venezia e la Biennale. I percorsi del gusto, exhibition catalogue (Galleria d'Arte Moderna Ca' Pesaro, Venice), Venice.

Verre de Venise : Trésors inédits, exhibition catalogue edited by E. Baumgartner (Musée Ariana, Geneva), Geneva.

'Vetri di Murano, una lampada di Venini', in *Antiquariato*, March.

1996

Gli artisti di Venini. Per una storia del vetro d'arte veneziano, exhibition catalogue edited by Fondazione Giorgio Cini, Milan.

Il bestiario di Murano. Sculture in vetro dal 1928 al 1965, exhibition catalogue edited by M. Barovier, A. Dorigato (Palazzo Ducale, Venice), Venice.

F. Deboni, *Murano '900. Vetri e Vetrai*, Milan.

M. Heiremans, *20th Century Murano Glass. From Craft to Design*, Munich.

T. Oldknow, *Pilchuck: A Glass School*, Seattle.

Sculture di luce. Murano, 1930-1965, exhibition catalogue (Galleria Soloarte, Rome), Rome.

1997

M. Barovier, *Carlo Scarpa. I vetri di un architetto*, exhibition catalogue (Palazzo Martinengo, Brescia), Milan.

Fragili e supremamente inutili, exhibition catalogue edited by W. Figliola (Palazzo Nervi, Turin), Turin.

Italian Glass. Murano-Milan 1930-1970, The Collection of the Steinberg Foundation, edited by H. Ricke, E. Schmitt, Munich, New York.

T. Oldknow, *Richard Marquis: Objects*, Seattle.

1998

Le arti decorative in Lombardia nell'età moderna 1780-1940, edited by V. Terraroli, Milan.

The Glass Skin, exhibition catalogue edited by S.K. Franz, V. Mizuta, H. Ricke (The Corning Museum of Glass, Corning).

Venini. Glas aus Murano, exhibition catalogue edited by A. Venini (Museum Bellerive, Zurich), Zurich.

Venini Venezia. Modern Glass, exhibition catalogue (The Finnish Glass Museum, Helsinki), Helsinki.

Il Vetro Italiano a Milano 1906-1968. Tra creatività e progettazione, exhibition catalogue edited by R. Barovier Mentasti, M. Chirico, G. Mori, A. Pansera, C. Salsi, (Castello Sforzesco, Milan), Milan.

1999

M. Barovier, *Il vetro a Venezia dal moderno al contemporaneo*, Milan.

Milano déco. La fisionomia della città negli anni Venti, edited by R. Bossaglia, V. Terraroli, Milan.

Index of Names

Aalto, Alvar, 48, 308
Albini, Franco, 307
Aloi, R., 205, 206, 210, 216, 218
Alpago-Novello, Alberto, 41
Andreotti, Libero, 21
Angeretti, designer, 54
Anti, Carlo, 214
APEM, factory, 305
Ashton, Don, 54
Aufiero, Tina, 188, 232, 307

Baker, Josephine, 196, 305
Barbiano di Belgioioso, Lodovico
   (called Belgioioso), 305
Barbini, Alfredo, 12
Barovier, Ceno, 305
Barovier, Ercole, 12, 13
Barovier, Giuseppe, 9
Barovier, glassworks, 9, 11, 214
Barovier, M., 15, 193, 196, 198, 199, 203,
   204, 205, 206, 207, 208, 209, 210, 211,
   212, 213, 214, 218, 221, 222, 228, 230
Barovier Mentasti, R., 25, 27, 43, 192,
   193, 194, 196, 198, 199, 200, 203, 204,
   205, 206, 207, 208, 209, 210, 211, 212,
   213, 214, 216, 217, 218, 220, 221, 222,
   227, 228, 229, 230, 231
Bartal, 224
Baumgartner, E., 193
Belgioioso, see Barbiano di Belgioioso,
   Lodovico
Benzoni, M.N., 39
Berman, Eugène, 50, 221, 305, 307
Bernasconi & Fiocchi, designer, 224
Bianconi, Fulvio, 14, 31, 41, 42, 50, 155,
   157, 160, 161, 163, 216, 217, 218, 305,
   307
Biasutto, Arturo (called Boboli), 45, 216
Binfarè, Francesco, 226
Boboli, see Biasutto, Arturo
Bonsembiante, Mario, 49
Bossaglia, R., 25, 43, 200, 216, 217, 218
Brozzi, Renato, 40
Brusatin, M., 210
Buzas, Stefano, 223
Buzzi, Tomaso, 13, 21, 22, 24, 25, 28, 29,
   40, 41, 42, 47, 48, 114, 115, 116, 117,
   118, 119, 121, 123, 124, 126, 127, 128,
   208, 209, 210, 305, 307, 308, 309

Cadorin, Guido, 25, 40
Cadorin, family, 21, 23
Cappellin, Giacomo, 11, 12, 15, 17, 19,
   20, 24, 27, 28, 29, 31, 39, 45, 52, 305,
   307, 308
Cardin, Pierre, 52, 224, 306

Carlsson, Birgitta, 231, 306, 307, 308
Caroli, Gio, 228
Carpenter, James, 33, 34, 36, 37, 43,
   186, 231, 306, 307
Carrà, Carlo, 192, 193
Carta, T., 228, 229
Casanova, Giacomo, 54
Cerutti, C., 192, 193, 217
Chiesa, Pietro, 21, 28, 47, 48, 202, 217,
   305, 307
Chihuly, Dale, 33, 34, 42, 53, 306, 307,
   308
Chirico, M., 43
Christofle, factory, 227, 305, 308
Cibau, Geminiano, 21
Colelli (master glassblower), 227
Copier, Andries Dirk, 13, 15
Cousins, M., 201, 213, 227, 228, 229

D'Annunzio, Gabriele, 21, 23, 24, 25, 40,
   47, 194, 305, 308
Dabbeni, Egidio, 22
Dailey, Dan, 306
Dal Co, F., 210, 211, 212
De Guttry, I., 196, 198
De Luigi, Mario, 51, 305
De Maria, Astolfo, 25
De Maria, family, 21
Deboni, F., 15, 192, 193, 194, 196, 198,
   199, 200, 201, 203, 204, 205, 206, 207,
   208, 210, 211, 212, 213, 214, 216, 217,
   218, 220, 221, 222, 223, 224, 227, 228,
   230
Del Debbio, Enrico, 223, 305
Del Giudice, Brenno, 23, 25
Dell'Oro, G., 203, 210, 211, 212
Diaz de Santillana, Alessandro, 31, 43,
   54, 55, 188, 232, 306, 307
Diaz de Santillana, Laura, 31, 43, 51, 54,
   55, 56, 186, 188, 226, 227, 231, 232,
   306, 307
Diaz de Santillana, Ludovico, 31, 33, 34,
   36, 42, 43, 47, 50, 51, 53, 54, 168, 172,
   174, 176, 202, 203, 206, 210, 212, 213,
   216, 217, 223, 224, 226, 227, 305, 306,
   307, 308, 309
Dorigato, A., 15, 43, 192, 193, 196, 198,
   199, 203, 204, 205, 206, 207, 208, 209,
   210, 211, 212, 213, 214, 216, 217, 218,
   221, 222, 223, 228, 229, 230
Durand-Ruel, Paul, 45

Eos, glassworks, 54, 307
Escritt S., 25

Fei, see Toso Ferdinando

Felice, C.A., 39, 41, 43, 198, 199, 200
Fellini, Federico, 54
Ferrari, Teodoro Wolf, 9
Ferri, Matilde, 308
Ferro E., glassworks, 214
Ferro, Rafael, 305
Fiocco, G., 19
Fontana Arte, factory, 47, 217, 308
Fontana, Lucio, 305
Fornasetti, Piero, 221, 305, 307
Fortuny y Madrazo, Mariano, 19, 40
Franzini, Alberto, 25

Gardella, Ignazio, 51, 305, 306, 307
Gardini, R., 54
Gariboldi, Giuseppe, 21
Gasparetto, A., 41, 43, 45, 204, 205, 211,
   212, 214, 218, 223
Gignous, Eugenio, 50, 307
Gignous Venini, Ginette, 42, 50, 204,
   221, 222, 305, 306, 307
Giraudon, C., 15
Glasfabriek, Leerdam, glassworks, 13
Grasso, Mario, see Tosi, Mario
Griselli, Italo, 21

Haslam, M., 25
Heiremans, M., 192, 193, 199, 200, 201,
   203, 204, 205, 206, 207, 208, 210, 211,
   212, 213, 214, 216, 217, 218, 220, 221,
   222, 223, 224, 227, 228, 230
Hillier, B., 25
Hoffmann, Josef, 11
Holbein, Hans, 45, 192
Hoog, M., 15
Hrstka, Miroslav, 185, 230, 308

Iittala, 42

Kämpfer, F., 192, 206
Keinänen, T., 43
Klein, D., 25
Klimt, Gustav, 308
Kormoso, Grete, 305

Labino, Dominick, 33
Labirinto (Labyrinth), group, 21, 23, 28,
   41, 47, 202, 305, 307, 308
Lancia, Emilio, 21, 28, 305, 308
Lebensold, 223
Leone, Giovanni, 308
Libensky, 308
Licata, Riccardo, 185, 221, 305, 308
Licitra Ponti, L., 49, 201
Liefkes, R., 15
Linzeler, R., 39, 43, 192, 193

Lipofsky, Marvin, 306
Littleton, Harvey, 33
Lorenzetti, G., 198
Lundgren, Tyra, 13, 15, 41, 164, 166, 167,
   217, 220, 305, 308, 309

MacNeil, D., 43
Maestri Vetrai Muranesi Cappellin & C.,
   glassworks, 20, 23, 25, 39, 307, 308
Maino, M.P., 196, 198
Maraini, A., 196
Marconi, P., 194
Marelli, Michele, 21, 28, 41, 47, 305,
   307, 308
Marenesi, Mario, 25
Mariacher, G., 192, 201, 203, 204, 205,
   206, 207, 212, 214, 218, 223, 224, 228
Mariano, E., 25
Marimekko, 222, 308
Marinot, Maurice, 13, 15, 45, 202
Marioni, Dante, 34, 36, 37
Maroni, Gian Carlo, 23, 25, 197
Maroni, Ruggero, 23, 24, 25
Marquis, Richard (Dick), 33, 34, 37, 42,
   186, 230, 306, 308
Martens, Dino, 31
Martini, Arturo, 49, 214
Martinuzzi, Napoleone, 12, 13, 19, 20,
   21, 22, 23, 24, 25, 27, 28, 29, 39, 40,
   41, 47, 48, 62, 64, 67, 68, 71, 72, 73,
   74, 75, 76, 78, 80, 81, 83, 84, 87, 88,
   89, 90, 92, 94, 95, 192, 193, 194, 196,
   198, 200, 208, 305, 307, 308, 309
Martinuzzi, P., 25
Marussig, Guido, 40
Mazzariol, G., 210, 211, 212
Mazzoni, Angiolo, 47, 305
Mazzotti, G., 228, 229
McClelland, N., 25
Menghi, Roberto, 229, 307, 308
Mestrovic, Ivan, 308
Milner, John, 306
Moore, Benjamin, 34, 36, 37, 42, 306
Moratto, Attilio, 305
Moretti, Vincenzo, 9
Mori, G., 43
Motta, E., 41, 43, 210, 214

Nane Patare, see Seguso, Giovanni
Nebbia, U., 40, 43, 200
Nourot, Michael, 306

Ojetti, U., 25
Oldknow, T., 230
Ongaro, Francesco (Checco), 34, 52, 232,
   308

Pansera, A., 43
Paolucci, E., 196
Papini, R., 20, 25, 28, 39, 40, 41, 43, 192,
    193, 196, 208, 209, 213
Pavanello, Malvino, 305
Pelzel, Franz, 49, 213
Peressutti, Enrico, 305
Perocco, G., 39, 43
Philips, factory, 224
Piacentini, Marcello, 22, 47, 51
Piano, Eliseo, 214
Piccinato, Luigi, 47, 202
Polak, A., 192, 200, 211, 212, 218,
    220
Poli, Flavio, 12
Ponti, Giovanni (Gio), 17, 20, 21, 29, 39,
    41, 47, 48, 49, 50, 51, 96, 98, 196, 201,
    204, 205, 206, 207, 210, 211, 212, 213,
    217, 218, 227, 305, 306, 307, 308
Portaluppi, Italo, 21
Powolny, Michael, 11
Pringle, William, 306
Prutscher, Otto, 11

Quesada, M., 25, 43, 196, 198

Radi, Lorenzo, 309
Ravenna, Ugo, 48
Richard-Ginori, factory, 20, 21
Ricke, H., 9, 15, 193, 194, 206, 212, 217
Riegl, A., 19, 25
Rioda, Andrea, 19, 307
Rogers, Ernesto Nathan, 305
Rosenthal, factory, 227, 307
Rossi Colavini, A., 25

S.A. Venini, glassworks, 214
S.A.L.I.R., factory, 13, 14
Sacchi, Bartolomeo, 25
Saetti, Bruno, 305
Salsi, C., 43
Salviati, Antonio, 9, 11, 15
Samonà, Giuseppe, 51
Sanquirico, Antonio, 309
Saponaro, Salvatore, 21
Sarfatti, M., 25
Sarpellon, G., 15
Scarpa, Carlo, 12, 13, 14, 15, 25, 29, 31,
    33, 34, 41, 42, 48, 49, 50, 51, 52, 130,
    134, 135, 136, 137, 138, 139, 141, 145,
    147, 148, 149, 150, 152, 204, 208, 210,
    212, 213, 214, 305, 308, 309, 310
Scarpa, Tobia, 31, 51, 213, 222, 223,
    305, 308, 309
Scheiner, Michael, 34
Schildt, Göran, 218
Schmitt, E., 15
Sciolla, G.C., 25
Scott, Kenneth George, 49, 221, 305, 308
Seguso, Archimede, 12, 31
Seguso, Giovanni (called Nane Patare),
    28, 305
Seguso Vetri d'Arte, glassworks, 28, 214
Sironi, Mario, 41
Stearns, Thomas, 31, 42, 52, 222, 305,
    308
Stonorov, Oscar, 42, 50, 206, 305

Tagliapietra, S., 43
Tait, H., 192
Terraroli, V., 17, 25
Thorssen, Ove, 231, 306, 307, 308
Tiepolo, Giambattista, 22, 307
Tiepolo, Giandomenico, 22
Tintoretto (Jacopo Robusti), 19

Tissot, Lyn Charles, 305, 308
Titian, 19
Toninato, T., 43
Toorop, Jan, 308
Tosi, Mario (called Mario Grasso), 37,
    310
Toso, Ermete, 304
Toso & Co., glassworks, 11, 194, 214
Toso Ferdinando (called Fei), 194

Ulrich, factory, 305

Ve Art, glassworks, 52
Venini & C., glassworks, 33, 214, 305,
    306, 307, 308, 309, 310
Venini Diaz de Santillana, A., 25, 42, 43,
    45, 305, 306, 307
Venini, Franco, 308
Venini, Paolo, 11, 12, 13, 14, 15, 17, 19,
    20, 21, 22, 23, 24, 25, 27, 28, 29, 31,
    33, 34, 36, 37, 39, 40, 41, 42, 43, 45,
    46, 47, 48, 49, 50, 51, 52, 54, 98, 103,
    104, 105, 107, 108, 109, 110, 111, 194,
    200, 202, 203, 204, 205, 206, 214, 217,
    218, 221, 222, 228, 305, 307, 308, 309
Veronese (Paolo Caliari), 19, 45, 192
Vetri Soffiati Muranesi Cappellin Venini
    & C., glassworks, 11, 19, 20, 24, 27, 28,
    39, 45, 305
Vetri Soffiati Muranesi Venini & C.,
    glassworks, 21, 24, 25, 28, 305, 307,
    308
Vignelli Valle, Elena, 54, 308
Vignelli, Massimo, 36, 50, 54, 56, 178,
    226, 227, 305, 306, 308
Visconti di Modrone, Carla, 21, 29, 305,
    308
Vuillard, Édouard, 307

Werkbund, 9
Wiener Werkstätte, 17, 19
Wirkkala, Sami, 230
Wirkkala, Tapio, 31, 42, 182, 229, 230,
    305, 308
Witwe Joh. Lötz, glassworks, 11, 12
Wright, Frank Lloyd, 50, 305

Yamasaki, Minoru, 54

Zanelli, Angelo, 308
Zecchin, Francesco, 23, 24, 25, 45, 308
Zecchin, Vittorio, 9, 11, 12, 13, 18, 19,
    20, 21, 22, 23, 24, 28, 39, 40, 45, 59,
    60, 61, 62, 192, 193, 194, 196, 305, 308
Zevi, Bruno, 50
Zuccheri, Toni, 31, 181, 227, 228, 305,
    308
Zynsky, Toots, 190, 232, 308

Index of Places

Asti
   private collection, *73*, 73, *82*, 83, *121*, 121, *147*, 147, *196*, 196, *198*, 198, *208*, 208, 209, 214, *215*

Bergamo
   Post-office building, 24, 47, *95*, 95, 198, *200*, 200, 305
Berkeley
   University of California, 306, 308
Berlin
   Staatliche Museen, 45, 192
Bern
   Städlicher Berner Waisenhaus, *176*, 176, *226*, 226
Boston
   Francesca Hillyer Collection, *202*, 202
   Laura Venini Hillyer Collection, *108*, 108, *204*, 204, *220*, 220
Brescia
   Hotel Vittoria, *22*, 22
Brussels
   Expo, 42, 50, *207*, 305

Catania
   Central Palace Hotel, 308
Chappaqua
   private collection, *216*, 216
Coburg
   Kunstsammlung der Veste, 230
Cologne
   Museen der Stadt Köln, Museum für angewandte Kunst, *59*, 59, *192*, 192
Corning
   The Corning Museum of Glass, *36*, 36, 51, *231*, 231, 308

Detroit
   Metalworkers Union (United Automobile Workers), 50, 206, 305
Düsseldorf
   Kunstmuseum Düsseldorf, Glasmuseum Hentrich, *10*, 11, *149*, 149, 194, *195*, 214, *215*

Ferrara
   Post-office building, 305
   Railway Station, 305
Florence
   Teatro Comunale dell'Opera, 305
Forlì
   Post-office building, 305
Fulda
   Schlosstheater, 51, 224, *225*, 306

Gardone Riviera
   Il Vittoriale degli Italiani
      Archivio dei correspondenti, 25
      Casseretto
         Gian Carlo Maroni's study, *81*, 81, *197*, 197
      Prioria
         Bagno Blu, *23*, 23, *68*, 68, 194, *195*
         Bagno delle Ospiti, 24, 76, *77*, *197*, 197
         Office Cheli, 24
         Office cucina, 84, *85*, *198*, 198
         Stanza Cicerin, 68, *69*, *74*, 74, 194, *195*, *197*, 197
         Stanza del Lebbroso, 64, *65*, 194, *195*
         Stanza del Mappamondo, *76*, 76, *197*, 197
         Stanza del Mascheraio, 24
         Stanza del Monco, *60*, 60, *193*, 193
         Stanza della Leda, 24, *94*, 94
         Stanza della Musica, 24, 40, *74*, 74, *75*, 75, *196*, 196
         Stanza della Zambracca, *23*, 23, *86*, 87, *90*, 90, *198*, 198
         Stanza delle Reliquie, *22*, 22, *23*, 23
         Stanza di Gasparo, 24
         Stanza Verde, 24, 78, *79*, *198*, 198
Geneva
   Musée Ariana, *61*, 61, *193*, 193
Genoa
   Palazzo Bianco, 307
   Palazzo Rosso, 307
   San Lorenzo, 307
Gorizia
   Post-office building, 305

Ivrea
   Olivetti, Headquarters, 52, *224*, 224

Lausanne
   private collection, *176*, 176, *226*, 226
Location unknown, *16*, 17, *20*, 20, *26*, 27, *29*, 29, *30*, 31, *41*, 41, *42*, 42, *44*, 45, *47*, 47, *108*, 108, *192*, 192, *193*, 193, 194, *195*, *196*, 196, *197*, *198*, 198, *199*, 199, *200*, 200, *201*, 201, *203*, 203, *204*, 204, *205*, *207*, 207, 210, *211*, *212*, 212, 214, *215*, *216*, 216, *217*, 217, 218, *219*, *221*, 221, *222*, 222, *224*, 224, *225*, *228*, 228, *229*, 229, *230*, 230
London
   Liliane Fawcett Collection, *227*, 227
   Victoria and Albert Museum, 307, 308

Lugano
   private collection, *114*, 114, *139*, 139, *140*, 141

Manchester
   Airport Lobby, 51, *223*, 223, 305
Maser
   private collection, 218, *219*
   Villa Barbaro Volpi, 22, 48
Milan
   Biblioteca Ambrosiana, *94*, 94
   former Stock Exchange building, 47, *202*, 202
   Fornasetti Collection, *221*, 221
   Galleria In. Arte, *103*, 103, *109*, 109, 111, *112*, *113*, *118*, 118, *124*, 124, *126*, 126, *152*, 152, *162*, 163, *166*, 166, *180*, 181, 206, *207*, *217*, 217, 218, *219*, *220*, 220, *227*, 227
   Marco Arosio Collection, *96*, 96, *201*, 201, *209*, 209
   Palazzo Accursio, 47
   Politecnico, 307, 308
   private collection, *80*, 80, *111*, 111, *114*, 114, *121*, 121, 130, *131*, 172, *173*, *197*, 197, *202*, 202, 206, *208*, 208
   Showroom Cassina, *226*, 226
   Triennales (from 1933), 21, 41, 42, 43, 48, 49, 50, 52, 203, 205, 206, 208, 209, 212, 213, 214, 216, 218, 222, 223, 305, 307, 308
   via Montenapoleone, 20, 21, 28
Montreal
   Place des Arts, Auditorium, 51, *223*, 223
Monza
   Biennales (1923, 1925, 1927; Triennale 1930), 20, *21*, 21, 39, 40, *41*, 41, 43, *48*, 48, 193, 196, 198, 200, 308
Munich
   Die Neue Sammlung, Staatliches Museum für angewandte Kunst, *59*, 59, *62*, 62, *192*, 192, *193*, 193
Murano
   Museo Venini, *42*, 42, 176, *177*, *185*, 185, *201*, 201, 206, *207*, 210, *211*, *226*, 226, *230*, 230, *231*, 231
   Museo Vetrario, 19, 20, 47, *72*, 72, *82*, 83, 186, *187*, *188*, 188, *196*, 196, *231*, 231, *232*, 232
   Palazzo Da Mula, 52, 308

Naples
   Forum, 305

Lugano
New York
   Altamira, 305
   Barry Friedman Collection, *105*, 105, *106*, *107*, 107, *110*, 110, *146*, 147, 157, *158*, *159*, *205*, 205, 206, *207*, *217*, 217, 218, *219*
   Bonniers, 305, 308
   Brooklyn Museum, 218
   Macy's, 221, 305, 308
   Martin Cohen Collection, *220*, 220, *222*, 222
   Museum of Modern Art, 50, 217, 227, 305, 308
   Olivetti Showroom, 305
   Oswaldo Costa Collection, *212*, 212, *222*, 222, 227, *228*, 228
   private collection, *186*, 186, *201*, 201, *222*, 222, *231*, 231
   School of Visual Arts, 43, 54, 306, 307, 308
   Wall Street Branch, Swiss Credit Bank, 224, *225*
   World Trade Center, 54

Padua
   Cassa di Risparmio, *201*, 201, 306
   Maurizio Graziani Collection, *178*, 178, *227*, 227
   private collection, 25, *66*, 67, *71*, 71, *83*, 83, 90, *91*, *115*, 115, *119*, 119, 168, *170*, 194, *195*, *196*, 196, *198*, 198, *199*, 199, *208*, 208
   Università degli Studi (University), 49, 152, *153*, 214, *215*, 305
Palermo
   Post-office building, 305
Paris
   Académie Ranson, 307
   Arcet, 305
   Beaubourg, 54
   Foire de Paris, Salon des Expositions de la Porte de Versailles, 224, *225*
   Fourrures Georges V, *226*, 226
   Louvre, 194, 308
   Maison Pierre Cardin, 224
   Musée des Arts Décoratifs, *145*, 145, *213*, 213, *221*, 221, 307
   Musée Nissim de Camondo, 25, *194*, 194
   private collection, *82*, 83, *88*, 88, *174*, 174, 198, *199*, *224*, 224
   Salon d'Automne, 196
   Salon des Artistes Décorateurs, 45, 202
Pavia
   private collection, *61*, 61, *193*, 193, *229*, 229

Piacenza
private collection, *89*, 89, *123*, 123,
128, 128, *199*, 199, *200*, 200, 208, *209*,
210, 210, *216*, 216
Pilchuck
Pilchuck Glass School, 34, 37, 53, 307,
308
Pola
Post-office building, 305
Private collection, *20*, 20, *32*, 33, *136*, 136
Providence
Rhode Island School of Design, 34, 306,
307, 308

Reggio Emilia
Railway Station, 305
Riyadh
Saudi Radio-Television building, 54
Rome
Enrico Camponi Collection, *227*, 227
Farnesina, *223*, 223, 305
Hotel Cavalieri Hilton, 307
private collection, *148*, 148, 214, *215*,
221, 221
Quadriennale, 21, 200
Quirinal Palace, 51
Teatro Sistina, 51
via Condotti, 305

San Vito al Tagliamento
Toni Zuccheri Collection, *228*, 228
Savona
Post-office building, 305
Seattle
Benjamin Moore Collection, *36*, 36
Dante Marioni Collection, 36, *37*
Pam Biallas Collection, *34*, 34
Richard Marquis Collection, 34, *35*,
186, 186, *230*, 230
Siena
Railway Station, 305
San Domenico, 305
Singapore
Mandarin Hotel, 54, 224, *225*, 306
Stockholm
Nationalmuseum, 48
Nordiska Kompaniet, *52*, 52, *53*, 205
Switzerland
private collection, *216*, 216

Ta'if
Royal Palace, 54
Tarzana
Artur Liu Collection, *126*, 126, *209*, 209
The Hague
Gemeentemuseum, *13*, 13
Tivoli
private collection, *223*, 223
Toledo
The Toledo Museum of Art, *38*, 39, 206,
207, 218, *219*, 307
Trent
Post-office building, 305
Railway Station, 305
Treviso
private collection, *67*, 67, *128*, 128,
138, 138, *145*, 145, *150*, 150, *209*, 209,
210, 210, *211*, 211, *213*, 213, 214, *215*,
218, *219*
Tunis
Great Mosque, *206*, 207
Turin
Galleria Ecodiforme, *84*, 84, *87*, 87, 96,
97, *98*, 98, *99*, *102*, 103, *116*, 116, *117*,
117, *122*, 123, 130, *132*, *133*, 141, *142*,

143, *168*, 168, *169*, 174, *175*, *198*, 198,
201, 201, *208*, 208, *212*, 212, *221*, 221,
223, 223, 224, *225*, *231*, 231
Gerard Figliola Collection, 168, *171*,
223, 223
Italian Pavilion, 51, 214, *215*
private collection, *87*, 87, *120*, 121,
128, *129*, *130*, 130, *144*, 145, *154*, 155,
167, 167, *181*, 181, 210, *211*, *228*, 228

Udine
private collection, 178, *179*, *227*, 227
Union City
Odetto Lastra Collection, *104*, 104, 124,
125, *130*, 130, *135*, 135, 150, *151*, *155*,
155, *156*, *157*, 157, *160*, 160, *161*, 161,
163, 163, *164*, 164, *184*, 185, *205*, 205,
209, 209, 210, *211*, *216*, 216, 218, *219*,
221, 221
United States
Millennium Pictures Collection,
104, 104, *134*, 134, *137*, 137, *141*, 141,
194, 194, *210*, 210, *211*, 211, *212*,
212, *213*, 213, 214, *215*
private collection, 214, *215*

Vaduz
Steinberg Foundation, *205*, 205
Venice
Alessandro Diaz de Santillana
Collection, *188*, 188, *232*, 232
Anna Venini Collection, *8*, 9, *18*, 19, 24,
58, 59, 92, *93*, *108*, 108, 188, *189*, *192*,
192, *199*, 199, 202, *203*, 203, *204*, 204,
206, *206*, *207*, 207, *212*, 212, *223*, 223,
224, 224, *225*, *226*, 226, *227*, 227, *229*,
229, *230*, 230, *231*, 231, *232*, 232
Biennales, 21, 39, 40, 41, 45, *47*, 47,
49, 49, 52, 54, 196, 198, 199, 203, 204,
205, 206, 207, 208, 209, 210, 211, 212,
213, 214, 216, 217, 218, 220, 221, 222,
223, 230, 308
Ca' Pesaro, 19, 27, 308
Ca' Rezzonico, 307
Carraro Collection, 206, *206*
Cassa di Risparmio, 51, *172*, 172, 206,
223, 223, *228*, 228
formerly Istituto Statale d'Arte, *208*, 208
Galleria dell'Accademia, 192
Istituto d'Arte e Accademia di Belle
Arti, 307, 308
Laura Diaz de Santillana Collection,
190, 190, *191*, *231*, 231, *232*, 232
Lido
Hotel Excelsior, 51, 196, 224, *225*,
305, 306, 307
Palazzo del Cinema, 51
Massimo Nordio Collection, 164, *165*,
220, 220
Palazzo Ducale, 194, *195*
Palazzo Grassi, 42, 206, *207*, 305
piazzetta dei Leoncini, 305
Ponte della Libertà, 49
private collection, *55*, 55, *70*, 71, 98,
100, *101*, *192*, 192, *196*, 196, *204*, 204,
205, *209*, 209, *212*, 212, *221*, 221, *229*,
229, *232*, 232
Residence Gritti, 307
Scuola di Architettura, 51, 307
St Mark Square, 48
St Mark, basilica, 20
Vienna
Opera House, 51
Österreichisches Museum für
angewandte Kunst, *192*, 192

Zülpich
Lösch Collection, 214, *215*, *217*, 217,
218, *219*, *220*, 220
Zurich
Museum Bellerive, 62, *63*, *104*, 104,
118, 118, *127*, 127, *148*, 148, *150*, 150,
182, *183*, 194, *195*, *205*, 205, *209*, 209,
214, 214
private collection, *208*, 208
Soland, 305